NORTHERN FRONTIER, NORTHERN HOMELAND

NORTHERN FRONTIER

NORTHERN HOMELAND

THE REPORT OF THE MACKENZIE VALLEY PIPELINE INQUIRY: VOLUME TWO

Design and Photocomposition:
Alphatext Ltd.

Available by mail from
Printing and Publishing
Supply and Services Canada
Ottawa, Canada K1A 0S9
or through your bookseller

Catalogue number:
English edition CP32-25/1977-2
French edition CP32-25/1977-2F

RR-0170-020-EE-A1
RR-0170-020-FF-A1

ISBN:
English edition 0-660-00777-0

Price: Canada $5.00; other countries $6.00
Price subject to change without notice

Table of Contents

This is Volume Two of a two-volume report. Volume One deals with the broad social, economic and environmental impacts that a gas pipeline and an energy corridor would have in the Mackenzie Valley and the Western Arctic. In it certain basic recommendations are made. This second Volume sets out the terms and conditions that should be imposed if, in the future, a pipeline is built and an energy corridor is established in the Mackenzie Valley

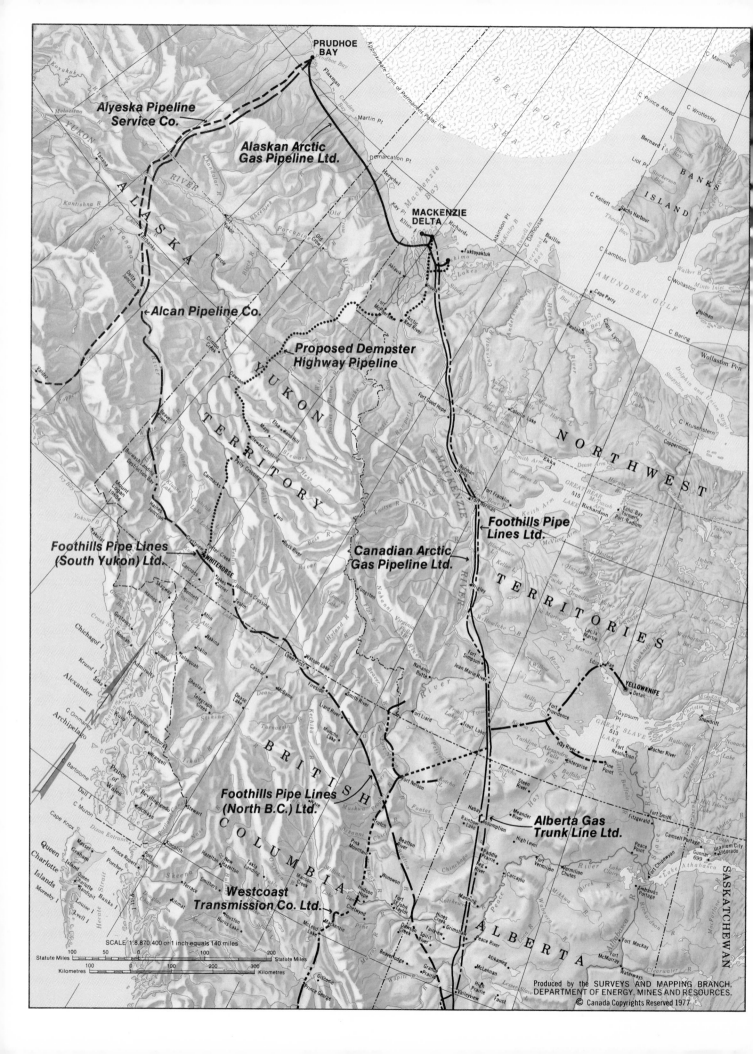

PRUDHOE BAY

Alyeska Pipeline Service Co.

Alaskan Arctic Gas Pipeline Ltd.

MACKENZIE DELTA

Alcan Pipeline Co.

Proposed Dempster Highway Pipeline

ALASKA

YUKON TERRITORY

NORTHWEST TERRITORIES

Foothills Pipe Lines (South Yukon) Ltd.

Canadian Arctic Gas Pipeline Ltd.

Foothills Pipe Lines Ltd.

YELLOWKNIFE

Foothills Pipe Lines (North B.C.) Ltd.

BRITISH COLUMBIA

Alberta Gas Trunk Line Ltd.

Westcoast Transmission Co. Ltd.

ALBERTA

SASKATCHEWAN

SCALE 1:8,870,400 or 1 inch equals 140 miles

100   50   0   100   200
Statute Miles |‾‾‾‾‾‾|‾‾‾| Statute Miles
100   0   100   200   300
Kilometres |‾‾‾‾‾‾|‾‾‾‾‾‾| Kilometres

Produced by the SURVEYS AND MAPPING BRANCH,
DEPARTMENT OF ENERGY, MINES AND RESOURCES.
© Canada Copyrights Reserved 1977

MACKENZIE VALLEY PIPELINE INQUIRY

COMMISSIONER
Mr. Justice Thomas R. Berger

Suite 600
171 Slater Street
Ottawa, Ontario K1P 5H7

The Honourable J. Hugh Faulkner
Minister of Indian Affairs and
Northern Development
House of Commons
Ottawa, Ontario

November 30, 1977

Dear Mr. Faulkner:

This is Volume Two of my report. In Volume One, which was tabled in the House of Commons on May 9 of this year, I recommended that, on environmental grounds, no pipeline be built and no energy corridor be established across the Northern Yukon. I found that construction of a pipeline along the Mackenzie Valley would be feasible from an environmental point of view, but I recommended that it be postponed for ten years to allow for a settlement of native claims. I also expressed the view that, if a pipeline had to be built to deliver Alaskan gas to the Lower 48, the Alaska Highway route was preferable from an environmental point of view. The National Energy Board reached conclusions similar to my own, and since that time, you and your colleagues have reached agreement with the United States on the construction of a pipeline along the Alaska Highway route.

Rejection of the Arctic Gas proposal allows the government to plan now for the preservation of the caribou, whales, wilderness and wildlife of the Western Arctic, and to settle native claims throughout the region. In Volume One, I outlined a number of broad recommendations to deal with these concerns, and I shall elaborate on them in this volume.

In its report, *Reasons for Decision: Northern Pipelines,* handed down on July 4, 1977, the National Energy Board indicated that, depending upon the extent of discoveries in the Mackenzie Delta and the Beaufort Sea, a pipeline should be constructed either along the Dempster Highway, to connect with the pipeline that is to be built along the Alaska Highway route, or along the Mackenzie Valley. If the reserves of natural gas in the Beaufort Sea turn out to be large, then in due course — at a time when they are needed, and following a settlement of native claims — they can be delivered by means of a pipeline along the Mackenzie Valley. In any event, there will be continuing exploration in the Delta region, and a pipeline along either the Dempster Route or the Mackenzie Valley Route will affect that area — an area about which I heard a great deal of evidence. Some of the recommendations in this volume will have a bearing on whatever pipeline route is finally selected.

Volume One and Volume Two

In Volume Two, as in Volume One, I have proceeded on the assumption that, in due course, the industrial system will require the gas and oil of the Western Arctic, and that they will have to be transported along the Mackenzie Valley to markets in the mid-continent. However, I have also proceeded on the assumption that we intend to protect and to preserve the northern environment, and that, above all, we intend to honour the legitimate claims of the native people. All of these assumptions are embedded in the *Statement of the Government of Canada on Northern Development in the 70's,* presented by the Honourable Jean Chrétien to the Standing Committee on Indian Affairs and Northern Development on March 28, 1972.

The social, cultural and political tensions in the North are closely linked to industrial advance. The intrusion of large-scale frontier development among native people has aggravated the cluster of pathologies that have become so familiar in the North: welfare, crime, violence, disease, alcoholism, and social and personal disarray. This is a hard fact to accept, requiring as it does a reconsideration of conventional wisdom, but it is supported by the evidence before the Inquiry. The evidence led irresistibly to the conclusion that, if a pipeline were built now in the Mackenzie Valley, its economic benefits would be limited, its social impact devastating, and it would frustrate the goals of native claims.

Because it perceived the problems of northern native peoples as arising out of individual poverty, the federal government has, during the past two decades, initiated many programs to increase their opportunities for wage employment and income. The idea was essentially a simple one: create enough job opportunities in the North (by developing mines, for example), give the people some training (as heavy equipment operators, for example), and the problems will eventually go away. But they are still there, because they are not simply problems of poverty, but of a people trying desperately to preserve their cultural identity. Thus the growth of government and bureaucracy and the coming of industry constituted a threat to their desire to affirm their identity as a people, and to gain control over their own lives and their own future — something they believe is essential to their well-being.

The condition of native people in the North today is, in many respects, the product of white domination of native people and native society. That this domination has often been benevolent does not at all diminish its devastating consequences for the patterns of collective and cooperative self-reliance that are the tradition of northern native people. Despite the benefits that the dominant white society has brought to native people — benefits that they readily acknowledge — this dominance, and the resulting weakness of their own society, have left native people, as a group, and as individuals, especially vulnerable to the impact of large-scale industrial development. In Volume One, I attempted to show how this historically established relationship between white and native society could not be separated from questions of impact, of native identity, and of the long-term prospects for economic and social well-being.

Rapid and large-scale industrial development is, in any circumstance, a potentially disruptive process; in the context of a northern society that has experienced many years of domination, this disruption contributes to the profoundest of social ills. It then becomes something that cannot be treated with ameliorative measures that may, in other historical or cultural contexts, be more or less effective. Because the various causes of these social ills are inextricably linked, a consideration of industrial development and social, cultural and political progress in the North cannot be separated from a discussion of native claims. It is through a settlement of their claims that native people see the way to social, economic and political advance.

I concluded in Volume One that certain adverse consequences of the construction of a pipeline and the establishment of an energy corridor could not be mitigated, and that it was unrealistic to proceed as if they could. I did say, however, that if the pipeline were postponed, and if steps were taken now to strengthen native society and the native economy through a settlement of native claims, the pipeline might be built in ten years' time, when the benefits of pipeline construction could be enlarged, and the adverse consequences mitigated. This volume deals with the measures that will have to be taken to achieve these ends.

Social and Economic Recommendations

My social and economic recommendations apply to renewable resources, employment, manpower delivery, urban centres, rapid growth, northern business and transportation.

I believe that, in the North, a strong native society and a strengthened renewable resource sector can exist side by side with large-scale, non-renewable resource development, but only if we change our priorities and strengthen the renewable resource sector before the pipeline is built. Postponement of the pipeline means that many alternate modes of social, economic and political development can be explored in the Mackenzie Valley and Western Arctic — alternatives that would otherwise have been foreclosed. Some of these alternatives can be explored only through the settlement of native claims, and some can be clarified only with more knowledge about the area's renewable resource development potential. I am, therefore, making certain proposals for more accurate measurement of the native economy, and for the development of the renewable resource sector as a whole.

It has been said that the choice for native people is stark: jobs on the pipeline or no jobs at all. This statement is, of course, false because it overlooks the fact that, for native people, the opportunities provided by pipeline construction will be limited. Moreover, it fails to recognize the persistence of the native economy, the possibilities for development of the renewable resource sector, the continuation of oil and gas exploration activity, and the role of the federal and territorial governments as employers. It ignores the fact that many native people have shown that they are not strongly inclined towards the type of employment offered by large-scale industrial projects. It disregards the long-term implications of employment in a volatile boom-and-bust sector, of which pipeline construction is an obvious example. And it overlooks the potential of the renewable resource sector. Jobs — permanent jobs — can be provided in logging and sawmilling, in the management, harvesting and processing of fur, meat and game, in fishing, in recreation, conservation and other related activities. Such ventures, given a fraction of the support extended to the non-renewable resource sector, could offer many opportunities to native people in the North. Ventures like these are also amenable to local or regional control, and would not, therefore, impede the goals of native claims. With such enterprises in place, there would be a diversified spectrum of job opportunities, no undue dependence on pipeline construction when it takes place, and no necessity for the kind of wholesale recruitment of pipeline construction workers from native communities that is presently envisaged.

Nonetheless, all northern residents who want to work on pipeline construction when it is built should have that opportunity. I recommend that pipeline construction be accompanied by preferential hiring on the basis of five years' residence in the North. Such preference would exist for any northerner seeking a pipeline job, and would help him over whatever obstacles might be presented by requirements for union membership and lack of adequate training. But a manpower delivery system of this kind should not be founded on the notion that pipeline employment is necessarily the preferred choice for northern people.

It is likely that the pipeline, when it is built, will attract large numbers of people to the Mackenzie Valley and the Mackenzie Delta, and cause major shifts of population within the region. The pipeline will have a particularly severe effect on some communities — I call them action communities — especially Inuvik, Tuktoyaktuk, Norman Wells, Fort Simpson, Yellowknife and Hay River. Most of these communities are already experiencing the socially harmful effects of rapid growth of government and industry, and the tensions between native people and white institutions. Because the pipeline will exacerbate these conditions, my proposals with regard to the action communities are ameliorative. My recommendations relate to methods for coping, first of all, with the social impact of the pipeline in the action communities, and secondly, with the physical and financial aspects of such impact. These communities cannot be expected to cope with many of the pressures that pipeline construction will place on them, and they will require impact funding from senior governments.

It has been argued that gas from the North should not bypass northern communities only to service industries and homes thousands of miles away. Yet the evidence presented to this Inquiry suggests that, if gas were made available, few northern communities would experience a cost reduction over presently available energy sources. There are, I believe, more effective, if less direct, methods of ensuring that northern communities benefit from the natural gas reserves of their region. I propose subsidization of northern energy costs, regardless of the fuel that is most efficient in a particular location. In this way, some of the benefits that will be experienced by southerners can be extended to northerners.

I have also considered the effects that a Mackenzie Valley pipeline could have on northern business. Many witnesses expressed concern that the pipeline may cause serious distortions in the territorial economy. The pipeline might generate overinvestment in pipeline-related activities, it might inhibit the ability of local firms to supply goods and services needed by northern communities, and it might generally interfere with orderly and sustained economic growth. But northern businessmen will quite properly want to use the pipeline as an opportunity for growth and expansion. Their ability to do so is limited in comparison with large firms domiciled in the metropolitan centres of the provinces. I am, therefore, recommending measures that relate to bidding on contracts, bonding, and the availability of capital. These measures are designed to place northern firms in a competitive position so that they can secure a reasonable volume of pipeline-related work and prosper in the long run. Native enterprises, whether proprietorships, cooperatives or corporations, should enjoy the same preferences as other northern firms.

If native cooperatives and corporations are set up as a result of a settlement of claims, then I anticipate that they will assume a place on the northern business scene, and that they could play a part in the economic activity generated by pipeline construction. I expect, however, that once in place, native cooperatives and corporations will undertake ventures in the renewable resource sector rather than in non-renewable resource enterprises, such as mining, and the oil and gas industry simply because they are on too large a scale. Native people should have the opportunity to participate in the management of enterprises that can be undertaken locally and regionally — economic ventures related to traditional values and experience, and based on skills that are already acquired or that can be developed and used within the community. The development of a strong renewable resource economy would reduce the vulnerability of the northern economy to the kind of boom-and-bust cycle that has characterized it in the past.

To a great extent, the social and economic recommendations in this volume are anticipatory. Postponement of the Mackenzie Valley pipeline means that the terms and conditions being formulated now will have to be enforced in an institutional and political context that cannot very easily be foreseen. I have sought to be specific, but in some areas, it would be implausible, if not impossible, to be precise. This is less of a difficulty in the case of environmental matters, still less in the case of engineering matters, and you will find that my recommendations in these areas are quite specific in many instances.

Environmental Recommendations

In Volume One, I made recommendations designed to protect caribou, whales, wildlife and wilderness. These recommendations were founded on the need to preserve critical habitat in perpetuity. Thus, my proposal that a wilderness park be created in the Northern Yukon is intended to protect this unique wilderness region, including vital habitat for wildlife and migratory birds on the Arctic Coastal Plain and Old Crow Flats, and particularly the critically important calving and summer range of the Porcupine caribou herd. My recommendation that no pipeline be built and no energy corridor be established across the mouth of the Mackenzie Delta, together with my proposals to establish a white whale sanctuary in west Mackenzie Bay and bird sanctuaries in the outer Delta, are designed to protect the unique land and water ecosystems that characterize the Delta and the margins of the Beaufort Sea. In addition, the bird sanctuaries that I have proposed along the Mackenzie Valley are intended to protect major populations of migrating and nesting birds at critical localities. In this volume, as in Volume One, I focus my concern on critical habitat and critical life stages of mammals, birds and fish and particularly on the limited tracts of land and water that are vital to the survival of whole populations of certain species at certain times of the year.

In view of the agreement between Canada and the United States to build a pipeline along the Alaska Highway route, it is appropriate to repeat one of the recommendations that I made in Volume One. I urged that Canada should undertake to establish a wilderness park in the Northern Yukon, and the United States should accord wilderness status to its Arctic National Wildlife Range, thus creating a unique international wilderness park: nine million acres on each side of the international boundary. I suggested that it would be an important symbol of the dedication of our two countries to environmental as well as to industrial goals.

Since the release of Volume One, the Carter Administration has recommended in proposed amendments to the Alaska National Interest Lands Conservation Act, that 43 million acres in Alaska, including the lands comprising the Arctic National Wildlife Range in northeastern Alaska, be set aside as wilderness. Thus, the United States has taken an essential step toward fulfilling the conditions that are necessary for the establishment of an international wilderness park. It remains now for Canada to include in our National Parks Act a provision for the establishment of wilderness areas, and then to designate the Yukon north of the Porcupine River as wilderness.

In Volume One, I drew attention to the impacts that the Dempster Highway will have on the migration patterns and winter range of the Porcupine caribou herd. Hunting will also increase because of the access the highway will offer. These concerns have been intensified by recent events on the Dempster Highway, and by the possibility that Mackenzie Delta gas will be transported by a pipeline along the route of the highway. The impact of such a pipeline has still to be assessed in detail.

The decision to build the Dempster Highway was made without adequate environmental assessment. However, the highway is now virtually complete, so we shall have to devise measures to deal with it. In particular, protection of the Porcupine caribou herd's winter range must be a principal concern. If we can devise measures to cope with the Dempster Highway, we may, in due course, be able to cope with many of the impacts of a pipeline along the same route. I recommend, therefore, that a restricted hunting zone extending two miles on either side of the highway, and on either side of all connecting access roads and seismic lines, be established within the winter range of the herd. Provision should be made, however, for the continuation of traditional use by native people. I also recommend that vehicle traffic and construction activity along the highway be controlled during caribou migration in the vicinity.

Turning to the Mackenzie Valley itself, I concluded in Volume One that the construction of a pipeline along the Mackenzie Valley was feasible from an environmental point of view. Consequently, in this volume, I have included a lengthy series of recommendations designed to protect the environmental resources of the Mackenzie Valley and the Mackenzie Delta. These environmental proposals are intended to serve as guidelines for the government in its review and approval of project designs and plans, and for regulation of the project in general. As these recommendations tend to be quite specific, I can only highlight a few here.

A pipeline along the Mackenzie Valley will result in disturbance to wildlife populations, because it will increase access. I recommend, therefore, that the same conditions I have urged for the Dempster Highway be imposed here: the establishment of a two-mile restricted hunting zone along each side of the pipeline right-of-way, along all temporary or permanent access routes, and around all pipeline facilities, with the qualification that traditional use by native people be exempted from this restriction.

The birds of prey — including the peregrine falcon and gyrfalcon — that nest in the vicinity of proposed pipeline routes constitute a significant portion of the surviving North American population of these species. During their occupation of nest sites in spring and summer, these birds are extremely sensitive to disturbance by machinery, aircraft or human activity; even repeated low-intensity noise can lead to desertion of nests and the loss of young. It is important to avoid disturbance in the vicinity of occupied nests, particularly those of the rare and endangered peregrine falcon. I therefore recommend that a Raptor Protection Zone be established around any nest site that may be adversely affected by the pipeline project, and that construction activities within these zones be controlled by permit.

If large volumes of gas are discovered in the Beaufort Sea, it is likely that a pipeline will be built along the Mackenzie Valley. Thus, it is only common sense to urge that lands for conservation purposes be withdrawn now, well before new pipeline proposals are made. I therefore recommend that the Government of Canada develop a northern conservation strategy — a strategy that recognizes the claims of northern native peoples, the constitutional situation in the North, and the special characteristics of the northern environment. Such a strategy would entail not only a program to set aside wilderness areas but also park lands, wildlife areas, wild rivers, ecological reserves, recreation areas and archaeological and historic sites.

I have already discussed the need for wilderness protection for the Northern Yukon and the Porcupine caribou herd. Wilderness protection should also be provided for the white whale sanctuary I proposed in Volume One for west Mackenzie Bay. These proposals are designed to protect the caribou and the whales in perpetuity.

What I am urging now, in addition, is that throughout the region, conservation lands should be identified and set aside. This, of course, should be done only after the fullest consultation with northern government and northern peoples.

Conservation lands can be set aside under Section 19 of the Territorial Lands Act. They should be set aside only on the basis that native hunting, trapping and fishing rights within these areas are guaranteed, and they would be subject to a settlement of native claims. It should be borne in mind that one of the objectives of native claims is the preservation of northern wildlife on which native people have long depended. To this extent, their goals coincide with the goals of setting aside conservation lands. In fact, the people of Old Crow have expressed their support for my proposal for a wilderness park in the Northern Yukon. No final disposition of any conservation lands should be made until native claims are settled.

I want to emphasize that a northern conservation strategy offers an opportunity to involve native people in the whole conservation lands program in the North: in fish and game management, in compiling inventories of environmental and recreational resources, and in managing wilderness parks and other conservation areas. This would offer native people employment, training in skills that are relevant to the preservation of their northern homeland, and a livelihood that would allow them to remain in their own communities and regions. There is no reason why the objective should not be for native people to manage these conservation lands.

Project Recommendations

The first issue to be addressed in the discussion of the project is location of the pipeline and its auxiliary facilities. Major routing issues were dealt with in Volume One, but there is still a need to refine the location of the right-of-way, ancillary facilities and access routes along the Mackenzie Valley. To reduce disturbance of land and waterbodies, to minimize impact in tributary valleys, and to protect wildlife and fish populations, I recommend that measures be taken to ensure the refinement of location of the pipeline right-of-way and its ancillary facilities. These measures will take into account present patterns of development, future plans, and the views of the communities along the route. Routing must not be decided by the Company simply in terms of engineering and cost. Rather, tentative locations and routes should be progressively refined by a process of successive Company proposals and regulatory responses that take all of these factors into account.

The existence of permafrost along the pipeline route necessitates departures from the engineering design and construction procedures commonly applied by the pipeline industry. I have discussed some of these in Volume One. In permafrost terrain, construction procedures for clearing, grading, drainage and erosion control, revegetation, and use of snow roads and snow working surfaces must not only meet the needs of the pipeline project, but also avoid chain-reaction impacts on land, on the environment and on people. Design measures and construction procedures are needed to control adverse effects of thaw settlement, frost heave, liquefaction of thawing soil and slope instability. In view of the uncertainties that still surround these matters — despite the vast amount of evidence brought before this Inquiry and the National Energy Board — I recommend that a geotechnical review board of independent experts be established to ensure the successful resolution of all outstanding problems.

If a pipeline is built in the Mackenzie Valley, snow roads and snow working surfaces will be needed in place of the graded, temporary winter roads normally used by the industry. In view of the importance of snow roads in reducing damage to permafrost terrain, and in view of the complexity of permafrost distribution in the southern part of the Mackenzie Valley, I recommend that snow roads be adopted for all pipeline construction North of 60, except where a different mode, such as graded winter road construction, is specifically approved.

The management of fuels and hazardous substances during pipeline construction and operation presents two problems: contingency planning and spill prevention. At present, government is concentrating on the contingency aspect, that is, spill clean-up. On the other hand, spill prevention — undoubtedly the best way to ensure protection of the enviornment — is not receiving enough attention. I therefore include detailed proposals aimed at preventing spills of fuels and hazardous substances during their transportation, transfer and storage.

Project recommendations should be both practical and enforceable. As an illustration, take schemes for the management of liquid and solid wastes — schemes designed to protect both public health and the environment. Because the public health aspects are already dealt with as a matter of routine, my recommendations focus on environmental issues and, in particular, on sewage effluent guidelines. For construction camps, I recommend standards less stringent than those set out in the Department of the Environment's current *Guidelines for Effluent Quality and Wastewater Treatment at Federal Establishments* and less stringent than those recommended for the pipeline by the National Energy Board. In my view, those more stringent standards are unnecessarily rigid for many of the pipeline's temporary facilities, and strict adherence to them is not practicable.

The pipeline project will require a considerable number of low altitude aircraft flights superimposed upon existing aircraft traffic in the region. Because these flights could have adverse impacts on populations of mammals and birds, I am making proposals for flight corridors, flight ceilings and regulation of flight schedules. In particular, I recommend the establishment of a Flight Control Group that would vet aircraft flight plans for the pipeline project and related activities. This group would deal with matters of routing, altitudes and scheduling in the context of current information on bird and mammal sensitivities.

Project Regulation and Design Review

The pipeline project will be immense in its scope and impact, and the necessity for a regulatory agency to supervise the project is inescapable. I assume that there will be a unified regulatory Agency, for the company building the pipeline should be answerable to one authority, not a multitude of them.

The changes that occur in the Northwest Territories during the next ten years may be as great as those in the ten years just past. The certainty of change makes it difficult at this time to offer specific recommendations on the machinery of regulation that should be established when a pipeline is built. But some principles are, I believe of paramount importance, and their importance will likely persist, no matter what changes occur in the North and its institutions over the next decade.

The Agency should be in business from the very beginning. By this, I do not mean that it should be in business at the start of construction, or even preconstruction, activity. Rather, the Agency should be operational just as soon as a permit for a right-of-way is issued.

In addition, the most careful definition of the Agency's authority will be necessary. I recommend that its mandate be confined to the enforcement of all terms and conditions, social and economic as well as engineering and environmental, on the pipeline right-of-way itself and on associated facilities, but that the powers and responsibilities of ordinary government departments and agencies should prevail elsewhere. If the Agency's mandate is not carefully defined, it could infringe unduly on the jurisdiction of northern governmental institutions.

The problems resulting from social, economic and environmental impact require measures that range all the way from the provision of services to in-migrants to the monitoring of caribou populations. These problems are so wide-ranging in their impact, and affect such a variety of interests, that they should be dealt with by appropriate departments of government at the federal, territorial, regional and local levels. To turn the regulation of such matters over to a monitoring and enforcement Agency would lead to the creation of a parallel government structure that would exercise perhaps greater authority than existing institutions; it would be subversive of any other structure of northern government.

Clearly, ordinary institutions of government, as well as other interests with legitimate concerns about pipeline impact, must be able to participate in, and have access to, the work of the Agency. For instance, those responsible for fish and game management should have access to the Agency at all levels, as should those branches of government that are responsible for the social conditions in the towns and settlements within the zone of impact. At the same time, public interest groups, such as those concerned with environmental protection, should also have access to the Agency.

Furthermore, the Agency should be responsive to the concerns of native organizations. This need may well have diminished by the time the pipeline is built, for native claims will have been settled by then, and a new structure of local and regional institutions will be in place. Nevertheless, native organizations at that time may assert a special interest in the impact of the pipeline – an interest that extends beyond the scope and capacity of northern institutions as they may exist a decade from now, and that calls for a response from native organizations outside the structure of northern government and northern institutions. In some respects, this will depend on the extent to which native people a decade from now consider northern government and northern institutions to be truly reflective of their interests.

I also recommend the establishment of an Impact Assessment Group. This group would consist of representatives from local, regional and territorial governments, and from public interest groups, and, of course, native organizations. It would advise the Agency on matters of local impact, but it would also exercise an ombudsman function in its relations with the regulatory Agency. The group would have the right to question officials and employees of the Agency, and review the Agency's documents. Although they would not in any sense be an appellate tribunal, since they would have no power to reverse the Agency's actions, they would have the responsibility to make their findings public. This assessment group would deal with the overall impact of the pipeline and the Agency's administration, as well as with specific problems of impact and specific complaints about the Agency's administration.

Conclusion

In Volume Two, my objective has been to distill the available evidence on a wide range of social, economic and environmental subjects. In this way, Volume Two is designed to serve as a convenient point of departure for those persons in both the public and private sectors who, in the years to come, will be engaged in planning for the Mackenzie Valley and the Western Arctic. The responsibility for such planning and its implementation will rest with the Government of Canada, and with the local, regional and territorial institutions that may evolve in the Northwest Territories as a result of the government's statement of August 3, 1977 on *Political Development in the Northwest Territories* and of a settlement of native claims.

Throughout both Volume One and Volume Two, I have sought to avoid rigid distinctions between the issues that are before us. At many points, social, economic and environmental matters overlap, and the question of native claims impinges again and again on virtually every aspect of northern life. At the heart of my recommendations is the need to settle native claims. This need bears directly on all of the social, economic and environmental subjects discussed in this report and indirectly, but no less compellingly, on all matters related to the North; it requires a recognition of the special and collective nature of the native interest in the North.

Yours truly,

Thos R. Berger

PART ONE

People: Social and Economic Concerns

THE REPORT OF
THE MACKENZIE VALLEY
PIPELINE INQUIRY

PART ONE —
PEOPLE: SOCIAL AND
ECONOMIC CONCERNS

1 Introduction: The Need for Balanced Development

Government policy for the economic development of the North has focused on extractive or non-renewable resource industries. In Volume One I discussed the difficulties resulting from this policy, and argued that the development of the northern economy should not be based exclusively on large-scale non-renewable resources. The same point may be expressed in terms of choice or options: economic development that is in the best interests of northerners will offer greater variety than the single possibility presented by industrial advance based on non-renewable resources. If the pipeline — the largest industrial development project ever proposed for the North — is to be in the best interests of northerners, a condition of its construction must be the prior adoption of other forms of development. In this way, the native people will be able to maintain the economic and cultural forms they regard as their own; they will not be forced into adopting an economic mode and a way of life that they may not want. Only by accepting this condition can we avoid aggravating the social and economic impact of pipeline construction.

Let me be clear about the implications of this position. It presupposes the continuation of the kind of economic development — mining and oil and gas exploration activity — with which the northern frontier has for some years been associated; more specifically, it presupposes that, in due course, there will be a gas pipeline and an energy corridor along the Mackenzie Valley. But these would not be the only forms of economic development: the development that would result from the pipeline and related activities would be balanced by a parallel development of the renewable resource sector of the economy. Many potential large-scale industrial developments in the North would be site-specific and, once established, they would offer employment opportunities at only a few locations. But if that is to be the only kind of development, the social and economic impacts of such activity will be magnified throughout the entire region: native people will be drawn to it for want of any alternative, and the social and economic consequences will proliferate in communities and families far from the project itself. Only balanced

economic development can ameliorate or avoid such effects. It is, therefore, vital that development of the renewable resource sector be given priority now. If it is not strengthened and thriving by the time a pipeline is built, native people will not be able to withstand the impact of the pipeline project and all that it will entail.

Non-renewable resource industries, including the oil and gas industry, sometimes produce uncertain and sharply fluctuating patterns of economic growth. Northerners must be protected, so far as is practicable, against the impacts of such uncertainty and fluctuation — another compelling reason for insisting on the development of an alternative, long-term and stable renewable resource sector. In addition, as the evidence referred to in Volume One shows, there are historical and cultural reasons for thinking that native people consider the land and its renewable resources to be of special importance to them and to their children.

All of these considerations demonstrate the importance of a mixed economy in the North. My report accepts the view that the development of Canadian frontier gas and oil is in the national interest, but if such development is to take place with the least disruption of native people and native society, it must be preceded by the development of its alternatives. Because alternative development has for so long been neglected, it must now be given priority. The social and economic recommendations made in this volume are designed to ensure that a Mackenzie Valley pipeline will come at a time when it will confer tangible economic benefits on the North and when its social impact can be mitigated.

Nonetheless, we must be aware of the problems that may be created by the potentially intensive effects of any large-scale industrial development. Its volatile patterns of growth, strongly-formed work conventions, and its effects on both local environment and local society, mean that the future relationship between the renewable and the non-renewable sectors of the northern economy will not be simple. Rather, that relationship must seek to minimize the direct dependence of the renewable upon the non-renewable resource sector, otherwise the whole renewable resource sector would be continually vulnerable to the economic interests and activities of the South. Development of the renewable resource sector must therefore aim at some considerable degree of independence from the non-renewable sector. In the following chapter on Renewable Resources, I consider some of the specific problems and possibilities to which this consideration gives rise.

Two Philosophies

Before turning to specific socio-economic considerations, I would like to make very plain the contrast between two philosophies of northern development. This subject, which was raised in Volume One, bears directly on the nature of the terms and conditions that should be applied to social and economic impacts.

On the one hand, there is the well-established opinion that large-scale industrial development will bring the benefits of employment opprtunities to all northerners. It is a point of view that emphasizes both the failures of the past and the possibilities of the future. The proponents of the philosophy concede that large-scale industrial development, both in the North and on other frontiers, has not always led to the employment of large numbers of native people or to their overall economic advantage. This failure has at times been regarded as lamentable, but as something that appropriate governmental intervention could set right. In other words, this philosophy emphasizes the economic potential of large-scale industrial development, and turns us towards terms and conditions that would guarantee the realization of that potential. It turns our attention towards ensuring that native people take their place at the industrial frontier, and it has led to a consideration of manpower delivery systems and of ways to provide the northern businessman with special preferences in connection with pipeline construction.

On the other hand, there is a philosophy of northern development that emphasizes the importance of the native economy and the renewable resource sector and the wishes of the native people themselves. It was this point of view that I emphasized in Volume One. This philosophy causes us to re-examine the conventional wisdom regarding the benefits that are always assumed to accompany the advance of the industrial system to the frontier. It is skeptical of the advantages to native people of large-scale industrial development and it urges us to strengthen the native economy and the renewable resource sector, including logging, sawmilling, fishing, trapping, recreation and conservation. It advocates the removal of all impediments to the development of renewable resources and the modernization of the renewable resource sector, with a view to securing the basis of the native economy for the future. This philosophy does not reject oil and gas exploration and the pipeline. Rather, it holds that a pipeline should not be built until the strengthened renewable resource

sector is in place and that, in the meantime, oil and gas exploration should proceed in an orderly way.

Advocates of the first philosophy often insist that the second is the outcome of sentimentality. But, as proponents of the second philosophy have pointed out, a policy of economic development in the North that ignores native society and the native economy must inevitably undermine that society and that economy. This neglect of the renewable resource sector forecloses the possibility of developing over time a truly diversified northern economy.

Since the publication of Volume One, I have often been asked why I place so much emphasis on the native economy, and on the renewable resource potential of the North. The answer is clear enough: the objective of northern development should be parallel economic sectors — large-scale industrial activity, where and when it is necessary and appropriate, co-existing with continuing development of the native economy and the renewable resource sector. But where the two economic forms exist side by side, it is the renewable resource sector that is likely to be at risk: large-scale industrial development in the North intrudes, often totally, on native peoples and their way of life. To ensure parallel development, the renewable resource sector, which has been neglected, must be defined. The point is that undue policy emphasis on the non-renewable resource sector results in undue dependency on that sector. Unless priority is given now to the renewable resource sector, the mixed economy of the North will inevitably evolve into a single, non-renewable resource economy. This kind of monolithic economic mode is not what native people want, nor, in my judgment, what most northerners or, indeed, most Canadians want.

Various Project Situations

It is important that parallel development be applied throughout the North, but we must not forget that circumstances differ from place to place, and that future development will not follow the same course in every part of the region. In particular, I have in mind the differences between the Mackenzie Valley and the Mackenzie Delta. Although I have argued for a ten-year postponement of pipeline construction along the Mackenzie Valley, I have anticipated that the search for resources in the Mackenzie Delta and the Beaufort Sea will continue. It is also possible that other exploration activities will take place in the Western Arctic, and that these activities will be acceptable to some of the native communities in the area. We must recognize that large-scale industrial activity in the Mackenzie Delta has come to stay, but we should try to limit the impact of such developments to Inuvik, Tuktoyaktuk, and the Delta, and not let them extend to the smaller communities on Amundsen Gulf. Therefore, our consideration of terms and conditions should take into account the differences in the prospects for these two areas.

Similarly, there are important differences between the larger centres, which I call action communities, and the small villages. In the larger centres there are communities of businessmen, predominantly white, and they should be the beneficiaries of certain preferences if northern business is to enjoy a reasonable measure of growth and expansion as a result of pipeline construction. I make certain recommendations in this regard in Chapter 5.

There are other differences that directly affect the native people and the kinds of future they are likely to want. In the larger and economically more developed communities, such as Hay River, Yellowknife, and Inuvik, native people do use and, in varying degrees, continue to depend upon the land and its produce. But their dependence upon wage employment — including employment by local, territorial and federal government, as well as industrial employment — is in some cases high. In the smaller settlements, dependence upon the land and its produce is greater, and development of the renewable resource sector there will be of great importance. Chapter 2, which pertains to the measurement and development of renewable resource potential, has important implications for the economic life of all the communities in the region.

The Past and the Future

The various philosophies of northern development have, of course, been reflected in different accounts of northern history: our views of the past are — perhaps inevitably — closely related to our broad views and concepts of human well-being and human purpose. Evidence given to the Inquiry showed repeatedly how differences in philosophy can reveal themselves. At times, these differences resulted in conflicting, if not opposing, conclusions, and there were profound disagreements on how events had shaped the northern scene — especially with regard to native people in recent times.

It is never easy to stand aside from differing interpretations of historical events and assess, from an informed but neutral position, their appropriateness and their implications. But, within the several historical overviews, there are, I believe, some crucial areas of consensus, and these areas relate to the domination of native society by white society.

Although the relative advantages and disadvantages of the fur trade have been judged quite differently by various historians of the North, they all more or less agree that the white presence — from the missions and fur trade to the advent of industry and the proliferation of government institutions — represented, and continues to represent, a domination of native society. Moreover, historians also agree that there is an intrinsic relationship between this domination and the cluster of social pathologies and economic difficulties that native people have experienced especially in recent years. This consensus, in relation to both dominance and its consequences, was epitomized in this way in the submission of Commission Counsel:

At both community hearings and in the form of overview evidence, this Inquiry heard many accounts of recent northern history. These suggested that dominance of native northern society by southern interests has constituted a pervasive and persistent problem, only marginally compensated for by the provision of a certain level of economic (as distinct from social) stability, and some well-intentioned ... support schemes. [Commission Counsel, 1976, "Basic Issues," p. 1]

Although witnesses did not agree on how best to resolve the present difficulties in the North, by and large they did agree that southern intrusion into and domination over northern social processes have generated serious problems. A number of these problems were mentioned repeatedly, and were, therefore, central to the arguments in Volume One: alcohol, violence, inter-generational strife, and some distinctive forms of individual disarray. It is, of course, extremely difficult to articulate the precise forms of such pathologies, and still more difficult to identify their precise and immediate causes. Insofar as experts have sought to identify the causes, they have pointed to the domination of native society by white interests; they have pointed equally to the speed of social change and to the difficulty native people inevitably experienced in trying to comprehend and adapt to the resulting transformations in their lives. A lack of control over their society and their economy lies at the heart of many of the social and economic difficulties.

It follows that, in seeking to resolve the difficulties, and to ameliorate or eliminate the real problem, we must focus on the question of fundamental social, economic and political relationships. If we do otherwise, we obscure the real issue and make believe, so to speak, that band-aids can cure illness. Thus the proposals made in this Part — indeed in this volume — should be read with the knowledge that there is a fundamental need to establish new institutions in the North. In this way, we can attack the problems of domination and begin to move towards the fundamental causes of northern malaise. The settlement of native claims offers the means to achieve this.

Unless the native peoples and other long-term residents of the North believe that they have and do, in fact, have a major role in the decision-making process, the old relationships will persist: no amount of short-term ameliorative measures will even begin to reverse the social and economic trends that I have identified in this report and that I have seen so often during the course of this Inquiry. Endorsement of this principle does, of course, mean acceptance of and confidence in the northern peoples themselves. We can ensure that appropriate southern skills and resources are made available in the North, but it is not for us in the South to say what native peoples should do about their society and its difficulties. If new institutions are properly structured, control of society will be accompanied by the identification and control of the society's problems. Many of the specific terms and conditions proposed in this volume cannot properly be considered until new institutions are in place. In this way, the historical tradition of dealings between white and native people on this continent will, for once, have been broken. This is the only means by which the basic causes of socio-economic and individual malaise in the North can be addressed.

THE REPORT OF
THE MACKENZIE VALLEY
PIPELINE INQUIRY

PART ONE —
PEOPLE: SOCIAL AND
ECONOMIC CONCERNS

2 Renewable Resources

The evidence before this Inquiry has clearly established the importance of renewable resources in the northern economy. This sector of the economy has provided and must continue to provide native people with employment and income and, therefore, we require adequate knowledge of its present status and future potential. Yet the statistical evidence on the use of renewable resources that was presented to the Inquiry was incomplete, inadequate and sometimes confusing. I have, therefore, asked my staff to compile and analyze the available data for the Mackenzie Valley and Western Arctic. They have brought together a great deal of valuable information including data from the region under study and from elsewhere that has become available since the hearings of this Inquiry ended. In the first two sections of this chapter, I have used these recent data and other information, in addition to evidence presented to the Inquiry, to review the data base and to analyze the production of and trends in the traditional economy.

In Volume One, I pointed out that the present lack of data is an indirect consequence of government policy; that is to say, the government, having decided that renewable resources did not provide a sufficient basis for economic development in the North, has made no attempt to estimate the present or potential contribution of these resources to the northern economy. So the tendency to ignore the potential of the renewable resource sector was reinforced. I therefore thought it worthwhile to prepare this discussion of the measurement and the production of the traditional economy. Game managers and wildlife biologists have long been aware of many of the shortcomings in the data that they have helped to record, and they may find little that is new in the ensuing discussion. It is clear from the submissions made to the Inquiry, however, that few economic analysts who have considered the northern economy have shared that awareness.

Most economic analyses are flawed by one or more of three major methodological errors. First, participation in the traditional economy is underestimated because employment in it is, in effect, defined to include only those activities that generate cash. Secondly, the volume of production is underestimated because of a frequently uncritical reliance on the government's fur and game statistics — figures that were not specifically designed to measure and, in fact, do not measure the total harvest. Thirdly, even if replacement costs are used as the basis for imputing value to country produce (and by no means all analyses do that), both the identification and evaluation of appropriate substitute commodities are incorrect because neither measurable nutritional differences nor intangible factors of culture and taste are properly taken into account. These errors combine to produce estimates that may be as little as a tenth of the real gross value of fur, fish and game production. Methods used to measure economic performance in an industrial society clearly do not work well when they are applied to a mixed economy with a significant domestic component.

The economic evaluation offered here is by no means intended to be the last word on the measurement of the traditional economy. The data sources are so doubtful, and there are so many compounding sources of error, that a wide range of estimates are at present possible. In presenting this evaluation, I am trying to provide a framework or a model for analyzing the native economy, and I also make some recommendations for the improvement of the methods of data collection.

In the third part of this chapter, I examine the potential for renewable resource development. The discussion is necessarily tentative because information that we have on the actual resource base is so limited. I am also concerned with the objectives of renewable resource development, particularly with the potential that may exist for processing and marketing, and I examine the implications of such development for employment and income in the North.

Finally, I review the problems that have bedevilled renewable resource development, both now and in the past. It is not my proper role to make specific recommendations for development — that would usurp the local initiatives that will be so essential to its success and to encroach upon areas that should be negotiated as part of native claims. Instead, I outline the context in which renewable resource development must occur and the criteria that any specific endeavour must meet, if it is to be successful in the long run. My chief concern here is that the development of renewable resources should go forward with native initiative and under native control. Governments ought to supply financial and technical assistance, but they should play a supporting rather than a leading role.

Inadequacies of Existing Data Bases

Any assessment of the productivity, value and significance of the traditional sector of the economy in northern Canada must be based on accurate statistical data. They in turn must be based on precise, agreed definitions of terms and of the purposes for which the data are collected, and on an efficient and workable system for collecting and maintaining the data. It is a measure of the neglect of the traditional economy in the development of public policy that neither of these requirements can, at present, be met. Very simply, there exist no systems for the regular collection of data that can provide simple, accurate indications of the numbers of people participating in the traditional sector of the economy, or of the volume or value of their produce. As a result, a variety of statistics and estimates have been placed before this Inquiry; on inspection, they differ in purpose and definition as well as in their absolute numbers. It is important, therefore, to examine the nature and causes of these differing estimates and to resolve these differences, so far as possible, to provide a clearly understandable statistical assessment of the traditional sector today.

Participation in the Traditional Economy

The wide variation in the estimates of the number of trappers in the Mackenzie Valley placed before this Inquiry (96 by Arctic Gas, 1,075 by the Indian Brotherhood of the Northwest Territories) was noted in Volume One. We saw there that the problem was one of fundamentally different definitions, rather than one of simple enumeration, and that neither the number of people defined occupationally as trappers nor the number defined by adherence to a way of life as trappers provides an adequate measure of the degree of participation in the traditional economy. Yet to judge the performance of that economy, it would be helpful to know how many people participate in it and benefit from it.

Unfortunately there are no precise estimates of the native population or of the native labour force in northern Canada at either the community or the regional level. In an examination of all of the censuses conducted by public authorities or private agencies in recent years, we find widely but inexplicably differing results. Few of these censuses explain their definitions or methodology. In Volume One, I estimated that

there are about 15,000 native people in the Mackenzie Valley and Western Arctic. Discounting for natural increase, the figure for 1972-1973 would have been a little less than 14,000. I shall use this figure for purposes of comparison with other data presented later in this chapter.

Estimates of the labour force are as inadequate and inconsistent as figures for population. If we assume that half of the native population is male, and that half of that population is under the age of 16, then the available male labour force may be estimated to be 25 percent of the native population or slightly less, if we discount for old people. This calculation suggests a native male labour force of about 3,000 for the region as a whole.

We can compare this figure with the number of General Hunting Licence holders, the number of people who trade furs, and the number who earn at least $400 annually from fur sales. These figures are presented in Table 1.1.

In considering these figures as indicators of participation, the following factors should be kept in mind. General Hunting Licences are issued annually free of charge, but not automatically, to native people. Usually, members of the immediate family are permitted to hunt on the licence of the head of a household. If everyone eligible to hold a General Hunting Licence actually obtained one, the number issued would be approximately the same as the number of native males of working age. Because the hunter must obtain the licence on his own initiative, it seems likely that those who do so actually exercise their hunting rights. It is possible that some people obtain General Hunting Licences for purely symbolic reasons and do not actually hunt, but I think their number — if any — is insignificant for the period under discussion. Available evidence suggests that, on average, at least one person per household obtains a General Hunting Licence, but there are no good figures for the number of native households in the Mackenzie Valley and Western Arctic.

Table 1.1 suggests that about three-quarters of the native males of working age in the region engage in at least some hunting, although not all of them provide the major part of their families' diets by hunting. We can assume that some of the food these hunters obtain is distributed to families that do not have active hunters, but again there is no basis for estimating the number of such families or the quantity of food they receive.

So far we have been discussing estimates of the number of native people engaged in hunting for food for themselves and their families. Now let us look at the native people engaged in trapping for fur, that is, for cash. The number of people who trade furs does not necessarily indicate the number of them who actually harvest furs. The number may be an overestimate because furs may, through a variety of circumstances, be given to non-trappers or an underestimate because furs trapped by members of a household may be traded for sale through the head of the household. The former consideration probably outweighs the latter, so that perhaps only about half of those who hunt also obtain furs (the number of hunters, if any, who obtain furs but no meat must be insignificant). If hunters who obtain furs solely from the spring muskrat hunt and hunters who set only a few traps at the edge of town are excluded, perhaps about one-quarter of those who hunt also set trap lines.

In the entire region under consideration, the number of trappers who earned over $400 in 1972-1973 was probably about 450 or about 15 percent of the native males of working age. In 1975-1976, however, 764 trappers in the region, or about one-quarter of native men, earned over $400. This difference is chiefly a reflection of increased fur prices, for the same level of effort would place more trappers over this mark, but it may also indicate increased participation, perhaps in response to market conditions or to a revival of interest in trapping.

Clearly, there are many more participants and, indeed, many more significant participants in the native economy than a census of those whose primary occupation is trapping would suggest. Equally clearly, only a minority of those who identify themselves culturally as trappers in fact earn their living, or even the greater part of their living, by trapping, although hunting is economically important to the great majority of them.

Unfortunately, I have no direct measurements with which to confirm these observations. I refer to the native economy, yet there are no standard figures for the numbers of native people who are the primary participants and beneficiaries of that economy. The basic unit of production in the native economy is the family or household, yet there is no standard, reliable census of households. Any analysis of the native economy must take into account the number of people who are actively engaged in fur, fish and game harvesting, and the extent to which they are involved in it. Yet there is not even a commonly accepted definition, let alone an enumeration, of these people. We can only make inferences from other forms of data that are available, but they are a poor substitute for the information that is really needed. Such inferences and estimates are subject to many kinds of error, only some of which have been described above. Put simply, no one can provide a clear picture of the participation of the native people in the traditional economy on the basis of the available information.

The Volume of Production

In economic terms, the volume of production is the number of animals taken by hunters and trappers that are potentially useful to them. This number is in contrast to the harvest as defined by a game manager: the total number of animals cropped from a population by hunting or trapping. Our statistics do not, therefore, include animals lost through wounding, waste or predation before retrieval. They do, however, include animals that may be lost through spoilage or

otherwise made unusable or unsaleable after retrieval. By retrieval is meant the use, storage or consumption of an animal at or near the site of the kill or the loading of all or part of the animal for transportation elsewhere for its subsequent use, consumption or sale.

The only uniformly and continuously maintained series of statistical data on wildlife harvests in the Northwest Territories are the Fur Export Tax Returns and the General Hunting Licence Returns kept by the territorial Fish and Wildlife Service. Both of these returns are aggregated annually by community. Officially compiled annual summaries of fur exports have been maintained since 1953, and statistics for hunting kills are available from 1963 onwards, although data have been obtained under ordinances made for both subjects since about 1930. Earlier tabulations are available, but they are generally less complete. Annual reports on game compiled by RCMP detachments are undoubtedly a valuable additional source of information, but they are not summarized by community and year and they were discontinued after 1972. In any event, they have not formed the basis of any presentation to this Inquiry on the volume of country food production. There are other, independent observations or sources of data on country food, but they are sporadic in time and place, of varying quality and reliability, and they are, therefore, rarely comparable.

Virtually all of the evidence on the production of country food placed before the Inquiry was based on the two series of returns maintained by the Fish and Wildlife Service of the Government of the Northwest Territories. Gemini North and the Environment Protection Board used these statistics unquestioningly. Dr. Michael Asch and Scott Rushforth, on behalf of the Indian Brotherhood of the Northwest Territories, and Dr. Peter Usher, on behalf of the Committee for Original Peoples Entitlement also used these two series, although all three witnesses questioned their validity. Usher made some estimates of the direction and magnitude of the bias of these figures, and both Rushforth and Usher provided some of their own field data.

Several government reports that provided important background material for this Inquiry also relied on the statistics of the territorial government, in every case without questioning their validity or adjusting them for possible error. These reports include two by Don Bissett on native resource use (one of which was prepared under the auspices of the Economic Staff Group), one on Old Crow by John Stager, all for the Environmental-Social Committee, and two earlier reports on the native economy by Chang-Mei Lu and John Palmer of the Economic Staff Group of the Department of Indian Affairs and Northern Development. Gemini North relied heavily on Bissett's work in particular.

The Fish and Wildlife Service statistics clearly provided the primary basis for measuring the production of the native economy, but do these figures really measure those harvests? Usher has emphasized that, in fact, they only approximate the actual fur and game harvests, and he examined the causes of their errors (Exhibit F656). More recent research on wildlife harvests in the Mackenzie Valley (Usher, 1977) and northern Quebec (James Bay and Northern Quebec Native Harvesting Research Committee, 1976) now enable us to assess the magnitude of error in these official statistics in more detail. The information from northern Quebec is particularly relevant, because of the attempt to deal practically with this problem in an adversary situation.

The fur export tax was first levied, as its name implies, on furs exported from the Northwest Territories to raise revenue to offset the administration costs; since 1967 the tax has been nominal, and the requirement for an export permit has been retained solely for the purpose of collecting data. These returns have always been the best indicator of the fur harvests in the Northwest Territories, and they have, therefore, been the basis for the official figures on territorial fur production. That, however, was not the primary reason for keeping these figures, and neither these returns nor any other existing system of keeping records was designed explicitly to measure the actual harvest of fur.

The purpose of the General Hunting Licence in the Northwest Territories has always been to control access to fur and game resources. Because the licence is supposed to be turned in at the end of each year, together with a declaration from memory of the holder's harvest of big game and birds (and, until 1961, of fur), it has also served as a means of keeping records. However, the requirement to turn in the licence is not enforced.

These systems of collecting data cannot be criticized for failing to reveal information that they were not designed to elicit, but anyone who uses the data they supply for different purposes should understand the risks in doing so. Clearly, both the Fur Export Tax Returns and the General Hunting Licence Returns have an inherent bias toward underestimating harvests because they record only furs exported raw and whatever big game and birds that the licence holders declare. We can examine the sources and magnitude of this bias on a species-by-species basis. Table 1.2 lists the economic species of wildlife and fish harvested in the Mackenzie Valley and Western Arctic with which we are concerned in this report. Other species are occasionally harvested, but they invariably constitute an insignificant proportion of the total volume of production. The discussion of the errors inherent in official statistics is limited to the figures gathered since 1965.

FURBEARERS

The volume of production of furbearing animals is approximated from summaries of the Fur Export Tax Returns. These returns do not include furs that are not recorded as exported from the Northwest Territories. Furs may be retained in the Northwest Territories for various reasons. Pelts retrieved by trappers that are of poor or unsaleable quality may be used for domestic clothing or handicrafts, or they may be discarded. In

some cases the meat of the animal is used, even if its pelt is not. Good quality pelts may be retained for domestic use, either in clothing or in handicrafts. The most popular furs for clothing are muskrat, beaver, lynx, coloured fox, wolf, coyote and wolverine, although fur preferences vary by region. The pelts of muskrat and white fox are probably the most commonly used in handicrafts. If there are quotas on the sales of pelt, the proportion of furs used domestically is likely to increase, and the number of furbearers taken only for food may also increase. Because export permits are required only for raw furs, it is of interest to note that, should a tannery be established in the North, furs exported after being worked would not be recorded under the present system.

In addition, as public transportation has improved in the North and as more and more outsiders have come to the North for work or pleasure, the scope for private sales by trappers has greatly increased. When the Fur Export Tax ordinance was enacted in 1929, furs were shipped out of the Northwest Territories only by water and there were but two export points for the entire region: Herschel Island and Fort Smith. The passage of people and pelts through these centres could be closely observed and controlled. Fur was then the basis of the regional economy and regulations concerning the fur trade were common knowledge. Today a trapper in even the most isolated settlement can sell furs to tourists or transient workers for good prices and immediate cash. There is no reason to suppose that deliberate smuggling of furs out of the Northwest Territories is or ever was widespread, but the number of pelts exported or sold in ignorance of the regulations is almost certainly increasing. The fact that tanneries in the South will not accept improperly tagged furs for processing must, however, act as a brake on this tendency.

How insignificant are these factors in relation to the total fur harvest? No accurate answer can be given without an intensive survey that would involve a large sample of trappers. Rushforth gave in evidence some estimates of the differences at Fort Franklin, and other unpublished information provides further indications.

In Table 1.3, the error in officially recorded figures for the fur harvest of each species is estimated for the Mackenzie Valley and Western Arctic as a whole, taking into account domestic retention only. These estimates are conservative and based on very limited information; they take no account of unreported exports, which cannot be estimated. All analyses of official records, including my own analysis, indicate a substantial decline in the number of furs taken in most of the Mackenzie Valley during the early 1970s. We cannot rule out the possibility that at least a part of this decline may be attributable to leakage in the form of unreported exports; if such is the case, trends in fur production will become more and more difficult to identify in the future. This example is but one of many to show how systems to collect economic data that were designed for the closed economy of yesterday's

North can no longer work in the more open and fluid economy that prevails today.

For comparison, Table 1.3 shows the estimates of error by species between official records and observed harvests in northern Quebec. In all cases, they are much higher than our own estimates for the Northwest Territories, and they are much more thoroughly documented. The research in Quebec is being carried out in connection with the James Bay and Northern Québec Agreement, and the question has assumed considerable significance. No doubt there are important differences in the official means of recording the fur harvest in the two jurisdictions, but the discrepancies in northern Quebec are so remarkable as to warrant a thorough review of the data base in the Northwest Territories.

The export of seal pelts has been recorded officially only since 1971, whereas local sales have been recorded since 1961. The same downward bias in recording applies, chiefly because of their use in handicrafts, but there are even greater discrepancies in the records for the total seal harvest. They are discussed below in the subsection on marine mammals.

BIG GAME

The kill statistics derived from General Hunting Licence Returns provide the basis for estimating big game harvests, except for muskoxen. Bear harvests are recorded by both General Hunting Licence Returns and Fur Export Tax Returns. There are quotas allocated by settlement on the harvests of both muskoxen and polar bears. Both quotas are normally filled, so recent harvests of these animals are assumed to be equal to the total of the quotas for the region, except where reliable records indicate otherwise. No polar bear hides, and probably no muskox hides, are retained for domestic purposes.

The Fur Export Tax Returns records do not distinguish between black and brown bears, although the General Hunting Licence Returns records do. Because the dominant proportion of the harvest is composed of black bears, the two species are combined for the purposes of this report. There appears to be a considerable retention of black bear hides for domestic use, because the General Hunting Licence Returns bear harvest totals are generally much larger than the Fur Export Tax Returns totals. Even the former totals, however, must be underestimates because of incomplete reporting.

Harvests of the ungulate species are all calculated exclusively on the basis of General Hunting Licence Returns declarations. These species provide a substantial proportion of the food supply for most communities, so it is important to appreciate the downward bias of their numbers in the official records because of non-reporting, non-recording, and misreporting. First, because not all licence holders make the statutory declaration, reporting is incomplete. Secondly, a hunter's declaration of his entire year's harvest is made wholly from memory, although the Fish and Wildlife Service has attempted at times to provide simple recording aids to

licence holders. Thirdly, there may be deliberate underreporting of some harvests, particularly of caribou and geese, if the native people fear that the authorities may be thinking of restriction or regulation of hunting.

All of these considerations bias downwards the official statistics for wildlife harvests. How far downward cannot be said for certain without more extensive research, although we do have some indications. For the years 1968 to 1973, the Fish and Wildlife Service has figures on the numbers of general hunting licences returned as well as issued, and these numbers are summarized in Table 1.4. The non-reporting rate is clearly high, and it is apparently increasing. It is impossible to know if non-reporting occurs at random, therefore I cannot simply apply these percentages in compensation to the kill statistics. For example, it may be that non-reporting is more common among less active hunters. The bias caused by non-recording is probably very small for big game species, for the great majority of hunters remember easily and accurately the number of such animals they have taken. Much more difficult to gauge is the magnitude of deliberate underreporting, because there is no direct evidence about it. Of the three factors taken together, however, non-reporting is undoubtedly the most important cause of downward bias for the harvest of big game.

Some evidence has been offered on the total difference between reported and actual harvests. Table 1.5A compares Rushforth's figures on Fort Franklin caribou harvests taken from interviews with those reported in the kill statistics. If Rushforth's data from Fort Franklin are indicative, then less than half of the caribou taken are recorded by the kill statistics. This difference is probably not equally great throughout the region as a whole because the percentage of General Hunting Licences returned is higher in most of those settlements, such as Rae, that account for the bulk of the regional caribou harvest.

Table 1.5B provides a comparison between Dall's sheep harvests, as determined by interviews, and those accounted for in the kill statistics. The interviews covered a substantial proportion of the total sheep harvest, and they may be representative of the region as a whole. No comparable estimates are available for moose, but, because moose kills are both memorable and widely reported locally, the bias in official statistics must be largely restricted to non-reporting. Bison are harvested under quota, and the reported totals for them are close to the allowable limit.

BIRDS

Four categories of birds are tabulated in the kill statistics: ducks, geese, ptarmigan and grouse. They comprise almost all of the birds harvested by native people. All the same reasons for the downward bias in the official statistics for big game are true of birds, but to a greater degree, because non-recording of bird harvests is much more prevalent. Hunters are less likely to keep an accurate mental count of bird kills than of animal kills, especially for ptarmigan, grouse, and probably ducks; these birds are usually obtained incidentally in the pursuit of other game and many may be taken by several members of a family under one licence. Geese are the objects of special hunts, so the numbers of them taken are more likely to be remembered — but here again the native people have reason to underreport their harvests. The kill statistics for birds are, therefore, highly unreliable. Table 1.6, which shows Rushforth's data based on interviews and some comparative evidence from other parts of the North, indicates that the actual harvests of birds are much higher than the kill statistics indicate.

OTHER SPECIES

We must also consider here the harvests of species that the official fur and game statistics fail to record and that most other studies have also ignored, no doubt for that reason.

In the Beaufort Sea region, marine mammals are important. The number of sealskins traded or exported are recorded, with the same errors noted above, but these numbers by no means tell the whole story. Many seals are used for food (chiefly dog food), the skins of which are not traded. Dr. Tom Smith's evidence from Holman, presented in Table 1.7, suggests that the difference between seals harvested and sealskins traded is substantial. Yet there are no consistent data on the actual harvest of seals as opposed to the trade in sealskins. The ratio of seals taken to sealskins sold varies significantly with price, and in interpreting Table 1.7, it should be kept in mind that prices were relatively much higher in the mid-1960s than in the 1970s. It is not possible, therefore, to suggest a reliable conversion factor by which the actual harvest may be estimated from official records. The harvest of white whales is recorded informally by the federal Fisheries and Marine Service, and their totals appear to be reliable, although they do not provide a consistent geographical break-down.

Throughout the region, fish are a major food resource, yet there is no regular tabulation of the catch nor even a uniform — let alone an adequate — methodology for making one. Occasional surveys of varying reliability have been conducted. Usually the catch is recorded by weight, but in some cases only the numbers of fish are recorded. The available data for some areas are apparently incomplete, so they would lead to an underestimation of the regional total. Because the techniques of observation and recording are never clearly stated, other causes of bias, and whether the bias is upward or downward, are not known.

Another important food source, particularly in the Mackenzie Valley, is hare. So far as I can find, there is not a single quantitative estimate of the hare catch in any part of the Mackenzie Valley and Western Arctic, except for Banks Island, where the catch appears to be far smaller than anywhere else. Yet, by all accounts, hares form a significant part of the diet among the Dene. Here again, estimates from the James Bay region may be useful. Hares are cyclic in abundance and, according to Martin Weinstein (1975), they provide between near zero and 25 percent of the total country food harvest at Fort George, depending on the point in the hare's population cycle. These considerations suggest that it would be appropriate to add perhaps five percent to the total weight of food calculated from the harvest of all other species to represent hare meat. The proportion would probably be lower in some communities, particularly those north and east of Great Slave Lake, where caribou form a large part of the diet, and on the Arctic coast, where the consumption of hare meat seems to be relatively low. Finally, we have no data whatever, and there are no estimates, on other supplies of country food, including eggs and plant products.

TOTAL NUMBERS OF ANIMALS

I should emphasize that this discussion of statistical recording so far concerns the Northwest Territories. It may not apply equally to the Yukon, although the Alaska Highway Pipeline Inquiry found that data on the traditional economy there was also inadequate. In the statistical tabulations given in the second section of this chapter, I have applied correction factors for the Northwest Territories to data from Old Crow. Because about 95 percent of the wildlife harvest we are examining is from the Northwest Territories, any different bias that affects the Yukon figures should not significantly affect the totals given here.

Table 1.8 provides estimates of error in the kill statistics for big game and birds. They are conservative estimates, based on the information and inferences discussed above. I believe that more accurate estimates based on adequate research will prove in every case to be higher.

Once the number of animals harvested is known, the next problem is to determine how much food they have produced. This answer is most easily calculated as the sum of the products, for each species, of the numbers taken and the average edible yield by weight per animal.

THE AVERAGE EDIBLE YIELD OF ANIMALS

There are no uniform, reliable measurements of the average edible yield of northern fur and game animals because of inadequate field data and lingering problems of definition. There are relatively few actual measurements of live or component weights of northern animals. A common technique for estimating the edible weight of an animal has been to use a set percentage of its live weight, based on estimates from meat packing houses (for example, 50 percent of the live weight of cow-shaped animals and 70 percent of the live weight of pig-shaped animals and of birds). The James Bay Research Committee calculated food weight value as the product of the average whole weight multiplied by the percentage of the whole weight that is convertible to food. Yet for some species, especially some of the larger mammals, there are very few records of their live weights.

Here are some of the problems in attempting to make useful estimates of average edible yields. First, different populations or races of the same species may have different growth curves and average sizes. The averages for one population may not, therefore, apply to another.

Secondly, the concept of the average individual live weight of population has relatively little meaning unless it can be related to the actual harvest. Some live weight records for big game, for example, have been obtained largely from specimens killed by sports hunters. Such records usually refer to the oldest males in the population. Native hunters, on the other hand, may select younger age classes or females. The age–sex composition of the subsistence harvest varies both geographically and culturally. An accurate weight index would, therefore, require two sets of data: the mean weights for males and females of each age class in a population, and an age–sex break-down of the subsistence harvest of that population. Rarely is either set of data available.

Thirdly, the relation of edible yield to live weight must be established. Ignoring cultural preferences for the moment, to establish this relation will require accurate data on the component weights of each species in terms of meat, fat, bone and edible and inedible viscera. Seasonal variations in these components, particularly of fat, and the seasonal break-down of the subsistence harvest must be known, because the weight and condition of every species varies significantly throughout the year. Certain definitions must be agreed on: for example, should edible weight include the bone-in portion of the dressed carcass. There is no general agreement on this point in the literature, nor are the methodology or the data recorded uniform. Adequate data on component weights would enable us to calculate potential edible yield, as well as actual edible yield, according to cultural preference. In the absence of such data, many researchers have used the standard meat packers' estimates referred to above.

Finally, cultural preferences and practices must be known in order to estimate the actual edible yields of animals. It is generally agreed that native people use more parts of an animal than are culturally preferred by southern Canadians. Conversion factors must, therefore, take into account the possible use of heads and some organs that are not accounted for in the packing house estimates. Native butchering techniques and native use of an animal varies with time and place. Information on these matters is sporadic at best.

Despite these problems of definition and of measurement, three attempts have been made to summarize existing knowledge of edible yields of northern animals. They were made by Don Foote (1965), Peter Usher (1971) and the James Bay and Northern Quebec Native Harvesting Research Committee (1976). Of these three, the last is the most reliable, because it is the most thoroughly considered and it is based on the most recent available data. The Committee's criteria for determining edible weights also have the merit of being the joint and agreed result of research undertaken by adversary parties in a situation involving conflict over resource use. Accordingly, unless otherwise specified, these criteria and figures are used in this analysis. Their acceptance by disputing parties does not automatically make them scientifically correct, of course, and the Committee has stated that a conservative interpretation of conflicting evidence has been the rule. For species not found in the James Bay region, or when the data from James Bay have not been applicable, other sources of information have been used. No figures are given here for individual fish species because the harvest records of fish are generally available by total weight rather than by numbers.

Table 1.9 provides the best estimates of the average edible weights of each species for each of the five regions discussed in this analysis. These weights are used to determine the amount of food produced by the native economy. The total harvest weights derived by this means (shown in Tables 2.5, 2.6 and 2.7) refer largely to flesh, as opposed to fat. The specialized food yields of animals that are high in fat, that is, marine mammals, are considered separately and are not included in the weight totals. The figures for average edible yield do not take into account waste or cultural variations in the use of parts of the animal.

Existing analyses of native food harvests have not been consistent in their use of conversion factors for edible weights, which has added to the confusion. The conversion factors used here should in all cases supersede those used in previous government reports and in earlier submissions to this Inquiry. The conversion factors previously used have shown no consistent directional bias, so recalculation of previous work using the present conversion factors will not consistently produce higher or lower results. The objective in recalculating previous work is to move toward uniformity of analysis.

1. There is a need to devise a standard methodology and to obtain data through field surveys.

The Value of Production

FUR

The primary source of data for the value of the fur harvest in the Northwest Territories is the Traders Fur Record Books, which record all of the furs bought and the prices paid by licenced fur dealers in the Northwest Territories. The average price per pelt paid to trappers is calculated from these data, and the total value of the harvest of each species is calculated by multiplying the total pelts by the average price. This calculation provides an underestimate of the income to trappers for several reasons.

The calculation does not take into account the substantially higher prices received by trappers who export their furs directly to auction or who take advantage of the Northwest Territories Fur Marketing Service. In some communities, a high proportion of the furs taken is marketed through these outlets. The calculation does not take into account private sales to local non-natives and tourists, for which usually substantially higher prices are realized. Also, it does not take account of the fact that trappers who divide their sales among local dealers, auction houses and private sales probably tend to reserve their poorest furs for the local dealers. The average quoted prices in the Northwest Territories may therefore refer to the lower grades of fur, and this may explain why these figures are consistently below the national average prices listed by Statistics Canada.

Without extensive further research, I cannot accurately estimate the magnitude of these causes of error, but the error could well be of the order of 10 percent.

FOOD

No one method is used consistently to evaluate the production of country food. Because this food rarely enters the market place, its value can only be imputed. The general principle that its imputed value must be reckoned on the basis of the cost of substitution was clearly established at this Inquiry on the understanding that we are dealing here with a question of economic welfare rather than one of the market value of production.

There is less general agreement on what, in fact, constitutes an appropriate substitute for country food and how to impute a price to it. Imported red meats appear to be the closest possible substitute for big game, imported domestic fowl for birds, and imported fish for local fish. Yet imported red meat and domestic fowl are not directly comparable to wild meat. Quite apart from such immeasurable qualities as preferences of taste and of cultural significance, they are not identical in nutritional content, particularly protein. Drs. Otto Schaefer and Peter Usher provided evidence to show that the protein content of country meats is significantly higher than that of their domestic counterparts. What is not clear from their evidence or from the supporting literature is the comparability of the samples from which the measurements were made. Although the weight of evidence clearly indicates the superior protein value of country meat, we must be cautious in using specific figures. It is not clear whether the higher percentages of protein reported for country meats are due to the absence of marbling in the flesh, or whether the protein content of wild flesh is higher than that of lean beef. Standard grade beef is reported to have a much higher protein content than prime grade beef.

2. *There should be an index of protein and fat, as a proportion of either the whole body weight or of the total edible weight of meat, uniformly defined, of all major wild and domestic species, as well as an index of the protein and fat content of directly comparable cuts of wild and domestic meats.*

Very few of these data are at present available. Accordingly, it may not be legitimate to apply a correction factor to imported meat prices to account for protein differences, so estimated values must at present be considered to be tentative.

3. *Other nutritive differences (in addition to fat and protein) between wild and domestic meats should be examined and accounted for, including the absence of hormones and chemicals in the former and possible differences in the composition of fatty acids.*

How do we determine the price of a substitute commodity? Usher used an approximate average of the per pound prices of whole meat cuts sold in Western Arctic food stores because they were the only available substitutes for country meats. Counsel for Foothills argued that a more appropriate price would be the average per pound delivered price of a side of beef. Foothills' argument is correct in that the relative price of individual cuts of meat reflects southern Canadian rather than native food preferences. On the other hand, as Usher argued, whole sides of beef or pork are neither actually nor practically available to native people in their present working and living conditions. The use of store prices for butchered meat can be made only in a situation where it is the only available substitute. Should imported red meat become cheaper through availability in bulk, or should locally produced meat, such as reindeer or commercially hunted game, become widely available, then the relatively high prices yielded by Usher's approach given in Table 1.10 would have to be revised downwards. Present or revised price equivalents, however, are used here only as a measure of the welfare contributed by harvests of country food, not as an index for compensation in the event of the loss of these resources. Despite these reservations, we have no alternative to using the prices of current, locally available substitutes to impute a value to Mackenzie Valley and Western Arctic food production. Ideally, country produce should be evaluated according to local substitute prices. In the absence of other specific data, we have applied prices in the Mackenzie Delta Region to all regions, except Great Slave Lake, where they have been reduced by 15 percent. This procedure reflects current cost of living indices by community.

When imputing values to determine income in kind, that is to say, as a measure of welfare, it is necessary to deduct the cost of production from the gross values. But these data, too, are rarely available, and their general applicability is uncertain. Usher suggested in evidence, on the basis of very limited data, that production costs might equal about one-quarter of the gross value of the product. This suggestion is approximately consistent with information from Grise Fiord (recalculated on the basis of the values determined above) cited by B.F. Friesen in a report to Inuit Tapirisat of Canada (1975). I shall use this 25 percent estimate in the absence of any other, but I should like to emphasize again the obvious need for further research into this important subject.

I also want to reiterate that this exercise of imputing a value to country food is strictly to determine the cost to the consumer of obtaining the closest possible substitute commodity. The substitution costs determined at this Inquiry cannot represent the real value of country produce to native people because they do not derive the same satisfaction from these substitutes. Substitution costs do not take into account the many intangible qualities of country food, and they therefore underestimate its true value in a welfare sense.

It is evident from the foregoing discussion that new reporting systems and new techniques of analysis of the traditional economy are required, and I make recommendations on these in section two of this chapter. Yet even now, on the basis of the considerations of volume and value of production I have reviewed here, it is possible to reinterpret existing data to arrive at a more realistic estimate of the output of the traditional economy.

Output and Trends in the Traditional Economy

Several estimates of the output of the native economy, as well as observations on trends in it, were placed before this Inquiry. All of these estimates were based on only one or on a very few years' accumulation of data, and it is plain that such data may well be unrepresentative. Even if several years of data were available, the identification of trends is difficult when the availability, harvest and value of the resources fluctuate in complex fashion over time. The use of annual data from even a five-year period, such as that submitted by Gemini North, can lead to inferences about and the extrapolation of long-term trends that do not, in fact, exist. By and large, the data presented in evidence, although helpful, failed to provide an adequate basis for establishing trends.

Accordingly this section gives output data for a ten-year period, 1965-1975, and it will compare the annual averages of two five-year blocks, 1965-1970 and 1970-1975. The use of five-year averages should smooth out much of the cyclic, as well as isolated or sporadic, variations in animal abundance and short-term price fluctuations. These variations obscure changes in hunting and trapping effort so that smoothing them out should make long-term changes of effort more apparent. The comparison of two five-year blocks, the first of which precedes most of the recent industrial activity in the Mackenzie Valley and Western Arctic, may reveal some noteworthy trends. It would be desirable to examine a series of five-year averages for trends, but time has not permitted that.

To compare the two five-year periods, we have used unadjusted government data so that, although the totals are low, they provide a reasonable basis for comparison. Totals are given for only the major fur and game species (Table 2.1) on the grounds that changes in the harvests of these species are better indicators of changing effort than are the harvests of minor species. Indeed, the harvests of minor species often reflect the strategies and effort devoted to the major species.

It has also been necessary to determine a means of allocating the data on a geographical basis. Harvests of fur, fish and game occur over broad areas and at myriad scattered points in the Mackenzie Valley and Western Arctic. For data collection purposes, however, they are reported at a much smaller number of points, generaliy the established settlements. The problem is to relate these reporting points to the collection areas in which the produce is harvested so that it is reasonably certain that almost all of the fur and game reported and recorded at locations in the area were in fact harvested within that collection area, and not in a neighbouring area.

Previous research has established the minimum level of data aggregation and the related harvest areas (chiefly Exhibit F656 for Inuit areas and a recent report by Usher on Dene harvesting). The boundaries of these minimum areas or harvest districts have been redrawn on the basis of additional information (Exhibits C31, F884 and Stager's Old Crow report). Although the Inquiry did not visit Snowdrift, that district has been included here in order to encompass all of the Dene communities in the Northwest Territories. In this chapter, all references to the harvest districts and regions of the Mackenzie Valley and Western Arctic, including Old Crow, refer to the areas delineated on the Map and detailed in the Legend. The 21 districts have been grouped into five regions, and all data are presented at the regional level.

The boundaries shown on the Map should be interpreted as rough delineations of core areas rather than as exact dividing lines between districts or regions, although they have remained more or less stable for at least the last 40 years. These harvest districts are not necessarily coincidental with past or present limits of native land use nor with the areas used by particular native social groupings. Nor are they necessarily the areas that any of these groups might identify or claim as their own. In some cases, there is significant movement across these boundaries for hunting and trapping or for other purposes, and some areas are shared by two or more groups. Native land use areas, so clearly understood by individual hunters and trappers, are only loosely defined in the aggregate, although in the lower Mackenzie and Arctic coast areas, Hunters and Trappers Associations have recently defined and registered their trapping areas in accordance with the Northwest Territories Game Ordinance.

Not all of the district boundaries are coincidental with the administrative boundaries of the territorial north. This is chiefly true of the Hay, Smith and Liard districts, which extend southward into the provinces. By the same token, some people from the northernmost communities of Alberta and Saskatchewan hunt and trap in the southern parts of the Northwest Territories. These cross-border harvests are in all cases small, and they do not significantly affect this statistical presentation.

Fur, Fish and Game Harvest Districts and Regions of the Mackenzie Valley and Western Arctic

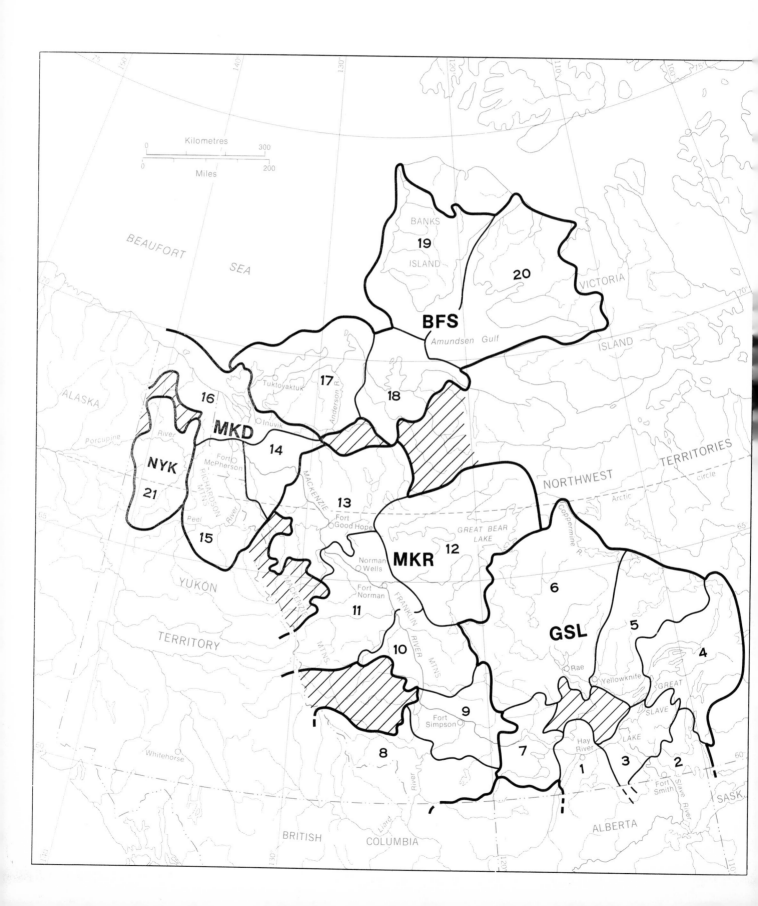

LEGEND

Northwest Territories

Great Slave Lake Region (GSL)
1. Hay
2. Smith
3. Resolution
4. Snowdrift
5. Yellowknife
6. Rae
7. Providence

Mackenzie River Region (MKR)
8. Liard
9. Simpson
10. Wrigley
11. Norman
12. Bear Lake
13. Good Hope

Mackenzie Delta Region (MKD)
14. Arctic Red
15. McPherson
16. Delta

Beaufort Sea Region (BFS)
17. Tuktoyaktuk
18. Paulatuk
19. Banks
20. Holman

Yukon Territory

Northern Yukon Region (NYK)
21. Old Crow

—— Regional boundary
—— District boundary   } These boundaries are in no way official
//// Areas not harvested at present)

Abbreviations Used in Tables

BFS — Beaufort Sea Region
GSL — Great Slave Lake Region
MKD — Mackenzie Delta Region
MKR — Mackenzie River Region
NYK — Northern Yukon Region

na — not available

GNWT — Government of the Northwest Territories

JBNQNHRC — James Bay and Northern Quebec Native Harvesting Research Committee

TABLE 1.1

Some Population and Participation Estimates, Mackenzie Valley and Western Arctic[1]

Native male labour force[2]	3,000
General Hunting Licence holders[2]	2,225
Number trading furs, 1972–1973[3]	1,200
Number earning over $400 from furs, 1972–1973[3]	450
Number earning over $400 from furs, 1975–1976[4]	764

[1] Excluding Old Crow.
[2] Average per year, 1970-1975.
[3] Estimated from incomplete data.
[4] Data provided by GNWT, Fish and Wildlife Service.

TABLE 1.2

Economic Species of Wildlife in the Mackenzie Valley and Western Arctic

Furbearers

Muskrat *(Ondatra zibethicus)*
Beaver *(Castor canadensis)*
Otter *(Lontra canadensis)*
Ermine *(Mustela erminea)*
Mink *(Mustela vison)*
Marten *(Martes americana)*
Fisher *(Martes pennanti)*
Lynx *(Lynx lynx)*
Coloured fox *(Vulpes fulva)*
Arctic fox *(Alopex lagopus)*
Squirrel *(Spermophilus parryii and Tamiasciurus hudsonicus)*
Wolf *(Canis lupus)*
Coyote *(Canis latrans)*
Wolverine *(Gulo gulo)*

Big Game

Black bear and brown bear *(Ursus americanus and U. arctos)*
Polar bear *(Ursus maritimus)*
Moose *(Alces alces)*
Caribou *(Rangifer tarandus)*
Bison *(Bison bison)*
Dall's sheep *(Ovis dalli)*
Muskox *(Ovibos moschatus)*

Small Game

Snowshoe hare *(Lepus americanus)*
Arctic hare *(Lepus arcticus)*

Marine Mammals

Ringed seal and bearded seal *(Phoca hispida and Erignathus barbatus)*
White whale *(Delphinapterus leucas)*

Birds

Ducks (various species)
Geese (various species)
Ptarmigan *(Lagopus lagopus and L. mutus)*
Grouse (various species)

Fish

Fish (all species)

Scientific names for mammals according to Banfield (1977).
Scientific names for birds according to Godfrey (1966).

TABLE 1.3

Estimates of Error in Officially Recorded Fur Harvests[1]

SPECIES	MACKENZIE VALLEY AND ARCTIC COAST[2]	NORTHERN QUEBEC[3]
Muskrat	1.1	1.9
Beaver	1.2	1.5
Otter	?[4]	1.7
Ermine	?[4]	3.9
Mink	<1.1	1.8
Marten	<1.1	1.5
Fisher	1.1	—[5]
Lynx	1.5	3.4
Coloured fox	2.0	4.7
Arctic fox	1.1	
Squirrel	?[4]	9.5
Wolf	2.0	—[5]
Coyote	2.0	—[5]
Wolverine	4.0	—[5]

[1] Total estimated or observed catch as a proportion of the catch recorded in GNWT Fur Export Tax Returns.

[2] Rushforth (1975); Asch, personal communication June 3, 1977; Smith, personal communication June 3, 1977; Usher, field observations.

[3] Feit (1975).

[4] No basis available for making estimate.

[5] Not reported in Feit (1975).

TABLE 1.4

Percentages of General Hunting Licences Returned, Northwest Territories, 1968-1973[1]

SEASON	REGION				TOTAL
	GSL	MKR	MKD	BFS	
1968–1969	70	79	71	67	71
1969–1970	75	76	61	75	71
1970–1971	64	65	64	65	64
1972–1973	45	37	30	74	42
Average	64	64	57	70	62

[1] GNWT, Fish and Wildlife Service, General Hunting Licences issued and returned, 1968-1973.

TABLE 1.5

Comparison of Data on the Harvest of Big Game from Kill Statistics with Data from Interviews

TABLE 1.5A
Caribou: Fort Franklin (Bear Lake District)

YEAR	KILL STATISTICS	GENERAL HUNTING LICENCE REPORTING RATE (PERCENTAGE)	INTERVIEWS[1]
1970–1971	12	14	200
1971–1972	4	na	185
1972–1973	340	0	350
1973–1974	159	na	290
1974–1975	92	na	285
Average	121		262

TABLE 1.5B
Dall's Sheep: Richardson Mountains (McPherson and Delta Districts)

YEAR	KILL STATISTICS	GENERAL HUNTING LICENCE REPORTING RATE (PERCENTAGE)	INTERVIEWS[2]
1967–1968	4	na	25
1968–1969	59	72	16
1969–1970	25	61	30
1970–1971	33	67	39
1971–1972	22	na	40
1972–1973	30	31	62
Average	35		42

[1] Rushforth (1975).
[2] Simmons (1973).

TABLE 1.6
Some Comparative Observations on Bird Harvests

TABLE 1.6A
Fort Franklin (Bear Lake District), 1974-1975

TYPE	KILL STATISTICS	INTERVIEW[1]	
		TOTAL KILL	PER CAPITA KILL
Ducks	95	1,500–2,000	4.3
Ptarmigan	200	750–1,100	2.3
Grouse	87	250–350	0.7

TABLE 1.6B
Alaska, 1956-1957 (58 villages, with a native population of 10,694)[2]

TYPE	TOTAL KILL	PER CAPITA KILL
Ducks	39,400	3.7
Geese	17,160	1.6
Ptarmigan	50,435	4.7
Grouse	3,268	0.3

In some cases, observational data indicated that the actual harvests of migratory birds were about three times those reported in interviews with game officials.

TABLE 1.6C
Hay Lake, Alberta, 1966-1967 (native population of 175; 30 regular hunters)[3]

YEAR	TOTAL DUCKS AND GEESE	PER CAPITA KILL
1966	8,600	48.0
1967	2,010	11.5

TABLE 1.6D
Northern Quebec Cree Communities, 1974-1975 (seven villages with a native population of 6,059)[4]

TYPE	TOTAL KILL	PER CAPITA KILL
Ducks	53,808	8.9
Geese	81,070	13.4
Ptarmigan	51,325	8.5
Grouse	16,542	2.7

TABLE 1.6E
Northern Quebec Inuit Communities, 1974-1975 (12 villages with a native population of 3,629; 807 males 18 and over; 646 potential hunters)[5]

TYPE	TOTAL KILL	PER CAPITA KILL
Ducks	14,870	4.1
Geese	31,225	8.6
Ptarmigan and Grouse	83,035	22.9

[1] Rushforth (1975).
[2] Hansen (1957).
[3] Macauley and Boag (1974).
[4] James Bay and Northern Quebec Native Harvesting Research Committee (JBNQNHRC) (1976), Part I.
[5] JBNQNHRC (1976), Part II.

TABLE 1.7
Comparison of Numbers of Sealskins Traded with Numbers of Seals Harvested: Holman

YEAR	SKINS TRADED[1]	SEALS HARVESTED[2]
1962–1963	1,726	2,250+
1963–1964	3,479	4,250
1964–1965	3,712	na
1970–1971	na	5,445+ (calendar year 1971)
1971–1972	1,096	
1972–1973	2,198	8,000 (calendar year 1973)
1973–1974	3,213	
1974–1975	2,876	na

[1] GNWT Fur Export Tax Returns.
[2] Usher (1965) for the 1960s; Smith (F18511ff.) for the 1970s.

TABLE 1.8
Estimates of Error in Officially Recorded Big Game and Bird Harvests[1]

SPECIES	ERROR ESTIMATE
Black bear and brown bear	1.3
Polar bear	1.0
Moose	1.3
Caribou	1.5
Bison	1.0
Dall's sheep	1.2
Ducks (various species)	3.0
Geese (various species)	3.0
Ptarmigan	5.0
Grouse	2.5

[1] Total catch as a proportion of catch recorded in GNWT Kill Statistics.

TABLE 1.9

Average Edible Weight (in pounds) Per Animal[1]

SPECIES	REGION				
	GSL	MKR	MKD	BFS	NYK
Muskrat	1.4	1.4	1.4	1.4	1.4
Beaver	17.4	17.4	17.4	—	17.4
Otter	10.5	10.5	—	—	—
Lynx	8.5	8.5	8.5	—	8.5
Black Bear[2]	210.0	210.0	210.0	—	210.0
Polar Bear[3]	—	—	—	175.0	—
Moose	438.0	438.0	438.0	—	438.0
Caribou[4]	112.0	120.0	120.0	90.0	120.0
Bison[5]	550.0	—	—	—	—
Dall's sheep[6]	—	75.0	75.0	—	—
Muskox[7]	—	—	—	300.0	—
Ducks[8]	1.7	1.7	1.7	2.5	1.7
Geese[9]	3.5	3.5	3.5	3.5	3.5
Ptarmigan	0.8	0.8	0.8	0.8	0.8
Grouse	0.7	0.7	—	—	—
Snowshoe hare	1.9	1.9	1.9	—	1.9
Arctic hare[10]	—	—	5.0	5.0	—
White whale[11]	—	—	232.0	232.0	—
Seals[12]	—	—	30.0	30.0	—

[1] According to JBNQNHRC (1976), unless otherwise noted.

[2] Includes a small proportion of brown bears; they are assumed to yield the same edible weight.

[3] The JBNQNHRC figure of 350 pounds is considered too high for the Beaufort Sea area, where many of the bears taken are from the younger age classes. Stirling (personal communication, June 7, 1977) suggests 150-200 pounds edible weight per animal is more reasonable, and therefore a median figure of 175 pounds is used here. This accords more closely with an earlier estimate, based on a small sample, of 250 pounds (Usher, 1971).

[4] Weighted averages are used that take account average weights for different herds and the proportion that each herd contributes to the regional harvest. Table 1.9.1 below indicates the basis for this weighting. The weight estimates are derived from Foote (1965), Kelsall (1968) and Usher (1971).

[5] Derived from dressed weights by age and sex class provided by Novakowski (1965). The harvest is assumed to consist chiefly of young adults (2.5 to 4.5 years), equally divided between males and females, on the basis of advice from Novakowski (personal communication, June 8, 1977). This gives an average of 513 pounds, which has been increased to 550 pounds to take account the use of the head and organs.

[6] Very few data are available. Those provided by Geist for older rams suggest live weights of nearly 200 pounds. Banfield (1977) estimates adult female weight at 125 pounds. As the native harvest includes a large proportion of females and juveniles (Simmons, 1973), the average edible yield per animal is estimated to be 75 pounds.

[7] Very few data are available. Application of the same general reasoning as for Dall's sheep (above) to the weights provided by Tener (1965) gives an estimated average of 300 pounds edible yield.

[8] The average edible weight for eider ducks (Usher, 1971) is used for the Beaufort Sea harvest.

[9] The average weight of snow geese is used here because this species makes up the bulk of the goose harvest in all regions.

[10] Estimate derived from Usher (1971).

Table 1.9, footnotes (continued)

[11] Estimate derived from Brackel (1977). In addition, Brackel estimates that each whale yields 30 gallons of muktuk and 20 gallons of edible oil. Estimating a specific gravity of 1.00 for muktuk, and using Bailey's (1952) figure of about 0.93 for whale oil, this converts to 300 pounds muktuk and 186 pounds oil.

[12] Application of McLaren's (1958) component weight percentages to Usher's data on live weight for ringed seals (1971) results in an estimate of 26 pounds edible weight for humans. This may be conservative, for the JBNQNHRC figure is 31.5 pounds. (There is, on average, another 7.5 pounds of blubber per ringed seal available for dog feed or for rendering into edible oil.) Taking into account the small proportion of the catch that consists of the larger, bearded seal, and applying Usher's catch and weight data for Banks Island (1971), the average seal, regardless of species, yields 30 pounds edible weight of food plus 8.6 pounds blubber.

TABLE 1.9.1
Weighted Determination of Average Edible Weights of Caribou

| SUBSPECIES (Rangifer tarandus) | AVERAGE EDIBLE WEIGHT (POUNDS) | PROPORTION BY REGION (PERCENTAGE)[1] | | | | |
		GSL	MKR	MKD	BFS	NYK
caribou	170	10	25			
groenlandicus	105	90	75		35	
granti	120			100		100
pearyi	80				65	
		WEIGHTED AVERAGE BY REGION (POUNDS)				
CARIBOU		112	120	120	90	120

[1] Estimate based on probable location of harvests by district, 1970-1975.

TABLE 1.10
Gross Imputed Values of Country Foods

| TYPE OF FOOD | SUBSTITUTE | AVERAGE PRICE/POUND[1] | CORRECTION FACTOR FOR PROTEIN | IMPUTED VALUE/POUND BY REGION | |
				MKR, MKD, BFS, NYK	GSL
		$		$	
Big game and hare	Beef	2.50	1.6	4.00	3.40
Edible furbearers[2]	Pork	2.50	1.2	3.00	2.55
Marine mammals	Beef	2.50	1.8	4.50	—
Birds	Chicken	1.50	1.3	1.95	1.65
Fish	Fish	2.00	1.0	2.00	1.70

[1] No adjustment made for bone content because there are no uniform measurements of edible yields of comparative wild meats.

[2] The leading edible furbearers — beaver and muskrat — have fattier meats; they are, therefore, more comparable to pork than to beef.

TABLE 2.1

Comparison of Average Annual Harvests of Major Fur and Game Species, by Region, 1965-1970 and 1970-1975[1]

REGION		MUSKRAT	BEAVER	MINK	MARTEN	LYNX	ARCTIC FOX	MOOSE	CARIBOU
GSL	1965–1970	56,709	3,471	3,106	2,073	1,226	222	464	4,497
	1970–1975	32,675	2,956	1,462	1,856	1,183	266	323	4,443
MKR	1965–1970	6,363	3,952	833	6,226	560	6	535	683
	1970–1975	2,817	2,453	439	4,104	1,234	17	284	660
MKD	1965–1970	138,577	1,034	963	928	619	570	75	1,376
	1970–1975	64,406	179	1,031	956	553	912	46	1,480
BFS	1965–1970	184	—	10	263	—	5,049	—	571
	1970–1975	1,480	—	17	211	—	9,019	—	1,152
Total NWT	1965–1970	201,833	8,457	4,912	9,460	2,405	5,847	1,074	7,127
	1970–1975	101,378	5,588	2,949	7,127	2,970	10,214	653	7,735
NYK	1965–1970	8,900	43	13	63	9	—	20	554
	1970–1975	11,852	29	31	61	22	—	19	516
Total all regions	1965–1970	210,733	8,500	4,925	9,553	2,414	5,847	1,094	7,681
	1970–1975	113,230	5,617	2,980	7,188	2,992	10,214	672	8,251

[1] NWT: GNWT, Fish and Wildlife Service, Fur Export Tax Summaries; Kill Statistics derived from General Hunting Licence Returns. Yukon: Stager (1974); information provided by Yukon Game Branch.

TABLE 2.2

Comparison of Value of Average Annual Harvests of Major Furbearers, by Region, 1965-1970 and 1970-1975[1]

		MUSKRAT	BEAVER	MINK	MARTEN	LYNX	ARCTIC FOX	TOTAL
		$	$	$	$	$	$	$
Average	1965–1970	0.93	12.32	16.67	10.87	23.81	13.45	
price	1970–1975	1.76	14.58	18.66	14.94	51.11	17.97	
Region								
GSL	1965–1970	52,739	42,763	51,777	22,534	29,191	2,986	201,990
	1970–1975	57,508	43,098	27,281	27,729	60,463	4,780	220,859
MKR	1965–1970	5,918	48,689	13,886	67,677	13,334	81	149,585
	1970–1975	4,958	35,765	8,192	61,314	63,070	305	173,604
MKD	1965–1970	128,877	12,739	16,053	10,087	14,738	7,667	190,161
	1970–1975	113,355	2,610	19,238	14,283	28,264	16,389	194,139
BFS	1965–1970	171	—	167	2,859	—	68,044	71,241
	1970–1975	2,605	—	317	3,152	—	162,071	168,145
Total NWT	1965–1970	187,705	104,191	81,883	103,157	57,263	78,778	612,977
	1970–1975	178,426	81,473	55,028	106,478	151,797	183,545	756,747
NYK	1965–1970	8,277	530	217	685	214	—	9,923
	1970–1975	20,860	423	578	911	1,124	—	23,896
Total all	1965–1970	195,982	104,721	82,100	103,842	57,477	78,778	622,900
regions	1970–1975	199,286	81,896	55,606	107,389	152,921	183,545	780,643

[1] Table 2.1; Statistics Canada, *Fur Production* (23-207 annual) 1967-1976.

TABLE 2.3

Average Annual Volume and Value of Fur Harvest, 1970-1975, Adjusted

SPECIES	FUR EXPORT TAX RETURNS TOTAL	CORRECTION FACTOR[1]	ADJUSTED TOTAL	VALUE PER PELT[2]	TOTAL VALUE
				$	$
Muskrat	113,230	1.1	124,553	1.76	219,213
Beaver	5,617	1.2	6,740	14.58	98,269
Otter	78	?	78	25.74	2,008
Ermine	2,181	?	2,181	.73	1,592
Mink	2,980	<1.1	3,200	18.66	59,712
Marten	7,188	<1.1	7,800	14.94	116,532
Fisher	27	1.1	30	23.28	698
Lynx	2,992	1.5	4,488	51.11	229,382
Coloured Fox	784	2.0	1,568	26.04[3]	40,831
Arctic Fox	10,214	1.1	11,235	17.97[4]	201,893
Squirrel (various species)	7,937	?	7,937	.52	4,127
Wolf	249	2.0	498	52.10	25,946
Coyote	42	2.0	84	19.43	1,632
Wolverine	58	4.0	232	64.16	14,885
Black bear and brown bear[5]	271	1.3	352	31.10	10,947
Polar bear	57	1.0	57	575.08	32,780
Ringed seal[6]	2,166	1.5	3,249	13.75	44,674
Total					1,105,121
Add 10 percent for undervaluation					110,512
Adjusted total value					1,215,633
Unadjusted total value[2]					897,915
Percent difference					35%

[1] From Tables 1.3, 1.8.

[2] Statistics Canada, *Fur Production* (23-207 annual) 1972-1976.

[3] Average for red fox.

[4] Average for white fox.

[5] Correction factor based on General Hunting Licence Returns under-reporting.

[6] Correction factor based on apparent non-reporting in Fur Export Tax Returns (*See,* for example, Smith and Taylor, [1977:4]).

TABLE 2.4

Average Annual Production of Food Animals by Region, 1970-1975, Adjusted

SPECIES	CORRECTION FACTOR[1]	REGION					TOTAL
		GSL	MKR	MKD	BFS	NYK	
Moose	1.3	420	369	60	—	25	874
Caribou	1.5	6,665	990	2,220	1,728	774	12,377
Black bear and brown bear	1.3	173	153	23	—	3	352
Polar bear	1.0	—	—	—	57	—	57
Bison	1.0	85	—	—	—	—	85
Dall's sheep	1.2	—	8	23	—	—	31
Muskox	1.0	—	—	—	30	—	30
Muskrat	1.1	35,942	3,099	70,847	1,628	13,037	124,553
Beaver	1.2	3,547	2,943	215	—	35	6,740
Lynx	1.5	1,775	1,851	829	—	33	4,488
Otter	1.0	71	6	—	—	1	78
Ducks	3.0	23,157	5,781	7,059	7,128	150	43,125
Geese	3.0	1,299	978	2,580	7,608	18	12,483
Ptarmigan	5.0	28,690	5,760	4,135	20,875	220	59,680
Grouse	2.5	11,600	3,288	—	—	—	14,888
Whales	1.0	—	—	70	50	—	120
Seals[2]	—[3]	—	—	250	6,000	—	6,250

[1] From Tables 1.3, 1.8.

[2] Estimated total harvest.

[3] Not calculated.

TABLE 2.5

Average Annual Weight (in pounds) of Food Produced, by Species and Region, 1970-1975, Adjusted

SPECIES	REGION					TOTAL
	GSL	MKR	MKD	BFS	NYK	
Moose	183,960	161,622	26,280	—	10,950	382,812
Caribou	746,480	118,800	266,400	155,520	92,880	1,380,080
Black bear and brown bear	36,330	32,130	4,830	—	630	73,920
Polar bear	—	—	—	9,975	—	9,975
Bison	46,750	—	—	—	—	46,750
Dall's sheep	—	600	1,725	—	—	2,325
Muskrat	50,319	4,339	99,186	2,279	18,252	174,375
Beaver	61,718	51,208	3,741	—	609	117,276
Lynx	15,088	15,734	7,047	—	281	38,150
Otter	746	63	—	—	10	819
Ducks	39,367	9,828	12,000	17,820	255	79,270
Geese	4,547	3,423	9,030	26,628	63	43,691
Ptarmigan	22,952	4,608	3,308	16,700	176	47,744
Grouse	8,120	2,302	—	—	—	10,422
Whales	—	—	16,240	11,600	—	27,840[1]
Seals	—	—	7,500	180,000	—	187,500[2]
Fish[3]	897,750	307,160	690,371	188,960	35,000	2,119,241
Hare[4]	50,000	27,650	33,600	10,000	7,000	128,250
Total	2,164,127	739,467	1,181,858	619,782	166,106	4,870,440

[1] Does not include 22,320 pounds edible oil and 36,000 pounds muktuk.

[2] Does not include approximately 40,000 pounds edible oil.

[3] Estimates based on literature sources.

[4] Estimates based on five percent of human food from all other sources, except as indicated in the text.

TABLE 2.6
Comparison of Estimates of Total Food Harvest by Weight (in pounds)

TYPE	GNWT RECORDS[1]	OWN ESTIMATES
Big game	1,338,937	1,895,862
Edible furbearers	282,510	330,620
Marine mammals[2]	92,820	215,340
Birds	54,735	181,127
Subtotal	1,769,002	2,622,949
Unrecorded by GNWT		2,247,491
Total	1,769,002	4,870,440

[1] GNWT, Fish and Wildlife Service, Fur Export Tax Returns summaries; Kill statistics derived from General Hunting Licence Returns.
[2] Not including edible oil and muktuk.

TABLE 2.7
Total and Human[1] Food Production by Type and Region (in pounds)

TYPE OF FOOD		REGION					TOTAL
		GSL	MKR	MKD	BFS	NYK	
Big game	total	1,013,520	313,152	299,235	165,495	104,460	1,895,862
	human	1,000,000	300,000	290,000	160,000	100,000	1,850,000
Furbearers	total	127,871	71,344	109,974	2,279	19,152	330,620
	human	100,000	60,000	50,000	1,000	15,000	226,000
Birds	total	74,986	20,161	24,338	61,148	494	181,127
	human	70,000	18,000	22,000	58,000	0	168,000
Marine mammals[2]	total	—	—	23,740	191,600	—	215,340
	human	—	—	10,000	50,000	—	60,000
Fish	total	897,750	307,160	690,371	188,960	35,000	2,119,241
	human	300,000	175,000	300,000	80,000	25,000	880,000
Hare	total	50,000	27,650	33,600	10,000	7,000	128,250
	human	50,000	27,000	33,000	10,000	7,000	127,000
All food	total	2,164,127	739,467	1,181,858	619,782	166,106	4,870,440
	human	1,520,000	580,000	705,000	359,000	147,000	3,311,000

[1] Human food estimated to nearest 1,000 pounds.
[2] Does not include edible oil and muktuk.

TABLE 2.8

Value of Human Food Production

TYPE	WEIGHT (POUNDS)	VALUE/POUND[1]		TOTAL VALUE
		$	$	$
Big game, hare	1,977,000	4.00	(3.40)	7,278,000
Edible furbearers	226,000	3.00	(2.55)	633,000
Marine mammals:				
meat	60,000	4.50	—	270,000
edible oil and muktuk	78,000	—[2]	—	25,000
Birds	168,000	1.95	(1.65)	306,600
Fish	880,000	2.00	(1.70)	1,650,000
Total	3,359,000			10,162,600

[1] Figure in brackets is GSL regional value.

[2] Local exchange values used due to lack of appropriate substitutes. Brackel (1977) quotes these as $1.50 per gallon of oil and $5.00 per gallon of muktuk.

TABLE 2.9

Average Annual Gross and Net Imputed Values of Primary Harvest in the Native Economy, Mackenzie Valley and Western Arctic, 1970-1975

ITEM	VALUE
	$
Human food	10,200,000
Dog food	1,000,000
Furs[1]	1,200,000
Other	1,240,000
Total, gross	13,640,000
Total, net (approximate)	10,200,000

[1] Cash value.

Trends

The harvest of moose and caribou meat appears to have declined by about 10 percent by weight, although the decline in moose kills is much greater than the increase in caribou kills. However, in view of the apparent decline of hunters reporting their kills during the second of the five-year periods, we must estimate that there has been no significant change in the meat harvest.

Changes in the fur harvest are much more pronounced, and they appear to be significant even if it is assumed that non-reporting of furs is on the increase. There was a severe decline in muskrat and beaver harvests, and almost as great a drop in the fine fur (mink and marten) harvests. Long-haired fur (lynx and fox) catches both rose, although, in view of the very long population cycle of lynx, and of the unusual succession of good years on Banks Island (where most arctic fox in the Mackenzie Valley and Western Arctic are taken), this rise is not necessarily the result of increased trapping effort. Overall, there appears to have been a significant decline in trapping effort, although higher prices for all furs resulted in an increase of about 25 percent in trapping revenue from the major species. Table 2.2, which shows the comparative values of fur harvest, should be interpreted cautiously because the total values are the product of average price and average harvest. Preliminary assessment suggests that this procedure has biased the value of the lynx harvest upwards and of the fox harvest downwards, but that it has had negligible effect on the other species. Returns for 1975-1976 indicate unusually high harvests of some species especially in the southern Mackenzie District, but we do not yet understand the cause or the significance of this change.

I am fully aware that all of these observations are based on a very crude examination of the data. A proper determination of trends must be based on a rigorous analysis of a longer series of data and it must include statistically sound procedures for isolating significant variables.

Output

I shall now attempt to establish the total output of the native economy by adjusting official data according to the factors of error identified in the preceding section. Annual averages are calculated for the five-year period 1970-1975.

FUR

Applying the foregoing correction factors to the fur harvest, we see in Table 2.3 that official statistics underestimate their total value by about 35 percent. One caution in using this table: to the degree that the adjusted value accounts for domestic retention of furs, it includes an imputed value as well as a cash income. The imputed value of furs in this case, however, is not its substitute value, it is the producer's value or opportunity cost. Accordingly, this procedure is appropriate for both market and welfare evaluations of fur production.

In any larger analysis of the native economy, the value of furs retained for garments or for handicrafts should be subtracted from the gross value of these final outputs. Minor considerations not accounted for in the table include the sale of muskox hides, which possibly amount to about $10,000 annually, bounty payments for wolves, and the small number of furs taken in the Yukon by trappers from Fort McPherson and the Mackenzie Delta. There do not appear to be any continuous records of furs or caribou taken by these trappers in the Yukon.

FOOD

Table 2.4 shows the adjusted harvest totals for each species, and Table 2.5 shows the weight of edible yield of this harvest. As outlined in section one of this chapter, hare harvests have been estimated at five percent of the total of all other human food production from the land, except for the Great Slave Lake and Beaufort Sea regions, for which best estimates have been made. Table 2.6 indicates that official records seem to underestimate the weight yield of the recorded species by about one-third and further, that these recorded species account for little more than one-half of all native food production.

Table 2.7 attempts to show the probable proportion of gross food production that is actually consumed by humans. This estimate is based on sources in the literature, but the data are so sporadic that some extrapolation has been necessary. I have tried to err on the side of caution and to underestimate the proportion that humans actually use. Of the total production of meat and fish, about two-thirds is used as human food and one-third as dog food, an estimate that takes into account the very great decline in the dog population throughout the Mackenzie Valley and Western Arctic during the 1970s. The amount of food production that is not used at all is thought to be very small and seems to be restricted chiefly to marine mammals and edible furbearers.

The value of human food production is estimated in Table 2.8. The total consumption of about 3.36 million pounds is valued at nearly $10.2 million. Assuming a native population of 14,000, the annual per capita consumption of meat is 240 pounds, which would have a replacement value of $726. The figure of 240 pounds is slightly higher than the figures earlier estimated by Asch (Exhibit F605) and Usher (Exhibit F676) for the Central Mackenzie and the Western Arctic respectively. Surveys conducted in 1974-1975 by the James Bay and Northern Quebec Native Harvesting Research Committee (1976) reveal much higher per capita harvests in northern Quebec: 327 pounds by the Cree Indians and 1,026 pounds by the Inuit. The figure for the Inuit is augmented by substantial harvests of marine mammals (40 percent by weight), not all of which may be consumed. Nonetheless, these figures, based on comprehensive research in northern Quebec, suggest that my estimates for the Northwest Territories are conservative.

The proportion used for dog food, valued conservatively at

$.50 per pound on a replacement basis, would be worth about $750,000. The use of inedible viscera and other waste products for dogs might bring the total value of dog food in kind to about $1 million.

TOTAL PRIMARY HARVEST

Finally, some account must be taken of domestic produce other than food or furs, such as caribou hides used for bedding, moose hides used for clothing and, in particular, wood used for fuel and construction. There is little quantitative information of these uses, and the total imputed value of these products might be in the order of 10 percent of all other production values. By far the greatest proportion of this amount, estimated at nearly $1.25 million, is accounted for by fuel wood, which, in heating value equivalent to fuel oil, is worth about $100 per cord.

Table 2.9 summarizes the values of all types of country produce. Deducting estimated production costs, we obtain a rough estimate of the average annual net value during 1970-1975 of the primary harvest in the Mackenzie Valley and Western Arctic of over $10 million. Now this is quite evidently not a definitive evaluation of the output of the native economy. Rather, the purpose here has been to outline the methods and considerations that would enter that evaluation and to demonstrate how far we are at present from being able to make that evaluation. Until there are improved reporting systems and firmer conversion factors, I think this is the best estimate that can be made.

Yet whatever modifications may result from more thorough documentation and analysis of the traditional economy, some conclusions may already be drawn. The level of participation in the traditional economy, and the volume and value of production from that economy, are considerably greater than estimates upon which government policy relating to resource development in the North has hitherto been based.

Comparison with Other Economic Sectors

The estimates offered above are valid only in considering the contribution of the primary harvest in the native sector to the economic welfare of native people. Adjusting the Gemini North data for the region defined here, native income from all sources in 1972 and 1973 was at most $12 million. Gemini North's estimates for native income (again regionally adjusted), however, suggest a gross income of just over $1.5 million from traditional pursuits, or little more than 10 percent of the total presented in Table 2.9. By a welfare measure (and I use this term as economists do: an indication of personal or social well-being rather than in the popular sense of a subsidy), native income in the region would in fact have been about $20 million, of which roughly half came from primary production. Whatever may be the need for more jobs and more cash, it must be made quite clear that in economic terms alone the renewable resources make a vital contribution to native well-being throughout the region.

It would not be valid, however, to use these estimates in direct comparison with the output of, for example, the mining sector. The market value of primary production in the native sector would be considerably lower than its welfare value, but for the reasons outlined at the end of section one of this chapter, I do not believe it is either practically possible or theoretically valid to attempt any direct comparison of the market values of output in the native and non-native sectors.

Recommendations for Data Collection

It is evident from the foregoing discussion that conventional measurements of the output of the traditional economy may produce estimates that are in error not just by a few percentage points, but by factors of up to ten. In no other sector of the Canadian economy would such a situation be allowed to occur, much less persist — but that reflects the cultural bias of southern Canadians. Few native people would think of measuring their economic production, much less devise elaborate methods for doing so. They are well aware of the value to them of the land and its resources, and the need to measure the output of the native economy exists only because of external encroachments on that economy. Yet, if the need for such measurement is external, the ability to meet it is internal. The systems of data collection in use at present do not meet the purpose of measuring or evaluating output, they do not work well, and they will probably work even less well in future. Output can be accurately totalled only on the basis of individual reporting by hunters and trappers, supplemented by regular surveys and observations. But this form of reporting will never work unless native people find that it is in their own interest to undertake these efforts.

4. Reporting systems used in other jurisdictions, for example, those recently developed in Northern Quebec, should be examined, particularly those that rely on voluntary reporting by hunters themselves.

The problem of measuring the performance of the traditional economy will be closely associated with both the future control and direction of game management and the settlement of native claims, especially if the settlement contains provisions or guarantees for the maintenance of the traditional economy.

5. Because future reporting systems, if they are to be effective, will require the approval and, indeed, the active support of hunters and trappers, both the institutional and technical problems inherent in such systems should be examined without delay.

The institutional questions are certainly political, and the initiatives must come from native people's own organizations.

I am aware that neither the federal nor the territorial game management agencies are ignorant of the deficiencies in data collection that I have discussed, and that they are now taking steps to improve harvest reporting. I would emphasize, however, that harvest surveys and related research to measure native resource use have objectives and implications that go well beyond game management or economic development. What is being measured is the use of a resource that native people consider their own by law, right and tradition, and it is, therefore, intimately related to the settlement of native claims.

6. *All aspects of harvest research, including technical aspects, must be devised in full consultation with, and implemented with the full agreement and cooperation of both the native people's organizations that are concerned specifically with game, and their political organizations.*

Harvest surveys or any other means of measuring the traditional economy will surely founder and produce questionable results if those most concerned have reason to question the motives or objectives behind such research.

In order for native people to find it in their own interest to report their harvests accurately, several conditions must be satisfied, among them the following.

7. *Native people must be involved in the direct management and control of the reporting system, through whatever bodies they designate or establish for that purpose. Technical expertise should be made available to such bodies as required.*

8. *Harvesters must be assured of anonymity in reporting. Accordingly, the reporting system must be entirely independent of regulatory and enforcement agencies, such as the Fish and Wildlife Service and the RCMP, in the same way that information collected from individuals for national censuses is neither collected by nor available to the Department of National Revenue. Aggregated data must of course be available to all government agencies and to the public.*

9. *Native people must be assured of their continued right and ability to harvest their traditional resources.*

This assurance will presumably require the enshrinement of native hunting rights, guarantees of control over access to the resources, and possibly guaranteed harvest levels. These guarantees, of course, are all matters for claims negotiations between native people and the Government of Canada. We can be sure, however, that if there is any suggestion that full disclosure of harvests will in any way threaten existing use and enjoyment of traditional resources, or lead to restrictive or punitive action on the part of government authorities, a voluntary reporting system will never work. On the other hand, a satisfactory settlement of native claims, as well as appropriate guarantees of compensation, should ensure that the interests of hunters and trappers would not be served by deliberately overreporting their harvests.

10. *Standard definitions, measurements, conversion factors and methodologies must also be devised. Significant progress in native harvesting research has been made in other*

jurisdictions, and the experience there should be brought to bear here. There is also much expertise in both federal and territorial government agencies to assist in the solution of technical problems. Research needs should be identified as soon as possible and cooperative arrangements should be made between native organizations and the appropriate governments to undertake the necessary research. The technical groundwork can be accomplished before any new reporting systems are established.

Potential for Renewable Resource Development

An assessment of potential economic development in the North must begin with an examination of the endowment of natural resources. For the purposes of this volume, when I speak of the renewable resources of the North, I mean specifically the natural resources that native people have traditionally used, as well as resources they can develop largely under local initiative, management and control. The two categories together include the full range of fur, fish and game resources, timber resources for selected purposes, the environment itself as a recreational and aesthetic resource, and agriculture. They do not include the development of water resources for hydro-electric power or the large-scale processing of wood for pulp and paper. I am not suggesting that the native people would not, under some circumstances, wish to take some part in such ventures (for example, as rentiers), but only that the people who addressed the Inquiry clearly indicated that direct participation in such economic developments would be incompatible with their style of life and their aspirations. However, as I pointed out in Volume One, the sort of development we are discussing here could extend beyond renewable resources to include certain small-scale, non-renewable resource developments, such as gravel pits and quarries.

The resource itself is of prime importance in determining whether or not the native people would wish to include an activity based on it in their economy. The scale of technology and organization that exploitation of the resource would demand is also an important factor. For native people, the scale of organization should not exceed the framework within which they make decisions in their communities. The community must always be able to control the venture and determine its development. The venture should not be of a kind or scale that would enable it to dominate the community.

There are two main aspects to the development of renewable resources: the first is to increase harvest levels and the second is to improve the marketing, processing and service activities that are based on these resources. Unfortunately there are no adequate or comprehensive assessments of the potential of renewable resources in the Mackenzie Valley and

Western Arctic. I can only suggest here, on the basis of limited evidence from biological research, historical harvest statistics, and previous northern experience what are likely to be the most promising directions for more detailed assessments.

Increasing Harvest Levels

FUR

Both Dr. Nick Novakowski and Robert Ruttan suggested in evidence that many furbearing species in the Mackenzie Valley are underharvested, a view that is widely expressed within the region as well. It appears to be a reasonable inference, if not a well substantiated fact, for we have virtually no quantitative data on the actual populations or sustainable yields of any of the northern furbearers.

Of the major furbearers, muskrat seems to offer the greatest promise for increased harvests. Annual returns of over 500,000 pelts, of which a much larger proportion than at present consisted of the more valuable trapped (rather than shot) muskrats, were frequent in the 1940s and 1950s. There do not appear to be any biological impediments to realizing such harvests again. Beaver and marten harvests have been double their present levels for extended periods in the past, although both species have been overtrapped in the past as well, which has led to highly restrictive quotas or closed seasons. Yet in some areas the potential for greater harvests of these species appears to exist, and beaver yields can be improved through management techniques. Lynx populations are extremely cyclic, and they appear to be vulnerable to overharvesting at their low points. The feasibility of increased harvesting is unknown, although lynx may be underharvested in some areas. Coloured fox harvests are at present only a small fraction of what they were many years ago, and there appears to be great scope for increasing their catch. Squirrels and ermine are thought to be underharvested, although their values per pelt are low. The remaining terrestrial furbearers do not appear to offer any significant potential for improved harvest.

No increase is foreseen for polar bears, and the seal situation is uncertain. Possible increases in muskox quotas will make more of their hides available for sale.

Ruttan and John T'Seleie, in their evidence, estimated that the overall fur harvest at Fort Good Hope could be increased threefold. Taking the Mackenzie Valley and Western Arctic as a whole, I believe that a doubling of the present output, assuming constant prices, is probably possible. Much of this potential can be realized only by harvesting areas that are at present unused, although improved game management practices will be important for some species. The cost per pelt retrieved will therefore be higher, given present trapping arrangements.

Fur farming provides additional possibilities of raising production. In the Soviet Union, the world's leading producer of arctic fox, feeding stations on the tundra and summer feeding of young foxes in captivity have raised pelt yields. In the 1950s, a mink farm was operated in the Mackenzie Delta under private ownership, but it failed because of the lack of feed. This problem should no longer be an impediment to successful mink ranching because the decline in the dog population has made available large amounts of food that are unsuitable for human consumption and much of which is at present wasted.

FOOD

Fish and wildlife are essential sources of protein in the North and, with improved management and development, they could supply both a growing population there and a limited export market. The most beneficial use to man of vast areas of land and water in northern Canada is for the production of protein. The regional potential for improving food harvests cannot readily be estimated, partly because many of the major food species found there are migratory and are, therefore, shared with users outside the region. The problem of game management is therefore also complex. A useful discussion of the economic potential of a number of the major food resources, based on research sponsored by Inuit Tapirisat of Canada, is contained in a recent report by B.F. Friesen (1975) and in another by Friesen and J.G. Nelson (1975). They do not, however, deal with the major freshwater fisheries in the Mackenzie Valley nor with terrestrial species common only in the southern Mackenzie District.

There are marked differences of opinion on the ability of the caribou herds in the region to withstand significantly greater hunting pressures, especially in view of increasing encroachment on caribou range by various developments in the northern parts of the provinces as well as in the territories. Nevertheless, improved management and harvesting practices should permit greater yields in at least some areas. The reindeer herd, despite its checkered history, continues to provide food and employment in the Mackenzie Delta region, although its full potential has never been realized. Moose and muskox harvests could be increased in certain areas. Experiments in other parts of the North indicate that muskoxen can be raised domestically to provide milk and wool as well as meat. Recent reports by G.W. Scotter (1970) and Scotter and E.S. Telfer of the Canadian Wildlife Service (1975) assess these possibilities in more detail. Other big game species do not appear capable of sustaining much larger harvests than at present. The potential for increased bird harvests is not known. Increased beaver and muskrat yields would, of course, result in additions to the food supply.

The best prospect for increased food production in the North is almost certainly fish. The annual potential fish yield in the North has been estimated at 20 million pounds, of which only about 7 million pounds are harvested at present. This harvest includes commercial fisheries, which have not been mentioned in the previous discussion of domestic food production. The decline in the dog population appears to have led to a marked reduction in the domestic fishery, and this slack could be taken up by harvesting fish for other purposes. At the same time, there may be as yet untouched fish populations, chiefly in marine waters, which could be harvested to advantage. The possibility of significantly increased yields through management techniques or aquaculture appears to be more promising with the fish resources of the North than with any other food source.

Quite apart from whether or not the kill of marine mammals can or should be increased, a reduction in the loss rate by sinking of all species through improved harvest techniques would yield a great increase in the food supply. The decline in the dog population has released large quantities of marine mammal protein, as well as of fish, for other uses, and no advantage has been taken of its availability to date. There are available also large unused, but potentially valuable, quantities of marine oils.

OTHER RESOURCES

The forest resources of the Mackenzie Valley are, by and large, at present underused. Most of the harvestable stands are located south of South Nahanni River. North of Fort Simpson, the available timber is concentrated in narrow stands on alluvial soil in river valleys. However, whether or not the more northern stands can provide a sustained yield is questionable because of the very long time — up to 200 years — that an average tree takes to reach maturity and because of the uncertain quality of timber. A method for successfully reforesting cut-over areas in much of the North has not yet been developed. In the Mackenzie Delta, there is evidence that once a wooded area has been cleared, tundra takes it over. In many ways, then, the northernmost parts of the forest can be functionally non-renewable.

Any program for increasing timber yields must therefore be based on careful management of the forest for long-term production. Large, short-term construction projects such as a pipeline, which might require substantial quantities of lumber and pilings, could lead to local depletion of the forest in some parts of the region and jeopardize the future viability of locally controlled enterprises that might be based on this resource.

11. Precipitous exploitation of forest resources must be avoided, and the long-term value of the forest must not be sacrificed to meet the short-term requirements of an industrial development. The allowable cut should be established before making any large-scale harvest, such as a pipeline may require, to ensure that the forest resource can be maintained for future local use. However, policies should recognize that short-term demands, if not excessive, could provide a starting point or boost for local forestry enterprises.

12. Future forestry programs must also recognize the importance of the forest as habitat, not only in terms of its ecological significance for wildlife, but also, and as a consequence, in terms of its cultural and economic significance to native people. Its aesthetic and recreational uses must also be considered. On balance, these values appear to outweigh the benefits of timber cutting in most areas. Yet, even where timber is to be harvested, the native people's interest in the wildlife habitat that the forest provides must receive adequate consideration. Any program for increased forest use should, therefore, be consistent with fur and game conservation and harvesting.*

Nevertheless, forest resources in some areas offer an excellent opportunity for integrated local development. A complex of small-scale enterprises based on logging, the production of logs and lumber, and the construction of houses (both locally and in other communities) could provide some communities with a substantial additional source of income and employment. There is already a serious housing shortage in the Mackenzie Valley and Western Arctic, so it cannot be argued that there would be no market for an integrated regional housing construction industry, an industry that could be based on small-scale local units. There are already housing cooperatives in some of the communities, but to date they have concentrated entirely on the final assembly of prefabricated housing modules shipped into the North by southern suppliers. The considerable economic and social rewards that might be offered by the use of local materials for housing have been largely ignored in official policies.

Limited agricultural prospects exist in the Mackenzie Valley, mainly in small-scale gardening for local markets. For example, in 1943 the Mackenzie Valley was largely self-sufficient in potatoes, having then a production of almost 160 tons from an estimated total cultivated area of 300 acres, only part of which was used for potatoes. However, the experience with both lumber and vegetables has been that, as transport links with the South have improved, imports have become cheaper than local produce. In part this is a result of public policy and economic accounting systems, and they are subject to change. New techniques in small-scale gardening operations in the South might be usefully applied in the Mackenzie Valley and, if a pipeline is built, the use of industrial waste heat for greenhouse operations, as Professors Ed Maginnes and George Green suggested at this Inquiry (C6092ff.), should be considered. I am by no means suggesting that native people ought to become farmers, in the way that the federal representatives who framed the Prairie Treaties had supposed. Small-scale agricultural enterprises are merely one of a variety of options that are open to community-based and community-controlled enterprises in the Mackenzie Valley.

An exhaustive review of the potential for expanding renewable resource production in the North is unnecessary. Many reports have examined these possibilities at greater length, and I recommend for further consideration the following: the submission of Ruttan and T'Seleie to this

Inquiry (Exhibit F683); the reports of the Renewable Resources Project sponsored by Inuit Tapirisat of Canada (1975); the report of the Special Staff Group of the Department of Indian Affairs and Northern Development on *Development Agencies for the Northwest Territories; the Report of the Royal Commission on Labrador; Northward Looking, a Strategy and a Science Policy for Northern Development,* by the Science Council of Canada; and two documents produced by the Canadian Council on Rural Development, *A Development Strategy for the Mid-North of Canada,* and *Working Papers, Seminar, Environmentally Appropriate Technology for the Mid-North of Canada.*

Neither biologists nor resource managers doubt this general potential for an expansion of the northern economy based on renewable resources, even though our knowledge of the resource base is inadequate in its specifics. It need hardly be added that prescriptions for expanding production are not universally applicable to the entire Mackenzie Valley and Western Arctic. Some areas are richer than others, and some species in some areas are already harvested to capacity. Perhaps some groups of native people, who live in areas that are relatively poor in renewable resources, cannot hope to increase their production of fur or food in any significant way.

13. Whereas there is an overall necessity to encourage and expand resource production, specific efforts must be tailored to the needs of individual communities and their local resource potential, in accordance with sound management principles.

THE NEED FOR CASH

The basic problem is not the adequacy of the resource base but the realization of a cash income from it. To illustrate this point, let me return to my estimates of gross and net value of fur, fish and game production. The calculations in section two of this chapter imply that persons participating in the traditional economy spend a total of almost $3.5 million a year to outfit themselves with nets, snowmobiles, canoes, outboard motors, rifles and ammunition, gasoline, aircraft charters, and so on. These expenses amount to nearly $1,600 for each General Hunting Licence holder, a sum that appears to be consistent with the few estimates that have been based on detailed research into the operating, maintenance and depreciation costs for hunting, trapping and fishing. The most active participants would certainly spend more than this amount, but there must be many licence holders who spend less: as an average figure, $1,600 seems to be reasonable, and it adds weight to our general estimate that production costs amount to about 25 percent of the gross value of total production. By far the greater part of this estimated $3.5 million is spent within the Northwest Territories, and it is therefore evident that an expansion of activities based on renewable resources will benefit the local businesses that serve that sector.

It is important to note that this estimated $3.5 million is three times the present cash yield from trapping and substantially more than the most optimistic potential yield from this activity. We have no estimates of the net income that is at present derived from secondary activities based on renewable resources, such as commercial fishing, handicrafts and garment manufacture, but it would at least partly make up the difference. This differential does, however, highlight the need for cash from other sources to support the viability of the traditional sector as it now exists, and it demonstrates yet again why so many persons who identify themselves as trappers also work — indeed, may have to work — for wages. In some smaller communities, transfer payments, such as family allowances and old age pensions, can be important sources of capital for hunting.

Too often it is supposed that the development of renewable resources simply means more hunting, trapping and fishing, and that those who argue for it seek only to preserve an idyllic but irrelevant way of life in a museum environment. I cannot overemphasize the fact that this point of view has nothing to do with the goal of developing a sound economy based on renewable resources. Even the most optimistic estimates of the harvest potential of renewable resources do not suggest that every man, woman and child in the territories can harvest enough, not only to eat, but also to pay for all the other things they might want. I have made it quite clear that there is a need for cash that goes far beyond what is at present earned from that sector. An economy based on renewable resources does not mean simply a subsistence economy, although it would certainly encompass a subsistence component, the benefits of which, as I have noted, have been so often underestimated.

The objective of increasing renewable resource production is not, in the main, to increase domestic consumption of country food, for it seems clear that most native people already eat well off the land. Expanded production makes sense primarily if the new production is, in fact, surplus to domestic requirements.

Surplus production would have two beneficial uses. The first is for redistribution: native people, particularly those who live in larger centres, who do not have good access to country food, could then obtain the nutrition they require and desire at reasonable prices. This arrangement would increase the possibilities for intersettlement trade. The second use, which is the real key to successful renewable resource development as a basis for the northern native economy, is to generate cash income. This result can be achieved by marketing the surplus directly for commercial sale, not only for redistribution among native people, but also to non-native northern residents, and by using the surplus in further processing as a basis of small-scale industrial enterprises.

MARKETING

The success of any attempt to expand renewable resource production for commercial purposes will depend heavily on the ability to market these commodities. In the case of raw furs, the markets are international and, on this scale, territorial fur production is small. Because it is virtually impossible for trappers to obtain adequate credit from local fur buyers, they have turned increasingly to selling their furs directly at auction. The Government of the Northwest Territories has taken positive steps to encourage this tendency, although further evaluation of the situation is necessary. Improvement of the prices paid to trappers can come only through cooperative efforts on the national level: it would be impossible for a territorial marketing board, if such a thing existed, to affect auction prices significantly by its own efforts.

Marketing food is a different problem. With the exception of some species of fish, it is generally considered that the production of food for export is impractical, for both biological and economic reasons. There is, however, a growing market for local sale, and it is not now satisfied by commercial caribou hunting, cropping the reindeer herd, and small-scale commercial fishing. This local market offers by far the most attractive prospects for commercial harvesting because it requires less marketing effort and lower transport costs to reach. It is also about the right size because, unlike the export market, successful entry into it would not create a demand so far in excess of supply that undue pressure would be placed on both the supply itself and on the suppliers' capacity to produce and distribute it.

14. There should be a thorough examination of the possibilities of marketing foods locally. Both the federal and territorial governments have the option of giving preference to local produce wherever the resource base might permit increased production for local sale.

Secondary Activities

Processing and manufacture of locally produced commodities could add significantly to employment and income. The chief opportunities in this direction appear to be fur tanning, garment manufacture, food processing, marine oil processing, sawmilling, log and lumber construction, handicrafts and similar cottage industries, and tourism. Enterprises that already exist in these areas could be increased or expanded. Others that have been tried in the past and failed should be re-examined in the light of present circumstances. Others that have never been tried may require innovative design and techniques. Many ideas for this sort of development have been suggested in the past, and there is no need to review them individually here.

Opportunities for native employment exist in the management of renewable resources, as well as in the design, technology, manufacture and maintenance of equipment for the harvesting and processing of these resources. Virtually no serious examination has ever been given to these latter possibilities and, although any major attempt to consider and implement these possibilities must await the settlement of native claims, thought should in the meantime be given to them.

15. We must not assume that, following the settlement of claims, events will logically and easily take their course. Preparatory work now will facilitate an orderly and balanced development of the native economy in due course.

Implications for Employment and Income

I have recommended nothing here that is really new. Many knowledgeable and capable people in both the public and private sectors have seen and discussed these possibilities. Some experiments have been tried, with mixed success, and I shall examine some of the reasons for their partial failure in the next section.

It should by now be evident that an economic sector based on renewable resources, which encompasses most or all of the enterprises listed above, is much more than subsistence activity that relies solely on traditional skills. The development of this economy will require scientific, technical, clerical, administrative, managerial and business skills. It will need the abilities and ambitions of younger people who have received schooling and training, and it will provide opportunity for them to stay in the North, to remain in their home communities. The oil and gas industry does not now offer these advantages in the same measure, and pipeline construction could not under any circumstances offer them.

It is not my purpose to estimate here how many jobs might be created by any particular occupation or enterprise or how many there might be in aggregate. Nor do I suggest that this sector could provide all the jobs that may be needed in the North of the future. The point that I do wish to nail down is that a healthy economy based on renewable resources offers employment and opportunities for secondary employment far beyond primary production, and it is employment of a type that native people repeatedly and everywhere told this Inquiry they want. Such an economy would offer a real choice to native people, not simply the imposed choice between industrial employment and welfare.

It is impossible to estimate at present the income levels, regional or individual, that might be generated by a fully developed renewable resource-based economy, but it would be nonsense to pretend that these could compete with wages earned on pipeline construction. Not many jobs anywhere do! But that choice is open to every Canadian: to work at home among family and friends and community, in a secure job and environment — or to go elsewhere in search of high-paying, if temporary and uncomfortable, even dangerous, employment. That is exactly why high wages are paid on the frontier, to induce people to work under these conditions. If native people are to have the choice that all other Canadians enjoy, then their own local economy must be strong enough to offer a real alternative. They will not be satisfied with less, nor would southern Canadians be satisfied if their only choice of employment lay between frontier oil development and subsistence agriculture.

Problems in Developing the Renewable Resource Sector

This is not the first report to emphasize the great potential that exists for development and modernization of the renewable resource sector of the northern economy, a potential that cannot be doubted and, that is greater than is commonly supposed. Yet potential is one thing, its realization is another. We saw in Volume One that the relative failure so far to realize this potential has been caused by the devaluation of renewable resource development in public policy and in federal priorities. Development policy for the North has proceeded on the premise that only the non-renewable resources found there can make a significant contribution to the national economy. By comparison, the maximum potential output of the renewable resource sector is small indeed. Yet, to suppose that the only hope of the native people of the North for their economic future also lies in non-renewable resource development flies in the face of the overwhelming weight of evidence heard before this Inquiry.

With the legacy of past policies and developments, the realization of the renewable resource sector's potential will not be easy. In this section, I shall examine some of the problems and their implications that must be faced. Previous difficulties with renewable resource development have occurred at two levels: individual enterprises and the renewable resource sector as a whole. The evidence of Ruttan and T'Seleie, Donald Snowden, Ralph Currie and Sam Stanley provided many useful observations on these problems at both levels. There is also the problem of access to the resources on which this development is to be based.

Problems at the Enterprise Level

Northerners, and those who know the North, are highly conscious of the failures of many small-scale projects or enterprises based on renewable resources. Almost all of them have been associated with government, which to many is explanation enough, and some of them are remembered as having been simply ludicrous in conception, design and implementation. To many ears, the very mention of renewable resource development carries with it the sound of failure.

This Inquiry heard a great deal of evidence and many opinions about actual renewable resource-based enterprises, in many cases from persons who were directly involved in them. Successful or not, they faced many of the same specific problems. The list is long and it includes inexperienced or even incompetent management and personnel, failure to develop appropriate technology, poor quality machinery and facilities, inadequate maintenance, slow resupply, inadequate

or insecure financing, lack of local involvement and control, improper understanding of the local situation, failure to take advantage of local expertise and skills, jurisdictional problems within governments, rapid turnover of administrative personnel in Ottawa or Yellowknife, bureaucratic red tape, and inability to make quick decisions and to take quick action. Many of these problems can be attributed to the difficulties inherent in direct government involvement and administration of local projects. Other problems are probably soluble with greater experience and understanding of local circumstances. Yet it appears that the solution of problems at the level of individual enterprises will be of little consequence unless the larger issues that face renewable resource development in the North are also resolved.

Problems Related to the Northern Economy as a Whole

Little attention has been given to the much larger forces that work to the detriment of successful development of renewable resources and the reason is clear. Because this kind of development has for so long had such low priority, those responsible for it or for promoting it have been distant, either geographically or hierarchically, from the centres of power. But what are these larger problems and how might they be overcome?

A variety of jurisdictions with differing and changing philosophies has initiated locally based development in the North. Sometimes cooperatives have been promoted, sometimes individual enterprises. A project may be started with overriding social goals, then abandoned because it does not make an economic profit. Some projects are nominally conceived as having distinctively Inuit or Dene objectives, then are expected to compete with non-native enterprises on the latter's terms. In all of these enterprises, native people are subjected to the whims of outsiders who have control. They are not told of the conflicting objectives that underlie otherwise mysterious changes in policy or abandonment of enterprises. If their objectives are both unclear and imposed, the participants can hardly be expected to work toward them effectively.

16. *The financial profit and loss of an individual enterprise should not be the only criteria of success. Social goals such as training, leadership, community solidarity and well-being, personal satisfaction from useful employment and reduced welfare dependence must also be counted against economic losses or subsidies to the enterprise. Too often the measure of success is imposed on local enterprise by the external agencies that control it, rather than being developed and understood by the community itself. Whatever the measures of success are to be, they must be consistent.*

The same observation can be applied to the northern economy as a whole. For example, although the unit capital cost of housing may be cheaper as a result of importing prefabricated modules, the total benefits to the North in terms of local enterprise, training, employment and income, would be far greater if houses were built from local logs and lumber. Louise Clarke, in her evidence, pointed out that the success of log construction in the North will depend on developing new technology and designs. Lack of adequate housing is one of the most serious social and economic problems in the North, and its solution could bring many social and economic benefits. Nevertheless, narrow economic accounting systems and narrowly conceived policy objectives stand in the way of this praiseworthy goal.

Renewable resource development has always been bedevilled by piecemeal approaches. The very idea of an integrated, locally based economy implies an interdependence among enterprises and supporting agencies that has never in fact existed. An enterprise that could flourish among other related and healthy enterprises could just as easily wither and die alone in a hostile environment. Snowden, in his evidence to the Inquiry, stressed the need for an integrated approach to renewable resource development in terms of the multiplicity of resource opportunities as well as of the combination of skills, innovations and organization needed to bring such projects to fruition. The example of housing illustrates the need for the integrated approach that has been lacking so far. In the case of fur marketing, piecemeal solutions at the local level will never amount to much unless the problem is also considered at the territorial and, indeed, the national level.

The Problem of Capital

I have already pointed out that subsistence activity combined with trapping usually cannot generate enough capital to sustain itself. Additional inflows of capital have in the past come from transfer payments and wage employment, increasingly from the latter. The mixed economy, which the majority of native people have told this Inquiry they want to maintain, means a continuation of something like this situation. For those who choose to trap full-time, grants and loans may be required, although they will serve the purpose only if they are large enough to outfit the trappers properly. Insufficient provision of capital for trapping (or, indeed, for other similar ventures) is a sure prescription for failure. One way in which this problem may be solved is for hunters and trappers to control the distribution of funds through their own organizations, because they are in the best position to know their members' needs. For many hunters, however, occasional trapping may provide a welcome addition to income, but the bulk of their cash requirements will have to come from employment. If this employment is to be generated by the renewable resource sector, then the kind of enterprises we have discussed must be established.

Employment, loans, grants and so on can meet only the individual's investment requirements. Investment at the level of enterprise or infrastructure cannot at the outset be generated by the personal savings of hunters and trappers or by any surplus they might generate by those activities. Financing at this higher level will have to be more generous than it has been in the past. More important, however, this financing must also have both greater administrative flexibility and longer-term stability and continuity than has characterized previous government-administered enterprises.

The various native claims proposals include provisions for the transfer of capital to native control, chiefly through royalties on non-renewable resource development. Evidence from Alaska suggests that this is not without problems: it can create rather than reduce dependence on externally controlled rapid industrial development. Capital transfers will not, in themselves, assure the appropriate financing of renewable resource development unless specific provisions for that purpose are incorporated in native claims settlements. Ultimately, renewable resource-based enterprises and, indeed, the sector as a whole may be able to generate their own capital requirements, but that is not possible now.

17. Until the renewable resource-based sector in the north is able to generate its own capital, government could make funds available as a matter of public policy pursuant to such programs as the Western Northlands, established under the Department of Regional Economic Expansion (DREE), or pursuant to the Agricultural Rural Development Act (ARDA).

The Problem of Access

Renewable resource development raises difficult questions about access to the resources themselves. There are at least three points of view about access to fur, fish and game in the North. One is to give open access to all northern residents regardless of ethnic origin, economic status or occupation. Another is to limit access to only native people, but again without distinction according to economic status or occupation. A third is to limit access to only one class of native people; those who are hunters and trappers by profession. Public policy has veered from one to another or to a combination of all of these options at various times in the past. The first option prevailed until the late 1920s in most of the Mackenzie Valley and Western Arctic, but was then replaced by the second. Since the 1960s, there has been a gradual shift back towards the first option. In the mid-1960s, serious consideration was given to a limited version of the third option, that is, to restrict trapping rights to native people who were without wage employment.

Native people have generally opposed the first option and have had mixed feelings about the third. Certainly all of the current claims proposals are at one in seeking to enshrine native hunting and trapping rights and to transfer control over access to native people themselves. The federal government's statement on the *Political Development in the Northwest Territories*, released August 3, 1977, contemplated that land and renewable resources will in some instances be turned over to the Government of the Northwest Territories and in other instances to native people. Whether or not access to fur, fish and game — or indeed to other renewable resources — ought to be in the control of or limited to native people will depend on the conditions that are attached to any transfers made by the federal government and on the decisions that the territorial government and the native people are disposed to make thereafter.

The choice between the second and third options is again a matter on which native people will have to pass judgment, but it is nonetheless worthy of some comment here. Access to resources is an essential feature of a subsistence economy. To limit that in any significant way must necessarily undermine the traditional basis and the continued viability of the subsistence economy. The idea of specialization and professionalization of harvesters, on the other hand, implies a division of labour and in such as case there might well be persuasive reasons to limit access.

Options for the Future

Whatever the course of renewable resource development in the North, two fundamental points should be made clear. Although these points have already been stated in the course of the argument in other chapters of this report, they are matters that should be emphasized in relation to the whole question of renewable resource development.

First, I am not assuming that such development should be the sole form of economic development in the North. Large-scale industrial development is obviously going to occur in parts of the North, and all northerners will become involved in some way with such development. It is the prior development of renewable resources that is of central importance: unless that option exists and unless it is able to offer real opportunities to native people of the North, the undue dependence on the non-renewable sector that I discussed in Volume One will occur.

18. *The critical thing is that priority be given to the strengthening of the renewable sector now. Parallel development is not, of course, without its problems: conflicts of land use and conflicts of interest between southern and northern objectives will occur. But the terms of a settlement of native claims must secure for those whose interests lie within the renewable resource economy an effective voice in how such conflicts are to be resolved.*

I have discussed this subject in Chapter 12 of Volume One. Only in that way can the long-term viability of an economy based on renewable resources be assured.

Secondly, none of the argument here should be understood to be a nostalgic look back towards some idyllic era in the recent or remote past to which native northerners should be urged to return. That was no part of their submission to the Inquiry, it was no part of the argument of Volume One, and it is no part of the argument of Volume Two. In the wake of a

settlement of native claims, native people will themselves manage the renewable resource economy. They will effect the balance between subsistence-oriented hunting and fishing, individual trapping for trade, and more elaborate development projects that are based upon renewable resources. In each of these activities there will be modernization. Indeed, such modernization has been taking place, at the individual level, throughout this century. Dene and Inuit adaptability as renewable resource harvesters ha⸱ been remarkable, and, given appropriate institutions and possibilities, they will continue to adapt.

19. *If renewable resource development is to succeed, then the continuing and serious impediments to it must be clearly acknowledged, understood and removed. A favourable climate must actively be created for such development, otherwise individual projects and enterprises of the type I have discussed will be operating in a hostile environment that will jeopardize their success.*

I have already reviewed some of the specific impediments that hobbled earlier attempts to develop renewable resources. It must also be recognized that, to some extent, the ideology and objectives of a native economy based on renewable resources are not the same as those of non-native economic enterprises in the North. Today, as in the past, we hear the suggestion that public support should be withdrawn from native enterprises because they constitute unfair competition to non-native business. Some people expect native enterprises to show quick profits to justify their existence. Some suggest, explicitly or implicitly, that enterprises based on renewable resources merit support only if they can generate large surpluses and tax revenues to support the existing structures of commerce and government in the North. These attitudes, which are clearly at odds with native people's objectives and their economic future, appear to be widely held, and they explain, in large measure, the lack of enthusiasm for renewable resource development. If they continue to prevail among the persons who make or influence policy, then an economy based on renewable resources that so many native people desire has no viable future, and native people will never have a real choice.

20. *The production and processing of renewable resources must be regarded positively as a desirable social and economic goal. Not only should the resource base be protected, but the well-being of the harvesters should also be promoted. Just as good farmland in the South needs able and willing farmers to make use of it, so the northern fur, fish, game and timber resources can become useful only with competent and adequately financed harvesters and processors in the North.*

This approach will be far more beneficial to northern people than a patchwork assemblage of individual assistance programs for one or another industry or enterprise. In the case of the fur industry, for example, floor prices, production subsidies, unemployment insurance for trappers — all of which have been proposed in the past — may serve to channel additional funds to individual hunters and trappers, but they cannot ensure the long-term health of the fur economy as a whole. Even the outpost camps and small settlements could eventually wither and disappear, despite assistance, in the face of an overwhelming orientation and drive towards industrial development based on the non-renewable resources of the North. I do not want to underestimate or belittle the importance of these specific programs, which are commendable in their intent and are presently meeting a real need in many parts of the North. Nevertheless, on their own they are not enough. However, in the context of a generally favourable climate and policy towards the renewable resource sector, even these programs could be made both more effective and more efficient.

The creation of this favourable climate will depend not only on a reorientation of government policy and programs towards that objective, but also on a clear understanding and commitment that an economy based on renewable resources must be developed under native control and on native initiative. Even the outpost camp and trappers' assistance programs cannot realize their full potential as long as their administration remains exclusively or even largely in the hands of government.

21. The rules by which outpost camps and trappers' assistance programs operate must be clearly understood and accepted by their users, and they must meet needs that have been identified by participants in the programs.

22. Native people consider renewable resources, particularly fur, fish, game and timber, to be essential to their identity and their way of life. These resources must be the cornerstone of native economic development, and neither the initiatives nor the benefits can be appropriated by others. It follows that any

attempt to develop these resources by means or programs that are non-native in design and execution are not only destined to fail in the long run, but they will also generate resentment and hostility.

23. A proper role of government, whether federal or territorial, is to facilitate the availability of capital and of technical assistance to the people under its care. The problem of capital should, as I have already said, be resolved primarily through the settlement of native claims, although funds from applicable existing government programs should be made available in the interim. If, however, funds continue to be made available, and programs continue to be developed and administered only under tight government control and regulation, then native people will be suspicious of both the motives and the benefits, and these programs will end in failure. The control and administration of such developments must lie in the hands of native people.

The viability of the native economy, based on renewable resource development, must depend on its being largely separate, both geographically and in orientation, from the operations of the non-renewable resource sector. The movement of native people between the two cannot and should not be excluded, but, if the renewable sector thrives, such movement will be minimized. Each native community and every individual will have to decide on which economic mode primarily to rely. Although the two economies may not be mutually exclusive, there will be a tension between them. Hard choices will have to be made both by individuals and by the organizations that represent them.

The task of developing the renewable resource sector will not be easy, either for native people or for governments. Both the history of failure and the potential for future failure must be overcome. But the evidence before this Inquiry leads me to the conclusion that, if native people are to be full citizens and participants in the North of tomorrow, it can and must be done.

THE REPORT OF
THE MACKENZIE VALLEY
PIPELINE INQUIRY

PART ONE —
PEOPLE: SOCIAL AND
ECONOMIC CONCERNS

3 Employment and Manpower Delivery

The Pipeline Guidelines call for an employment system that would give northerners, particularly native people, preference in obtaining employment during the construction of the pipeline. Such a preference is based on the assumption, which the government has followed during the past decade or more, that northern native people should be encouraged to take wage employment on large-scale industrial projects.

The native people have not entered industrial employment in large numbers. The reasons for this were set out in Volume One. Suffice it to say that the industrial system has presented native people with a wide range of conflicts with their own land-based economy. In Volume One, I proposed a series of measures by which these conflicts could be mitigated, and by which a diversified northern economy, based on both renewable and non-renewable resources, could be established.

In Volume One, I also commented on the contradictions that are implicit in the government's policy on employment, and on the statistical and analytical mistakes on which it is based. In this chapter, I deal with the question of employment at two levels. Because of the broad thrust of the evidence placed before this Inquiry and because of my own apprehension that the experience of the native people with the industrial system has not been adequately understood, I feel compelled to comment here on some of the fundamental problems that affect northern employment. They in turn lead to specific recommendations regarding manpower delivery and the principles on which any manpower delivery system should be based.

We are, of course, considering the construction of a pipeline that is not going to be built immediately but may well be built ten years in the future. When the time comes to build it, no doubt many of its technical characteristics will have changed, and its construction will require a different mixture of labour and capital than it would require today. Such a change would alter the demand for labour, including northern labour. If, as I have recommended, the development of renewable resources is given priority, then the supply of local northern labour available for pipeline work might decrease considerably. That result is greatly to be wished for: my thesis throughout has

been that we should create the conditions that would enable the native people to strengthen the renewable resource economy in the North and thereby reduce their vulnerability to the social and economic stresses that industrial employment has, in the past, visited upon them.

There is a strong possibility that even the most careful forecast of labour supply and demand will not prove reliable over time. The following analysis therefore uses present-day information on the construction of pipelines, on the kinds of labour required, and on the quality and availability of northern labour. This is the best information we have; but it will have to be updated in the future.

In Volume One, I estimated that the present population of the Mackenzie Valley and Western Arctic is about 30,000, consisting of approximately equal numbers of native and white people. Ten years from now, this population may have increased considerably. But the proportion of the total population, or more accurately, of the total labour force, that will want jobs on the pipeline is difficult to predict. I would suggest that only a small part of the permanent white population of the North will not already be fully employed. Some of them may wish to work on the pipeline, but I think that most of them will prefer the security of the jobs they have to the possibly more lucrative, but certainly (for them) short-term jobs the pipeline may offer. If there is a negotiated settlement of native claims, and if the renewable resource economy is successfully developed and enlarged before the pipeline is built, then it seems unlikely that a large number of native people would want pipeline jobs, or would feel compelled to take them because they had no other means of livelihood. Thus the underlying rationale for widespread recruitment of native people on pipeline construction will, I hope, no longer apply. This will mean that the number of native people who will be working on the pipeline if it is built in ten years' time will be considerably less, as a percentage of the work force, than we would expect to see if the pipeline were built today.

The Demand for Northern Labour

Government and industry have placed considerable emphasis on the effect the pipeline could have in solving the problems of unemployment and underemployment in the North. How much employment could the project provide to northern residents? Could such employment help northerners, particularly native northerners, to obtain careers as skilled tradesmen or industrial workers? Could it provide them with the kind of certification that would be acceptable in the labour markets of the South? Or would the pipeline employ northern residents only as short-term labour?

Arctic Gas' plans called for the construction of a pipeline along the Mackenzie Valley during four or five winter seasons, each season lasting about four months; actual pipe laying would take place during two of these winter seasons. Some additional time will be required to build compressor stations and other facilities, but this will not greatly extend the life of the project. Thus, although such employment could be beneficial to the northern resident in terms of experience, it would not go very far in helping him to meet the standards that have been laid down for apprenticeship and training. Some kinds of work associated with pipeline construction, such as skilled labourers, some classes of heavy equipment operators, and welders, do not have a designated apprenticeship period. The ease or difficulty of entry into these jobs varies considerably, but it is unlikely that native northerners could readily gain entrance into trades that require substantial experience and skill. The employment of native northerners would be largely restricted to work as unskilled labour, and such employment would bring them into the industrial economy at a relatively low level and without any prospect of permanent employment.

Many skills and trades require an apprenticeship that extends well beyond the time needed to build the pipeline and related facilities. For example, plumbers, painters and sheet metal workers require a four-year apprenticeship. Cement masons, insulators, and gasfitters require a three-year apprenticeship. In general, construction of the pipeline will not offer a period of continuous employment long enough to enable a northern resident to attain the status of journeyman. Of course, some apprentices might move south when the pipeline is completed, but the number of persons likely to do so would not be large. Some promising northern apprentices might be retained on contractors' payrolls all year round, rather than only seasonally, or they might find some related work during the off-season, but again the number of such persons will not be large.

Turning then to pipeline employment as short-term employment, as opposed to a means of acquiring a trade or a skill that would equip a northerner for permanent wage employment in the North: the project would offer short-term employment to many people. Many of the jobs on the pipeline will require low to moderate levels of skill. Les Williams of

Arctic Gas divided the total pipeline labour force into four groups. Group one respresents the highest skill levels, such as those required by operating engineers, hot-pass welders and warehousemen; group two includes equipment operators, electricians and carpenters; group three includes apprentice equipment operators, welder's helpers and swampers; and group four includes common labourers and bull cooks. Williams said that 100 percent of the jobs in group one and 90 percent of the jobs in group two require extensive industrial experience. However, no extensive industrial experience was necessary for any of the jobs in the other two groups. "Extensive" has not been defined, but it seems clear that northerners who have had at least some experience of industry or wage employment could probably qualify for a considerable range of pipeline jobs.

Williams did not translate his skill categories and percentages into actual numbers in the evidence that he gave, but there is a useful breakdown, based on Arctic Gas data, in a study prepared by MPS Associates and filed with the Inquiry as Exhibit F727. MPS Associates indicate that the mix of skills in the pipeline labour force, as measured by the average number of workers required on northern spreads during the winter construction season, would consist of 2,313 skilled workers (or 56 percent of the average winter labour force), 1,280 semi-skilled workers (or 31 percent of the average winter labour force), and 536 unskilled workers (13 percent of the average winter labour force). Most of the jobs that would be available to native people are to be found in this latter category, although there could also be some jobs available in the semi-skilled category.

According to MPS Associates, there would also be an average of some 1,780 jobs available in the North during the summer, of which 211 would be unskilled and 479 would be semi-skilled. Presumably all of the unskilled jobs and some of the semi-skilled jobs would be open to native people. It is unlikely, however, that many of the 1,090 skilled jobs available in summer would be filled by northerners (MPS Associates, 1976, pp. 7-8). Neither the winter nor the summer estimates include jobs on related projects, such as the construction of gas-gathering facilities, or jobs in continued or accelerated oil and gas exploration.

Now, what about the operating phase? It is said that this phase will offer the prospect of the acquisition by northerners of long-term jobs, useful skills, and tradesman's status. But only 200 to 250 workers will be needed as permanent staff to operate the pipeline and man the northern administrative and maintenance facilities. Thus the number of northerners who can make a permanent career on the pipeline will necessarily be small. Moreover, most of the jobs associated with the operations phase require high levels of training. It is not likely that very many native people will be able to meet the high entry standards. The number of opportunities open to a particular trade at any given facility, such as a pumping station or a maintenance headquarters, is limited. Some exceptions may be made in order to accommodate northern native people, but the young native worker who may initially have found employment at Inuvik may, within a few years, find himself and his family in Alberta — if he wishes to advance his career. In the past, native people have often rejected such a move or, if they have not rejected it, they have found adjustment to it very difficult.

In general, then, the northern labour force is not likely to figure prominently in the skilled jobs that the pipeline will provide during either the construction phase or the operating phase. Only a limited number of northerners would be in a position to use the pipeline as a first step on a career ladder; this would be especially true of native people. They might learn much about the labour market and about working in an industrial setting but, for the majority of northern workers, the knowledge and experience they may gain will not result in certification or enhanced status within the labour force.

Labour Supply Considerations

White northerners should not have much difficulty in fitting into pipeline employment. Most of them are used to meeting job-skill requirements, joining unions, and working standard industrial hours while on the job. But this is not typically the case with northern native people who come from a non-industrial culture. Only very recently have they attended schools, and, in the schools, levels of achievement have been disappointing. In terms of the requirements that prevail in the modern labour market, most young native people, and virtually all older native people, are regarded as undereducated, unskilled, inexperienced and, to a great extent, immobile.

Arctic Gas commissioned a study undertaken by the Boreal Institute at the University of Alberta on the question of recruiting native people for pipeline employment. The results of the study are of interest. Of the 8,358 residents of the Mackenzie District that this study classed as native people in 1969 (Treaty Indian, Inuit and Metis), 162 had completed grade ten; 112 had completed grade eleven; and only 118 had completed grade twelve. Only 23 people had obtained a first university degree or technical diploma, only five had gone on to a second degree or diploma, and only three had completed a third degree or diploma. (Vol. 14.f, App. D, Part I, pp. 16-21, 26, 34.) It would appear from the Boreal Institute's data that not a single person had completed a graduate university degree. In percentages, these figures mean that only 1.4 percent of the total native population had completed grade 12, and that only 0.28 percent had gone on to complete some kind of formal post-secondary training. Although the situation has improved since 1969, the levels of educational achievement by native people, when measured against those of northern whites, are still low.

The problems of the native people are all the more obvious when compared with national standards. According to

Gemini North, in 1970, 93 percent of the native population of the Mackenzie Valley and Western Arctic had attained an educational level of grade eight or less. Two-thirds of this population had no schooling at all. In Canada as a whole, in 1973, only about 30 percent of the population had attained grade eight or less, and of this number, only a very small fraction, perhaps five percent, had no schooling at all. Just over 70 percent of the national population had completed high school, technical school or university, whereas in 1970 only seven percent of the northern native population had completed high school or technical school and none had completed university (Gemini North Ltd., 1974, Vol. 2, Table 7.38, p. 723). Thus, in a labour market in which emphasis is placed on educational attainment, the native people are at a very serious disadvantage.

Yet it would be wrong to suggest that native people have no knowledge or experience that would be useful in an industrial setting. Many native people have had experience of working on exploration crews, on highway projects, and in other industrial roles. During the 1960s, many of them were involved in one of the largest projects undertaken in the North up to that time, the Great Slave Lake Railway: they worked in varied jobs, including some that required unusual powers of comprehension and skill. Before that, they had been involved in the construction of the DEW Line stations, the building of Inuvik, and in a number of mining ventures.

The problem is not, therefore, that native people cannot perform industrial jobs. It is more complicated than that. On the one hand, government and industry have, in many ways, encouraged native people to take industrial wage employment. One of the results of this encouragement has been that, in some parts of the North, many native people have been dislodged from their own economic base. On the other hand, the entry standards that government, industry and the unions have set for various kinds of jobs in the industrial and bureaucratic labour markets place native people at such a great disadvantage that they are unable to compete. They are, therefore, simultaneously drawn into a particular path and then prevented from following it. Until a more rational approach is taken toward the whole question, native people will continue to have great difficulty in participating in employment programs, and many will find it impossible to do so. In Volume One, I outlined the nature of the problem in some detail and I proposed changes in our approach to education and to industrial development in the North that would enable the native people to come to grips with the problem.

There is, moreover, a cynicism about industrial employment that will have to be overcome if native people are to work effectively on projects such as the pipeline. Many northern native people have already had wage employment, but it has rarely lasted long enough in any one locality, or paid well enough, to provide them with permanent jobs and adequate income. Such work has come and gone, at times slowly, at times quickly, but it has never lasted. Given such experiences, people are disinclined to believe that wage employment offers greater security than their own way of life. The study prepared by the Boreal Institute says that:

A reality about employment in the North is that most job opportunities generally provide employment for periods averaging from a few weeks to about four months. Many employers pay more than the minimum wage requirement stipulated by the government (which appears extremely low relative to living costs in the North), yet fail to provide the common labourer with a living wage. Thus, one poorly paying job is seen to be as good as another and the present job is regarded as a temporary event. If consideration is given to the kinds of labouring jobs offered to the northerner, [for example] unloading cement from barges or other menial chores requiring little more than brute strength, one becomes aware of some of the reasons contributing to the formation of present attitudes toward work held by the northern labourer. [Arctic Gas Application, Vol. 14.f, App. D, Part I, p. 54]

The prevalence of such a pattern of employment makes it difficult for northerners to form any strong or favourable impressions of such terms as "permanent wage employment" or "careers in industry." Moreover, the cyclical and volatile nature of northern industrial activity has had its effects on the employability of northern native people. Ironically, it is the northern worker, and not the erratic manner in which industrial activity has been carried out in the North, that has come to be viewed as unstable. The Boreal Institute study explains:

Part of the problem of hiring people in the North, either for jobs or for training, is that the work history (if available) of the "successful southern employee" may very well be completely different from that of the "successful northern employee." The nature of employment in the North is generally short-term and seasonal (logically following from the "boom or bust" cycle of industrial development), and thus, work history showing short periods of employment followed by unemployment are, by southern standards, not looked on as favourably as a work history of unbroken employment. It even goes deeper than this when personnel managers, concerned about lowering the labour turnover rates and thereby decreasing costs, are understandably less apt to take a chance on the person with a broken history of work than the person from the South who has a continuous work record, even though the employment opportunities in the North may well necessitate spotty employment histories. [Arctic Gas, op. cit., p. 57]

Manpower Delivery

The pipeline project, enormous by any standards, will bring to the Northwest Territories contractors that rank among the biggest in the world and which have vast assets and resources at their disposal. It will mean that, for a period of some years, major international unions will be active in the North. All of this activity will be on a scale and of a complexity that is far beyond the experience of northern people, both native and white. These organizations, both the corporations and the unions, have commitments to their shareholders and their members — commitments that extend well beyond the North. For instance, though the unions have offered their cooperation to the development of programs for northern hire, the attitude of the unions toward preferential treatment of northerners may be expected to vary with the national employment situation in the trades they represent. It would be difficult to imagine that it could be otherwise.

Let me turn then to the question, how is northern labour to be recruited and given an opportunity, where they wish it, to work on pipeline construction? The answer is that a manpower delivery system must be established, and northern preference in hiring must be enforced. Whether a northern resident gets a fair deal with regard to pipeline employment will depend on the effectiveness of the rules that are worked out beforehand between government, industry, the unions, and the native people. Unless the rules are clearly spelled out, understood and accepted by all parties, and made known right down to the first line supervisors and union officials, a northern employment preference system simply will not work.

A new manpower delivery system should be established to handle the employment function. The task of referring persons for pipeline employment should not be given to existing agencies, such as the federal Commission of Employment and Immigration, or to the territorial government's Employment Division because they will be busy enough supplying manpower to employers other than the pipeline, and providing training and other assistance that the northern labour force will continue to require.

The function of the manpower delivery system will be to deal only with the emergency situation of pipeline construction. It should not overlap or intrude upon the responsibilities of the Commission of Employment and Immigration and the Employment Division of the territorial government. To find employment on the pipeline for northern people will require a special concentration of expertise and knowledge. During the construction period, the manpower delivery system will often have to react quickly and vigorously; that kind of reaction would be difficult if parts of the system were diffused throughout the bureaucracy or if there were jurisdictional conflicts among them. The entities with which the manpower delivery system will have to deal represent enormous power. To ensure that they do what is required of them, it will be necessary not only to lay down well defined rules but also to ensure that they can be enforced.

Those in charge of the manpower delivery system should deal directly with the pipeline company, the contractors and the unions with regard to the employment of northerners on the construction spreads and at the compressor station sites. They should have complete access at all times to the Agency in charge of the regulation of pipeline construction, so as to be in a position to call for the assistance of the Agency in securing compliance with terms and conditions established to ensure northern hire.

The Problem of In-migration

One of the most difficult aspects to plan for and control in boom economies is the large movements of population that they induce. The North American frontier has always attracted large numbers of people to relatively unpopulated regions. In cases such as the Klondike Gold Rush, most of the people left when the boom faded, but in other cases, such as the Alaskan gold rushes, a large number of people stayed to settle permanently.

David Boorkman, an urban sociologist, gave evidence on Alaskan population growth, focusing particularly on the recent growth induced by the Alyeska pipeline. The construction of that pipeline attracted many tens of thousands of migrants to the state because of three factors: the special character of Alaska as a romantic frontier, the magnitude of the Alyeska project and the widespread publicity that it received, and the prospect of obtaining high-paying construction jobs. These factors were enhanced by circumstances that arose from Alaskan legislation on local hire, by the fact that most of the union hiring halls for the pipeline were located in Alaska, and because the state did not fully enforce its legislation on local hire. Even for a region as developed (relative to the Northwest Territories) as Alaska, the population inflows were large enough to cause serious problems, which I discussed at length in Volume One.

Other population movements occurred within Alaska. Of particular note was the migration of native people from the smaller towns and villages of Alaska to centres such as Fairbanks, Anchorage and Barrow to seek jobs on the pipeline and in related work. A study undertaken by Professor Larry Naylor and Dr. Lawrence Gooding of the University of Alaska indicates that substantial numbers of native people from all parts of Alaska went to the main recruiting centres to obtain pipeline work. The distance of their home community from the pipeline did not seem to have much bearing on the numbers of migrant workers. Probably factors such as regional employment opportunities (or lack of them) and previous experience with the industrial labour market were important, but Naylor's and Gooding's material does not go into this.

In Alaska, the movement by native people between the pipeline, the larger urban centres, and their home communities, must have been substantial. The study indicated that 4,888 native persons (out of a native population of about 60,000) held a total of 20,280 pipeline jobs, which works out to an average of about four jobs per person. When one considers that some native workers would have been much more stable employees than others, a significant part of the native labour force must have been highly mobile during the period of construction.

In the evidence that Arctic Gas presented to this Inquiry, comparisons between Alaska and the Canadian North, including comparisons of in-migration, were downplayed. But even if it is granted that the in-migration resulting from pipeline construction in the Northwest Territories may prove to be of a smaller scale than it was in Alaska, it will still be enormous in relation to the population and to the economic base that exists there now. Migration to the pipeline region and movements within the area of construction are likely to dwarf all experience in northern Canada so far. These movements of people will raise problems notwithstanding a claims settlement and despite strong ameliorative measures. I comment further on the problems that migration could cause in the chapter entitled Action Communities.

Recommendations

Not all of the recommendations that follow can be appended to a permit for a right-of-way. The responsibility for some of them clearly lies with government, and others may require extensive negotiations involving government, industry, the unions and the native people.

Residency Requirements

Evidence presented to the Inquiry suggests that there is a consensus among government, industry, the trade unions and some of the native organizations on the need for a preferential hiring system for northern residents.

Arctic Gas supported the idea of a preferential hiring system. Indeed, they have already had discussions with government officials and with representatives of the Canadian Pipeline Advisory Council (a joint union-management organization), and some informal contact with native organizations and native people. Frank Hollands, General Manager, Employee Relations and Public Affairs for Arctic Gas, described some of the problems associated with a northern preference system. Because they lack education, experience, skills and mobility, native northerners might have difficulty meeting standards for union membership, and qualifications for jobs. To overcome these obstacles, special membership considerations could be extended to native people, and job qualifications and standards could be relaxed in some cases to accommodate northerners who do not have adequate experience or education.

Jack Witty, Chief of the Employment Division of the Government of the Northwest Territories, outlined a priority placement system based on residency criteria, that the territorial government felt should be applied to individuals seeking jobs. First priority consideration would go to persons who were born in the Northwest Territories and had lived there all their lives; second priority, persons who were born in the Northwest Territories and had lived there for most of their lives; third, persons who were raised in the Northwest Territories and had lived there for a substantial part of their lives; and fourth, persons who had lived in the Northwest Territories for at least four years.

The United Association of Journeymen and Apprentices of the Plumbing and Pipe Fitting Industry of the United States and Canada, represented at the Inquiry by Russ St. Eloi, defined a northern resident as a person born in the northern areas where the pipeline is being built, that is, the Northwest Territories or the Yukon Territory, or born to a family originally from the North, whose sons and daughters were born in the South and have returned to their family homeland. Jack Dyck of The Labourers' International Union of North America, Irv Nessel of the International Union of Operating Engineers, and Joe Whiteford of the International Brotherhood of Teamsters, Chauffeurs, Warehousemen and Helpers of America urged that a northerner be defined as a person resident in the North for six months.

The Canadian Pipeline Advisory Council expressed confidence that every bona fide northern resident genuinely interested in pipeline work would have the opportunity for employment in construction or related work. The Council, recognizing the problems associated with in-migration, urged strict control of hiring policies. It rejected the idea of a quota system, but accepted the principle of priority placement in training and employment for qualified northern native people.

All parties agreed that some system — but not the quota system — would have to be devised to ensure that the preference system actually placed native people in jobs. The preference system would require components to train, evaluate and counsel, and would have to include services such as transportation to and from the employee's home community. A priority placement system would apply to all northerners, based on the length of residency in the North. Residency would have to be defined, and several definitions were suggested. Finally, inasmuch as union membership presents a problem, the cooperation of unions would be needed on the admittance of northerners who cannot meet normal union standards.

Commission Counsel's proposal for a manpower delivery system did not specifically differentiate between native and non-native workers, but it did suggest the development of a hierarchy of preference that would favour persons with longer residency. This hierarchy of preferences would give native northerners a significant degree of preference over other northerners, without creating a classification system based on race. Commission Counsel proposed that pipeline jobs be extended first to qualified permanent northern residents, and then to other northern residents.

1. To qualify for preferential treatment with respect to pipeline employment, a person must have resided in the Northwest Territories or Yukon Territory for a period of five years prior to the commencement of pipeline construction. Preferential treatment should proceed on the basis of "right of first refusal," and quota systems should not be used in its application.

Some of the disadvantages that native people experience in the labour market are caused not by deficiencies in their own skills and experience, but by a rigid approach to the classification of jobs and to the application of job standards. A solution to this problem lies in a thorough review of entry requirements for the various categories of employment that native people might be able to undertake.

2. A panel composed of representatives of government, the contractors, the unions and the native people should be established by the manpower delivery system and should be responsible for determining the entry standards that would apply to northerners. If entry standards for some jobs are unreasonably high, they should be lowered, and preference in hiring should be given to native people.

3. It is essential that unions admit as members all qualified northern residents found acceptable by the employment system for pipeline work. The unions have offered their support in this endeavour.

Single Agency Referral System

The Committee for Original Peoples Entitlement suggested the establishment of a single agency with strong powers of enforcement to deal with all aspects of pipeline employment, recruitment, training and union membership. The Canadian Pipeline Advisory Council also supported a single agency to deal with all employment matters. This agency would include representatives from the pipeline company, the contractors, the unions and native groups, but it would be a government agency and would coordinate the pipeline employment activities and requirements of all other government departments and agencies. Although Arctic Gas strongly favoured the concept of a manpower delivery system, they opposed the proposal to set up a single agency.

In their study, *Alaskan Native Participation in the Trans-Alaskan Pipeline Project,* which was prepared for the Department of Indian Affairs and Northern Development, Gemini North proposed a manpower delivery system that, although separate from contractors, unions and existing government agencies, would rely on the resources of these existing agencies.

I do not share the view that a manpower delivery system should be developed solely from existing government agency programs. A pipeline employment service will certainly draw extensively upon these programs, but existing agencies should concentrate on their non-pipeline and continuing functions; otherwise, there will be a tendency to neglect the non-pipeline sector. Moreover, I am not convinced that compliance and enforcement provisions would be adequate in a manpower delivery system operated by existing agencies.

4. *A new manpower delivery system for pipeline construction, that is, a single referral system to deal with the pipeline contractors, the pipeline company, the unions and the potential clientele of an employment system, should be established. It should have one central office that would hold the whole system together and provide a point of reference for both employers and employees.*

5. *The native people must have control over those aspects of the manpower delivery system that most affect their communities, and over the relations between the system and the communities. Each community, for example, should have the right to determine whether the manpower delivery system would be allowed to provide information about pipeline jobs and to recruit within that community.*

Native workers could, of course, still go to work on the pipeline as individuals. The point is that the manpower delivery system should not enter a community without the agreement of the community itself.

Functions and Establishment of the Manpower Delivery System

Commission Counsel's submission deals specifically with the functions and organizational structure of the manpower delivery system. Although I accept the general intent and scope of the recommendations, they are more applicable to a pipeline that is to be built immediately rather than in ten years' time. The general functions that I consider appropriate for a manpower delivery system are as follows.

6. *The manpower delivery system should establish, staff and operate a central office and associated services; acquire and operate support services as required; establish active liaison with line agencies responsible for the delivery of training and related manpower services; and coordinate and direct programs to disseminate information, and orientation programs. It should register applications from northern residents for pipeline-related jobs and training; assess, screen, evaluate and process those applications in terms of skills and experience; and, where necessary, refer clientele to training programs. If necessary, it should prescribe and initiate pre-employment training. In all these functions, the manpower delivery system should assist the unions in their dispatch of northern residents. Finally, it should assemble data and monitor the performance of the employment system, with particular attention to northern participation in pipeline employment and training.*

7. *There should be a two-year planning period for the establishment of a manpower delivery system. The Company and its contractors should provide the manpower delivery system with detailed information on their labour force requirements before they request personnel for particular positions. The use of existing community employment and labour pool services should be mandatory.*

8. *The manpower delivery system should be prepared, at any*

time, to inform its client groups or the general public about its work and how it operates. That is, any agreements that are made with the Company, its contractors, the unions, or the native people, should be matters of public record.*

Hiring Halls and In-migration

Although they expected the pipeline to cause some in-migration, Arctic Gas said they would try to prevent an influx of non-northern workers seeking employment on the pipeline. One deterrent proposed by Arctic Gas was that non-residents would be hired only in southern centres. In other words, only northern residents would be referred to pipeline employment from a northern manpower delivery system. Arctic Gas anticipated that the establishment of a coordinating council of representatives from the government employment agency, unions, native organizations and employers would eliminate the need for hiring halls in the North. Foothills proposed to enforce a northern preference policy by ensuring that all southerners were hired through halls in the South, for example, in Vancouver or Edmonton. This, they said, would prevent southern contractors from hiring anyone other than northern residents in the North. The Committee for Original Peoples Entitlement also argued that hiring halls for non-residents should not be established in the Northwest Territories: southern workers should be hired only in southern locations.

Strong measures will be required to control migration from southern Canada to the Mackenzie Valley and Western Arctic during the pipeline boom. As in Alaska, there will be many people who will want to go north in the hope of finding work with high pay. These people will not only hinder or prevent northerners from securing employment, they could cause a variety of difficult problems for the territorial and local administrations.

I have already proposed that the minimum period of northern residence should be five years: that is, a person should have lived in the Northwest Territories for at least five years before becoming eligible for preferential treatment with respect to employment on the pipeline and related projects. This residency qualification provides the primary means of controlling undesirable in-migration; but it may not be adequate.

9. *To control in-migration, hiring halls in the North should be available only to northern residents; all other persons who want to work on the pipeline should have to apply for employment at southern hiring halls.*

The government should publicize this fact to all Canadians, and inform them, in clear terms, of the steps they must take to secure a job on the pipeline. Prospective pipeline workers not resident in the North must be convinced that they cannot expect to secure jobs on the pipeline and directly related projects by going North. To this end, there should be a publicity campaign that would make extensive use of the media.

Detailed information provided by other employment agencies, especially the Commission of Employment and Immigration, should be incorporated.

During the construction period, migration within the Mackenzie Valley and Mackenzie Delta will take two forms: from small communities to larger communities and from one area within the region to another. Control of such migration could be managed in several ways. To control migration from one area to another, zoning for employment purposes might be considered. Under such a scheme, persons living in the central Mackenzie Valley could apply for employment at only a single place, say Norman Wells; they would be discouraged from applying at other locations. Of course the most important factor in ensuring that there is not excessive outward migration from the smaller communities will be the development of a strong local and regional renewable resource economy after the settlement of native claims.

10. The manpower delivery system for the pipeline should not require a northern resident to be present at a hiring hall before dispatch to a pipeline job. In southern Canada, most unions can dispatch a member directly to a job by using a telephone or telex referral, and the same facility should exist in the North.

Training

Arctic Gas suggested that prospective employees who could not meet even related union qualifications should be given special training to upgrade skills to a level satisfactory for employment. Arctic Gas also intended to provide an orientation and counselling service to meet the needs of employed northern workers.

The preference system for northern resident employment outlined in Commission Counsel's submission should also be applied, in the same manner, to on-the-job and pre-employment training. Commission Counsel suggests that emphasis be given to the acquisition of skills in the apprenticing trades, preferably matching these to the long-term requirements for skilled labour in the region. Commission Counsel also suggested that contractors and unions be required to submit a joint plan of procedure outlining the number of training slots that would be available, the ratio of journeymen to apprentices on the job, and proposed programs of trainee supervision and assessment. This approach would be workable only if the single agency responsible for a manpower delivery system has the power to initiate and coordinate training.

11. Government, with the advice of the Company, the unions and the native organizations, should be responsible for the conduct of training programs.

12. Preference in pre-employment and on-the-job training should be offered to northern residents.

13. In some special cases, employees may have to be trained outside the North, but this number should be kept to a

minimum; *training should be available as close as possible to the home community of the trainee. This may mean the establishment of training facilities at major northern communities — which will be an expensive proposition, but if we are serious about employment preference for notherners, those costs will have to be borne.*

14. On-the-job training must, of necessity, be a large part of the overall training program. Journeymen, tradespeople and other personnel who provide on-the-job training must have a special awareness of the problems that may be encountered in training native people for employment in industry. This may be best accomplished by having native organizations participate in the presentation of orientation and training programs.

Conditions of Employment

Arctic Gas proposed to extend to all northern residents employed in pipeline construction the benefits and privileges offered to non-resident employees. In an effort to accommodate the personal and community commitments of northerners, Arctic Gas planned to ensure flexible work schedules for northerners working on sections of the pipeline close to home areas. As well, transportation would be provided to native communities during the scheduled rotational leaves of northern workers.

The Canadian Pipeline Advisory Council did not endorse the idea of preferential treatment for northerners while on the job. They took the position that northerners should be subject to the same disciplinary measures as all other employees.

15. Standards for on-the-job conduct and deportment should, for reasons of safety and non-discrimination, be the same for all employees.

Nevertheless, in the Mackenzie Valley and Mackenzie Delta, several cultures exist and several languages are spoken. This will mean the provision of an interpreting service in all of the languages and, where there is a written form of the native language, it will mean that printed materials, including forms and manuals, must be provided in the native languages. It is essential that terms under which native people are employed, and which recognize that they are culturally distinct, are fully observed.

16. Conditions of employment must reflect the fact that native workers are people of distinct cultures speaking distinct languages. Serious efforts should be made to provide support services and counselling to native people entering an industrial employment situation for the first time. The way in which workers are accommodated, fed and entertained in the construction camps must reflect native as well as non-native values.

Labour Pools

A labour pool or cluster hire system can be an effective way to ensure that a local work force, particularly native people, is retained on components of large projects that are amenable to the pooling concept. Commission Counsel, in his submission, outlined the advantages and disadvantages of a labour pool system. For the employer, the principal advantage is the ability to control labour attrition. For employees, the principal advantages are the closeness of work activities to the home community, flexibility of working hours and flexibility of tenure. The principal disadvantage is that work suitable for a labour pool system is limited to low-skill and labour-intensive activities.

17. Where northern residents indicate that this is what they want, efforts should be made to develop community labour pools for work on the pipeline project.

Accommodation, Food and Recreation

I have assumed that unions negotiating contracts with pipeline contractors will make adequate provision for acceptable accommodation, food and recreation standards in camps, and that these provisions will, in turn, reduce labour turnover. The standards specified for accommodation, food and recreation in such contracts have typically been high. However, the employment of native people on the pipeline will require special provisions that will have to be incorporated through collective bargaining.

18. The Company and its contractors should conform to the industry norm with regard to the provision of accommodation. Rooms should be designed for singles or couples; accommodation for couples and for women should be in separate sections of the camp facility. All rooms should be bright and clean; they should be equipped with electrical outlets, proper locks for security, and ample and modern shower, washroom and toilet facilities. Adequate laundry facilities for personal use and separate washroom facilities for women should be provided.

Collective agreements in the construction industry are extremely specific in terms of the quality, quantity and type of food that is to be served to all personnel on the site. The fact that there will be native people living at the construction camps must not be overlooked in the negotiation of agreements.

19. The Company and its contractors should make adequate provision for the food preferences of native people in construction camps. This should include provision of country food. In this regard, the Company and the unions should consult with the native associations.

In recent years, there has been a trend toward better and more complete recreation facilities in construction camps. However it may not be possible to install in the temporary and mobile camps of the Mackenzie Valley pipeline project recreational programs and facilities that are designed for more permanent camps.

20. The Company and its contractors should provide adequate recreational facilities and recreational programs for workers in construction camps. Facilities may include television, movies, library services, reading rooms, supervised card rooms, games rooms and equipment such as shuffleboard and pool tables. Provision for other sports activities, such as cross country skiing, and for self improvement programs, such as crafts, public speaking and culture appreciation, should be considered. Facilities should be provided for the controlled use of alcohol.

21. Any negotiations regarding recreational programs and facilities must consider the recreational modes and needs of the native people.

22. Camp security provisions should not be so strict that pipeline workers and other construction staff will not occasionally be allowed out of camp bounds. It would be unrealistic to expect that there would be no pressures from workers toward pursuing such activities. Of course, the circumstances under which they can leave camp to pursue recreation must be carefully controlled so that there is no contravention of native and environmental interests.

Security

Both pipeline companies have stated that they will give full support and cooperation to the RCMP with respect to normal police activities, but they both intend to have a private security force to police camps and construction security. Of course, the duties and authority of these private guards must be completely defined. Their ability to detain and search workers over security matters will be very limited, and problems relating to contraband (liquor, drugs and weapons), for example, will remain within the control of the relevant police authority in the region. Moreover, these guards will have to work carefully and diplomatically if they are not to have a negative effect on camp moral. The major task of the private security force relates to the actual policing of criminal acts, fights and so forth in camps.

23. At all times, there must be complete cooperation between the relevant police authorities and the camp security force.

24. At all times, the Company shall cooperate with the appropriate authorities with regard to policing and security aspects of the project and its impacts.

Police authorities shall have complete access to construction sites. All matters outside normal guard entry and exit security shall be referred to the relevant police authorities. The Company shall provide the appropriate authorities with any information it has relating to the discharge of undesirable persons from the project and to known or anticipated illegal acts within the construction areas.

The Company shall implement adequate education pro-

grams for security staff to ensure that they are aware of their own responsibilities in relation to those of other authorities.

Work Schedules

Work schedules and periods of rotation have not yet been established: these questions are normally left to the contractors and unions to negotiate. It has been suggested that workers on the project may work twelve hours a day, seven days a week.

Although these questions have to be settled through negotiation, there are some recommendations that I believe should be considered by the parties involved.

25. *The work schedule should generally be long enough to ensure sufficient overtime to encourage workers to accept and continue to endure the rigours of project employment.*

26. *Negotiations relating to hours of work should recognize the need to provide on-the-job training, apprenticeship and classroom training as part of the normal working day.*

Rest and Recreation Leave

Construction of a pipeline in the cold and dark of winter, in isolated locations, for a 10- or 12-hour day, seven days a week, is very taxing on workers. The psychological effect on people working in such conditions can be extreme. Regular periods of rest and recreation at intervals that are frequent enough to ensure that psychological problems do not develop are essential: they are essential for safety reasons and for camp morale. In Alaska, the work schedule was nine weeks of work and then one or two weeks of rest and recreation. The average period on the job, however, was between five and six weeks. After six weeks in camp, the average worker left the job and either went to his home community or to one of the major centres such as Anchorage or Fairbanks. All too often, he failed to return to the job. With regard to the Mackenzie Valley pipeline, there have been various recommendations for rotational periods, both from the pipeline companies and from the unions.

The pipeline companies have indicated that they would pay transportation costs to fly all southern workers to and from Edmonton for their rotational leave and, in addition, they will return all southern workers to Edmonton when employment is terminated. I should point out that there is usually a stipulation in the contract that a worker spend a certain time on the job before return transportation to point of hire is paid.

Whatever the normal rotation is to be for employees from the South, the pipeline companies have indicated that they would permit a more flexible rotation period for northerners. The pipeline companies plan to pay northern employees a sum equivalent to the cost of rotating a southern worker to and from Edmonton. This sum will be pro-rated over the normal period scheduled for a term of employment in the North. Thus, if the rotational period is six weeks and it costs,

on average, $250 to fly a person to and from Edmonton, a northerner who leaves after three weeks employment would be credited $125 for his transportation to and from his community. Anything in excess of that would be charged to the northerner and deducted from his pay entitlement.

27. *A northerner who leaves the work site before his normal tour of duty is completed should report to a manpower delivery system office when he is ready to return to work. The manpower delivery system should refer such workers to employment positions on a first-come first-served basis. (A northerner who works his full term and takes his normal rest and recreation period would return to his job automatically at the end of that period).*

The question of a bonus system to encourage both northern and southern employees to remain beyond their normal rotational term has been discussed. I cannot endorse this idea because such workers may become a danger to themselves and to the people with whom they work.

Safety on the Job

Both the pipeline companies and the unions have stated their positions regarding the safety of workers on the project. It is expected that adherence to stipulations in collective agreements and to various safety ordinances, together with briefing sessions before workers begin their employment, will deal adequately with the issue of job safety. There will, no doubt, be safety committees, scheduled meetings and established procedures. But there seems to be a need to channel safety information to the men on the job through special training programs, and in particular to native persons who may not have had experience with the construction industry and its hazards. It will be necessary to ensure that such safety training information can be provided to native employees in their native languages.

28. *Industry practices with respect to safety on the job and training for safe practices can be expected to be maintained on this project. Nevertheless, the magnitude of the project, the nature of the climate and environment in which the project will be conducted, and the presence of less experienced, northern workers and trainees, make it necessary to initiate special safety training and to maintain rigorous safety standards on the job.*

29. *Instruction in training and orientation programs related to safety should be given to native employees in their native languages.*

Conduct of Employees on the Job

The unions have stated emphatically that there should be only one standard of conduct for all workers, whether they are northern or southern, native or non-native. This position is a matter of principle for the unions because they believe that all workers must be treated alike and that it is unfair to permit one group to follow a less severe standard of conduct. Furthermore, the adoption of double standards implies that the individual worker is not responsible or accountable for his actions, and this, in turn, leads to bad work habits. This, the unions say, would hinder, not help the native people, because other employers will not apply a preferred standard to native people.

At the same time, we must recognize that a native worker on a construction site, particularly a person who has had only limited exposure to wage employment, is in a situation in which he faces new and difficult problems of time, punctuality, supervision and so on; his predicament must be viewed with flexibility and compassion. The danger is that too flexible an approach could create a double standard that could lead to abuse.

Some of these problems can be solved through training programs and orientation for job stewards, supervisory staff and employment advisers. In large measure, however, the successful participation by native northerners in the pipeline project will depend on a positive response to their needs.

30. There should be one standard of conduct for all employees on the pipeline project. The same degree of compassion that is extended to southern workers with special problems should be extended to northern workers in a similar position. Because of the inexperience of the northern work force, northern employees may face more than the usual number of problems. Extra attention should be given to these.

Money Management

Although individual rights with respect to the disposition of pay cheques must be maintained, workers, particularly northern workers, would probably benefit from orientation and training programs that deal with money management. There must also be facilities and services for workers to dispose of their earnings. The problems arising from the failure to provide money management counselling and credit union or banking services are apparent from an examination of the Alaska experience and of construction experience in other parts of Canada. In contrast, the Labourers' International Union included money management in its life skills training program at Keyano College, Fort McMurray, and this program has been partially successful in helping native workers on the Syncrude Project manage their earnings more effectively.

31. Banking and other financial services should be provided in camps so that workers can spend, save or invest their earnings or send money back to their families. The exact forms of these facilities and services must be determined through discussion and negotiation between the unions and contractors.

32. Money management counselling and orientation programs should be available to all employees, whether northern or southern, native or non-native. Counselling should include discussion of union membership dues, obligations, withdrawal dues and initiation fees. As part of a pay policy, the unions and contractors should make provision for deferred or installment payment of initiation fees.

Women in the Work Force

Hundreds of women were employed on the construction of the Alyeska pipeline in nearly all types and levels of work. And in Canada, too, more and more women are taking part in construction. At Keyano College, where workers on the Syncrude Project at Fort McMurray are trained, approximately one-half of the students graduating from courses for labourers are women.

33. The Company shall ensure that there will be no discrimination against women and that access to training, northern preference and the manpower delivery system, union membership and dispatching shall be afforded equally to women and to men.

THE REPORT OF
THE MACKENZIE VALLEY
PIPELINE INQUIRY

PART ONE —
PEOPLE: SOCIAL AND
ECONOMIC CONCERNS

4 Action Communities

Once construction of the pipeline and related projects is underway, those communities that have become the centres of urban, industrial and bureaucratic growth in the North will undergo a special impact. These communities include Inuvik, Norman Wells, Fort Simpson, Yellowknife, Hay River and, because of its role as a transshipment centre and its emerging importance to Beaufort Sea oil and gas exploration, Tuktoyaktuk. I think it will be useful to refer to these communities as action communities.

The action communities represent major forces for social and economic change in the northern hinterland. It is there that white society and native society come face to face and what happens in and around them will have a large bearing on how northern society as a whole will evolve. It is by means of the agencies and institutions that it has located in the action communities that the dominant society has brought the northern hinterland under the sway of the metropolis. It is through the action communities that decisions about government services or industrial development, taken thousands of miles away, are implemented. The growth of these communities and a dependence on services that they provide have drawn the native people closer into a way of life dominated by government and the industrial system.

With the great build-up of governmental institutions and the growth of mining and oil and gas exploration, the action communities have grown substantially in recent years. The growth of their populations, based largely on in-migration, has outstripped that of the native communities, (which can rely only on natural increase). During the 1961-1971 Census decade, Inuvik grew at an annual rate of 7.82 percent and Hay River grew at an annual rate of 6.19 percent.

In some of the action communities, the native population is at present a significant part of the total population. They are the majority in Tuktoyaktuk, about half the population in Inuvik and Fort Simpson. In Hay River, Yellowknife, Pine Point and Norman Wells, however, they are a minority (their numbers were never significant in the case of the latter two communities). Present native populations in the action communities comprise both persons who have traditionally been located near the communities, and persons who have migrated to the communities from smaller settlements or from the land. The white population of the action communities consists of a mixture of government employees, people in local business, and representatives of business interests from the South.

As construction of the pipeline proceeds, action communities will encounter two kinds of problems: those that derive from the mixed white and native populations within the communities, and those that derive from the physical and financial capability of such communities to absorb more people and activity than they have to cope with at present, and to provide for future growth. The first category encompasses several pathologies that have been observed with increasing — even alarming — frequency during recent years in the cities and towns that have borne the brunt of the northerly expansion of the urban, industrial and bureaucratic frontiers. The second category encompasses a number of issues critical to the question of how communities might meet the costs of, and derive benefits from, the pipeline. These issues relate to such things as town planning and impact funding.

Not all of the problems and issues I discuss affect only the action communities, and, to some extent, the points that are made in the following pages apply to all of the communities of the Mackenzie Valley and Western Arctic. But they derive from a consideration of the impact of pipeline construction in the action communities.

Consequences of Rapid Growth

The relationship between white and native people is complex, but the overriding fact is that white people have been dominant and native people subservient. Native people have had to give way before the imperatives of the white man, and they have been urged to modify their values, attitudes and social structures in response to white society. At times, such as the long years of the fur and mission era, this challenge was not overwhelmingly difficult to meet. Even today, in the outlying native communities, where native culture is still highly visible and where the white presence is limited, native people have found it possible to make accommodations and adjustments. In the action communities, however, where the white presence is dominant, and where it has intruded so completely into the native people's lives, the native people have found it far more difficult to adapt. In these communities, they have become hemmed in; their cultures and languages have become surrounded and have been overwhelmed by the dominant culture and language. They have also lost some of their access to the land and its resources.

The native people of the action communities have become split off from their own means of production, are unable to move out of the way of the dominant society, and are incapable of fully understanding or striking back at the forces that have come to cramp them into restricted physical and psychological ghettos. Their response to these pressures has been violence directed against themselves: drunkenness and alcoholism, beatings, child neglect, and suicides. It is the violence of people who take out their anger and frustration on one another. Death by violence, including suicide, is many times more frequent among native people than among other Canadians. It is currently the leading cause of death in the Northwest Territories, and most violent deaths are alcohol-related. Even the most cursory examination of the causes of social pathology reveals how essential it is to strengthen native society before the next wave of white in-migration takes place.

In addition to the violence, the predicament of the urbanized native people has had other, less obvious, consequences: greatly reduced access to their traditional diets and substitution of less nutritional foods, a weakening of the extended family leading to the breakdown of the support systems, such as care for indigent and aged family members, on which native people once relied. In fact, many of the health and welfare measures that government has initiated and expanded throughout the North are direct responses to this breakdown, which has coincided with the spread of the industrial system throughout the North.

I do not mean to imply that native people are the only group that finds the action communities difficult places in which to live. Many white people do not feel at home in them either, even though these communities represent frontier extensions of mainstream North American society. The severe climate, the tensions between white and native people, remoteness from their own home and families, and difficulties in adjusting to new and usually very different circumstances have led to problems such as alcoholism among white northerners. But their condition is in no way comparable to that of the native people.

Many well-adjusted native individuals and families can be found in these communities to prove exceptions to what I have been saying. My thesis must always be understood as referring to the dominant and overriding pattern, to the basic conflict that is fundamental to life in the action communities. To point only to the successful native entrepreneur or bush pilot is to overlook the fact that most native people who live in the action communities live on the margins and often in a state of continuous crisis.

Whatever occurs in the North, many native people will, either by choice or by necessity, continue to live in the larger communities of the Mackenzie Valley and Mackenzie Delta. If there is a movement back to villages and the land, it will take time to gather momentum to have any real effect on the distribution of population. Meanwhile, oil and gas exploration and development will continue, and we may assume that a pipeline will be built in due course; the impact of such industrial development on the populations of the action communities will be large. And, in these communities, it will be necessary to try to mitigate the problems that these impacts are likely to cause for all residents, both native and white.

Pathology of Rapid Growth

The mitigation of socially related medical problems, such as malnutrition, alcohol-related injuries and deaths, injuries due to violence, and suicides, is a major concern of all northerners, but especially of the native people. The conditions that breed such pathologies will likely intensify in the action communities if the pipeline and related projects are built: houses will become more crowded, the already high costs of living will increase, and the native people of the action communities will have even less access to the land. There will be an intensified need to provide and maintain the, at times, inadequate level of health services now available in the Northwest Territories.

1. Every effort should be made now to identify the kinds of problems in health care delivery that will undoubtedly occur during pipeline construction. Funding mechanisms and special programs should be in place well before the construction phase to ensure that the health care and delivery system will be able to cope with the problems brought by the pipeline.

2. In the action communities, planning for health care delivery during pipeline construction should involve not only both senior levels of government, but also local white and native spokesmen.

3. Control of native health care delivery should be in the hands of the people themselves. This would allow them, for example, to establish programs for the training of native para-professional health workers. Models that could be useful in the Canadian North include the North Slope Borough health program in Alaska, which trains and employs residents in each community to be primary providers of health care in the community; and the tradition in Greenland of para-professional involvement in health care services.

The Alaska Community Mental Health Services Act of 1975 was enacted to help communities plan, organize and finance community mental health services through locally developed, administered and controlled programs.

4. Legislation similar to that enacted in Alaska should be enacted in the Northwest Territories to help the people of the action communities deal with the stress that will inevitably accompany the changes brought by pipeline construction and related activities.

Mental health will not be the only area of health care that will require substantial community action and participation. However, there is a lack of understanding generally in society about the problems of mental health and particularly in a cross-cultural setting like that of the North. The practices that are applied — if any are applied at all — are often culturally irrelevant and may be based on serious misconceptions of what the problems are. This is why community involvement in mental health treatment is so important: the community often understands itself much better than does the outside professional.

Crisis intervention centres, also called distress lines or suicide prevention lines, exist in about 95 communities in Canada. The entire Northwest Territories are served by the distress lines established in Yellowknife in 1972. The telephones are manned by volunteers who provide a listening and referral service; some callers need help with a personal crisis, and others simply need referral to another agency. Ideally, the lines should be staffed on a 24-hour basis, but at the very least they should be operating when other services are not available. However, the lack of permanent, stable funding (the line was orginally operated with Local Initiatives Program (LIP) funds) has meant irregular hours of service and may lead to a complete shut-down of the facility.

5. At a time when the stress of changing lifestyles in the North is becoming greater, there is a vital need for at least one crisis centre, staffed by a paid co-ordinator and sufficient trained volunteers. The effectiveness of a crisis handling service for northern communities during pipeline construction depends upon early funding so that distress lines will be a well-established and familiar service to those in need of help. For those without a telephone or not familiar with its operation, friendship centres, which are described later in this section, should be available, particularly during the height of construction.

The fact that most deaths among native people are caused by alcohol-related injuries, accidents and violence indicates that the problem of alcohol abuse is extensive. The effects of alcohol abuse are also reflected in the incidence of child neglect, crimes of violence, violations of the liquor ordinance, family breakdowns and other social problems. The evidence

suggests that, because of increased access to alcohol and because of changes to the social and cultural fabric of the community at a rate that exceeds the capacity of the community to adapt, we should anticipate a rise in alcohol consumption during pipeline construction.

The decrease in alcohol consumption that has occurred since 1974 may be attributed to a new awareness by the native people and their determination to solve their alcohol problem. Recently enacted legislation on local option has resulted in some communities electing to go dry by prohibiting the sale of alcohol in their communities. Unfortunately, this approach is unlikely to be effective in the action communities where the non-native population is predominant, and where drinking is socially accepted. Even if the native people of these communities choose to go dry, bootlegged liquor will be available, and there will be strong pressures on people to continue drinking.

Adequate legislation and enforcement policies may be useful preventive measures in matters such as serving liquor to minors and to those already intoxicated.

6. To control liquor sales and consumption to and among pipeline personnel during the construction of the pipeline, the Company and its contractors should operate licensed premises within the camps, in full compliance with the Northwest Territorial Liquor Ordinance. Pipeline workers should have only restricted access to communities, especially those communities that prohibit alcohol. Workers found taking liquor or drugs into any community, or bootlegging to local people, should be fired immediately and returned to point of hire. The enforcement of drug-use legislation within camps should be carried out by the RCMP.

The Alcohol and Drug Co-ordinating Council of the Goverment of the Northwest Territories provides funding for an approach to alcohol problems that involves greater community control of alcohol use and the consequences of its abuse, in accordance with the perceptions of each community or of each group within a community. The success of these programs to date indicates that if native people are given the time and the opportunity to develop these programs before major industrial developments begin in the areas, there is a good chance of some success.

7. Funding for community-based programs to control alcohol use should be continued and strengthened. By relying on the support systems that are available in any community, some progress in controlling alcohol dependence can be made.

In Volume One, I referred to evidence that I heard on this subject in communities such as Fort McPherson and Fort Simpson. Alcohol abuse can be beaten if the people themselves are fighting it, and if they feel that they have at least an even chance of winning. But they will not always win.

8. Funds for facilities such as detoxification and rehabilitation centres will be needed if the communities are to be able to cope with new problems created by the pipeline or existing problems aggravated by it.

Development of the native economy, enlargement of the renewable resource sector, and participation by native people in the orderly development of the non-renewable resource sector will greatly reduce welfare dependence among native people in the action communities. In the meantime, however, those people who cannot cope with the pressures of change and development will need support. As well, in-migrant job-seekers who are unable to secure employment will also likely require welfare.

We can expect the cost of living to rise during pipeline construction, just as it did in Alaska. This would create new strains for people on fixed incomes, and for people receiving relatively low non-pipeline wages.

9. *Government social assistance payments must be increased to meet the higher cost of living that pipeline construction will bring.*

Communities in the Mackenzie Valley and Western Arctic, particularly the smaller communities, could lose, at least temporarily, significant parts of the local work force. This may put great pressure on the social welfare agencies: for example, women who take jobs directly on the pipeline, or who replace local men who have done so, would require day care services; and family and marital stress may increase under the pressure of difficult work conditions.

10. *To strengthen and expand programs and staff to deal with such problems, local people should be trained to work with professional social workers. Native para-professionals should be trained to work with the families of native workers that have accepted pipeline employment. As ,well, financial counselling should be available during this period of increased wage employment and cash flow to give native northerners a better understanding of money management.*

Solutions offered for the social problems of the Northwest Territories are typically those that have had some success in the South, particularly in urban areas, where the practice of social work and social administration has developed, and where the social workers have been trained. Such solutions may have little relevance in the North, where distinctive cultural conditions have resulted in different behavioural patterns and responses.

Physical and Financial Aspects of Growth

Several attempts have been made to predict how rapidly the major communities of the Mackenzie Valley and the Mackenzie Delta will grow during the construction of the pipeline and related gas gathering and processing facilities. In 1975, Stanley and Associates, an Edmonton consulting firm, prepared a fairly detailed forecast for the Northwest Territories Association of Municipalities. This forecast relied heavily on forecasts contained in community plans that had previously been prepared for Mackenzie Valley and Mackenzie Delta communities by a number of consultants.

In the case of Inuvik, Stanley and Associates predicted that under conditions of normal growth — that is, if a pipeline is not built — the population would increase from a projected figure of 3,500 in 1975 to 5,800 in 1985, and that thereafter it would continue to grow at an annual rate of 5 percent. Under conditions of accelerated growth — that is if a pipeline and associated developments are undertaken — the population would increase from a projected figure of 4,100 in 1975 to 10,000 in 1985. With the pipeline, therefore, the 1985 population is expected to be almost double what it would be without the pipeline. Similar patterns were projected for Fort Simpson and Hay River. Normal growth in Fort Simpson would see the population increase from 1,180 in 1975 to 2,120 in 1985, whereas accelerated growth would raise it from 1,310 to 3,020 in those same years. At Hay River, normal growth during the period 1975-1985 would see the population increase from 3,730 to 5,960, whereas accelerated growth would take it from 3,920 to 8,740 (F26981-82).

Since the Stanley report was published, construction of a pipeline along the Mackenzie Valley has been postponed for a period of years. But when the pipeline comes, we can expect the rate of population increase to be similar to that indicated by the accelerated growth figures. In Volume One, I cited evidence on the rapid growth of Alaskan communities, particularly the city of Valdez. Figures collected by the Fairbanks North Star Borough Planning and Zoning Department, and presented by Susan Fison as evidence before the Alaska Highway Pipeline Inquiry in July 1977, indicate that the Fairbanks regional population rose from 50,450 in 1973 to 73,519 in 1976, an increase of about 23,000, or 46 percent (Alaska Highway Pipeline Inquiry, Exhibit 124, p. 5).

The predications made by Stanley and Associates appear to assume smooth growth at a relatively constant annual rate for both normal and accelerated growth situations. In reality, the growth of a frontier community that is experiencing a boom is quite different. If a pipeline is built, there will probably be large annual variations in the rate of growth in the action communities, with the highest growth rates probably occurring just before and during the initial years of pipeline construction. When construction is completed, population growth will likely taper off substantially, but this will depend on what other projects are anticipated. In Alaska, for example, growth has slowed temporarily now that the oil pipeline is completed, but with the advent of projects such as the construction of the Alcan gas pipeline, drilling on the outer continental shelf, and exploration in Naval Petroleum Reserve Number 4, the population is expected to increase once again. Typically, there is nothing smooth about growth on the frontier.

The Stanley report does not say where the new residents of the Mackenzie Valley and Delta communities will come from, nor who they will be. A reading of the report indicates that it was assumed that the growing population will be relatively homogeneous. Pipeline construction workers are not included in the population growth figures, because these people will be housed in camps away from the communities. The report is concerned only with those people who will remain in the communities for some period of time, however variable. Some of these people will be employees of large corporations, such as banks and department stores and of government; they and their families will be moved there by their employers. This group should not cause many difficulties for planners and local and regional government officials because the employers would normally provide their housing. Moreover, when large employers have a substantial body of local employees, they often invest in a community and provide facilities that the community itself cannot easily afford. Property owned by the companies can be a significant source of tax revenues for the community. As well, the employees are usually well-paid, responsible residents who often take an active part in community affairs.

Many of the new residents, however, will be persons who have come to the region on their own in the hope of finding some kind of work, but with no commitment to stay. If they do find employment, they might remain for a time; but frequently they would leave after a few months or even weeks, only to be replaced by others like themselves. It was transients like these, and the families they brought with them, that created a wide range of problems in Alaska: they put a strain on community resources, but contributed little toward meeting community costs.

Transient workers should be viewed as an unattached and highly mobile body of labour that moves around within a large region in the hope of finding short-term employment. Although it should be possible to estimate the size of this population and to predict its movements on a regional basis — for example, Western Canada, the Maritimes — it would be impossible to predict how many of them might arrive at any particular northern community as it became the scene of a boom. Much would depend, for example, on preconceptions about the community itself, and about employment conditions elsewhere, and on attempts made to discourage in-migration. Even then, the most careful predictions of local impact could be wrong by a considerable margin.

Another component of population in a northern boom community will be native people who have come from the smaller settlements in search of employment, and who decided to stay for a time. Because it will be a low income population, its demand on community resources will probably exceed its contributions to community revenues. It will probably put additional pressures on housing, which will already be in very short supply. Native areas within the action communities will no doubt become even more overcrowded.

Planning required for the regular growth assumed by Stanley and Associates differs substantially from that required by the disjointed growth that is likely to take place on the frontier. Growth of the type projected in the Stanley report, whether normal or accelerated, involves simply looking ahead along a growth curve to determine when the capacity of municipal infrastructure and services needs to be expanded. Even with normal growth, there would be some miscalculation, but by and large, targets would be met.

Planning for the rapid and disjointed growth induced by a pipeline and related projects will be far more difficult. A flexible approach is needed that allows for smooth growth by some parts of a community's population and for erratic growth by other parts. In addition, there must be ready access to both expertise and funding, and there must be a way of obtaining quick and reliable data on what is happening to the community. These data will assist in determining the proportion of the in-migrant population that will remain after the pipeline project is completed, and the proportion that is transient.

Fairbanks, Alaska, because it has experienced more boom-induced growth surges than most North American communities, provides an example of how to handle community planning during periods of rapid and unpredictable growth. With the coming of the Alyeska pipeline, the Fairbanks North Star Borough established a Pipeline Impact Information Center, whose job was to define and measure the various components of growth, and to present this information to the city and borough in a manner that would provide a basis for planning. The Fairbanks North Star Borough is one of the wealthiest in Alaska, and had substantial resources to back up its planning. It also received impact funding from the state government.

Some things, however, the borough did not handle well. Housing was a major difficulty throughout the pipeline project, but no satisfactory system of providing additional or emergency housing was devised. Those persons that could afford high rents or mortgage payments obtained housing, others did not. The transient native people who came into the main hiring centres from the remote villages of Alaska simply hung around town while they were waiting for jobs on the pipeline. No special hostel or half-way facilities were provided for them. Indeed, the borough gave no special attention to the difficulties that these culturally different people encountered in an urban setting.

Information, Planning and Impact Funding

Postponement of the pipeline project has given us the time we need to initiate and establish processes that will help northerners cope with the pipeline, and the transformation that it will bring. The conditions exist now for information gathering, planning and impact funding in a way that reflects the wishes of the local people.

The planning process that I outline in the following paragraphs gives residents of the action communities a substantial role in planning. The people of the communities must be fully involved in the identification of issues, and the formulation of measures to deal with them. The people must also be involved in setting priorities so that impact funds, which will inevitably be limited, can be spent most effectively. A real concern about the future of their communities will ensure that planning that is undertaken locally is responsible and realistic. By the time we are ready to build a pipeline in the Mackenzie Valley, we should be in a position to set up the machinery needed to carry out the recommendations that follow.

11. Impact information centres, modelled on the Fairbanks North Star Borough Impact Information Center of Alaska, should be established. There should perhaps be one centre for the Mackenzie Delta, one for the middle Mackenzie and one for the Great Slave Lake area. The centres should be funded by government; they should be established well before construction of the pipeline begins and should continue for an appropriate follow-up period, such as two years, after construction is completed. Each centre should operate openly, and should distribute its information to government, to the pipeline company, and to any other person or group that needs it.

12. The centres should gather and distribute data on variables such as employment, income, prices, costs, shifts in local supply and demand, the changing status of particular groups, incidence of crime and violence, and alcohol consumption. Each impact information centre should be concerned not only with the action community in which it is located, but also with any nearby communities that might be influenced by the pipeline project or by the impact of rapid growth in the action community. In this way, information gathered by the centre could assist in regionally coordinated planning, as well as in local planning.

Planning is difficult in an area in which the future is as uncertain as that of the Mackenzie Valley. Before planning can start, a number of basic questions need to be answered. What is an appropriate time frame for planning: will the planning be concerned only with short-range problems, or will it apply to a prolonged period, say ten years? What geographic or societal unit should planners deal with: should they plan for individual communities, for groups of communities, or for a broad region.

13. Planning related to the pipeline project should be kept as simple as possible; it should have a local focus and deal with those communities that will be immediately affected by the pipeline. Apart from a reasonable period for follow up, such planning should not extend beyond the period of pipeline construction.

In this report, we are concerned with planning for extra-normal circumstances that may be caused by the pipeline and related developments. These circumstances will have their greatest impact at the local community level, and local people should, therefore, be in a position to modify and control them. We are not concerned here, for example, with the planning and construction of normal community facilities. Rather, we are concerned with how communities should meet extraordinary demands that could occur rapidly and that could be transitory. If, for example, more classrooms are needed, the community would decide, on the basis of what it considers best for its children, whether to use portable facilities or to double-shift existing facilities.

I am not saying these difficulties can be resolved before construction of the pipeline begins, but I hope that we can make a good start toward their resolution. If they are not dealt with, the divisions that presently characterize the action communities of the Mackenzie Valley may become aggravated.

There remains the definition of planning objectives. What exactly are we trying to resolve? At what level of government must action be taken? Will the problem respond to short-term solutions, or is it something that will go away or turn into some other kind of problem with time? Can the problem be solved with money, or is it a physical bottleneck that no amount of money can alleviate in the time available? What institutional factors impinge on the development of a solution to the problem?

14. Local planning to ameliorate or modify the impact of the pipeline should be closely related to the procedures of the Agency and to the activities of regional and territorial governments. It should be underway well before construction of the pipeline begins and should be an integral part of the final review of the pipeline design.

Local planners should assess the data assembled by the impact information centres, as well as other pertinent information and, with the help of professional staff from government and the Agency, should develop programs to moderate the local impact of the pipeline. Thereafter, as pipeline construction proceeds, the programs should be revised to match changing circumstances. In this way, each community would be able to evaluate the local effects of the project and draw up its own measures to deal with them, both before and during construction of the pipeline.

Planning, no matter how detailed, is useless unless it leads to a practical program. Moreover, in the communities that will be affected by the pipeline, the practical results will have to come swiftly: the time between the identification of needs, the setting of local priorities, the review of these priorities, the release of funds, and the implementation of the particular proposal, must be kept short. Some projects, such as the provision of additional housing, additional hospital beds, additional detoxification centres, and additional professional staff to man such facilities, may involve substantial sums of money.

15. To ensure that ameliorative measures can be implemented without delay, someone in the planning sequence should be empowered to hold funds, including major funds, and to release them quickly as the need arises.

Current plans call for the major part of pipeline construction to take place in winter. As a consequence, significant numbers of people could be without jobs for a considerable part of the year. Projects to moderate the impacts of the pipeline could be carried out during the slack season, providing that the technical and resource conditions governing them permitted this, and they could thus be used to counter the cyclical nature of pipeline construction in the region.

Specific Problem Areas

There are a number of major problems that could only become aggravated, unless steps to resolve or at least modify them are taken before construction of the pipeline begins.

16. Although the medical requirements of pipeline workers and other in-migrants will probably impose a severe strain on existing health facilities and services in the North, the provision of medical services to pipeline employees must not be allowed to jeopardize the health facilities or health programs of the communities of the Northwest Territories.

Under the Northwest Territories Public Health Ordinance, the pipeline company and its contractors will be responsible for providing medical services for their employees. Although the pipeline companies have said they will not use community facilities and staff, emergency situations and pressures on the Company's facilities may require them to do so. It is especially important to establish the nature and extent of the facilities and services that the Company will need. The pipeline is to be built during the arctic winter when darkness and intense cold impair not only productivity, but also alertness and awareness. Under such circumstances, and even with the best possible safety measures, there will be accidents, medical problems related to exposure to cold temperatures, and pyschiatric problems arising out of reactions to cold, darkness and isolation. The Company should be prepared to

cope with all of these problems, and cannot be allowed to burden facilities in nearby communities because of inadequacies in its own planning.

17. Realistic projections of both the pipeline employees' and the public's needs should be available before construction of the pipeline begins, so that the medical problems that will have to be met during construction can be properly estimated and provided for.

As I said earlier, it is difficult to estimate the size and distribution, and therefore the demands, of the transient population, and of the native population that will be attracted to the action communities. Planning for these populations should focus on the development of quick and flexible means to meet their requirements. Portable facilities, such as hospital units and nursing stations may be one solution.

18. Although some upgrading and expansion of hospital facilities in the major communities will be necessary to handle pipeline-related effects, the long-term needs of the communities must take precedence over the short-term needs of pipeline personnel.

19. Demands on sanitation programs will, without doubt, increase during construction of the pipeline. More environmental health officers for inspection and enforcement services will be needed as the water and sewer requirements of construction camps are added to those of rapidly growing communities. The problems of human waste disposal must be addressed now to ensure that conditions of good public health prevail before pipeline-induced rapid growth occurs.

The pipeline project and related activities will undoubtedly impose a burden on the school facilities of the major communities, and it is likely that it will be possible for only a part of the increased enrollment that may result to be accommodated in existing classrooms.

20. Planning to accommodate in the school system the increased number of pupils that will result from pipeline-induced growth should start soon and should include forecasts of the numbers and needs of pupils.

Accurate forecasting should become easier as the final design stage is approached. Planners must always distinguish between short-term problems, for example, temporary overcrowding, which may be resolved by measures such as double shifting, and problems resulting from long-term population growth, which could require the expansion of school facilities and staff.

Construction of permanent schools and classrooms financed out of normal government revenue must, even during peak pipeline construction, reflect the long-term needs of the individual communities. Students entering the school system during population surges that accompany pipeline construction could be accommodated in modular classrooms.

In Alaska, it proved difficult to ameliorate the housing crisis that accompanied the construction of the trans-Alaska pipeline, not because the United States lacked the resources to build houses, but because housing, traditionally, is not an area of government involvement. Housing is regarded as an area for private initiative, and government, to a great extent, lacks the agencies and funds necessary to deal effectively with housing shortages. Because Canadians tend to regard housing, especially in the North, as more of a public responsibility than the United States does, the problem might not be as severe in Canada as it was in Alaska. Nevertheless, there could be significant housing problems.

The influx of people into the North with the advent of pipeline construction will put pressure on the poor housing situation that exists at present. The Northwest Territories Housing Corporation, which uses federal funds through the National Housing Act and through Treasury Board directly, has inadequate funds to redress the housing situation. Indeed, the corporation cannot keep pace with new family formation, cannot match the existing shortfall, and does not have sufficient funds to rehabilitate and repair the existing housing stock. As the housing demand grows, overcrowding, use of substandard units, inflated building costs, and in general, an inadequate housing supply are likely to become more common. In addition, the supply of land to meet the present allocations of housing is restricted, and servicing is falling behind because of lack of planning.

21. The fundamental requirement to ensure the smooth delivery of serviced land is a survey of current housing adequacy, and a land use and site development plan for each community. Although the Company intends to provide its own housing for permanent staff, its housing plans must be consistent with community development objectives and must be subject to community regulation. The Company and the federal and territorial government should share equally in the cost of assembling and developing serviced land in the action communities.

The Northwest Territories Housing Corporation's housing policies to encourage home ownership are still inconsistent with its staff housing policy, which offers considerable benefit to persons who rent. Also, the Housing Corporation's policy of charging 25 percent of income for rental conflicts with the low maximum rents that exist in housing provided by government and major private sector employers. The Company should provide low-interest mortgages in place of and at better rates than rental allowances, which would encourage home ownership and stability. Rental subsidies to Company employees should conform with existing public housing subsidies in the Northwest Territories.

There must be safeguards to ensure that the supply of materials for housing construction in the Northwest Territories is not adversely affected by heavy demand that pipeline construction places on northern transportation systems. Funds for housing construction should not be reallocated

from other parts of the Northwest Territories or from smaller communities to larger ones. Mobile housing units that could be transferred rapidly from one location to another offer one solution to the problem of extraordinary surges in accommodation demand that will occur. The impact information centres, described above, should advise in-migrants on the unavailability of housing in the communities, and zoning regulations should be strictly enforced to avoid indiscriminate trailer and camp settling, which, on unserviced land, can create serious health problems.

Government's first priority is to ensure adequate housing for northerners at a time when pipeline construction activities will create a high demand and short supply. Estimates of housing needs should be frequently reviewed, in light of the difficulty of predicting the overall level of future activity in such an unstable region.

Camps and Communities

In the chapter Employment and Manpower Delivery, I dealt with the conditions that should prevail within pipeline camps regarding such matters as food, recreation, accommodation and security. I shall now consider the relationships that should prevail between construction workers housed in the camps and residents in near-by communities. My recommendations apply to all communities in the Mackenzie Valley and Mackenzie Delta, and not only to the action communities.

Many misconceptions have arisen about construction camps and their occupants. The fact is, construction workers are decent human beings who are trying to make a living and to save some money, and who must work long hours to do so. According to Professors Bering-Gould and Bennett, the attitudes and aspirations of the thousands of people living in the pipeline camp near Valdez, Alaska did not differ significantly from those of the residents of Valdez.

Workers who have comfortable housing facilities, good food and accommodation, proper recreational facilities and access to liquor (under controlled conditions) present fewer problems than workers who are poorly housed, badly fed, and treated like adolescents. The collective agreements that govern pipeline construction and that will apply to the Mackenzie Valley pipeline require a high standard of accommodation for pipeline workers. The quality of life in camp is not the only thing that determines whether a labour force will be easy to manage or not: treatment on the job and conditions of leave are also important factors. Nevertheless, the quality of camps has a major influence on the behaviour of workers during off-hours both in camp and in nearby communities.

22. Construction camps must be of a high standard and should meet the requirements set out in the chapter on Employment and Manpower Delivery.

Persons living in even the best of camps will want and, under certain conditions, should have access to nearby communities. However, the degree to which communities or groups within communities can accommodate or tolerate visitors varies. Although larger communities, such as Inuvik and Hay River, have had long experience with exploration crews, barge crews and construction crews and a considerable part of the local economy is based on expenditures by transient populations, not all parts of the populations of these communities are equally tolerant of outside intrusion. Native populations of the action communities have proved vulnerable to exploitation by unattached and irresponsible transients. However, in general, and within certain limits, action communities have established means of dealing with transients.

The smaller communities of the Mackenzie Valley and the Mackenzie Delta, those in which native people form the majority of the population, are far less able to withstand the influx of considerable numbers of visitors. The stability of relationships within such communities is important to their continuity and harmony. The intrusion of a few visitors, under conditions which the community can control, will not generally pose a problem, but should such visits occur at a frequency and under conditions with which the community cannot cope, the community may be presented with social problems of the most serious kind.

23. *Insofar as technical constraints governing pipeline construction will allow, camp facilities should be located far from communities, so that access to towns and villages is difficult and camp residents are discouraged from going. However, access to the action communities should not, and probably cannot, be restricted; workers who want to go to town will find some means of getting there.*

24. *Behaviour on the part of pipeline employees that is anti-social and disruptive to the well-being of the communities should not be condoned. Employees found guilty of disorderly and drunken behaviour, assault, and destruction of property, should be dismissed and returned to point of hire.*

25. *In action communities, facilities such as bars that pipeliners would frequent should be located away from residential areas.*

26. *Pipeline workers should be discouraged from visiting the smaller, largely native communities of the Mackenzie Valley and Delta. Means of restricting access to the small communities should be the subject of discussions between the native people, the Company, the unions, and the Agency.*

People from the communities will be attracted to pipeline construction camps for a variety of reasons. Local people who wish to learn about the pipeline or the camp, or who wish to visit relatives who are working on pipeline construction should not be prohibited from visiting camps.

27. *Access to camps, and to facilities for visitors within camps, must be of a kind that is not hazardous to the visitors, and that does not interfere with the normal operations of the camp. Access to camps must be carefully monitored and controlled by the Company.*

28. *At each camp, a comfortable lounge, or similar facility, should be provided in which pipeline workers and local people can meet and visit with each other. If a sufficient number of local people want to visit a particular camp, perhaps because several local people are working there, special arrangements should be made with respect to transportation and to accommodation of visitors. However, no such arrangements should be allowed to interfere with the prime purpose of the camp, which is to house people who are there to build the pipeline.*

Community Energy Supply

A gas pipeline in the Mackenzie Valley should provide two things for northerners an assured energy supply and a reduction in energy costs. At least that is the way northerners feel about it — they believe it would not be right that gas from the North should pass by northern communities only to service industries and homes thousands of miles away. I think the case they have made is a good one.

29. *To assure energy supply to communities close to the pipeline, the Company should either provide valves and fittings at appropriate locations along the trunk line or guarantee to provide them at a future time but at costs current at the time of the trunk line construction. The Company should enter into a commitment that will last as long as the operating life of the pipeline lasts, to make gas available to communities as and when it is requested to do so.*

The reduction of energy costs could be more difficult to accomplish. Evidence presented to this Inquiry suggests that, if gas were made available to communities, only Inuvik, Norman Wells and Fort Simpson would clearly experience a cost reduction over currently available energy sources. Benefits to smaller communities are likely to be insignificant or non-existent. However, economic studies are very sensitive to assumptions about oil (and gas) prices and market growth, and it is therefore impossible to be precise in marginal cases.

Whether energy costs to communities will be reduced or not depends not on the price of the gas itself but on the capital cost of installing lateral lines and distribution grids. Capital costs are heavily influenced by economies of scale: the higher the volume in any market, the lower the per capita cost. This fact, of course, benefits the action communities and works against the smaller communities in the North. However, even the largest communities of the Northwest Territories represent markets of minimal size in terms of recovering the full costs of supplying natural gas to them.

A number of subsidy schemes have been proposed to ensure that natural gas would be more widely available in the Mackenzie Valley and Mackenzie Delta. Foothills proposed to lower the price of gas service to residential and commercial customers in several communities by passing the cost on to southern users of northern gas. The Northwest Territories Association of Municipalities showed that if Inuvik, Norman Wells and Fort Simpson, all of which would experience substantial energy price reductions through the use of gas, were to pass some of these gains to other communities, energy costs in most communities in the region could be lowered. In addition, the Association recommended that any royalty on non-renewable resources ought to be applied first to achieve a reduction in energy costs throughout the Northwest Territories, to a level equal to the average energy cost reduction that is experienced by communities that can be economically supplied with natural gas.

Another factor is that energy costs vary considerably throughout the region. Norman Wells provides its customers with lower oil-product prices than are paid almost anywhere in Canada, and in some northern communities and for certain classes of consumers, the price of electrical energy is lower than in many major southern Canadian cities.

In my opinion, northerners should receive the benefit of reduced energy costs from northern gas production. This reduction could be achieved in two ways: through an inter-regional pricing policy that would ensure that southern users subsidize northern customers, and a system of cross-subsidization in the North within particular regions.

30. Some form of rent or special tax should be levied against gas owners, gas field operators and pipeline operators and the returns should be used to lower energy costs on a per unit of consumption basis by class of customer, throughout the region (Industrial customers are charged less for gas and accordingly would receive a smaller subsidy than residential customers.)

Costs should be reduced to the point where residents, businesses and industries in the most favoured communities (from an unsubsidized energy cost standpoint) in the North would pay energy prices equivalent to the most favoured communities in the South.

This does not mean that annual energy costs for northern consumers will equal those of the southern basing-point. The severe climate and longer winter of the North would still militate against northerners. But it would mean a considerable reduction in user-costs over those that apply in the North at present.

The benefits from extensive subsidy schemes that would result in an equal price for natural gas or, indeed, any form of energy to all larger communities are, in my opinion, questionable. There is already an artificiality and distortion of regional activity patterns, and the imposition of energy pricing policies that do not to some degree reflect local cost variations would further aggravate this trend. There is not much to be gained from action communities subsidizing each other's energy costs. And, in the same way that it is inappropriate for Hay River to share totally with Inuvik the economic benefits it derives from being a rail terminus, so it is undesirable for Inuvik to share totally with Hay River the economic benefits it receives from its proximity to a pipeline. But it does seem appropriate for action communities to subsidize the cost of supplying energy costs to the smaller communities in their local area of influence.

Thus Inuvik would subsidize communities in the Mackenzie Delta, Norman Wells would subsidize Fort Good Hope and Fort Norman, and Fort Simpson would subsidize Wrigley. I am not saying that energy prices should be the same in all of these communities but that natural gas-induced cost reductions in the larger communities should be used to reduce energy prices in the smaller communities.

31. In the region, there should be an area pricing scheme for energy by which the cost savings obtained by larger communities from use of natural gas would be passed on to the smaller communities in their local area.

THE REPORT OF
THE MACKENZIE VALLEY
PIPELINE INQUIRY

PART ONE —
PEOPLE: SOCIAL AND
ECONOMIC CONCERNS

5 Northern Business

This Inquiry heard a considerable body of evidence on the present state of northern business and about the expectations that northern businessmen had formed with respect to the proposed Mackenzie Valley pipeline. On the basis of this evidence, I now advance several recommendations designed to promote the orderly long-term growth of the northern business community and to ensure that it will derive appropriate benefits from the pipeline project whenever it may be built. Some of my recommendations are made to protect existing northern businesses; others are concerned with the promotion of a healthier and more competitive regional business economy.

Northern-based firms are in a poor competitive position relative to firms that do business in the North but whose main operations are in the South. Firms that are exclusively or largely dependent on the North normally operate in small and uncertain markets, and they do not have such a large volume of sales, over which they can spread overheads and other fixed costs, as their southern-based competitors have. Their markets are, moreover, likely to be distinctly seasonal, particularly in construction. Typical northern firms do not earn revenues during as much of the year as do southern firms. Northern firms are less favourably located with respect to suppliers, which means they have higher transportation costs and a more limited choice among suppliers of certain goods or services. Their labour costs are, on the average, higher, and the local labour force is often less skilled and less productive than the labour force in the South. Services that southern firms take for granted are frequently unavailable to northern firms, or available to them only at considerable expense.

Southern firms have generally left the northern market to northern firms when business in the South has been thriving or when projects in the North have not appeared attractive. However, when business has been slack in the provinces, or if a particular project is regarded as attractive, southern firms have vigorously entered the northern market. I do not suggest that existing northern firms can at present handle the full range of business opportunities that may occur in the North.

There are many projects they simply cannot tackle because they lack the necessary resources and experience. However, in certain fields, especially construction, southern-based firms have often been able to underprice northern firms by a considerable margin even on jobs that northern firms could undertake. Southern firms are thus in a position to skim the cream off the northern market, to move in and out as seems favourable to them, to take advantage of only the most rewarding projects, and to avoid the less attractive ones. Northern firms do not have this flexibility; they must work within their limited market and take advantage of whatever opportunities may come their way.

Not all problems faced by northern firms can be attributed to the market and to location. Although there are many competent businessmen in the North, there are some that are relatively inexperienced in identifying investment opportunities and in running a business. Native northerners, whose entrepreneurial traditions are mainly based on trapping, trading and riverboat transportation, do not fit easily into the business sector that is now taking shape in the North.

The northern economy, moreover, is and has always been pervaded by uncertainty, primarily because the region's major resources are sold in distant markets and because there is virtually no control within the North over these markets or over the development of these resources. Most of the decisions that affect the growth and development of the regional economy and that determine, therefore, whether or not its businesses will thrive are taken far beyond the region's boundaries. By the time these decisions have been transmitted to the northern business community, they have often been distorted by rumour and speculation and they generate unrealistic expectations.

My recommendations, therefore, recognize the need to improve the quality of northern management and to increase the range of services that are available to the northern business sector. More generally, they pertain to the growth of the northern economy as a whole because it is important that this economy should develop beyond its present limited capabilities and capacity if it is to survive the pipeline and, more positively, to benefit from its construction.

The nature and scope of the settlement of native claims will greatly influence the degree to which, and the methods by which, the native people of the Mackenzie Valley and Western Arctic will be able to participate in economic activity related to the pipeline project. It may well be that, as a result of the settlement of native claims, native enterprises, whether they are cooperatives, corporations, or proprietorships, will become an important element in the providing of goods and services in the North. As they evolve, they should enjoy the same advantages that I am recommending for northern resident firms, provided, of course, that this is consistent with the wishes of the native people.

The pipeline will introduce many new elements into the North for which most northern businessmen are, at present, ill-prepared. Not only will the project be one of the largest ventures ever undertaken by private capital, it will bring north powerful international unions. If a negotiated settlement of native claims has by then been achieved, there will also be a much larger native presence in the economic affairs of the region, the nature, scope and effect of which cannot be predicted at present. Thus, within a short time, the northern businessman's world will be reshaped and transformed, and he must be prepared to meet the challenge that these changes pose. My recommendations are aimed to help him in this adaptation.

Definition of a Northern Resident Firm

For the purpose of this chapter, I accept the definition of a territorial firm offered in *Report of the Task Force Formed to Study Problems Encountered by Northern Businessmen in Obtaining Federal Contracts*. The government of the Northwest Territories applies this definition to determine whether or not a firm is eligible for favourable treatment with respect to bid differentials. It requires the head and the administrative offices of a firm to be located in the Northwest Territories, that more than half of its business be carried out in the Territories, and that 50 percent or more of its capital assets be located there. Although this definition has given rise to certain problems and should be re-examinined, it is in principle a sound one.

1. Northern resident firms should be defined as those whose head administrative offices are located in the Northwest Territories, who carry out more than half of their business in the Northwest Territories, and who have at least 50 percent of their capital assets located there.

The definition of a northern resident firm is less of a problem than its application. If government seriously wants to create a viable northern business sector, it must be prepared to deal with resident firms on a preferential basis and should make exceptions to rules, such as the residency requirements, only when there are very special reasons to do so.

Bid Differential

The territorial government has maintained for some time a bid differential in letting contracts for construction. Late in 1976, the federal government announced that it would continue to follow this practice, but it has since retracted this statement. All contracting firms that meet the criteria set by the Task Force on northern business in its definition of a northern resident firm are given a 10 percent preference on territorial government contracts under $500,000 and a five percent preference on contracts over this amount. Preference here means that the bid of a northern resident firm can be higher, up to the relevant percentage, than the lowest bid by a southern firm. Thus far, only construction firms that are able to meet the residency criteria set by the Task Force on northern business are eligble for this preference.

2. The federal government should establish a bid differential and extend it to all northern resident firms that bid on government contracts or on contracts with private sector projects that require government approval. This change should be made soon so that it will have had a real impact in strengthening northern business well before the pipeline is built.

3. During pipeline construction, the bid differential should apply to the construction of all project facilities, as well as to those contracts defined above. However, to prevent a situation of permanent or potentially damaging dependence on measures such as bid differentials, there should be a thorough review of the subject both before and after construction of the pipeline project. The review before construction should focus on the adequacy of the measures that have been taken to that time. The review after construction should examine the need for the continuation of a bid differential.

Regional Purchase of Goods and Services

Industrial and commmercial growth usually depends on the ability of a few key industries to grow rapidly and to create capital and income for additional growth. For this reason, governments have typically encouraged the growth of leading industries and sectors of the economy by a variety of incentives and by market protection.

In any regional economy, the leading industries are usually those associated with exports from that region. In some cases, they include industries that are particularly vulnerable to shifts in market forces or that are under the control of external decision-makers who have little interest in the region beyond its resources. The result is that, instead of the relatively smooth growth that can be predicated on economic models, growth takes on an unpredictable character. This kind of growth has certainly been characteristic of the northern economy, where economic activity has been cyclical.

The purchase by the pipeline company of goods and services from firms resident in the Northwest Territories should not lead to a situation in which, by the time that the pipeline project is over and the regional purchasing programs have ended, a large proportion of the region's commercial and productive capacity depends solely on the pipeline project.

4. *The regional purchase of goods and services requires careful planning by the Company, all levels of government, and the regional business community. Well before the final design phase, the Company and regional businessmen should hold a series of meetings to determine the details of the procedures the Company will use for local purchases.*

Planning should focus not only on how some firms may benefit directly from the Company's purchases of goods and services, but also on how other firms may benefit from performing services for each other. Planning should also consider how the pipeline project might contribute to the growth of regional capacity and the quality of regional services, without making the northern business sector unduly dependent on the pipeline.

In planning the purchase of goods and services from resident firms, care should be taken to ensure that the volumes these firms undertake to supply are realistic. Resident firms should not undertake to supply goods and services to the Company in volumes that are likely to create shortages in local markets.

5. *The pipeline company shall instruct its prime contractors to ensure payment within 30 days to northern resident firms. This promptness is necessary because, among other things, northern subcontractors may have to meet conditions in their collective agreements that could impose strains on their cash flow position.*

Local purchase procedures for the pipeline may be complex and difficult to work out; the more experience that northern businesses have with such procedures before the pipeline is built, the easier it will be to apply them when the construction of it begins.

6. *Before the pipeline is built, government should establish and adhere to a local purchase program, and it should require large private companies in the North to do the same. Government should be flexible and willing to experiment with such programs, although not in a manner that would impose costs or confusion in the private sector.*

7. *Regional purchasing and other programs, including education programs, should encourage innovative solutions, such as the joint venture, in which two or more firms combine to provide goods or services or to bid on a particular contract. Joint ventures between northern firms, and between northern and southern firms, should be encouraged both in the long and the short term. They could provide the means of securing the risk capital that will be needed to complete special projects of limited duration, and they could facilitate the participation of northern resident firms in development projects.*

8. *Crown corporations, such as the Northern Transportation Company Limited, when they perform services for the pipeline company, should ensure that they involve local private firms to the maximum degree. In the meantime, and well before the pipeline is built, crown corporations should contract to northern resident firms some of the services they currently provide for themselves so that adequate local services, such as trucking, can be developed before construction of the pipeline begins.*

Tendering Procedures

Construction and the supply of materials are key activities in the North. Firms active in these fields provide considerable employment and income in the larger communities of the Mackenzie Valley and Mackenzie Delta. They could, moreover, be one way whereby significant numbers of northern residents could find their way into pipeline-related employment without being employed directly by the pipeline company or its major contractors. Excessive reliance of northern resident firms on the pipeline would be undesirable, but nevertheless assistance to northern suppliers and contractors is necessary to give these firms a position of equality with their southern-based competitors.

9. *Before pipeline construction begins, the pipeline company and its major contractors should prepare a list of goods and services they will require. This list should be developed with the assistance of the Government of the Northwest Territories and representatives of northern businesses and should be made available to northern suppliers and construction contractors.*

Where possible, this list should be broken down into increments or lots that coincide approximately with the scale and volume at which the northern firms can operate. It should also indicate how exacting the tolerances for a particular item or service may be and what substitutes may be allowed.

10. *All contractors and suppliers, whether they are based in the North or in the South, should be required to submit bids FOB point of use rather than FOB point of supply; that is, full transportation costs should be included in all bids.*

11. *Contracts that are compatible with the capacity of resident northern businesses should be tendered first in the locality in which the goods and services in question are to be consumed. To facilitate this recommendation, a list of pre-identified, registered northern resident businesses should be compiled by locality.*

12. *Standard procedures for tendering should be developed. All notices for tenders that are within the capability or competitive range of northern resident firms should be published in the North.*

Bid Depository

A bid depository is usually operated under the auspices of a contractors' association. Tenders are submitted before a specified time, and they are opened before an impartial committee. Strict rules ensure that all bids are submitted and opened by identical procedures. The cost of operating a bid depository is not great, and it should be financed through the sale of envelopes to contractors.

A bid depository has been in operation in Whitehorse for a number of years, but there are none in the Northwest Territories. The bid depository most frequently used by contractors in the Northwest Territories is in Edmonton, and that is another reason why contractors resident in the Northwest Territories are at a competitive disadvantage, relative to non-resident firms, in bidding on contracts for construction projects within the Northwest Territories. This competitive disadvantage is enhanced by the distances between contractors and their suppliers. Because the suppliers' bids are usually not available until moments before the bid depository closes the northern contractor must often travel to the bid depository to submit his bid on time. If bid depositories were located in the major communities of the Northwest Territories, they could be used, as well as those in southern centres, for the deposit of bids for major development projects in the North.

13. One or more bid depositories should be established in the Mackenzie Valley. During pipeline construction, bid depositories should be operating in all of the major centres within the Mackenzie Valley.

Because the initial volume of envelope sales will be low, the Government of the Northwest Territories should provide seed funding to a territorial construction association to develop a bid depository.

Labour Relations

It is federal policy, as stated in the Pipeline Guidelines, that any work that is directly associated with the construction of the proposed pipeline and its related facilities will be subject to collective agreements between prime contractors and a number of unions representing workers in the pipeline and building and construction trades. This regulation will, of course, have important implications for northern workers, who will have to join unions to be eligible for direct pipeline employment. The northern businesses that seek contracts associated with pipeline project construction will also be affected, because there will be provisions in collective agreements that stipulate that all subcontractors working on site for prime contractors are to be bound by the provisions of the collective agreements. In other words, the northern firm will have to pay the wages, offer the benefits, and provide the working conditions that are outlined in collective agreements.

With a few exceptions, this will be a new and perhaps trying experience for northern businesses.

A report prepared by Manforce Research Associates, *Trade Unions and the Northern Business Community*, suggests that the presence of unions in the North and the stipulations of collective agreements could significantly alter the hiring practices of northern businesses. Businesses directly associated with the project will have to ensure that the members of their work force meet union entry requirements. The increased expectations arising from union-negotiated wage-and-benefit packages could make it difficult for northern businesses to attract or to keep workers during the period of pipeline construction and to maintain worker satisfaction after it is completed. The report also indicates that administrative and bookkeeping chores are likely to increase: most collective agreements stipulate, for example, that workers must be paid on a weekly basis, that a cheque-cashing service must be provided, and that dues must be deducted from wages and forwarded to the union.

To the extent that construction of the pipeline will stimulate continued development of hydrocarbon resources in the Western Arctic and promote the growth of infrastructure in its larger communities, the stronger union involvement in the North will become. Representatives of the northern business community, in their submissions before the Inquiry, expressed concern over the impact that trade unions and collective agreements could have on their present operations and on their ability to obtain contracts associated with pipeline construction.

14. In preparing for pipeline construction, the Government of the Northwest Territories, in consultation with the northern business community and the trade unions representing workers in pipeline construction, should undertake a comprehensive review of trade union practices and their potential impact upon business operations in the North.

15. Before construction of the pipeline begins, a program should be created to inform northern businesses more fully of federal government policy with regard to unions and collective agreements. A similar program should be established to inform the trade unions about business conditions in the North.

Information and Forecasting

Many uncertain and unpredictable elements in the North affect the course of economic life in the region and make it a very difficult place in which to operate a business. These uncertainties are particularly strong in the region's major communities; their dependence on the hydrocarbon industry, the mining industry, and on government projects and activities has in the past led to large variations in activity. This problem has two aspects. First, northern businesses need better information about the plans and prospects that are now affecting the behaviour of industry and government both in the North and elsewhere. Secondly, better forecasts of what is likely to happen in the future are needed.

Large corporations and government have always been very selective in choosing the information they wish to make available to northerners, and they have tended to release only the information that could help them achieve a particular end. When they believe that no information is likely to further their interests, no information is made available. Not surprisingly, such behaviour has had a whole range of negative consequences. It has led to the excitement of great expectations about projects such as the Mackenzie Valley pipeline, which in turn has led to the misallocation of regional labour and capital resources.

It is very difficult to forecast with any degree of accuracy for a region such as the North, but it should be possible to separate out from the enormous range of events that might occur those that are most likely to occur. Even the roughest indications of what the likely course of events is going to be could give businessmen and potential investors something on which to base their decisions. Such crude forecasts would not only be helpful to the business community, all northerners could also benefit from their availability. However, they would have to be conducted in a responsible and professional manner to be of any real usefulness.

It is therefore appropriate to make recommendations with respect to the degree to which both government and large corporations should supply more and better information to an interested public. Fuller access by the public to such information will probably come about only with time and, even then, probably only with legislation.

16. *There is, at present in the North, a great need for better information so that the people there can comprehend the implications of a vast undertaking such as the proposed pipeline. Procedures to supply this essential information should be formulated and implemented as soon as possible.*

17. *The Government of the Northwest Territories should continue its efforts to assemble northern businesses into regional associations so that it will be easier to supply information to individual businessmen and to provide a forum in which the problems of the businessmen themselves can be discussed with representatives of government and industry. These organizations may require initial government support.*

18. *With assistance from the Government of the Northwest Territories, these regional business associations together could operate a business information centre, which should work closely with the impact information centres I recommend in Action Communities. The business information centre should be staffed by persons who are familiar with northern business and with the operation of both the territorial and federal governments. Under the direction of the business community, the centre should serve as a liaison with government and industry and inform businessmen of developments that are*

likely to affect their operations, review forecasts and maintain statistics.

Skills of Management and Enterprise

Although northern businesses have economic and geographical problems, the calibre of northern entrepreneurship and management is not always high, and these qualities could be improved in the long term by educational and management development programs, especially in the more isolated communities.

Several programs related to the development of managerial skills are now available to northerners through the Government of the Northwest Territories and the Federal Business Development Bank. The territorial government has designed a series of teaching modules on small business management. It may be difficult to persuade owners and managers of small businesses to set aside the time required to complete the sections of the course that are relevant to their own specific needs. A small businessman may be busy just making ends meet and he may be reluctant to undertake work that he considers merely academic. And, even with good management, probably many small northern businesses will not become more successful because of the geographical and market difficulties facing the northern economy. The northern businessman must, therefore, be persuaded of two things: that his business has a better chance of survival in the long run if he learns to run it more efficiently and that the management development course will be of real use and benefit to him.

Some incentives could be provided to induce the northern businessman to take a course to improve his managerial skills. For example, employees at the management level could be given bonus pay for successfully completing business management courses that their employers think may be useful to them. In addition, individuals could be reimbursed for course fees and costs.

19. *Businessmen should be encouraged to take advantage of the courses on management that are already available in the Northwest Territories, and new courses covering subjects that would prove useful in the event of pipeline construction should be devised and made available.*

20. *The government should assist northern firms to procure better management expertise. This could be done by providing funds to hire persons with management skills who could work with the resident owner and operator for a period of time, or by placing young northerners who show promise of business ability in management trainee positions in the South, to obtain management expertise through on-the-job experience.*

21. *Northern businessmen seeking contracts will require knowledge of a variety of special techniques and arrangements that are peculiar to industry, such as preparing bids, tendering procedures, bonding applications, job costing and* *labour relations. An advisory service for these procedures should be available within the Government of the Northwest Territories.*

Availability of Loan Capital

Loan capital is essential to the operation of a small business to ensure that sufficient funds are available for the acquisition of assets, the provision of working capital, and the financing of inventories, which must necessarily be larger in the North than in the South because of isolation and transport cost. Although there is now a special Agricultural and Rural Development Act (ARDA) program for the North, through which grants are made available to northern businessmen, loan capital will still be needed for equity and bridge financing until enough work has been accomplished to meet the requirements under which ARDA grants are made. The expansion of loan funding is important to the development of a healthy business community in the Mackenzie Valley. In the long term, and in anticipation of the construction of a pipeline, it is essential that sufficient funds are available for the establishment of new resident northern businesses and for the expansion of existing businesses.

At present, there are five major sources of capital available to residents of the Northwest Territories. The chartered banks and credit unions supply only limited loan capital because they have stringent collateral requirements and, in the case of credit unions, loan capital is in short supply. The Federal Business Development Bank is a major lender for the purchase of fixed assets in the Northwest Territories. The Small Business Loan Fund of the Government of the Northwest Territories lends capital for the purchase of fixed assets and the financing of inventories. This fund allows limited guarantees and limited grants. Upon being transferred from the federal government to the Government of the Northwest Territories, it was restructured, and the ceiling on loans was raised from $50,000 to $100,000. The fund will be replenished by $600,000 annually to a maximum of $5 million. Loans are amortized over a maximum period of 15 years at an interest rate set by the Federal Business Development Bank. The fund is now administered by a board made up of four businessmen and two government officials. The Eskimo Loan Fund provides financing to Inuit for risk and inventory capital at an interest rate well below the prevailing bank rates, and the Indian Economic Development Fund, which is administered federally, provides financing for risk and inventory capital for Indian and white entrepreneurs active in native economic development.

Thus limited risk capital is available through the Federal Business Development Bank, the Eskimo Loan Fund and the Indian Economic Development Fund. All other financing is limited to the purchase of fixed assets and, in the case of the Small Business Loan Fund, to the financing of inventories. There is a serious need, particularly in the construction industry, for loans to finance working capital. If a diversified service sector is to be developed in the North, it is absolutely essential that such capital be made available. Moreover, to the extent that business risk is a function of poor management, that problem can be met by providing incentives to businessmen who are willing to couple their borrowing with management training.

22. When pipeline-related activity begins, the Small Business Loan Fund should be expanded and the ceiling on loans should be raised to allow for the financing of the expansion of businesses so they can participate in primary and secondary pipeline activities. Such funds should be directed particularly toward activities that are likely to remain important in the pattern of regional employment and income base following completion of the pipeline.

23. Offices to administer the various northern loan funds should be set up in the main communities of the Mackenzie Valley and Mackenzie Delta, and perhaps throughout the North, to ensure that all regional businessmen have access to them.

24. The Federal Business Development Bank should be directed to locate and staff one or more regional offices in the Mackenzie Valley and Mackenzie Delta.

Bonding

Northern contractors who testified before the Inquiry stressed the difficulties they have encountered in obtaining bonding from surety companies. Bid bonding is usually required on tenders above a minimum value of between $5,000 and $10,000. This requirement is based on the need for owners and prime contractors to be assured that a contract will be completed in the time and manner specified in the contract. It is a form of prequalification of bidders in an industry that has long been troubled by defaults and bankruptcies. Owners obtain their protection through the bonding of prime contractors, and they in turn require the same protection from their subcontractors. A contractor who can obtain a bid bond will have no difficulty in obtaining the required performance and material bonds, therefore a bid bond has come to be regarded as a means of separating qualified from unqualified bidders.

Surety companies examine the applications for bonding to ensure that the contractor is not only in a financial position to complete the contract, but also that he has the capability and expertise to perform the work in a satisfactory manner. Applications must be supported by financial statements, summaries of experience on previous contracts, references from suppliers and bankers, and any other information that will persuade the surety company that the contractor has the experience and resources to fulfil his contractual obligations.

The northern contracting industry is still young and it shares the problems inherent in new business operations. Many contractors lack experience and management expertise, and they cannot provide the necessary assurance of their capability to execute a contract properly. Moreover, the contracting industry in the North is very competitive and has grown rapidly, thereby placing a greater demand on the surety industry to finance bonds. Competition for a limited amount of bonding capital places an additional obstacle in the way of new northern-based contracting firms. Furthermore, the surety companies do not have bonding agencies throughout the Territories, and they are not familiar with the special problems of northern contractors.

25. Pipeline contractors should use regional contractors, so far as possible, without requiring them to obtain bonding, provided that the pipeline contractor believes that commitments can be met and provided that those commitments will not place undue strain on the regional firm.

Bonds are not insurance, and a surety company has the right to recover from a contractor the full extent of its loss on a defaulted contract. The contractor should not, therefore, be bonded on contracts that are larger than he can handle.

Pipeline and Economic Problems

I have already said that the effects of the pipeline will intrude heavily into all aspects of economic life in the Mackenzie Valley and Mackenzie Delta. Major problems that may take years to resolve could arise out of the introduction or the extension of such massive new forces as large corporate interests, big unions, and unprecedented government intervention into the northern economy. Locally, these new forces could lead to permanently higher cost structures, price inflation, particularly in rents, and shortages of skilled labour. To counter such effects, I could recommend such measures as the subsidization of some costs, the indexing of incomes, and the establishment of rent control boards, but I am not convinced that these measures would be effective or beneficial. However, some problems can perhaps be modified or made less severe if action is taken now along the following lines.

26. In every possible way, government must ensure that unrealistic expectations are not built up in the minds of northern residents around the idea of the pipeline project.

In the early 1970s, the federal government's promotion of the Arctic Gas project, at a time when gas reserves in the Mackenzie Delta were questionable and the environmental and social impact of the proposal had not been subjected to independent scrutiny, led to great expectations of growth and expansion among businessmen of the region, expectations that have not been fulfilled. The proposals that I have already made with respect to the provision of fuller information and to forecasting would help to avoid disappointments in future. Other steps include an information program that would describe the negative as well as the beneficial aspect of the proposed pipeline and continued research on the probable local effects of the project. By placing local people in direct communication with union officials and corporate executives and by ensuring that their questions are properly answered, much confusion can be avoided. It will also be useful to report on conditions in regions, such as Alaska and later, the Yukon, that have experienced the construction of a pipeline.

I recognize that postponing the construction of a Mackenzie Valley pipeline has created hardship for some northern businessmen who may have believed that the project was imminent and who may have made investments they would ordinarily not have made. Of course, those who invest with a view to making a profit must expect to bear losses when they occur. So there is little that government can be expected to do directly about the problems of these firms. However, indirect measures could alleviate their plight and that of the local labour force that may have come to depend on them. Some local construction programs, proposed for the future, could perhaps be undertaken now to ease the transition for northerners who had expected the pipeline to be built almost immediately. I am not advocating unnecessary projects nor a round of pump priming for a pump that does not work. Such local projects should make sense in terms of the ordinary community and regional growth and renewal.

27. Procedures should be established to avoid, as far as possible, the bunching of major projects during peak pipeline construction. If they are not taken in advance of pipeline construction, various public works that government would normally undertake should be deferred, if possible, until the pressures generated by the pipeline have passed. Private ventures should be discouraged in the region during peak construction.

To some extent, this process will occur automatically: there will be severe shortages of labour and industrial capacity while pipeline construction is underway, and the resultant higher costs should discourage any but the most immediately profitable or, in the case of public works, the most necessary projects from going forward. Some public and private projects may have to proceed, despite their possibly disruptive effects and high costs. If, for example, there is a severe housing shortage, more houses will have to be built, and it may be impossible to postpone the construction of badly needed municipal structures.

28. Government should always be fully informed about when and where additional capacity exists in the Canadian economy so that, if necessary, it can draw quickly on goods, services and expertise. Where practicable and in keeping with other recommendations made in this report, the development of such capacity should be fostered in the North.

There is a widespread view, well-grounded in economics and law, that procedures such as northern preferences and bid depositories restrict the free functioning of industry and commerce and that they inhibit rather than enhance the operation of the market system. I agree with this view. No restrictive measures should be adopted — indeed, they should not be necessary — in a mature market where competitors are in a position of approximate equality. But the northern market is not such a market.

Northern businessmen, although they affirm their belief in free competition, insist at the same time on government assistance and enforced preferences. I do not see how they can do otherwise. Firms that must operate exclusively or largely in the North are at serious disadvantage in comparison with firms that do only a part of their business in the North. Northern-based firms operate at much higher levels of uncertainty and cost, and they do not generally have the same access to institutions of government, such as administrative tribunals, or to private professional services, such as lawyers, consulting engineers, and management consultants, as firms that are based in the South.

Because of this disadvantage, I feel that northern businesses require assistance in the form of protective and supportive measures of limited duration. The purpose of such assistance is to give the northern businessman a reasonable chance of surviving the pipeline project and to continue to serve in the private sector of the northern economy in the future. In other words, this assistance is primarily directed toward business-men who are able to demonstrate that they have a long-term commitment to the region and its economy.

THE REPORT OF
THE MACKENZIE VALLEY
PIPELINE INQUIRY

PART ONE —
PEOPLE: SOCIAL AND
ECONOMIC CONCERNS

6 Transportation

Project Logistics

The transportation associated with the pipeline construction will have a broad range of impacts on the region. Pipeline-related freight moving north from Hay River will more than double the total volume carried on the Mackenzie River in 1972, the peak year to date. If the pipeline is to be completed according to schedule, the region will have to accommodate similarly increased transport requirements in passenger travel and in the use of small aircraft and helicopters.

The existing regulatory machinery of the federal and territorial governments and the plans put forward by the pipeline companies are not adequate to ensure that the necessary protection against adverse effects is given. Past events have demonstrated the inadequacy of regulatory mechanisms and planning to cope with boom-and-bust situations in the North, situations that have invariably involved transportation. During the oil and gas exploration boom of the early 1970s, aircraft flying at environmentally hazardous low levels could be controlled only where there was a project-specific basis for such control and when land use or similar project-specific regulations could be applied. In the same way, because of large annual variations in the volumes of freight, the planning of transport capacity has proved to be difficult. A part of the Mackenzie River fleet, expanded with government approval during the period of the oil and gas exploration boom, is now in storage.

In considering the logistics of the proposed pipeline in relation to the regional transport system, we must remember that construction of the pipeline is likely to be postponed for ten years. By that time, transport systems and pipeline construction techniques will probably have changed considerably, but we must base our present view of this problem on the proposals put forward by Arctic Gas and Foothills.

Any examination of the environmental and the socio-economic impact of the pipeline project must consider the specific location, scheduling and method of operation of transport facilities. Inadequacies in consultation, planning and site-specific studies for transport facilities and inadequate control of the facilities during operation could create seriously adverse effects on northern people, northern business, existing and future patterns of land use, fish and wildlife resources and archaeological sites.

The response of communities to plans for transportation facilities may range widely. Action communities, particularly Hay River, Fort Simpson and Inuvik, may want improved facilities, whereas others may not wish to have anything to do with wharves or stockpile sites.

1. During review of the design phase of the project, consultation with the people of each community regarding the facilities to be constructed or used at or near that community will be essential.

Construction of a pipeline will require the transportation of enormous volumes of materials and equipment from the South to many sites in the North. Arctic Gas' plans called for the movement of about 1.5 million tons down the Mackenzie River over a three-year period. The transshipment operation at a typical Arctic Gas wharf and stockpile site would include 2.6 million gallons of fuel, 45,000 tons of pipe, 500 tons of explosives, and 9,500 tons of miscellaneous camp facilities and heavy equipment. These materials and equipment will be moved by various means, and the necessity of transporting them will bring about improvements in and additions to the transportation infrastructure that exists at present in the Mackenzie Valley. New wharf sites will be built and others will be up-graded, and there will be new stockpile sites, both at wharves and at compressor stations, new airstrips and heliports, and new access roads to serve these and other facilities.

Both Arctic Gas and Foothills proposed to use the Mackenzie River and Arctic Ocean routes for heavy equipment supplies. During the shipping season, equipment and supplies will be off-loaded at wharves along these waterways and stored either at the wharf site or at the stockpile sites farther inland until the winter construction season begins. Both Arctic Gas and Foothills concede that use of the Mackenzie Highway, while not absolutely necessary to them, would be an asset during the construction and particularly during the operation of the pipeline. Futhermore, witnesses from Alaska expressed the view, based on their experience with the oil pipeline built there, that an all-weather road is essential for pipeline construction and operations. Thus, whether or not the highway is extended is an important variable.

Both pipeline companies plan to make extensive use of snow roads. I have recommended that snow roads must be used if terrain damage is to be kept to acceptable standards. There are, however, two fundamental problems — scheduling and the sufficiency of snow. In Volume One, I described these problems and the techniques that have been proposed to overcome them and I consider them again in the chapter Terrain Considerations: Snow Roads.

I am particularly concerned by any plans that may be advanced to rely on helicopters rather than on fixed-wing aircraft. Helicopters have a limited freight capacity, they are much less able than fixed-wing aircraft to cope with bad weather conditions, and they are more likely to disturb wildlife. Contingency procedures will have to be developed for any plans that rely heavily on helicopters for pipeline construction and operation.

The proposals of Arctic Gas and Foothills for transportation are, in many respects, preliminary and tentative. Arctic Gas has drastically altered its logistics plan, first to accommodate the concept of multiple staging areas, then to accommodate a development plan that Hay River proposed for itself. Both pipeline companies have based their plans, at least in part, on overly optimistic and unproved (or invalid) assumptions, such as the capacity of the winter road between Fort Simpson and Inuvik to carry high levels of traffic,' the ability of helicopters to fly under adverse weather conditions, and the availabilty of community wharf sites and airstrips. Neither Arctic Gas nor Foothills have offered any contingency planning. Both proposals depend on a variable but short summer shipping season on the Mackenzie River. Other transportation routes and modes of transportation are available, but the companies' planning has not reached the stage in which these other possibilities might be used to handle major freight movements.

Nevertheless, although the pipeline companies' proposals for transportation are still in a preliminary form, many of the measures that will be necessary to minimize the undesirable effects of pipeline construction and operation on the regional transportation system can already be discerned from them. They are described below.

Existing and Proposed Public Facilities

The difficulties in planning logistics stem in part from uncertainty about government programs, especially with regard to facilities that will be available to the pipeline company. For example, in their original applications, the pipeline companies assumed that the Mackenzie Highway

would extend as far north as Fort Good Hope. During the course of this Inquiry, however, the federal government changed its highway program. Extension of the road is still included in the government's long-term plans, but the northern terminus of the highway will be, for an indefinite period, a location near Wrigley. However, work on the Fort Simpson–Fort Nelson Highway, which had been suspended, is now under consideration. This road could serve as an alternative to supply routes through northern British Columbia.

2. Government should make an early statement as to its policy for the public facilities in the North that will be available to the Company. This statement should include the exact nature, location and standard of all public works that government or crown corporations will undertake, a definitive timetable for such works, and a description of the locations and the principles of cost-sharing for major new facilities or additions to existing facilities that may be required by the Company but that would be of value to the region after pipeline construction.

At the same time the Company should make its own transportation plans known so that government can assess them and integrate them into long-range plans for the Mackenzie Valley. In this way, government can ensure that the natural and socio-economic environment is disrupted as little as possible.

At the hearings, Foothills stated that they hope to make considerable use of the Fort Simpson–Inuvik winter road and Edward Mirosh, Manager of Engineering, even declared that it "would serve the same purpose as the Mackenzie Highway" (F9746). The grades, route and width of this winter road limit the speeds and loads that can be carried on it, and, in its present form, the road does not appear to be suitable for the requirements of transportation during pipeline construction. Any proposal for using it should be looked at carefully, for it will probably then require up-grading and rerouting, with consequent environmental and socio-economic impacts.

3. The government should explicitly declare its plans for an all-weather road in the Mackenzie Valley. If the government does not intend to continue the Mackenzie Highway, it should state clearly its policy with regard to the Fort Simpson–Inuvik winter road.

Facilities

Transportation activities generated by pipeline construction will create both opportunities and problems. The project will provide useful additional facilities, such as the airstrips, wharves, warehouses and stockpile sites that the Company will have to install. But these facilities will have to be maintained. Moreover, they are an extension of non-native activities into the northern frontier: they will increase the mobility of outsiders within the North and will interfere in many ways with traditional native activities.

Operations related to the construction and operation of the pipelines may disrupt the normal resupply of the communities along the Mackenzie River. The demands on transport during pipeline construction have been forecast only on a theoretical basis, and there is no information on the amount by which this demand may be exceeded. The National Energy Board has already pointed out that an additional volume of freight will be required to counter the problem of frost heave. Because it takes time to bring into service some forms of equipment used along the Mackenzie River, especially tugs and barges, the impact of excess demand on the existing transportation system and on the people who now depend upon it could be severe.

Problems and opportunities must be considered from the point of view of the users, the carriers and the affected communities. Each may be significantly affected, but in different ways. To reduce this complexity, I shall discuss pipeline-related transportation problems in terms of facilities and services.

From the standpoint of facilities, the construction of a pipeline in the North could be similar to earlier construction projects there related to national defence. Facilities were built with little or no thought given to their short- or long-term advantages. Many of these facilities, however, proved to be useful, and some of these are now essential to the regional transport system. At the same time, these legacies are not without their costs: the Alaska Highway, for example, has required expensive maintenance and rebuilding over the years, and some of the airports are poorly located and too big. A facility created by this means is often too expensive to keep, but too good to throw away.

The pipeline project will require considerable augmentation of existing marine and air facilities and, although present services may be improved and of use in the longer term, we must ensure that, as far as possible, new or up-graded facilities created to serve the pipeline will not be only an added burden to the North.

4. *The Company should provide all the facilities and equipment that are required to increase the regional transportation system's capacity to accommodate pipeline-related traffic, and so far as is feasible, in a way that will ultimately reduce the costs of serving normal traffic and that will improve the quality of service.*

This should be the general principle, but there will be problems of implementation unless there are also available sufficient details about the Company's plans, firm commitments by the government with respect to transport infrastructure, and at least the basic elements of a multi-modal plan for the infrastructure of transportation in the Mackenzie Valley. One special aspect relating to the improvement of transport facilities in general is the improvement by the Company of existing facilities. Improvement and expansion that do not disrupt the social and economic fabric of the community is clearly desirable, but they could lead to conflicts in demand between the Company and the communities.

5. *The cost of expanding or improving existing facilities to accommodate traffic related to pipeline construction shall be borne entirely by the Company and shall not be assessed against traffic to resupply the communities.*

6. *During the period of pipeline construction, community resupply traffic shall have priority wherever facilities are jointly used. Normal operating and maintenance personnel shall not be displaced in favour of pipeline employees.*

The remaining problem is one I mentioned earlier: a new or improved facility may be too expensive to keep, but too good to throw away. This problem can be alleviated if the pipeline facilities are integrated into transport plans for the region. Nevertheless, the question of who will maintain facilities that are not required regionally remains unanswered.

7. *The design for improving and expanding existing facilities and the way in which they are built should permit them to be readily scaled down when they are no longer needed for the pipeline project. All improvement and expansion should be of a high enough standard to ensure that long-run maintenance costs are minimized.*

In addition to these general recommendations, specific problems include the use of community airports, the development of pipeline staging areas in the southern part of the Northwest Territories, and the use and maintenance of roads.

Community Airports

Arctic Gas originally intended to make major improvements to the airports at Fort Good Hope, Fort Norman and Wrigley. These improvements would have had to be in place before pipeline construction began and would have supplanted those planned by the federal government as part of its Northern Air Facilities Program. Subsequently, Arctic Gas indicated that, in response to representations made at community hearings, they would locate the necessary airstrips away from these settlements.

Throughout my report, I have stressed that pipeline construction must not intrude on native communities against the wishes of the communities. This principle should apply to government agencies as well as to the Company. The revised Arctic Gas proposal to construct the airports away from communities, in response to local desires, is entirely appropriate; it should be taken as a model in similar situations and should be formalized as a process during the preparation of plans.

Staging Sites in the Northwest Territories

In the chapter on Action Communities, I discuss some of the problems and benefits that will accrue to these communities as a result of development. Two of these communities, Hay River and Fort Simpson, could be greatly affected by the choice of staging sites in the Northwest Territories.

Hay River, at the head of rail, is the more important of the two staging sites in the Northwest Territories. Some of the residents, local businessmen and the town council want it to retain this pre-eminence, and they have prepared a master plan according to which Hay River will be the staging site for all pipeline traffic. If this plan were implemented, it would cost more than $30 million and create dock space and other facilities that would far exceed the foreseeable needs of the community, the transportation industry, or indeed the pipeline company. Future maintenance costs of these large installations would also be high. Fort Simpson, the other staging site, is the present terminus of the Mackenzie Highway for all practical purposes. Fort Simpson has not actively sought to expand its transport facilities, but business has gone there both because of its position at the end of road and because it has an enterprising barging company based there. Although Fort Simpson has not proposed plans similar to those of Hay River, it would like to retain at least its present share in the staging business and perhaps to expand it.

Both pipeline companies have proposed to establish a major marine staging area at Axe Point, a good natural site for such a purpose with enough flat land for associated facilities and fairly close to the Mackenzie Highway. Barge traffic going from Axe Point down the Mackenzie River would avoid the hazardous crossing of southwestern Great Slave Lake and the Providence Rapids. If this new staging area is built, Hay River and Fort Simpson will be able to handle all of the regular traffic, and the normal community resupply requirements will not be disturbed during pipeline construction. Both pipeline companies propose to deactivate Axe Point when the project is completed, but that may not happen: not only will the investment in Axe Point be substantial, but the leases there are held by Northern Transportation Company Limited (NTCL), and it is likely to have its own interests in view rather than those of the communities. If Axe Point is not deactivated, continued use of its facilities could reduce by as much as 12 percent the transportation costs on freight that enters the Northwest Territories by truck for furtherance by barge. These savings would be effected at some cost to the Hay River economy and to the governments that would have to serve the new community at Axe Point and deal with the socio-economic problems of Hay River.

Two other factors complicate the picture. Hay River has a major economic advantage as a port because it is also the head of rail. But vessels moving down the Mackenzie River from Hay River must navigate the Providence and Green Island rapids above Fort Simpson. If the channel there is not dredged,

and if costs for moving dry cargo by truck and air continue to decrease through better transportation techniques, the advantage for trucked-in dry cargo would pass to downstream locations, such as Axe Point and Fort Simpson. Hay River would maintain its superiority only with respect to petroleum products, which arrive by rail in bulk. Petroleum products account for about half the freight moved on the Mackenzie River. If indigenous natural gas replaces imported petroleum for heating and electrical generation, transport requirements and associated facilities will be drastically changed.

The solution of problems related to staging sites must be sought in a long-term plan for transportation facilities in the southern part of the Northwest Territories. However, such a plan cannot be drawn up until native claims have been settled and until decisions are taken regarding the use of indigenous energy supplies and the dredging of shallow areas in the Mackenzie River.

Although I cannot settle the controversy over staging sites, I can recommend that the following steps be taken toward achieving a resolution.

8. *Government should develop a plan for transportation facilities in the southern Northwest Territories that takes into account both energy supply and river dredging.*

9. *The Company should not be permitted to construct facilities at Hay River or Fort Simpson that do not conform to the principles of the government's transportation plan.*

10. *Facilities that will not be required to support the demand for transport in the Mackenzie Valley during the foreseeable future should be constructed away from communities and should be deactivated on completion of the project. To ensure that such deactivation takes place, the federal and territorial governments should hold as crown land, until they are required, all potential port sites between Hay River and Fort Simpson and reacquire all such sites that are now leased. (The NTCL leases at Axe Point expire between 1978 and 1982). In addition, the federal government should control any roads that extend from the Mackenzie Highway to potential port sites.*

Roads

The major effects of pipeline-generated traffic on roads are maintenance costs and dusty conditions. Evidence from Alaska indicates that there was a substantial increase in maintenance costs on some state highways because of increased traffic on them during pipeline construction and, in some places, highways had to close daily for extended periods so that they could be maintained. Construction of a pipeline along the Mackenzie Valley will be based on river transport rather than on road transport, so the impacts in Canada, although similar, will probably be less severe. In the Yukon Territory and Northwest Territories, government revenue generated from fuel taxes and licence fees approximately balances the costs of road maintenance. If care is taken to maintain this balance, maintenance costs should not pose a problem. However, the time required to carry out maintenance activities may well become a problem.

11. Before construction of the pipeline begins, permanent roads that will be used for project purposes should be reconstructed to a standard commensurate with the traffic that is expected on them during the construction period. The Company should bear the cost of any reconstruction that exceeds foreseeable local needs. Where the reconstruction represents an acceleration of planned improvements, the Company should bear the cost of the acceleration.

12. The territorial government should develop a highway maintenance policy for the period of pipeline construction that will give adequate consideration to the Company and to residents of the Northwest Territories.

Except for a few short paved stretches, northern roads are surfaced with gravel. In dry, unfrozen conditions, vehicles passing over them raise great clouds of dust; meeting or overtaking a vehicle in these conditions is unpleasant and dangerous. Dust abatement through the application of calcium chloride is carried out where traffic warrants it and, if higher traffic levels are reached, the road is paved. According to present policy in the Northwest Territories and subject to the availability of funds, dust abatement is introduced when traffic reaches 250 vehicles per day, and the road is paved when traffic reaches 500 vehicles per day. Application of calcium chloride is considered to be a maintenance expense, and it needs no special consideration beyond that given above to road maintenance generally. Paving, on the other hand, is a capital program. It would be wrong to charge the total cost of paving a road to the Company, if use of it by a few vehicles caused the arbitrary number of 500 vehicles per day to be exceeded.

13. If traffic is forecast to exceed 500 vehicles per day during pipeline construction, the road should be paved before pipeline construction begins. The Company should bear the full cost of any paving that would not be required in the foreseeable future; where paving represents an acceleration of planned improvements, the Company should bear the cost of the acceleration.

In Alaska, much of the highway north of Valdez had to be rebuilt because of frequent use by heavy vehicles during the period of pipeline construction. Permanent roads in northern Canada might require similar work after construction of the pipeline is completed.

14. After pipeline construction is completed, the Company should be required to restore the highway system in northern Canada to its previous standard. The amount of reconstruction and major maintenance to be carried out should be specified by government, and the work should be completed within

three years of the date that gas begins to flow through the pipeline. The Company shall bear the cost of this work.

Services

The completion on schedule of the proposed pipeline will depend on a transport system that operates with clockwork efficiency. The pipeline companies have stated that they would rely on dedicated services, which they would provide for themselves to whatever extent might prove necessary. It seems clear that the Company will have to provide at least some of their own transportation to avoid overstraining the existing services.

Although probably the basic requirements of the Company can be predicted and handled by the existing transport system, emergency situations will no doubt have to be accommodated. They will include emergencies during pipeline construction and during pipeline-related activity, such as government monitoring, gas plant construction, and oil exploration. There will also be increased demands by northern businesses that are responding to pipeline opportunities and increased spending by Mackenzie Valley residents based on income derived from work associated with the pipeline. The transport system must continue to meet the normal demand of northern communities, but there are justifiable fears that emergencies may cause a shortage of freight and of air transport capacity and drive the present rates upward.

SURFACE FREIGHT CAPACITY

The tug-and-barge system, which is the lifeline of the communities down river from Fort Simpson, will equally be the lifeline for pipeline and gas plant construction and for oil and gas exploration. Because NTCL, a crown corporation, has a near monopoly of the freight business along the Mackenzie River, the situation may not be difficult to control.

15. Northern Transportation Company Limited should be directed to give first priority to the delivery of shipments to resupply the northern communities. NTCL should also set a guaranteed delivery schedule for any dry cargo and for emergency shipments of bulk petroleum assigned to it.

I make the following recommendation to ensure that emergency requirements of the project do not disrupt the normal resupply of the communities.

16. Whenever the Company or its subcontractors unexpectedly require transport service, the use of which would mean the withdrawal of service from territorial residents, the Company should be responsible for the full cost of providing emergency replacement service to communities. The replacement service (for example, aircraft to replace water transport) should be provided through the Agency after consultation with the Company.

The problem of pipeline-related activities remains unsolved, and it should not be underestimated. Between 1971 and 1972, barge traffic on the Mackenzie River increased more than 40 percent because of increased oil and gas exploration in the Mackenzie Delta. The barge traffic that is related to hydrocarbon exploration and development should be integrated with the traffic for pipeline construction.

17. All items of freight destined for the oil and gas industry in the North that weigh more than 100 pounds should be forwarded by the Company, through a joint-industry transport group.

Such a group would ensure that critical development-related and construction-related shipments do not compete with discretionary shipments related to exploration and that the ultimate allocation of priorities for the hydrocarbon sector is not left to the carriers.

I am not impressed by arguments about the difficulty of distinguishing between shipments for the oil and gas industry and shipments for community resupply. Cargo destined for Swimming Point is cargo for the oil industry, whether it is shipped by Gulf Oil or by a food wholesaler. Nevertheless, some cargo ultimately destined for hydrocarbon activities may be handled through the communities. This is not of great concern, because such routing will benefit business in the northern communities.

The problems of truck freight have received somewhat less attention than those related to barge freight. However, the potential problems are just as great for communities, such as Yellowknife, Rae-Edzo and Fort Simpson, that rely on truck transport, and for communities, such as Fort McPherson and Inuvik, that will become more dependent on this mode of transportation if the Dempster Highway is completed. As with barge freight, the problem of truck freight could be solved by the use of a crown corporation.

18. The three previous recommendations should also apply to NTCL's subsidiary, Grimshaw Trucking and Distributing Ltd. To ensure that this corporation can carry out its task, it should be granted temporary authority to operate in the Yukon.

In making these recommendations, I have been concerned about effects on local businesses, especially on trucking businesses, which, because of low capital requirements, lend themselves to northern entrepreneurship. The thrust of my recommendations is to ensure a base level of service rather than to establish monopolies responsible for carrying out the resupply of communities. If NTCL and Grimshaw Trucking are required to carry only the traffic that is offered to them, the field will be held open for northern transport businesses to compete, if they wish to do so.

AIR PASSENGER AND AIR FREIGHT CAPACITY

The problems related to the availability of air services differ from those associated with freight services in at least two ways. First, because both companies plan to use dedicated air services, the problems of air freight capacity — indeed, the problems of the availability of air services in general — are less likely to be caused by the Company's actions than by the boom in related activities, such as oil and gas exploration. Secondly, there are two distinct parts to air services: mainline jet service to the action communities, and the use of small aircraft, in many cases on an irregular basis, to native communities. It is difficult to separate vital air services from those that may be said to enhance the quality of life. I do not consider this distinction useful in a northern context; I believe that transportation services, whether in support of real or perceived needs, must be as readily available to northern residents as, for example, health care.

19. Northern residents shall have priority as passengers and for cargo on mainline flights that follow a published schedule for up to 12 hours before flight time.

20. To ensure that air services to small communities are not affected, carriers providing non-scheduled unit-toll services shall be required to convert to scheduled unit-toll service during the period of pipeline construction, and northern residents shall have the same 12-hour preference on these carriers as well. The scheduled service should be at least as frequent as the service that is in effect when the National Energy Board grants a certificate of public convenience and necessity.

RATES

Many northerners fear that pipeline construction and related activities will create a supply shortage and exert upward pressure on rates or cause the withdrawal of common carrier services, if they convert to private or contract carriage. Previous recommendations should make the latter alternative unavailable. The problem of increased rates, however, is more difficult because the carriers will argue that they must be able to pass on costs caused by pipeline-induced inflation. The effect of passing on these costs, of course, will be an inflationary spiral, with costs and prices chasing each other.

21. Because of the pervasive effects that the means of transportation have on all aspects of life in northern Canada, I consider a freeze on transportation rates to be an essential and integral part of a program to control inflation in the North during the period of pipeline construction. Legislative authority to control rates already exists. The basic philosophy of the freeze on transportation rates is that only increases in fuel costs, depreciation costs on the acquisitions of new equipment not related to pipeline activity, and wages up to the national average could be passed on through rate increases. The Company must be held responsible for other costs and must ensure that the carriers' financial positions do not deteriorate from what they were when the certificate of public convenience is issued.

It would be unfair to the Company, however, to leave the above provisions entirely open-ended.

22. *To ensure prudence on the part of the carriers, the Agency should designate which northern carriers may be eligible to participate in the program to control rates described above. The Company should have the right to appeal to the Agency if it believes that excessive costs are caused by imprudent or inefficient practices by a carrier.*

23. *When construction of the pipeline is completed, the freeze on transportation rates should be reviewed. Any subsequent increase in rates must be related to general rate increases in southern Canada.*

POSTCONSTRUCTION PROBLEMS

After rates, surplus vehicles, particularly tugs and barges, will be the major transportation problem in the postconstruction period. Trucks, because of their short life, and aircraft, because of their mobility, present no significant problems. However, when the two peak shipping seasons proposed by the pipeline companies are over, there will be a large surplus of floating equipment that was specifically designed for operation on the Mackenzie River and that will be useless during years of normal shipping. Arctic Gas have estimated that $57 million will represent 80 percent of the amortized cost of the 13 barge sets they will require. Only another major construction project, such as an oil pipeline, would give this equipment more than salvage value.

There are two fears with respect to this equipment: first, a large part of its cost may find its way into increased rates for the resupply of communities; and secondly, the equipment may find its way into contract or private carriage, thereby destroying the economies-of-scale that exist in the present system of near monopoly by a crown corporation.

24. *Project-related barging equipment should be costed as part of the pipeline project and controlled by the Company. In turn, the Company should be enjoined from disposing of this equipment under ordinary circumstances except to a common carrier company who had prepurchase licencing approval from the Canadian Transport Commission. To gain such approval, the carrier should have to demonstrate public convenience and necessity as defined under the federal Transport Act.*

Reference was made above to disposal of the equipment under ordinary circumstances. However, it is possible to foresee extraordinary circumstances — the construction of an oil pipeline. To accommodate such a situation, it would also be appropriate to permit the Company to dispose of its equipment in any manner that met the approval of the Minister of Indian Affairs and Northern Development.

Communications

Communications, although equally as pervasive in the socio-economic environment of northern Canada as transportation, are not nearly as visible. This may be because high-speed communications are recent phenomena in the North: only a relatively few years ago the airplane that brought in passengers, freight and mail represented the most common method of communications. Until fairly recently, the only voice communications along the Mackenzie Valley were those set up by private organizations or government agencies to serve their own requirements. Canadian National Telecommunications, the common carrier for the region, has systematically been expanding public facilities to make the services there comparable to those available in southern Canada. Despite major and rapid improvements in various phases of communications, unique features in the North have made expansion difficult. The market area is small and does not generate sufficient revenue to support the high cost of technologically advanced systems. As a result, cross-subsidization from revenues generated in the South and assistance from the federal government through such programs as the Northern Communication Assistance Program has been necessary.

Operations of the pipeline will offer little opportunity to improve public facilities because the systems proposed by the pipeline companies cannot be fully integrated into community service. Both the satellite system favoured by Arctic Gas and the terrestrial system favoured by Foothills are to be private, dedicated systems. Improvements could be made during the construction phase, however, because the telecommunications system will require expansion to support both the general increase in economic activity and the specific needs of pipeline construction. Such expansion could be carried out so that private dedicated systems are kept to a minimum and can easily be interconnected with the public system.

25. *The government should ensure that the pipeline project does not cause upheavals in telecommunications and that pipeline construction serves as a vehicle for improvement of telecommunication services for all residents of the North.*

Telephone and Business Communications

During construction of the trans-Alaska pipeline, telephone systems in Alaska were unable to cope with the demand; indeed, they were barely adequate before pipeline construction began. During construction, the systems bogged down, not because of excess use by the pipeline company, which had its own telecommunications system, but because activity in the state increased generally. At Valdez, for example, a person might have to dial 80 or 90 times to complete a telephone call.

26. To avoid the problems caused by an inadequate telephone system in northern Canada, the government should establish contingency plans for expansion, based on anticipated traffic demand patterns.

We must also consider the communications requirements of businesses in northern Canada. Because the market for advanced telecommunications services in the North is small and scattered, these services have been available to northern businesses only slowly. Telex, for example, is still not available in many communities. During pipeline construction, small businesses in the North will be faced with a wide range of opportunities; it would be unfortunate if they had to let these opportunities fall to large, non-resident firms because communications techniques were unavailable or because their financial resources were inadequate to order specialized services on a dedicated basis.

27. To ensure that improvements and advances in telecommunications are provided, as far as possible, by the common carriers and broadcasting companies, and to ensure that the dedication of services is kept to a minimum, the federal government policy in this regard should continue in the North.

28. Improvements and expansion should be carried out in advance of construction to ensure that common carrier services are not relegated to a low priority position and thus possibly not become available generally until pipeline construction and induced demands have levelled off.

PART TWO

Environment
and Land

7 The Physical Environment

Many people assume that the vastness of the North and the sparseness of its human population preclude the possibility that its land, water and air could ever become polluted. This assumption, I believe, is false. Although large areas of the North still remain relatively pristine, there is ample evidence to suggest that they may not always remain unpolluted. Over the years, and especially during recent years, human activity has progressively extended disturbance from small, isolated centres to much larger areas. We can now see a marked contrast between the untouched wilderness on the one hand and, on the other hand, the lands and waters that surround the settlements and the extensive areas in the Mackenzie Valley and Mackenzie Delta that have been subjected to intensive exploration and development.

There is a tendency to underestimate the dimensional and cumulative aspects of human impacts on the northern landscape and to overestimate the capacity of the environment to absorb them. The concentration of polluting activities that follows projects of a linear nature, such as seismic lines, the proposed pipeline, highways, and transportation corridors in general, means that such impacts are not only becoming more extensive but also that they are becoming interlocking and interdependent. People and their polluting activities are generally found together, and the overlap and cumulative build-up of successive environmental changes they create tend to be longer lasting in the North than they are in more temperate regions. Our technological needs and capabilities are leading us to undertake very large-scale projects in the North, and these projects necessarily involve very large-scale environmental impacts and risks.

For these reasons, I do not believe that the vastness of the North and the relative sparseness of its population will be any protection from serious degradation of environmental quality. Furthermore, northern ecosystems are vulnerable because certain important species within them have critical habitats and critical life stages; thus, some human activities and some areas of wilderness will have to be excluded from industrial development, if we are sincere in our commitment to protect the northern environment. Some kinds of environmental damage that are self-healing in the South, or are at least capable of rehabilitation, are, in the North, virtually permanent, and they therefore tend to be cumulative. It is this kind of cumulative effect, however slowly it may develop, that I see as the most serious threat to the northern environment in the long run.

Environmental Priorities

The evidence of hundreds of witnesses at the community hearings makes it quite clear that cumulative environmental impacts in the Mackenzie Valley and Mackenzie Delta have already reached a level that disturbs the people who live there. It is impossible for me to compare analytically past and probable future rates of accumulation of environmental impact. In the past, the rate was no doubt hastened by a general insensitivity to environmental concerns, and our ability to mitigate these effects was less advanced than it is today. In the future, the rate may be slowed by a greater corporate, governmental, and personal concern for the environment, but it might equally be intensified by our now greater technological ability to advance massive industrial developments.

Subject to the recommendations in this volume, I am convinced that a pipeline can be built in the Mackenzie Valley with an acceptable level of environmental impact. But we must bear in mind that any individual "acceptable" level of impact may be the beginning of a significant impact that will result from insignificant increments. How often and in how many locations can "acceptable" levels be tolerated before cumulative impact has produced an "unacceptable" level? This question is important. It seems to me that an "unacceptable" level is determined by, among other factors, both the absolute extent of the change involved and the public's perception of the environmental quality base that is being changed. It may be that undamaged areas are likely to be regarded as worthy of protection from even minimal or "acceptable" damage. On the other hand, areas that have already been changed and that need protection to preserve their remaining environmental qualities may not be considered worthy of such protection. Often a crisis situation has to develop before action in the form of ameliorative measures is thought necessary.

Environmental protection cannot be viewed in isolation from man's perception of what is right and proper. It involves decisions on which elements of the environment warrant protection for their own sake, which elements should be protected to meet man's needs for renewable resources or his desire for aesthetic enjoyment, sport or recreation, and how far protection should be relaxed to meet his priorities for industrial development. Thus, priorities for environmental protection depend upon individual attitudes, and they will differ among the various segments of any society.

1. Priorities for environmental protection must reflect not only those of government and of the Company, but also those of native people and of other residents of the North, together with those of citizens of other parts of Canada. Of necessity, standards and measures for environmental protection must be developed and implemented. In practice, public officials will carry out this function, but interested segments of society must be permitted to have a voice in the formulation and the means of implementing controls. This is in recognition of the fact that, in the North, regulation of land use and protection of the environment are closely related. Environmental impact of an industrial development project will involve not only the project itself but it will also lead to changes in the renewable resources and lands and will therefore affect their ongoing use by others.

I am aware that there are many codes, standards, and regulations that apply generally to the environmental questions raised here, and that there are guidelines and standards specifically designed to apply to pipelines in the North. It is not my intention, in this report, to supersede such existing standards and regulations; rather, my purpose is to place on record some of the insights gained during the Inquiry process. I hope that my comments will supplement and complement existing measures and that they will be useful in the drafting of an environmental code and guidelines for the pipeline. (See Project Regulation and Review.)

Environmental Atlas

The interrelationships among the elements of an ecosystem are complex. Once one of the primary elements, such as land, water, vegetation, air or wildlife, is badly abused, it is difficult to prevent that damage from spreading to the other elements. Also, effects within an ecosystem are often felt in time and space far from the point of initial impact. For these reasons, damage to a highly visible element in the environment cannot be ignored or used as an excuse to avoid taking action that would prevent further degradation of that element. The northern environment must be viewed as an integrated entity.

Except in a very few localized situations, development in the North has not yet greatly abused the environment. Nevertheless, few large areas apart from the Northern Yukon can justify absolute protection measures solely on the basis of their wilderness condition. Most of the Mackenzie Valley and Western Arctic environment is in a state of early development and of sporadic impairment, a state that unfortunately evokes a somewhat apathetic response in any consideration of its environmental values. This apathy facilitates and serves to condone incremental damages that can, in the areas of critical habitat and life stages, quickly surmount the threshold of acceptability.

As an aid to understanding the wide range of environmental issues, I have been impressed with the usefulness of the environmental and wildlife maps prepared by the two pipeline companies and, in particular, by the atlas prepared by the Environment Protection Board and subsequently revised by Carson Templeton (Exhibits F135, F834 and F835). These documents present the various elements of the northern ecosystems, of present and projected land use, and related subjects in a visual format that is easily understood.

2. I recommend that a large-scale, detailed, environmental atlas be prepared jointly by the Agency and the Company to show environmental sensitivity and land use priority for the use of all interested parties during design review, construction surveillance and project monitoring.

Environmental Quality Index

How much "acceptable" damage can be tolerated before the situation becomes "unacceptable"? This question could be answered if we understood both the nature and extent of the accumulated damage and the public's perception of that total. I heard much evidence on the need for and the means of project and environmental monitoring, often of a subject-specific, species-specific or site-specific nature. However, I heard very little about how this valuable information could be used to appraise in a general way changes of broad environmental quality or changes over broad geographic areas.

Statistics bearing on changes in environmental quality already exist but they are frequently inaccessible, irregular in coverage and in time, or isolated from other related data. We need some measure of overall and cumulative environmental change to which the expert and layman alike can refer. In final argument, such a measure was proposed by Commission Counsel in his recommendation for environmental quality indices along the lines developed by Inhaber (1974) in Canada and by the Council on Environmental Quality in the United States (Thomas, 1972). Properly developed environmental quality indices would permit trends to be easily seen, would not hide assumptions, would be easily understood, and would be meaningful indicators of changes in, for example, air, water, land, and in biological and total environmental quality.

Air quality indices already exist for some metropolitan areas, for example Toronto, and the principle is firmly entrenched in our everyday lives by such well-known, continuously updated measurements as the gross national product (GNP) and the consumer price index.

Research by government and industry in the Mackenzie Valley has provided adequate environmental data to begin establishing indices for water, air quality, land and various biological components. Many measurements upon which such indices would be based are purely scientific. They are free from the cultural bias that the Committee on Original Peoples Entitlement stated, in its response to Commission Counsel's recommendations, would result from the imposition of non-native values on an index. Indices relating to things such as renewable resources could possibly be established that would take into account both the values of native people and their interaction with the environment.

Arctic Gas criticized severely the idea of indices, saying that it is "nothing but a futile attempt to portray in simple, meaningful ecological terms the complexity of ecosystems" (*Responses of Canadian Arctic Gas Pipeline Limited to Commission Counsel Submissions*, Vol. I, p. 11-91). I think that response misses the point. An index is not an attempt to provide a model of a system; rather, it is designed to give a general overview of a complex situation without an immense volume of reports, studies or detailed statistics. It is one means, admittedly a general means, for experts to communicate with both their peers and the layman.

3. *The government should establish a system of environmental indices for the Mackenzie Valley and Western Arctic so that there will be a readily available and easily understood measure of the state of the regional environment and a baseline against which short- and long-term changes can be assessed.*

The Northern Landscape

During pipeline construction and operation, large and widely distributed parts of the landscape will be subject to major disturbance. Compressor station sites will be the foci of activity, with associated wharves, gravel pits, landing strips, roads and other facilities affecting large areas around them. Permanent disturbance and sources of pollution will be introduced for the first time into areas where land, water and air are now virtually unimpaired. Large blocks of land, still in their natural state, will be split by the pipeline and held open by permanent access routes and sources of pollution.

We have been assured by the pipeline companies that deleterious environmental effects associated with short- and long-term disturbances of land and waterbodies, degradation of landscape values, and increases in air and noise pollution

levels will be held to "minimal" or "acceptable" levels. Nonetheless, I believe these effects will be significant.

Of course, some environmental damage is acceptable and some is unavoidable. However, this fact does not negate the need for protective measures; rather, it emphasizes such a need if we are not to foreclose other uses of the environment during the selection of land for a pipeline and the pipeline's use of it. Similarly, conflicts over land use can be exacerbated by environmentally inappropriate selection and use of land. Clearly there is a need for broad measures that will help mitigate these kinds of problems.

4. *As a general principle of environmental conservation, the areas of land and water used by any part of the project or physically disturbed by it should be kept to a minimum. Furthermore, the right-of-way, roads and sites for facilities should be selected so that their geographic distribution ensures minimal infringement upon other existing or potential uses of land. This principle of minimal pre-emption and disturbance applies to the routing, siting, design, construction, operation and, ultimately, the abandonment phases of the project.*

Sensitive Terrain

In Volume One, I described the characteristics of northern terrain that make the Mackenzie Valley much more sensitive to engineering ventures than topography alone would suggest. The Valley was formerly flooded by extensive postglacial lakes, which means that much of the region is now underlain by silts and clays. These soils cause engineering problems that are made yet more difficult by the presence of permafrost, which increases northward in the Valley. Under permafrost conditions, fine-grained soils frequently contain excess ice. When such areas are disturbed, the thermal regime can be altered so that the ice melts and the soil loses its strength and stability, leading to subsidence, slope failure and erosion.

5. *For environmental as well as for purely technical reasons, the pipeline route and facilities should avoid, wherever practicable, areas of sensitive terrain and particularly areas in which terrain disturbance could adversely affect nearby waterbodies or lands important to wildlife.*

The importance of the insulating properties of the organic mat that overlies permafrost is well-known. Irreversible and progressive environmental damage is often the inevitable result of disturbance of this mat.

6. *In permafrost terrain, and particularly in areas of sensitive fine-grained soils, disturbance of the organic mat and the vegetation that protects it should be minimized to avoid or reduce a wide range of environmental and engineering problems that could develop from permafrost degradation.* (See Terrain Considerations: Ground Surface Preparation.)

7. *Any organic mat and surface vegetation that has been disturbed should be restored, rehabilitated and stabilized. In* *permafrost terrain with fine-grained soils, the progressive nature of thermokarst degradation, slope failure and erosion requires quick and efficient remedial measures.*

Importance of Valleys

In Volume One, I noted the special importance of valleys in the landscape:

> Although the valleys crossed by the corridor may constitute only a small proportion of the total landscape, they are the locations of disproportionately high land use and are of particular environmental, aesthetic and recreational values. They define essential fish and mammal habitat and the vegetation along them is more varied and abundant than elsewhere. Valleys have always been and still are the preferred areas for many native people.... Valleys ... are the foci of the regional ecosystem. [pp. 78-79]

One of the most important elements of any valley, in environmental terms, is the bank of the river or stream. Here, the "edge effect" brings together for many species, including stream dwellers, their complex requirements of food, cover and water; it is a zone of very high biological productivity and diversity. The setting — the collective land-water contrast — is also a vital element of the scenery. From this perspective, shorelines can be considered to be environmentally sensitive areas that, if damaged by construction, will tend to broadcast the effect far out of proportion to the immediate and local circumstance.

8. *The potential for the pipeline project to cause land use conflicts, unacceptable damage to aesthetic values, or degradation of wilderness or areas important for recreation is particularly great in valleys and around waterbodies. The project should be adjusted to avoid or minimize impacts of this nature. Careful consideration must be given to the location of pipeline crossings, roads, water intakes, sewage and waste disposal sites, wharves, stockpile sites, work pads, camps, compressor stations and borrow areas where such facilities may impinge on valleys and waterbodies. Wherever possible, facilities (particularly groups of facilities) should be kept out of valleys and away from waterbodies and buffer strips should be left undisturbed. The land-water interface should be accorded special attention because of the special environmental values and geotechnical sensitivity associated with them. Water crossings should be kept to a minimum, and the pipeline route and roads should avoid closely paralleling watercourses.*

Wetlands

Swamps, marshes and wetlands constitute a unique natural landscape. Although they are recognized by some as vital habitat with high values for wildlife and water conservation, they are more often treated as wastelands or nuisances — something to be drained or filled in.

Wetlands must not be regarded simply as wastelands. In this regard, I cite the following statement made by President Carter to Congress on May 23, 1977, in a message about the environment:

> The important ecological function of coastal and inland wetlands is well-known to natural scientists. The lasting benefits that society derives from these areas often far exceed the immediate advantage their owners might get from draining or filling them. Their destruction shifts economic and environmental costs to other citizens ... who have had no voice in the decision to alter them. ... We must now protect against the cumulative effects of reducing our total wetlands acreage. [p. 13]

9. *To protect the hydrologic and biologic values of wetlands, they should be accorded the same level of protection as other elements in the landscape and environment.*

Aesthetic Values

In relation to the amount of direct evidence presented on aesthetic impacts of the project, the Inquiry heard a disproportionately large amount of cross-examination and discussion. This reflects the difficulty of coming to grips with such an abstract concept. The cross-examination was unsuccessful in demonstrating the existence of clear ameliorative measures, but it was useful in highlighting gaps in our knowledge and in delineating various aspects of the problem.

Arctic Gas stressed the subjective nature of aesthetic judgments, saying that perceptions vary so much from individual to individual that contradictory assessments can be made of the same situation. This extreme view tends to down play the importance of aesthetics. I agree that aesthetic judgment has a strong subjective component and that, as appeared in cross-examination, we know little of the influence of culture on aesthetics, particularly with regard to native people. However, whatever subjectivity and cultural influence there may be in aesthetic judgment, I believe there is a general consensus on what is pleasing and displeasing, on what is good practice, and on unacceptable aesthetic design. Although difficult to quantify or to protect, aesthetic values are an important component of environmental quality, and they must be viewed in this way in all aspects of the project.

10. *All aspects of the pipeline project should be designed and the right-of-way and facilities should be located to protect the natural aesthetic attributes of landscapes and waterbodies. All installations (and not simply those in areas of high sensitivity or visibility) should be constructed so that, as far as possible, the surrounding area is left in its natural state.*

Cumulative Effects of Development

Although the Mackenzie Valley covers a vast area, it will not be long before conflicts over land use within it intensify. The wildlife of the region has certain requirements. The native people will continue to need extensive lands for their own purposes. Industrial developers will need land, and still other areas may be designated for conservation and recreation. Each designated use will diminish the availability of uncommitted land, and competition for such land will increase.

The environmental effect of industrial development will often preclude or inhibit the ongoing use of the land by others. This problem is exacerbated by a tendency to view and assess each industrial development as a single and exclusive event. In considering the effect of a project like the pipeline, not only its direct and immediate impact but also the effect of all ancillary and spin-off activities, and the effect of other developments that can be reasonably anticipated over the life of the project, must be taken into account.

11. The pipeline project should be designed and located so that its effects on the ongoing use of the region by others, such as the native people, are kept to a minimum. In so doing, the cumulative effects of all construction, operation and abandonment activities shall be considered, along with the effects of other developments that can be reasonably anticipated in the region over the life of the project.

Two particular aspects of the pipeline project that are related to cumulative environmental impact warrant special mention. The first deals with the operation of the project after construction. It is established engineering practice to minimize long-term costs by judicious allocation of costs between initial capital construction costs and annual maintenance and repair costs. An essentially maintenance-free project is generally not feasible. In many locations, however, environmental considerations may render maintenance and repair activities too unacceptable to allow standard economic trade-offs to be employed. If the environmental protection of sensitive areas is to be taken seriously, there must be a shift in the ratio that normally exists between capital costs and annual maintenance costs to reflect more firmly the impact of maintenance activities on the environment.

Let me cite one example. Pipeline maintenance and repair, particularly in summer when the active layer is unfrozen and the ground surface is soft and when waterfowl or fish may be concentrated nearby, could be much more damaging and disturbing than the original construction activity.

12. The Company should locate, design and construct the pipeline and related facilities so that maintenance and repair activities that could damage the landscape and disturb wildlife over the life of the project are kept to a minimum. In permafrost and other sensitive terrain, the Company's designs may, as a result, have to be significantly more conservative than is usual in established pipeline engineering practice.

The second aspect related to cumulative environmental impact is of broader concern. It refers to both the current use of local resources by others and the possible future demand on those resources by further development. It is likely that there will be sections along any route where water, gravel and other resources that are essential to virtually all developments will be in short supply, or where they will be

regionally depleted before there is a comprehensive plan to share a scarce resource among present and future users.

13. The use of resources such as gravel and water by the pipeline project shall be compatible with the demand made on such resources by local activities and by developments that can be reasonably anticipated in the future. In particular, the pipeline Company shall employ designs and construction practices that minimize the use of limited local natural resources so far as practicable.

Water

Water, as an element of the physical environment, has innumerable domestic, commercial and industrial uses; as an element of the landscape, it is the essential element of marshes, ponds, lakes, streams, rivers and springs. In both of these functions, the quality of water is a prime consideration and it is this aspect that I develop in this section.

Much of what I have to say about other aspects of water is contained in other parts of this report. In the chapters on Fish and Wildlife, I deal with the biological aspects of waterbodies. Elsewhere I recommend measures to protect the land–water interface — the shorelines, the river banks and the stream edges — measures that would indirectly protect the waterbodies themselves.

Just as I recommend that the pipeline should avoid wilderness areas and specific, important natural areas to protect their intrinsic values, I also recommend that:

14. Wherever possible, lakes should be avoided, and the crossings of watercourses should be minimized to protect water resources. For example, the pipeline route should be adjusted where practicable so that meandering rivers are crossed only once.

Fluctuations in flow and water levels are natural, and certain plants and animals find their habitat in intertidal zones, floodplains, intermittent stream channels or sloughs that result from such changes. On the other hand, drastic changes in water levels, either natural or man-induced can cause destructive environmental changes. Although aquatic vegetation, furbearers, waterfowl and fish can tolerate a certain range of natural or seasonal fluctuations in water level, untimely changes may cause effects ranging from significant to severe. After a severe disruption, populations depending on such an environment may take generations to attain previous stable levels. It would be prudent, therefore, to eliminate or to minimize large-scale, man-induced effects of this kind. Such man-induced changes could occur if streams were overused as water sources, particularly in winter when flow is low, or if surface and subsurface drainage were impeded by the construction and operation of a chilled gas pipeline.

15. Site-specific review of water withdrawal proposals shall be required to ensure that any drawdown of water that exposes shorelines, shrinks channel flow or depletes stream pools does not cause unacceptable vegetative or faunal changes. (See Water Withdrawals.) Similarly, designs or construction activities that result in ponding or flooding shall be deemed unacceptable practice, and they shall require modification to mitigate these adverse impacts. (See Terrain Considerations: Drainage and Erosion.)

It is the pristine quality of water in the North that gives the waterbodies their great value. To the extent that southern Canadians have some idea of an undefiled northern landscape, it is probably based on their impression of pure lakes and streams rather than on unspoiled tracts of land. But the waterbodies in the North are highly susceptible to industrial pollutants. Permafrost restricts downward filtration so that spilled contaminants move laterally into surface waters rather than into deep soils and bedrock, where self-cleansing might take place. Permafrost also restricts groundwater movement so that many waterbodies are separate and isolated, rather than forming parts of a connected system, as they would in a region lacking permafrost. The cold temperatures also greatly inhibit biodegradation of pollutants, so they persist longer and often have a more devastating effect in northern waters than they would in the South.

Our experience with water pollution, competing demands, and conflicting interests over water resources in southern Canada should provide the motivation necessary to avoid these problems in the North. In southern Canada, we are now learning the great environmental, social and economic cost of water pollution and the difficulty of trying to restore the surface water to an acceptable quality. In the North, except for a few isolated localities, the surface waters have not yet been badly polluted. In allowing development to proceed, we have an obligation to maintain the high quality of water where it now exists. We must emphasize that here we would be maintaining the relative purity of northern water, a contrast with the current emphasis on water pollution control programs in southern Canada. Such a maintenance program must have two parts. The first is to control what goes into the water. My recommendations in this regard are found under Waste Management and, to a lesser extent, in other chapters such as Management of Fuels and Hazardous Substances. The second involves monitoring the quality of the receiving waters.

Following waste management procedures and adhering to effluent standards will not in themselves guarantee that the quality of receiving waters will be maintained. The treatment of effluent is limited by current technology, and it relies to some extent on the natural assimilative capacity of the receiving waters. Effluent standards are only one part of the administrative mechanisms directed at environmental (and public health) protection. They are not an end in themselves.

Each waterbody in its natural state has its own unique chemistry — its own unique quality. The development and use of effluent standards require judgment to determine how effluent can be released without adverse impact. Watercourse and effluent volume, flow or exchange rate, method and timing of effluent discharge, downstream water use and, of course, receiving water quality must all be considered.

I have not found a fully satisfactory compilation of the limits within which receiving water quality parameters must be kept, but Commission Counsel has examined a number of sources and combined the findings of three excellent and authoritative works: *Water Quality Criteria, 1972,* U.S. National Academy of Sciences and National Academy of Engineering; *Surface Water Quality Criteria, Province of Alberta,* Government of Alberta; and *Standards Methods for the Examination of Water and Wastewater,* American Public Health Association. Commission Counsel's compilation is included below as standards for the Agency and the Company.

Many of the streams and waterbodies that will be selected to receive effluent discharges are likely to be used for this purpose far into the future. There is no reason to believe that either the period of pipeline construction or the life of the project itself will terminate effluent discharges into them. Only by long-term monitoring will it be possible to make rational decisions that will maintain ambient water quality.

16. To ensure that receiving waters maintain the water quality standards imposed by the Agency, a program to monitor the streams and waterbodies into which effluents are discharged shall be established. Both the Company and the Agency should take into account the information made available by the Department of the Environment's Water Resources Document Reference Centre (WATDOC) and the National Water Quality Data Bank (NAQUADAT). These two computerized services shall be supplied with all relevant new information that is assembled during the design, construction and operation of the pipeline project.

Water Quality Standards

17. Unless otherwise specifically approved by the Agency, wherever effluent is released into a waterbody the Company shall adhere to the following limits for water quality:

a) Bacteria: at least 90 percent of the samples (not less than five samples in any consecutive 30-day period) shall have a total coliform density of less than 5000 / 100 ml and a fecal coliform density of less than 1000 / 100 ml. These standards are the upper limits; in certain cases, they may have to be substantially altered to guarantee that public health is protected. (See Waste Management.)

b) Dissolved oxygen: shall not go below 6.0 mg / 1. If natural conditions are below 6.0 mg / 1, effluent shall not be released into the waterbody unless the Company can demonstrate that discharge will not adversely deplete the oxygen level.

c) *pH: shall not be altered by more than 0.5 and shall be maintained in the 6.5-8.5 range.*

d) *Temperature: shall not be altered by more than 3°C.*

e) *Odour: shall not exceed the threshold odour number 8 at 20°C (see American Public Health Association, op. cit., p. 252).*

f) *Colour: shall not be increased more than 30 colour units above background.*

g) *Turbidity: see Fish.*

h) *Phenolics: shall not exceed 0.005 parts per million. Fish flesh shall not have any detectable change in taste or odour as determined by a government agency taste panel.*

i) *Oils and greases: no visible iridescent sheen shall be present.*

j) *Inorganic chemicals: shall not exceed the following levels expressed in mg /l:*

Boron	0.5	Nitrogen	1.0
Copper	0.02	Phosphorus	0.15
Fluoride	1.5	Sodium	30-75
Iron	0.3	Sulphide	0.05
Manganese	0.05	Zinc	0.05

k) *Pesticides: only air-fogging pesticides shall be permitted. No persistent chemicals shall be used.*

l) *Toxic chemicals: shall not exceed the following levels expressed in mg /l:*

Arsenic	0.01	Lead	0.015
Barium	1.0	Mercury	0.001
Cadmium	0.01	Selenium	0.01
Chromium	0.05	Silver	0.05
Cyanide	0.01		

18. *Samples for the water quality criteria shall be taken at points determined by the method outlined in Fish. Dissolved oxygen shall be measured in stream pools and locations in lakes where depleted oxygen levels could be expected because of organic loading.*

19. *Testing for the parameters listed above shall be carried out according to the methods outlined in Standard Methods for the Examination of Water and Wastewater, American Public Health Association, 1974.*

Air

There can be little doubt that, from a global perspective, there is little man-made air pollution in the North. However, the contrast between localized areas of human activity and the large intervening wilderness areas illustrates the high potential that exists for problems related to air quality, even with limited human activity. These problems range from the emissions of certain industries, to ice fog in communities and dust problems along the gravel highways. While the pipeline project would cause many problems that would have to be dealt with by the Agency, my principal concern here is the environmental effect of major sources of pollution at given points, such as compressor stations. Unless we formulate comprehensive standards for such permanent emissions now, we will be faced in the future, after successive industrial developments, with the problems and costs of trying to clean up these emissions.

Most of us do not think about problems of air quality when we have clean air, but quickly become obsessed by the sight and smell of pollution when, apparently from nowhere, the reward of our negligence is inflicted upon us. It is not surprising, therefore, that pure air is taken for granted throughout most of the Mackenzie Valley, whereas the residents of Toronto keep an anxious eye on their air quality index, and the citizens of Fairbanks and Inuvik suffer through the inconvenience and hazards of ice fog.

We can sometimes conceal or walk away from lands and waters that have been degraded, but we cannot walk away from air pollution. It envelops and pervades all aspects of our lives. No doubt that is one reason why, during the growth of environmental awareness in the 1960s, air quality was among the first aspects of the physical environment to receive widespread attention. Air quality is an issue that is personal, regional, national and international in scope.

Air Quality Objectives

The Department of the Environment has established National Ambient Air Quality Objectives for a number of common air contaminants. These objectives are divided into three levels — maximum tolerable, maximum acceptable and maximum desirable — with standards applicable for various periods of discharge. The most stringent standard, the maximum desirable level, is meant to "define the long term goal for air quality and provide a basis for an anti-degradation policy for the unpolluted parts of the country and for the continuing development of control technology" (*The Canada Gazette*, Part I, August 7, 1976, p. 3898).

In uninhabited areas, where there is no foreseeable threat of air quality degradation, an anti-degradation policy means little. If an anti-degradation policy is to be implemented anywhere, it should, I think, be applicable in the Mackenzie Valley and Western Arctic where the present air quality is high but is threatened by industrial development. The following recommendation therefore seems to me to be in keeping with stated government policy.

20. *Emissions from pipeline development shall be controlled in the Mackenzie Valley so that ambient air quality figures do not exceed "maximum desirable levels" as defined in the Clean Air Act: Ambient Air Quality Objectives (The Canada Gazette, Part II, Vol. 108, No. 11, and Vol. 109, No. 3).*

But is this control practicable under normal conditions? Temperature inversions must be regarded as normal, for this condition prevails from one-half to two-thirds of the time in winter in the Mackenzie Valley. During a temperature inversion, pollutants are discharged into the air as though into a closed container, the lid of which is removed only when the weather changes. As a result, under inversion conditions, emissions often accumulate for days at a time, and ice fog forms spontaneously if the temperature drops below -40°C.

21. *Constraints placed on the pipeline project to maintain air quality must reflect northern conditions, such as temperature inversions, which inhibit dilution and dispersal of atmospheric pollutants. (See Facilities Complexes and Equipment Operations.)*

Noise

The control of noise is as much a part of environmental conservation as the maintenance of water quality and of natural landscapes. The only redeeming features of noise pollution are that it is often of short duration, and that it usually leaves no visible scars when it stops. Nevertheless, intermittent or sustained noise has an overwhelming influence on overall environmental values from both a human and a wildlife perspective. Noise cannot be ignored because its effects, although not necessarily the sound itself, can and do linger on in the form of abandoned wildlife ranges, staging areas and nesting sites, and a general lessening of the usefulness of the region. In yet another sense, and one that I do not discuss here because it is adequately dealt with in existing codes, noise can be an occupational hazard for health and safety reasons.

Environmental Aspects of Noise

Noise is measured in decibels (dBA) on a scale that is not linear, but is based on doubling the apparent loudness of noise to the human ear with every additional seven to 10 dBA. Zero dBA, the lower end of the scale, is at the threshold of hearing. The level of conversation is about 65 dBA, and 120-140 dBA is at the threshold of pain. To place environmental noise levels in context, in a tundra environment under calm conditions, natural noise levels are less than 15 dBA (Dr. George Thiessen, National Research Council, Ottawa, personal communication, August 1977); in an open alpine meadow, with the rustling of grasses and brush and the distant sound of tree movement, Dailey and Redman reported the background level to be about 30 dBA under low wind conditions of three to five miles per hour, but to increase to about 35 dBA in a mature coniferous forest under the same conditions (*Guidelines for Roadless Area Campsite Spacing to Minimize Impact of Human-Related Noises*, 1973, p. 12). They also pointed out that noise must be reduced to 15 dBA *less* than the background level of

the setting before it is muffled by background noise (p. 16). Generally, noise levels decrease by six dBA for each doubling of the distance from its source. This figure may be increased or decreased by topography, vegetation and meteorological conditions.

In recent years, environmental noise pollution has received increased attention from the public and law-makers, a fact attested by the proliferation of arcticles and studies on the subject and by noise control legislation at all levels of government. The sound emission standards for construction equipment recently passed by the Province of Ontario, (Ontario Ministry of the Environment, Publication NPC-115 in Schedule 1 of *Model Municipal Noise Control By-Law*, Revised May 1976), are a good example of an approach that aims at maintaining environmental, and not simply occupational, quality. This trend toward noise abatement as part of the maintenance of overall environmental quality is directly applicable in the North and to the pipeline project in particular. Despite the present use of planes, trucks, snowmobiles, outboard motors and diesel motors in many communities, the North is still a relatively quiet place. This silence is a vital aspect of the habitat for many species of wildlife and is also one of its main attractions for both residents and visitors.

I shall not discuss here the complexities of the production, propagation, attenuation and measurement of sound and the enforcement of its control. But central to all these problems is the fact that sound is both a physical phenomenon and a perceived sensation. The first is objective, scientific, measurable; the latter is highly subjective and personal.

The recommendations I make, here and elsewhere in this report, require compliance with certain standards — in this case, with noise levels measured in decibels. It is a quantitative approach, such as regulatory agencies have traditionally felt bound to use for public health. The approach is not as satisfactory as a protection of environmental quality, but I nevertheless advocate its continued use for that purpose.

This approach, however useful it may be to quantify the problem, is quite inadequate to solve it. It seems to me that the crucial difference is the perceived difference between sound and noise. The distinction should not be made on the basis of intensity or of a decibel reading on a sound meter. The distinction should be made on the basis of acceptability or non-acceptability — on the basis of pleasantness or disagreeableness, of annoyance or disturbance — however difficult it may be to assess these qualities.

Low intensity sounds — lower than noise standards are ever likely to be set — can still be perceived as noise, and they can therefore be considered a disturbance. Disturbance to wildlife need not be manifested in fright or flight reactions to be real and harmful.

Subjective judgment must therefore be added to the quantitative approach to noise control. In attempting this change, we shall have to follow the advice of wildlife experts and to accommodate the feelings of the public. A solely quantitative approach to noise is limited in its application by the very fact that response to it is subjective according to species.

The Environment and Project Noise

It is clear that pipeline construction and operation in the Mackenzie Valley, which will have noise levels in the range of 90 to 140 dBA, will often produce noise that may be considered environmental pollution over an area several miles from its source. Noise will pervade a greater area than any other form of pollution generated by the project. The commonly held impression that transportation by pipeline is quiet is no doubt based on the public's experience with gas mains, water mains and sewage systems in urban areas. But such an analogy is wrong. The pipeline will be a noisy business, both in its construction and in its operation.

Of course, I cannot recommend that pipeline construction and operations should be silent: that is patently impossible. No technology exists (and it may never exist) that would eliminate the variety of noises associated with the construction and operation of industrial developments. But technologies do exist to reduce noise levels. Although noise is increasingly attenuated in the interests of public health and worker safety, we must begin to consider the importance of attenuating noise as a means of mitigating environmental pollution.

When compressor stations are operating, the gas turbine engines, which are comparable to jet aircraft engines, will emit constant noise of very high intensity. Maintenance blowdown (depressurizing the pipeline), with its intermittent but startlingly loud noise, will be confined mainly to compressor station sites, but similar noises will be generated elsewhere along the line, for example during purging. My recommendations on pipeline operations noise are dealt with more fully in the chapter Facilities Complexes and Equipment Operations. As a general principle however:

22. *The pipeline project should be designed in accordance with good noise abatement practice to minimize environmental disturbance, particularly at times and at locations that are critical to wildlife populations and to traditional land use by local people.*

Pipeline construction will employ thousands of pieces of heavy equipment, machinery and vehicles that have the potential for environmental disturbance by making noise. Crawler-type tractors, earth-moving and ditching equipment, air compressors and drills, to name only the most familiar machines, generate noise in the 85-115 dBA range. These noise levels will be generated at wharf sites on the Mackenzie River, at borrow pits, which are scattered over a wide area, and along the right-of-way. Only slightly lower intensities will be generated by road construction and haulage activities.

There seems to be no justification to diminish environmental quality through noise pollution because noise reduction technology is available. Sound emission standards for construction equipment are common in the South, and new standards have been developed for 1980 (Ontario Ministry of the Environment, op. cit.), so there is ample and practicable precedent for standards of noise attentuation in construction activities.

23. *Environmental standards for noise associated with the operation of construction equipment should be developed by the Agency in keeping with the best practicable technology. Special noise abatement practices should be developed for activities in sensitive areas for wildlife. (See Wildlife.)*

Construction noise will be accompanied by noise from associated transportation activities. The movement of supplies and personnel will increase barge, vehicular, helicopter and fixed-wing aircraft traffic, and commercial air traffic will also increase greatly. These sources of noise are discussed further under Facilities Complexes and Equipment Operations and under Wildlife. Blasting, another construction-related noise, is separately discussed under Terrain Considerations: Blasting.

Monitoring and maintenance activities, which will be carried out mainly by aircraft, will produce most of the transportation noise during the post-construction period. The major concerns about this form of continued disturbance are discussed at some length in the chapters entitled Wildlife and Aircraft Control.

Archaeological Sites

Archaeological sites are one aspect of the physical environment that we often overlook. In Volume One, I referred to the prehistory of the North as it is known through archaeological discoveries that have so far been made in, for example, the Old Crow Flats, but I said nothing about the impact of the pipeline upon the part of our national heritage that is represented by as yet undiscovered sites.

Archaeological sites constitute not only an irreplaceable element of our national heritage, they are also an integral part of the history of northern native peoples. The little that we know of the prehistory of the Mackenzie Valley and the Western Arctic suggests that sites there may be rare and small. Their smallness makes them hard to find and particularly susceptible to destruction. As J.V. Wright wrote in his article, "The Destruction of Canada's Prehistory," "Any human or natural force that alters, buries, or floods the earth can be regarded as being potentially destructive to archaeological data" (p. 5). Obviously, such forces include pipeline construction and associated activity. Preliminary studies in the Mackenzie Valley and elsewhere have shown that some disturbance and destruction of archaeological sites is inevitable in a project the size of the proposed pipeline.

Paradoxically, the very process of disturbing the northern

landscape is often the means of finding an archaeological site. The numerous borrow pits, the ditch excavation, and the excavations for other facilities involved in the pipeline project will provide unprecedented opportunities for archaeological and paleoecological studies that would further our knowledge as much as, if not more than, the disturbances would hinder it. This is an opportunity not to be taken lightly. Sites are difficult to find in the boreal forest and logistics are often complex and expensive. Moreover, the density of human population may always have been quite low so that archaeological sites may, in fact, be relatively scarce. We must, therefore, take advantage of any opportunity to provide future generations with a more complete record of past human occupation and environmental evolution in the North.

Existing legislation clearly stipulates that archaeological sites should be protected from both wilful and negligent destruction. The Territorial Land Use Regulations prohibit industrial excavations or other land use operations within 100 feet of a known archaeological site, and whenever an operation encounters a previously unknown site, the operator is instructed to suspend his work and notify the engineer or an inspector of the location and nature of the occurrence.

Embodied in the Yukon Act and the Northwest Territories Act are Archaeological Sites Regulations that stipulate that all archaeological investigations must be conducted under permission of the Minister of Indian Affairs and Northern Development.

It appears that existing law provides a legal framework for the protection of archaeological resources from construction projects, but on a large-scale venture such as the pipeline only the organization of an adequate archaeological project can ensure that this will be done. It is certainly in keeping with this position that the pipeline companies have proposed archaeological work as a complement to the pipeline project.

25. An archaeological program shall be established to identify, protect, excavate and investigate archaeological sites and associated paleoecological materials on or adjacent to lands used by or for the pipeline project. This archaeological program should be funded by the Company and organized under an arrangement between the Company and the Agency with the especial involvement of the Archaeological Survey of Canada, National Museum of Man. The program should be in operation from the time field operations of the Company begin until the pipeline is commissioned and all archaeological field studies and reports are completed.

8 Wildlife

A number of the principal environmental concerns identified in Volume One of my report will be alleviated by implementation of the major environmental recommendations in that volume. My recommendations that no pipeline be built and no energy corridor be established across the Northern Yukon, and that a wilderness park be created in that area, are designed to protect this unique wilderness region. This region includes vital habitat for wildlife and migratory birds on the Arctic Coastal Plain and Old Crow Flats, and, in particular, the critically important calving and summer range of the Porcupine caribou herd.

My recommendations that no pipeline be built and no energy corridor be established across the Mackenzie Delta, together with the recommendations for the white whale sanctuary and bird sanctuaries in the outer Delta area, are designed to protect the unique land-and-water ecosystems that characterize the Delta and the littoral of the Beaufort Sea. Only in this way will it be possible to safeguard the critical life stages of the migratory birds, whales, and other mammals and fish that depend upon this fertile and productive area. In addition, the bird sanctuaries that I proposed along the Mackenzie Valley are designed to protect major populations of migrating and nesting birds at critical localities.

Beyond these recommendations, there must be a wide range of specific measures designed to avoid or to mitigate the adverse effects of construction and operation of a pipeline on mammals, birds and fish. In this chapter and the following chapter on fish, I present the criteria, approaches and standards that I consider appropriate for the protection of these valuable but vulnerable resources.

Of course, the pipeline project will inevitably have some environmental impacts that cannot be mitigated. So I emphasize the importance of minimizing disturbance and of maintaining land, water and air, insofar as possible, in their natural state. With regard to mammals, birds and fish, I focus my concern on critical habitats and critical life stages — on the tracts of land and water of limited size that are vital to the survival of whole populations of certain species at certain times of the year. The recommendations I made regarding

withdrawals of land for a wilderness park, a whale sanctuary and bird sanctuaries offer the firmest protection to such habitat, but further measures are needed. My recommendations for the protection of birds relate to their migration routes and their nesting, moulting and staging areas; those for mammals concentrate on calving, lambing or den sites, on winter habitats, and on travel routes. I emphasize protection for species that are harvested by local people, as well as rare species, such as the peregrine falcon, the survival of which is of national or international concern.

The great challenge we face in the Mackenzie Valley is to maintain its living resources, a challenge that demands the same resolve with which we plan the development of northern energy and transportation systems.

Mammals

Caribou and Reindeer

In Volume One, I discussed in some detail the importance and vulnerability of the Porcupine caribou herd and why I was convinced that a gas pipeline should not be built across the Northern Yukon. My major recommendations that no pipeline be built across that area, but that a wilderness park be established there, were designed to offer the firmest protection for the habitat of this herd. I also mentioned the Bluenose and Bathurst caribou herds, which winter close to the Mackenzie Valley; the woodland caribou, which are year-round Valley residents; and the semi-domesticated reindeer, which live in the Tuktoyaktuk peninsula.

According to testimony before the Inquiry, the Bluenose herd once wintered in the Mackenzie Delta and ranged west across to the foothills. In recent years, this herd has been reoccupying winter range near the Delta, and it is possible that gas production facilities and the pipeline may disturb the herd in that region. The herd's apparent increase in numbers and its expansion of range is and will continue to be an important feature in the renewable resource economy of the people of the Mackenzie Delta and of the lower Mackenzie Valley.

The large-scale movements of migratory caribou herds allow them to use a wide range of habitat and environmental conditions. Nevertheless, the loss of any particular portion of a herd's total range may reduce its vitality and potential population.

The construction of a gas pipeline, the completion of the Mackenzie Highway, other developments, and increased access along the east bank of the Mackenzie River may, in my opinion, halt the continued westward expansion of this herd. The reduction of territory into which this herd might expand is, of course, significant, but it does not have the same serious implications for the future of the herd that the Dempster Highway and a pipeline along it would have on the Porcupine herd.

DEMPSTER HIGHWAY

In my discussion of the Porcupine caribou herd in Volume One (pp. 42-43), I drew attention to the impacts on the herd during migration and on its winter range caused by the existence of the Dempster Highway, by traffic on the highway, and by increased hunting related to the highway. These concerns have now been reinforced by the National Energy Board's decision to favour the possibility of a gas pipeline along a Dempster Route as well as by recent experience on the Dempster Highway.

The Dempster Highway and any pipeline along it would dissect the herd's winter range and might cut the herd off from a substantial part of that range. Although the Dempster Highway is not yet complete, there is evidence that the access it now provides to the herd's winter range and migration routes has greatly increased both subsistence and sport hunting in the region. Canadian Arctic Resources Committee, the Yukon Conservation Society and others, including Ronald Jakimchuk, a biologist who has spent years studying this herd, believe that the Dempster Highway poses a threat to its well-being. The threat comes from uncontrolled harvesting and from the obstruction to herd movements that the highway itself and traffic along it represents.

The whole point about the Dempster from an environmental point of view is that the decision to build the highway was made without adequate environmental assessment. But the highway is in place now. It is virtually complete, so we shall have to devise measures to cope with it. The highway must be our principal concern so far as protection of the Porcupine caribou herd's winter range is concerned.

I consider that measures are needed now to protect the Porcupine herd on its wintering range near the Dempster Highway. If we can devise measures to cope with the highway, we may, in due course, be able to cope with a pipeline along the same route if it comes. I deal with these measures in detail in the section on Wildlife Management

and Research, but I think this recommendation is appropriate here.

1. A restricted hunting zone should be established that extends two miles on either side of the Dempster Highway and of all connecting access roads and seismic lines within the winter range of the herd, but with provisions made for continued traditional use of this land by native people. All vehicle traffic and construction activity on the Dempster Highway should be controlled during the caribou herd's seasonal migrations through the region.

The Alaska Highway Pipeline Inquiry, in its report, made this statement on our present knowledge of the environment along the Dempster Highway:

> First, there is not sufficient information, nor has there been adequate study, of the Dempster Highway as a pipeline route. Further environmental, economic, and social research is necessary before this route may be seriously considered as an alternative to a pipeline along the Mackenzie Valley. There is an urgent need for detailed and extensive studies on the Porcupine caribou herd, and for studies of the probable impact on the herd of increased human activity along the Dempster Highway. Time is essential to permit adequate study of these subjects.
>
> Apart from the Porcupine caribou herd, there are other environmental consequences of a pipeline along the Dempster Highway that must be studied. No doubt much may be learned by the experience of constructing a pipeline across the southern Yukon, but, until we know much more about the Dempster Highway route, we cannot make an informed comparison of the advantages and disadvantages of that route and the one along the Mackenzie Valley. We therefore recommend that at least five years be given to studies of this nature. [p. 130]

I cite this recommendation because it is fundamental to the protection of the caribou herd and to the pending decisions regarding a pipeline along the Dempster Highway.

2. Before a pipeline along the Dempster Highway is given further consideration, the recommendation of the Alaska Highway Pipeline Inquiry should be implemented and a thorough comparison should be made of the alternative routes.

BARRIERS AND DIRECT MORTALITY

The possible effects of roads and other obstacles as barriers to caribou herds vary from minor diversions in the line of travel to delay in herd movement, increased exposure to hunters or to predators in unsuitable habitat, and abandonment of part or all of a traditional range. It has been demonstrated in Scandinavia and Alaska that highways and railways do not in and of themselves cause reindeer or caribou to abandon their ranges. However, in conjunction with heavy traffic and with hunting, which is of special concern (See Wildlife: Wildlife Management and Research), the herds are likely to abandon their ranges, with the result that a herd's population declines — perhaps drastically.

During construction, it should be possible to avoid most contact with the migrating caribou by the careful scheduling of work, including contingency planning, and by continuously monitoring the progress of the migration. Despite wide annual and seasonal variations in the use of ranges and of travel routes, the traditional use of certain locations, such as river crossings, allows observers to make some predictions about migration.

A number of activities related to pipeline construction could constitute both a physical barrier and a direct threat to caribou. An operating spread, complete with open ditch, strung pipe and operating equipment, or a well-travelled highway or haul road could present a formidable hazard to a migrating herd or to individual animals. Snow fences in unbroken lines perpendicular to a migration path, deep-drifted snow associated with roads or fences, steep road embankments, and elevated portions of the pipeline and feeder lines could also be serious barriers to caribou movements.

The main concern, as I emphasized in Volume One, is the Porcupine caribou herd. There is no similar large migrating herd in the Mackenzie Valley, although the fact that the Bluenose caribou herd winters not far east of the proposed route and part of the herd winters in the vicinity of the route, suggests the possibility of some impact on it. Woodland caribou in the Mackenzie Valley could also be affected, but their low density and relatively local migrations should keep the impact on a minor scale.

3. The Company shall schedule construction and all other activities associated with the project so that barriers to groups of caribou during migration or on their winter range are minimized. The Company shall, therefore, prepare detailed schedules, including contingency plans, to handle annual variations in the patterns of migration and occupation of wintering grounds. These schedules shall be approved by the Agency before the Company proceeds with construction.

4. Before and during construction, a monitoring program shall be maintained to define the seasonal distribution and day-to-day movements of caribou during critical periods. This monitoring program will form the basis of the Company's contingency plans to safeguard the well-being of caribou.

5. The Company shall submit to the Agency for approval, measures that will prevent caribou from being obstructed or entrapped by project-related activities. These measures may include but are not limited to the scheduling of construction to minimize the time lapse between trenching and backfilling; the construction of earthen plugs in open trenches to permit the animals to pass across or to escape from the trench; and the skewing or stacking of pipe strung out along the right-of-way to enable the animals to move freely.

6. The Company shall submit for approval by the Agency steps that will be taken to minimize any disturbance of, or interference with, the movement of concentrations of caribou that approach a construction site. These measures may

include, but are not limited to, backfilling parts of the trench, moving pipe strung out along the right-of-way, and shutting down operations.

7. The Agency should ensure that the design and maintenance proposals for any of the project's rights-of-way guarantee free and easy passage to the caribou. In particular, the Company shall design and maintain roads to ensure free and easy passage of caribou. Snow shall be controlled and cleared so that caribou movements are not impeded by long, unbroken stretches of snow fence or of deep drifts or snowbanks caused by snow fences or by road clearing. Snow fences shall be removed in spring before the caribou arrive.

8. To keep to a minimum the number of caribou killed as a direct result of increased hunting in the project area, the Agency, in cooperation with the Company and the relevant government departments, should restrict access to the pipeline right-of-way and related facilities to personnel directly associated with the project. (See Wildlife: Wildlife Management and Research.)

9. To avoid disturbance and mortality to caribou, a highway traffic management plan should be developed by the appropriate authorities for areas in which there are concentrations of caribou. Such measures as speed limits, convoying and staggered scheduling of traffic, and periodic closures of highways should be considered.

HABITAT AND DISTURBANCE

In the Mackenzie Delta and Mackenzie Valley, the construction of gas plants, feeder lines, compressor stations and the main pipeline will not pre-empt any significant portion of the range of the woodland caribou, the Bluenose caribou herd or the reindeer. There are, however, some overall concerns about habitat that are related to fire and to emissions from facilities, especially because the production facilities and the pipeline are concentrated in the Delta, where a major part of the reindeer range and part of the Bluenose caribou herd's range is located.

The destruction of critical winter range by wildfires must be considered, although such fires will not necessarily be caused by activities associated with the pipeline project. There is some disagreement over what use caribou can make of recently burned areas, but it is evident that the animals avoid areas that have recently burned. The regeneration and growth of the lichens that are a major part of the caribou diet is very slow in the North, and for many years burned areas are unsuitable for pasturage. Although the number of fires may increase because of activity associated with the pipeline, better communications and improved access may help to reduce the total acreage burned.

10. The Company shall develop contingency plans for the suppression of fires and give high priority to fire prevention and control in areas of important caribou habitat. (See Terrain Considerations: Forest Fire Prevention and Suppression.)

Disturbance from a number of pipeline-related sources, including aircraft flights, machinery, human presence and compressor station noise, is potentially one of the most serious impacts on birds and mammals and is particularly significant for caribou. Although construction is scheduled for winter, a time when most animal species are widely dispersed, it is a time when the food supply is low and the animals' energy reserves are becoming depleted. The effects of disturbance can be severe.

Uncontrolled aircraft flights are probably the most serious form of disturbance. I deal with this in detail in the chapter on Aircraft Control, and make only one general recommendation here.

11. To minimize aircraft disturbance to caribou, the Company shall control the flying heights and the frequency of project-related air traffic over occupied caribou range.

Hunting and the increased presence of humans, which follows from easier access to a region, are other major forms of disturbance, both of which I discuss in more detail in Wildlife: Wildlife Management and Research.

If disturbance of wildlife is to be kept within acceptable levels, a number of regulations will have to be imposed. Many of my recommendations on this subject apply equally to birds and fish, and they may be found in relevant sections. Others that are related to project activities are contained in the appropriate chapters of Part Three: The Project.

White Whales

In Volume One, I dealt extensively with white whales and recommended that a whale sanctuary be established in the west Mackenzie Bay area and that no pipeline be built across Shallow Bay. These measures are necessary if we are to protect the calving areas of the Beaufort Sea population of white whales, but they will not totally protect the whales. The sanctuary is, in itself, a compromise between the needs of the oil and gas industry and the necessity for preserving critical habitat of the whales. Thus, my concern for the well-being of these marine mammals does not end with those measures. As I explained in Volume One, there is a great deal of gas and oil exploration going on in the Delta and offshore in the Beaufort Sea. This activity will not cease, even if a gas pipeline is delayed or is not allowed to cross Shallow Bay. Exploration and other activities, which will extend well into the future, continue to pose a danger to the white whales of the Beaufort Sea through increased disturbance from water and air traffic and because of the risk of oil pollution.

Investigations to date have not been detailed enough to draw firm conclusions about the effects of disturbance on white whales. In *The 1975 White Whale Study*, Slaney and Company summarized their four years of investigations on the impact of construction of offshore drilling islands and of barge traffic on the whales in this way:

Boat traffic has, in some instances, resulted in short-term changes in whale distribution. Reaction of whales to boats is variable, probably due to the interaction of a complex of factors....

The possibility of adverse effects on whales and whale hunting as a result of current levels of industrial activity does exist, however, there is no evidence suggesting that the overall pattern of whale movement and/or hunting has been affected. [p. 41]

Dr. David Sergeant and Wybrand Hoek, in their testimony before the Inquiry, suggested that more detailed studies of the effects of waterborne noise on whales are required. They cited evidence from Churchill, Manitoba, where whales, because of increasing and continued disturbance, are believed to have abandoned their traditional calving area in favour of another area where they are not disturbed. The evidence stated that the white whales were most sensitive to waterborne disturbance during calving and were somewhat less sensitive to airborne disturbance.

Many aspects of the white whale's life cycle are not yet well understood. My concern is that whales outside of the proposed sanctuary may be adversely affected by the host of activities that are, and will be, impinging upon the white whale habitat in the Beaufort Sea as a consequence of oil and gas exploration, development, production and transportation.

Although existing levels of activity are producing only short-term effects, increased activity could result in long-term changes in the whale's pattern of behaviour, with consequences that could lead to a decline in the Beaufort Sea population of the species. Such changes could, of course, have a serious effect on the economy of native people who harvest white whales.

12. Shipping corridors should be established in the waters adjoining the outer Mackenzie Delta to avoid disturbing white whales, particularly during their calving season.

13. The Company, the Agency and the responsible government departments shall protect the white whales from disturbance by prohibiting harassment by low flying aircraft and water craft. Also, because information on the effect of air cushion vehicles on white whales is lacking, these vehicles should not be operated near the whales during their critical seasons.

Oil spills, whether from a blowout or from a tanker accident, are another potential threat to the whales. Although most adult whales could probably avoid an oil slick, females that are calving or nursing might be reluctant to move from the warm estuarine waters. And, if they did move, probably many newborn calves would lose body heat and die in the cold oceanic waters. An oil spill could also taint the whales' food.

14. Oil spill contingency plans prepared by government and industry shall outline measures to protect and clean up areas used by white whales for calving. (See Management of Fuels and Hazardous Substances.)

15. The design and construction of feeder lines that connect offshore wells to the onshore pipeline shall avoid the areas and seasons that are of critical importance to the white whale population of the Beaufort Sea.

Moose

Throughout the Mackenzie Valley, moose are an important species in the native economy. Moose range widely and are found throughout the forested region and, occasionally, above the tree line. The greatest cause for concern is that improved access will lead to increased moose hunting during and after pipeline construction. According to Dr. Peter Lent, a biologist with the University of Alaska, this has already happened in Alaska.

16. To help control access and hunting, the Company, the Agency, and the relevant government departments should restrict access to the right-of-way and to related facilities to personnel performing work on the project. (See Wildlife: Wildlife Management and Research.)

During winter, when the movement of moose is impeded by deep snow, weather and limited habitat, they gather in areas such as river valleys that provide shelter and food. Moose are sensitive to disturbance at this time, when, like the caribou, they are in a negative energy situation. Additional stress caused by disturbance would be detrimental to their well-being.

17. Wherever practicable, the pipeline right-of-way and facilities, such as haul roads and compressor stations, shall be located to minimize disturbance to critical moose wintering areas and, in particular, to class 1 moose habitat (as defined by Watson et. al., 1973.)

18. The Company shall minimize disturbance to moose by instituting measures such as those recommended in the section on Caribou and Reindeer above and in the chapter on Aircraft Control.

Foxes and Wolves

Many witnesses from northern communities explained their fears of hydrocarbon developments in general and of oil spills in particular by describing what might happen to the arctic food chain. I dealt with this subject at some length in Volume One, but foxes and wolves are good cases in point. Arctic foxes are known to scavenge the seal kills of polar bears. Seals could be regionally depleted as a result of an oil spill, so although not directly involved, the arctic fox could certainly be affected in a serious way by activities associated with industrial development. Similarly, the decline of any of the ungulate populations, especially the barren-ground caribou herds, would affect the wolf population. We have to view foxes and wolves — indeed all animals — in the overall context of the food chain, but my discussion of them here will be limited to the species themselves.

The pipeline project will affect only local populations of arctic foxes, coloured foxes and wolves. The concerns for these species arise mainly in two areas: the disturbance of the animals and their habitat; and the attraction of these animals to waste disposal sites.

All three of these species den in high, well-drained soils — soils that frequently provide prime borrow materials for construction. Because the pipeline will be constructed during the winter, disturbance during the denning period may not be a problem since these species occupy their dens in the spring. However, the danger remains that denning sites may be altered physically or destroyed by the alignment of the right-of-way or by their exploitation for borrow material. This could be significant because all three species tend to use the same den sites year after year.

Many of the reported arctic fox dens are on the Yukon Coastal Plain. My recommendation for a wilderness park there should protect the habitat of that species as well as of the wolf population. Throughout the Mackenzie Valley and Western Arctic the dens of arctic fox, together with those of the coloured fox and wolf, will need protection.

19. During final design, the Company shall identify all arctic fox, coloured fox and wolf dens within one-half mile of the right-of-way and other pipeline facilities so that the project can be designed, located and scheduled to avoid prime denning areas. Unless authorized by the Agency, construction shall avoid such areas by a distance of at least 100 yards.

The habituation of foxes and wolves to waste disposal sites and other camp facilities has always been a problem in the North and it was of concern during the construction of the Alyeska pipeline. Concentrations of these animals around campsites may become a nuisance, and could cause problems associated with rabies.

20. Every effort shall be made to prevent foxes and wolves from becoming a nuisance around campsites. To this end:

The feeding of foxes and wolves shall be prohibited.

The Company shall manage all domestic and other waste in a manner that will minimize the attraction of foxes and wolves to construction sites and facilities. Fencing shall be installed around all incinerator, food storage and domestic waste handling areas. (See Waste Management.)

Bears

Grizzly, polar and black bears inhabit the Mackenzie Valley and Mackenzie Delta in varying densities. The grizzly bear of the Delta and central Arctic, referred to as the barren-ground grizzly, may be taxonomically distinct from the grizzly bear of the Yukon. If this is the case, the barren-ground grizzly bear would be considered endangered. Its special relation to the tundra environment gives the species evolutionary interest and significance, and every effort should be made to maintain a healthy population.

Interactions between men and bears are usually viewed as threats to human safety, and bears are therefore usually eliminated from areas in which there is human activity. As is the case with foxes, the concerns for bears arise mainly in two areas: the attraction of waste disposal sites and disturbance of the animals and of their denning habitat.

Because of ineffective waste management practices in the North, bears have been attracted to areas of human activity and many of them have been destroyed in the name of human safety. This is a problem that can be solved only by improved techniques of waste disposal. Except when human safety is immediately threatened, only an authorized government representative may dispatch the animal as the last resort after all other possibilities have been exhausted.

21. The Company shall collect, store and dispose of all domestic waste in a manner that will minimize the attraction of bears to construction sites and facilities. (See Waste Management.)

22. The feeding of bears should be regarded as an act that threatens human life. Any person feeding bears should be immediately dismissed, reported to the Agency, and then returned to point of hire. Persons or companies who, through negligence or otherwise, provide bears with an opportunity to become habituated to waste materials should be prosecuted.

23. The Company shall ensure that each working unit (survey crew, right-of-way clearing crew, etc.) likely to encounter bears is equipped and familiar with the use of approved devices to scare bears away from centres of human activity. Each working unit shall be equipped with only one sealed firearm for use only when there is a real and immediate threat to human safety. Each firing of this firearm should be reported, and it must be resealed without delay by an authorized representative of the Agency.

24. The Company shall immediately report to the Agency any bear that may be considered a nuisance or that threatens human safety.

Although construction of the pipeline will alter bear habitat only minimally, certain critical habitats must be protected. Denning sites are found on high, well-drained slopes, which are also good locations for borrow material. Bears occupy their dens during winter, and any occupied dens must be protected from disturbance. If a bear is disturbed and forced to abandon a den in winter, the lack of food, inability to dig a new den in the frozen soil, and the cold would certainly lead to the bear's death. At other times of the year, extended harassment might deplete stored reserves of energy or cause death by physical exhaustion or overheating.

25. During final design, the Company shall identify bear dens within one-half mile of the right-of-way and other pipeline facilities so that the project can be designed, located and scheduled to avoid these sites. To prevent disturbance to denning bears, construction activities, especially blasting, shall avoid occupied dens by a distance of at least 500 yards, or as otherwise approved by the Agency.

26. The Company shall institute measures to ensure that there is no harassment of bears by aircraft and vehicles and that encounters or conflicts between men and bears are minimized. (See Facilities Complexes and Equipment Operations, and Aircraft Control.)

All three species of bears are hunted for food and sport, but the polar bear and grizzly bear are regarded as prize trophies. The harvest of polar bears is controlled by a quota system, whereas the harvest of grizzly and black bears is controlled by Territorial Game Regulations. Improved access, increased numbers of people and better facilities could have an adverse impact on the grizzly bear population.

27. To prevent overharvesting, the government should review existing game regulations respecting grizzly bears. Particular consideration should be given to suggestions made by Pearson (1976) regarding new game regulations that might reduce overharvesting and permit bear populations to be maintained.

Birds

It may be difficult for many Canadians to understand why it is necessary to make recommendations to preserve birds and their habitat. There has been a tendency to downplay the concerns expressed about northern bird populations by biologists and by others for whom birds are important. In most cases, I think this dismissive attitude is based on a misunderstanding of what is now at stake in northern Canada. The distribution of birds in the North is very different from what most of us have seen in southern Canada.

As I explained in Volume One, the Mackenzie Valley and, to a lesser extent, the shores of the Beaufort Sea, are major flyways for millions of geese, swans, ducks, gulls, terns and the many other species that converge on this region every summer to nest and raise their young. During these critical periods of their life cycles, these international bird populations rely on the habitat provided by the Mackenzie Valley, the Mackenzie Delta and the Beaufort Sea coast. Nature, political boundaries and treaties have made these populations a Canadian responsibility.

At least 230 species in 41 families of birds are nesters, migrants or casual visitors in the Western Arctic. Many of these species are continental in their distribution, so the proportion of their total population that might be affected by pipeline-related activities is small. Some species, however, are vulnerable to pipeline construction and operation either because a total population is relatively small or because a significant proportion of a total population gathers within the project area at some vital stage of its life cycle. For some species, a significant proportion of their critical habitat lies within the proposed project area.

Every species of bird that is found in the area is an integral part of both northern and continental ecosystems. A rational approach to the problem of protecting these birds requires us to define exactly what is at stake and then to devise a practical means of ensuring that what must be protected is protected. No amount of research and certainly no recommendations that I can offer will afford complete protection to all of the birds everywhere in the region. Our objective, therefore, is to permit both international migratory populations and local populations to continue to use this region year after year without having their numbers progressively diminished.

With this in mind, I turn now to the critical habitats and critical life stages of northern birds, to those tracts of land and water that are vital to the survival of whole populations of birds at certain times of the year.

There are three major groups of birds that must be protected and, if measures are taken to ensure their protection, many other species will also be protected. The first group comprises the rare or endangered species, such as the peregrine falcon, the whooping crane and the Eskimo curlew, that are of national or international concern. Raptors and, in particular, the peregrine falcon, gyrfalcon, bald eagle, golden eagle and osprey make up the second group. Finally, there are the waterfowl, especially the species that nest in colonies or form large, vulnerable congregations during moulting and staging.

Areas Important to Birds

In Volume One, I made recommendations to protect critical habitats and life stages of birds by specially designating certain land areas that are vital to them. It was, in part, the very heavy avian use of the Northern Yukon that led me to recommend the creation there of a wilderness park. I also recommended that human use of certain areas be strictly regulated to protect important waterfowl and falcon habitats and I proposed the outer Mackenzie Delta, the International Biological Programme sites at Campbell Hills–Dolomite Lake, Willow (Brackett) Lake and Mills Lake as bird sanctuaries. I also noted that many islands in the Mackenzie River are important to migratory waterfowl and, I suggested that, at some time, some of them should be designated as bird sanctuaries.

The designation of lands on which industrial activity should be prohibited or appropriately controlled is only one way of protecting birds. When we have in view a specific project, such as a pipeline, a second method — that of specific regulations — is also appropriate. In my opinion, the protection of birds and their habitat can be achieved in three ways. First, the pipeline route and the location of its associated facilities can be adjusted. Second, engineering designs that minimize impact can be used: noise attenuation devices fall

into this category. Third, the timing of construction activities can be scheduled so that birds would not be disturbed during their seasonally critical life stages.

28. *Birds and their habitat shall be protected from adverse effects associated with surveying, construction, operation and maintenance of the pipeline. Before construction begins, the Agency shall identify important and restricted areas and periods for birds, particularly for raptors, and waterfowl, and shall devise whatever restrictions may be necessary on project location, engineering design, project scheduling, access and aircraft activities in these areas and during these periods.*

PROTECTION FROM SPILLS

Spills of oil, fuel and other hazardous substances are one of the greatest threats to birds and their habitat. Biologists spoke at length at the Inquiry about the devastating impact of oil spills on birds and emphasized that we are not able to rehabilitate birds that come into contact with oil, even in temperate climates. Waterfowl in particular are threatened by such spills. If extensive areas of waterfowl habitat or small areas used by large numbers of individual birds are affected by a spill, the effect could be catastrophic.

I dealt with the problem of spills at some length in Chapter Six of Volume One and I make specific recommendations elsewhere in this volume on the means of minimizing the chances of a spill. But because our ability to handle large spills is rudimentary and because the effects could be so severe, I make the following recommendation with specific reference to birds.

29. *The Company's plans for the transportation, handling, storage and disposal of fuels, lubricants and other toxic materials shall demonstrate that bird habitat, and particularly waterfowl habitat, will be avoided or in some other way protected from the risks of spills. Contingency plans shall demonstrate that the Company has fully considered and has the technical, logistical and financial ability to protect critical waterfowl habitat. (See Management of Fuels and Other Hazardous Substances.)*

PHYSICAL DISTURBANCE OF LAND AREAS

Other general issues related to bird habitat warrant mention. The bars and islands of the Mackenzie River constitute important mating and resting areas for migrating birds in the spring. Physical alteration of these areas may affect the birds' chances of breeding success and survival during the summer. I have already recommended in Volume One that these islands be designated as bird sanctuaries.

Specific activities related to the project will affect various aspects of terrain and water that are important for birds, particularly waterfowl, which tend to congregate in large numbers at various times in their life cycle. For example, trenching and other activities in wetland areas may lead to the draining or drowning of waterfowl nesting and feeding habitat, and excess siltation from stream crossings could affect waterfowl food supply. The mouths of the tributaries of the Mackenzie River are particularly important habitat.

30. Degradation of important bird habitat such as the river islands of the Mackenzie River, the beach bars of the Arctic Coast, wetlands and the riparian vegetation of streams and lakes shall be avoided, wherever possible, and shall otherwise be kept to a minimum. Critical habitat that has been degraded shall be restored following the construction period.

DISTURBANCE FROM NOISE AND PEOPLE

There is much more to the disturbance of birds than simply startling them. If that were the only problem, the birds would probably fly from the area, alight elsewhere and carry on as normal. The problems of disturbance are far more complex. The disturbance of birds during critical life stages or in critical areas may lead to abandonment of nesting sites and death. Take the case of the snow geese: because they nest in colonies, any continuous disturbance of them during their nesting season could cause the loss of one year's brood through exposure of the eggs or young to the weather or predation; similarly, if snow geese were harassed on their fall staging grounds and were, therefore, not able to store up enough energy, large numbers of them could die on their southward migration.

Most construction activity will take place in winter when there are few birds in the area. Nonetheless, during the summers of the construction period, there will be movements of aircraft and barges, activities at stockpile sites, compressor sites and airfields, and perhaps operations at gravel pits and other activities along the pipeline route. During the operation of the pipeline, there will be noise from compressors and from pipe blowdowns, aircraft and barge movements, vehicles, and repair and maintenance work. I make specific recommendations on many of these activities in Part Three: The Project, but it is worthwhile to review here the scope of the problem in its ornithological context and to make appropriate recommendations to mitigate the adverse effects.

31. As far as practicable, construction and maintenance activities shall be scheduled for winter or for other times of the year when birds are not present. Activities undertaken when birds are in the area shall be strictly controlled to limit the extent and level of disturbance.

There will be substantial numbers of people working at wharf, stockpile and compressor station sites during the summer. The amount of disturbance to the bird populations near any given facility will depend on the type and frequency of the disturbance emanating from the site, its effects on surrounding vegetation and topography, and the sensitivity of particular species to disturbance.

The location of pipeline facilities and of ground-based activities will be critical to the well-being of raptors and colonial nesting birds. Any source of disturbance that is immediately adjacent to the nesting areas of these birds could

have a serious effect on them. Both groups are particularly sensitive to human presence when they are nesting and rearing their broods. Unrestricted human access to their nesting areas could lead to reduced reproduction of these species.

Compressor stations located near sensitive wildlife areas are of particular concern. I note that the National Energy Board has accepted Foothills' undertaking to keep noise from compressor stations down to 60 decibels (dBA) at the fence line. However, research commissioned by the pipeline companies has suggested that even that level of noise can have significant effects on bird populations. Staging snow geese vacated an area within 1.5 miles of a compressor-station-sound simulator that had a noise level of 50 dBA at 1,000 feet, and it was suggested that a level of 56 dBA at 1,000 feet would cause geese to vacate an area within a 2.5-mile radius. Extensive observations of geese during the drilling of Imperial Oil's gas well at Taglu suggested that staging geese would vacate an area within a 5- to 10-mile radius around a compressor station, depending on the amount of aircraft disturbance associated with the site.

32. The Company shall locate all facilities and design all devices associated with those facilities to minimize disturbance to birds. In particular, noise attenuation devices shall be installed on all appropriate equipment to reduce noise to the lowest practicable level. In certain locations and at certain times that are deemed to be sensitive for birds, the Agency may require special noise attenuation equipment and procedures. (See Facilities Complexes and Equipment Operations.)

33. Upon request, the Company shall provide the Agency with all data used to assess the cost-effectiveness of various levels of attenuation and to assess the impact of various levels of noise on birds at any construction site.

Of all the forms of disturbance to birds that may be caused by industrial development in the North, uncontrolled movement of aircraft is potentially one of the most serious. The degree of susceptibility to such disturbance will vary among the species, depending on the season, weather and location.

Ornithological studies submitted to Arctic Gas have suggested that aircraft disturbance may cause gyrfalcons to abandon their nests and that staging snow geese may be disturbed within nine miles by a light aircraft flown at an altitude of 10,500 feet. The results of many of these studies are inconsistent, and firm conclusions based on them are not possible. However, because aircraft will be a major means of transportation during construction and operation of the pipeline, some form of control will have to be exercised to regulate the altitudes and frequencies of aircraft flights.

The protection of birds through the regulation of aircraft is such an important issue that I discuss it in a separate chapter entitled Aircraft Control. There I make proposals for flight corridors and the regulation of flight ceilings and schedules so that critical locations and life stages of the bird populations that are susceptible to disturbance may be avoided.

Increases in river traffic during the construction and operation of the pipeline and related facilities are also a source of disturbance for birds. The Mackenzie Valley is one of North America's most important flyways. In spring, the northward migrating birds generally pass through before the barging season on the river begins. But in years when waterfowl, especially geese and swans, may not have stored up enough energy for their flight south, the islands and bars in the Mackenzie River become extremely important to them as resting and feeding areas. Barge traffic at this time might so disturb the birds that many of them would fail to complete their flights south. Increased barge traffic may also disturb ducks in the Beaver and Mills Lakes areas, but it is in the Mackenzie Delta that disturbance from such traffic would be most serious. There waterfowl use the river islands and channels for moulting and staging sites from July to September.

34. *The routing and scheduling of water traffic shall be regulated to minimize the impact on birds and their habitats during sensitive periods in the Mackenzie Delta and elsewhere along the Mackenzie River. Water traffic shall avoid areas identified as critical to bird populations. Similarly, docking and other shoreline facilities shall be located to avoid the disturbance of such areas. (See Facilities Complexes and Equipment Operations.)*

Rare or Endangered Species

At present in Canada, there is no official federal recognition of any rare or endangered species, and because there is no national policy or legislation for dealing with such species, the designation of a species as rare or endangered may be highly subjective. Under these circumstances, it is difficult to ascertain the relative significance of the designation of a species as rare, uncommon or endangered.

During the Inquiry, mention was made of many species, the majority of which are birds, that biologists consider to be rare or endangered. The peregrine falcon, whooping crane and Eskimo curlew are the best known of this group, which also includes the Hudsonian godwit, buff-breasted sandpiper and Thule white-footed goose. Except for the peregrine falcon, little attention was focused on any of these species, perhaps because our knowledge of them is limited. My concern for the peregrine falcon is dealt with below in my recommendations on raptors. The breeding habitat of the whooping crane is already protected, and it is unlikely to be affected by the present alignment of the pipeline. So little is known of the ecology of the other rare and endangered birds that it is impossible at present to make recommendations to protect them. Continuing research will reveal more information about these birds, but in the meantime recommendations to protect other species will hopefully protect rare species.

We have an obligation to do all we can to ensure the survival of species of birds that may be in danger of extinction, especially if that danger is caused by human disturbance.

35. *The government should develop a national policy and should draw up legislation to provide for the protection of rare and endangered species of birds.*

Of course, the problem of rare and endangered species goes well beyond bird species. The bowhead whale inhabits the offshore waters of the Beaufort Sea and is listed by the International Whaling Commission as being endangered. The barren-ground grizzly bear that I mention in Wildlife: Mammals may also be considered rare or endangered.

Raptors

The raptors (birds of prey), that nest in the Western Arctic constitute a significant proportion of the remaining North American populations of these species. There are nesting sites all along the Mackenzie Valley and, in particular, in the Campbell Hills and Franklin Mountains.

Raptors such as the falcons, bald eagles, golden eagles and ospreys are fairly common in the North, although their populations elsewhere in North America are low. It is necessary to give northern populations of all raptors attention, but it is the peregrine falcon that requires particular protection. Here is what Finney and Lang said in a report prepared for Foothills Pipe Lines Ltd.:

> The population [of the peregrine falcon] is at a dangerously low level and there is no indication that recovery is imminent. Due to the sensitivity of the peregrine population, developers have to face the fact that the destruction of a single nest site or interference with nesting in a single year is a serious and unacceptable impact. These constraints apply to no other bird species regularly nesting along the proposed pipeline corridor. [Finney and Lang, 1975, *Biological Field Program Report: 1975*, Vol. VI Section 4, p. 32]

The recommendations I make for raptors therefore apply primarily to the peregrine falcon.

The maintenance of wilderness within critical distances of the nest sites is of paramount importance because raptors are extremely sensitive to disturbance by men, machinery and aircraft. Such disturbance could cause direct destruction of the eggs or young by exposure, predation or accidental ejection of the eggs or chicks from the nest, or it could reduce the wilderness seclusion of the area around the nest so that it was no longer acceptable to the breeding pair. Low-intensity, repeated disturbance over a period of time frequently has a cumulative effect that leads to permanent desertion of the nest. We can best protect raptors by isolating their habitats from the disturbances caused by the project.

36. *The pipeline and its related facilities shall be located, designed, constructed and operated in a manner that avoids disturbance to raptors and their habitat.*

37. *For purposes of project review and control, the Agency shall designate Raptor Protection Zones around regularly and irregularly occupied raptor nest sites that are considered to be threatened by project activities. Such zones should be applicable to peregrine falcons in particular but may also apply to other raptors. These zones should be approximately two miles in radius or of the size that is required to protect the nest site. Access to these zones shall be prohibited unless authorized by permit.*

Applications for an access permit to Raptor Protection Zones shall be accompanied by sound biological evidence that the proposed activity will not jeopardize the raptors during their nesting period and will not adversely affect the nest site itself.

Because of the need to provide complete protection for raptors and their habitat, the Company must understand that there may be lengthy delays if it plans to undertake activities in a Raptor Protection Zone.

38. *To limit disturbance to raptors, barging operations and other movements of pipeline material that infringe on any Raptor Protection Zone during the periods of occupancy shall be subject to site-specific limitations imposed by the permit.*

39. *The frequency and altitude of aircraft flights over Raptor Protection Zones shall be controlled by the Flight Control Group. (See Aircraft Control.) In general, aircraft shall maintain an altitude of at least 3,000 feet above ground level over any Raptor Protection Zone during a sensitive period. Flights at lower levels shall be diverted around the zone. Airstrips and heliports shall be located so that approaches and take-offs avoid Raptor Protection Zones. Pipeline surveillance flights at less than 3,000 feet above ground level, helicopter landings and motorized terrestrial access for maintenance or repair shall be prohibited within a Raptor Protection Zone during the period of occupancy, except as specifically authorized by the Agency.*

Waterfowl

The Beaufort Sea coast, particularly the Blow River–Shallow Bay area and, to a lesser extent, the coastal plain out to Herschel Island, provides important nesting habitat for whistling swans. Brant, many species of ducks, loons, gulls, and other species use the coastal lagoons, beaches and islands of the Beaufort Sea as resting, nesting and moulting areas. From June through August, the tundra lakes of the Yukon Coastal Plain are important nesting, feeding, brood-rearing and moulting areas for many species of swans, geese, ducks, loons and shorebirds. At any one time in the late summer and autumn, between 300,000 and 500,000 geese, swans and ducks gather on the Yukon Coastal Plain and Shallow Bay for a period of concentrated feeding to build up their energy reserves for the long southward migration. Snow geese are most numerous during this period and, on any one day in late August, almost the entire Western Arctic population of this

species might be gathered on the coastal plain between Bathurst Peninsula and the Canning River in Alaska. Old Crow Flats, in the Yukon interior, are second only to the Mackenzie Delta as a critical waterfowl production area in northwestern Canada.

In Volume One, I recommended that no pipeline be built and no energy corridor be established across the Northern Yukon and that a wilderness park be created in that area. This recommendation was intended, in part, to protect vital habitat for waterfowl there.

The Mackenzie Delta is also an important waterfowl production area and it has breeding populations of several hundred thousand ducks and geese. Of particular concern are the snow geese at Kendall Island, where there is a colony of 1,200 to 8,000 breeding birds; approximately 20,000 whistling swans nesting in the Eskimo Lakes–Liverpool Bay area; and the rare trumpeter swan, which has been reported nesting near Moose Channel. Many parts of the Delta are critical for moulting ducks, swans and geese during summer. For example, in any given year the Delta may be as vital as the Yukon Coastal Plain to the snow geese. Normally, the majority of the snow geese stage on the Yukon coast, but, in 1975, when the geese arrived in early September it was covered with snow and most of the geese moved into the Shallow Bay area of the Delta. The peak number of geese there, at that time, was an estimated 325,000 out of the region's total population of 375,000. Snow geese are easily disturbed by aircraft movements of the kind that would be associated with the construction and operation of a pipeline and production facilities.

In Volume One, I recommended that a bird sanctuary should extend across the outer part of the Mackenzie Delta, thereby giving the Canadian Wildlife Service jurisdiction to regulate industrial activity in the area.

The Mackenzie Valley, one of North America's major flyways, is used by many species of birds that breed in the Western Arctic and sub-Arctic. In May and early June, large numbers of migrating waterfowl find the only available open water around islands in the Mackenzie River between Camsell Bend and the Mackenzie Delta and in some of the lakes near the river. At this time, these areas of open water are heavily used for mating, nesting and feeding. As many as 100,000 northbound geese and swans may be concentrated on sandbars, spits and island fringes. These same areas also provide resting areas vital during the fall migration in years when young birds have been unable, for any reason, to store adequate reserves of energy to complete their long southward migration. With so short a season, the waterfowl cannot be delayed, and disturbance of them must be kept to a minimum.

Large numbers of ducks, some Canada geese, sandhill cranes, loons and various other species, nest in the forest and forest-tundra habitats of the Mackenzie Valley. The Ramparts River, Mackay Creek, Willow (Brackett) Lake, Mills Lake and Beaver Lake areas are the most important nesting, brood-rearing, moulting and staging areas for water-oriented birds in the Mackenzie Valley between Great Slave Lake and the Mackenzie Delta.

In Volume One, I recommended that Willow Lake (Brackett Lake) and Mills Lake, which were identified under the International Biological Programme as sites important to waterfowl, be designated as bird sanctuaries.

In addition to the designation of sanctuaries, regulations will have to be developed to control the adverse effects on waterfowl of activities associated with pipeline construction. Disturbance to populations of waterfowl could increase stress and alter normal behaviour patterns during critical life stages, such as spring migration, nesting, moulting and staging for fall migration. Disturbance could also decrease reproduction success and cause birds to desert traditional areas, such as nesting sites for which there may be no suitable alternative. The impact of disturbance on a particular species is a function of the type and intensity of the disturbance, as well as of the time of year, location, distribution of the species, and its sensitivity to disturbance and its ability to avoid the sources of disturbance. These variables become more important farther north, where shorter summers impose even tighter limits on the hatching and raising of healthy young in time for the fall migration.

40. The Company shall control, restrict and otherwise alter its terrestrial and airborne activities and those of all its contractors and subcontractors to avoid disturbance to waterfowl and their habitat and to comply with restrictions of access and activity in important waterfowl areas, as defined by the Agency. Such measures should include the designation of corridors for air traffic and the designation and regulation of flight altitudes. (See Aircraft Control.)

a) Habitat critical during the spring migration throughout the Mackenzie Valley, including islands, deltas of tributaries, and adjacent marshes. Within these critical habitat areas, concentrations of birds should be protected from disturbance by a two-mile-wide buffer-zone. The period of restriction would generally be from May 1 to May 31. In addition, if these areas are used in the fall by migrating geese and swans, contingency plans should provide for the adequate protection of the birds and this habitat during such periods.

b) Areas in the Mackenzie Delta where there are concentrations of migrating, nesting, rearing, moulting and staging geese and other waterfowl. In general, construction activities should be minimized and personnel should be restricted to their immediate work areas from May 5 to October 5.

c) Areas critical for snow geese. All construction and other activity likely to cause disturbance and all human access should be strictly controlled within two miles of occupied areas from about August 15 to October 15.

d) Waterfowl habitat in the Mackenzie Valley forest areas between Great Slave Lake and the Mackenzie Delta.

41. Because of the extensive disturbance created by air cushion vehicles to waterfowl while they are nesting, rearing their young and staging, these vehicles shall be prohibited within the critical waterfowl areas described above, while birds are concentrated in them.

Wildlife Management and Research

It became evident during the Inquiry that, although the North has abundant wildlife resources, relatively little scientific information is available about wildlife populations. In this respect the North is still very much a frontier area. Much of the information that is available has been gathered as a result of gas and oil exploration and the proposal for a gas pipeline. As I stated in Volume One, much more information is needed if the populations of northern birds and mammals are to be managed scientifically for the benefit of northerners and conserved for all Canadians.

At present, five separate agencies are responsible for the management of northern wildlife resources. The Yukon Game Branch and the Northwest Territories Fish and Wildlife Service are responsible for the management of mammals and non-migratory birds, including raptors, within their respective territories. The Department of Indian Affairs and Northern Development is responsible for land management within the Yukon Territory and the Northwest Territories. The Canadian Wildlife Service, Department of the Environment, is responsible for the management of migratory birds, and the Fisheries and Marine Service, also part of the Department of the Environment, is responsible for the management of marine mammals.

During the Inquiry, I heard from representatives of all of these government agencies. The general conclusion was that, without more intensive wildlife management, a gas pipeline could have severe and long-term effects on many wildlife populations. Although there has been industrial development of various kinds in the North for some time, the pipeline is regarded by many as the first in a series of large-scale industrial developments there. I concur with this view; as I stated in Volume One, construction of a gas pipeline will trigger a series of other activities, and the pipeline should not be viewed in isolation. Without effective wildlife management programs many of the now abundant populations will decline.

Northern Wildlife Management

The essence of wildlife management is the manipulation of an animal population or its habitat for the benefit of man. The territorial government's wildlife management programs are, for the most part, directed towards the benefit of native people. Dr. Norman Simmons, Director of its Fish and Wildlife Service, described territorial policy to the Inquiry: "The management programs of the Fish and Wildlife Service are designed primarily to satisfy the food and psychological requirements of [the] indigenous people." (F20898) Whereas management policy may have these objectives at present, that has not always been the case. Commission Counsel summed up what I think has been, and is still, an essential fact about wildlife in the North:

> The recent history of the North is replete with examples of the ability of mechanized man to decimate animal populations. These include not only the well-known nineteenth and early twentieth century examples, such as fur seal, sea otter, baleen whales, muskoxen, and caribou, but also more modern instances of wildlife depletion by northern residents, witnessed by the wildlife vacuums surrounding all northern centres of habitation. Where abundant wildlife populations still exist in the North, it is generally due in large part to limited human access. This isolated position of large areas in the North is rapidly being reduced. Without corresponding large scale increases in wildlife management efforts in the North, this loss of isolation will be accompanied by rapid depletions in many animal populations. [Commission Counsel, 1976, "Wildlife Protection: Wildlife Management and Monitoring," p. 1]

In the previous sections that describe individual species, I repeatedly mentioned the two most important causes of impact: disturbance and increased access. These causes may have long-term effects and may cover a much larger area than the actual right-of-way of a pipeline. Having already discussed this problem as it relates to individual species, I shall discuss later the measures necessary to mitigate disturbance from specific aspects of this project.

Increased use of many areas that are still virtually wilderness areas will be a direct result of the greater numbers of people and of better and more facilities in the North. This threat to many wildlife populations is recognized by, and accepted to be, the responsibility of the wildlife management agencies. The success of a game management policy, whatever it may be, depends to a considerable degree on the staff and the funds that are made available. Even today, these agencies do not have adequate resources to meet their full range of responsibilities.

If northern wildlife is to be preserved, funds for management and research are required, whether or not a pipeline is built tomorrow or ten years from now. Not only will the wildlife aspect of the Agency have to function during the construction of the pipeline, but the management functions of the various wildlife departments will have to be increased to meet a broad range of demands stimulated by the pipeline development. Because these increases will in part be directly attributable to the pipeline construction, it is logical that at least some of these costs should be borne by the Company. This is not a new concept: the development of the James Bay hydro-electric project has involved Hydro-Québec financially in the surveys of native harvests now going forward.

42. In addition to funding the Agency so that it may undertake its functions related to wildlife, the government should ensure that the funding of various other agencies and organizations before, during and after pipeline construction is sufficient for them to meet increased responsibilities related to wildlife management and research in the face of a major industrial development. In so doing, the government should ensure the meaningful involvement of native organizations in all aspects of wildlife management in the region and should specify the extent and nature of the financial and professional involvement that will be required of the Company during the life of the pipeline.

In Volume One, I indicated that certain areas should be excluded from industrial development and that certain other areas, such as bird sanctuaries, should be closely managed by the responsible government agency. The wilderness park in Northern Yukon and the whale sanctuary in the Beaufort Sea come into the first category, whereas the expansion of the Kendall Island Bird Sanctuary and the designation of the Mills Lake and Brackett Lake sites as sanctuaries come into the second. So far, in this volume, I have recommended that protection zones be set up around raptor nest sites, especially those of the peregrine falcon; that a game preserve be established along both sides of the right-of-way and around all pipeline facilities; and that a similar game preserve be established along both sides of the Dempster and Mackenzie highways. These areas of excluded or restricted access that I have identified are a major tool of wildlife management. There are, however, a variety of other means to effective management that must be used to protect wildlife populations so that they may continue to be used as renewable resources. I shall deal more explicitly with these other means in the following paragraphs. Because aircraft are considered a major source of impact, I have dealt with this subject in a separate chapter entitled Aircraft Control.

Wildlife Management and Pipeline Regulation

During the Inquiry, it became apparent that, at all stages of the pipeline project, programs dealing with the enforcement and adaptation of regulations, the rehabilitation of habitats, and contingency plans are central to ongoing comprehensive wildlife management. For example, advice from wildlife specialists will be needed to review designs and to approve schedules, the location and relocation of facilities, and equipment.

The inspection and enforcement of regulations governing pipeline construction activities will be very difficult tasks, especially since they may lead to delays or work stoppages. Field inspection staff will have to be given pragmatic training and the authority to carry out their duties effectively. If they do not have that authority, there will be needless delays, frustration and non-compliance. The greatest emphasis must be placed on having knowledgeable and experienced people in the field while construction is underway.

During the construction phase it will be necessary to document changes in the numbers and the movements of animals, damage to habitat, success of mitigative measures, and so on. Without collection and assessment of this type of information, the impact of the pipeline would not be apparent nor would mitigative techniques and methods be progressively improved.

43. *To ensure that the concerns for wildlife that have been expressed are considered and incorporated during all stages of design and that regulations concerning wildlife are enforced during the construction of the proposed pipeline, the Agency staff shall include specialists and high-level administrators to review and approve designs, to inspect and to enforce regulations, to design mitigative measures, and to collect and evaluate data on both the project and wildlife activities. These activities must be done in close coordination with the appropriate wildlife management agencies of government and must involve consultation with and input from native organizations.*

The regulation of the pipeline operation will involve protection of mammals and birds from the noise and disturbance involved in starting up the pipeline, in the routine operation of compressor stations and other facilities, in routine maintenance and repairs, and in contingency repairs. I assume that the Agency will be terminated soon after construction of the pipeline is completed and, therefore, that the regulatory tasks necessary during operation of the pipeline will become the responsibility of the permanent wildlife regulatory bodies under whatever arrangements may apply after the settlement of native claims.

44. *Before the Agency is disbanded at the end of the construction period, the roles of ongoing wildlife agencies and the responsibilities of the Company should be established. Consideration should be given to factors such as who will assume specific Agency functions during the operation and abandonment phases of the pipeline, and the funding and staff requirements necessary to maintain a comprehensive monitoring and management program.*

Hunting and Access

One of the major concerns that I have mentioned throughout this chapter and in Volume One is that the construction of this pipeline will afford easier access to areas that have, until now, been relatively inaccessible to man. This improved access, together with the increasing number of residents and tourists in the North, will undoubtedly increase stress on many wildlife populations through direct mortality (hunting), by increased disturbance, and by habitat loss or alteration.

Both Foothills and Arctic Gas have stated that movement of pipeline personnel will be restricted and that they will not be allowed to hunt on company property. The pipeline companies will similarly restrict access to the right-of-way and to the pipeline facilities to company personnel. However, in view of the large number of people that will be attracted to a major project of this sort, it will be difficult for the Company alone to enforce these good intentions. Therefore, to protect the wildlife populations and the traditional harvest of them, a number of measures are required that will go beyond the Company's jurisdiction.

It will be necessary to control in some manner access to the right-of-way and to all access roads, wharves and other pipeline facilities. Otherwise many wildlife populations will decline or they will abandon certain areas.

One particularly important aspect of game management is the need to protect the Porcupine caribou herd in the vicinity of the Dempster Highway, both from the adverse effects of the highway and its traffic and from increased hunting pressure that has followed the highway. In Volume One, I quoted Ronald Jakimchuk on this subject. After publication of Volume One and of the National Energy Board report, he wrote to me about his observations along the Dempster Highway this spring. He said, "The herd is in existing and continuing jeopardy from the Dempster Highway." He urged "a commitment by government to implement timely regulations ... to ensure free and unimpeded movement of migrations and to monitor and regulate the kill," and he added, "The proposed wildlife range does not solve these problems as it does not encompass the Dempster" (Jakimchuk, personal communication, June 17, 1977).

In view of the continued work on the Dempster Highway and the undoubted increase in traffic and hunters on it when it has been completed and particularly in view of the endorsement that the National Energy Board has given to the idea of a pipeline along the Dempster Highway, I consider that it is of great importance for government to institute measures as soon as possible to protect the herd when it is near the Dempster Highway and to reinforce these measures whether or not a pipeline is built along the highway.

45. *A two-mile restricted hunting zone should be established along both sides of the pipeline right-of-way and all access roads and around all pipeline facilities. A similar restricted* *hunting zone should be established along the Dempster and Mackenzie highways and all access roads that are within the winter range of the Porcupine caribou herd. Within this game preserve, traditional native harvesting would be allowed to continue, provided that the wildlife populations can support such harvesting.*

46. *The government should develop a traffic management plan for the Dempster Highway and other rights-of-way in areas that are important to caribou. When caribou are present in such areas, regulations such as slower speed limits, convoying or the staggered scheduling of highway traffic, and periodic closures of sections of the highway that may be the locations of large-scale caribou crossings should be instituted.*

47. *During construction the Company shall limit access to its facilities to only those persons who, in the course of their employment, need to be there. All haul and access roads, the right-of-way, and all airstrips and helipads built and operated by the Company shall be closed to public access, except in emergency situations or as approved by the Agency.*

48. *After pipeline construction is completed, the Company shall remove or otherwise make unusable (in an approved manner) all access facilities and structures that are not necessary to the continued operation of the pipeline.*

49. *To help control hunting during and after pipeline construction, revisions to the hunting regulations should be contemplated. Measures such as increasing the length of the residency requirement to obtain a hunting licence and restricting hunting areas and seasons, should be actively pursued. (See Renewable Resources.)*

Wildlife Research and Monitoring

In Volume One, I drew attention to our lack of knowledge about northern birds and mammals, which, according to the biologists who gave evidence before the Inquiry, has hampered them in predicting the impacts of pipeline development. This lack of knowledge will also hamper the development of measures for the protection and management of wildlife during construction and operation of the pipeline.

50. *Wildlife studies should be undertaken before, during and after pipeline construction to gauge the nature of populations, to develop comprehensive mitigative responses and to assess the effectiveness of ameliorative measures on both a short- and long-term basis.*

MONITORING

The monitoring of animal populations involves repeated checks or surveys of the populations to determine whether or not there are changes in the health, demography or distribution of a population. Monitoring is also used to document the movements of migrating animals. Should a migrating population come into contact with development activities, the knowledge gained from monitoring permits appropriate

precautions to be taken. Both short-term and long-term monitoring programs are necessary in any management plan to protect wildlife.

Obviously it is not possible, at this time, to specify which mammal or bird populations will have to be monitored, or where and when the monitoring will have to be done. These matters will have to be worked out by the relevant wildlife management bodies, the Agency and the Company.

51. *Because a wildlife monitoring program is vital to any successful plan to observe and to mitigate impacts on wildlife resources, a comprehensive short-term monitoring program shall be an integral part of the work of the Agency. This program shall be designed to locate migrating mammals or birds and sites of concentrated wildlife activity and, on the basis of this information, to alter pipeline project activities that may cause unacceptable impact. This monitoring should also be used to assess the effectiveness and improve remedial measures.*

52. *The long-term monitoring program associated with continuing wildlife management in the region should be the responsibility of ongoing wildlife management agencies. Such a program should start before construction and continue through the life of the project and afterwards, to determine the health of populations and to develop comprehensive management programs that relate to all aspects of the wildlife resources in the region. This, of course, must include a harvest monitoring research component. (See Renewable Resources.)*

WILDLIFE RESEARCH

The Inquiry was presented with a variety of proposals regarding the research that is needed to understand the impact of pipeline development on mammals and birds and to serve as the basis for programs of wildlife management and protection. Such proposals can be found in material presented by Canadian Arctic Resources Committee, Committee on Original Peoples Entitlement, Environment Protection Board and Commission Counsel, in the evidence of witnesses, in exhibits filed with the Inquiry, and in the final arguments before the Inquiry. For example, Canadian Arctic Resources Committee's "Final Arguments and Recommendations" contains a multitude of recommendations for wildlife studies, including 39 separate research proposals related to caribou.

The studies that have been proposed differ greatly in urgency, practicality and utility for wildlife management as it relates to pipeline development. But it is clear that there are important gaps in the knowledge that is required for effective wildlife management and that a great deal of field research is needed to fill these gaps.

53. *Concrete plans for research that is essential to wildlife management in relation to pipeline development should be prepared by the agencies that regulate wildlife. The government should make funds available for this purpose so that* *independent government research may be started well ahead of the commencement of construction of the pipeline.*

To those charged with planning this research, I particularly commend Commission Counsel's proposal for disturbance studies (Commission Counsel, 1976, "Wildlife Protection: Wildlife Management and Monitoring," p. 7).

54. *The effects of various forms of disturbance, such as aircraft, noise from fixed facilities, blasting, ground transport and watercraft, on wildlife populations should be studied in some detail to allow more precise prediction of these effects. The following groups of animals and birds are pointed out as species that deserve particular attention in these studies: all species of geese, swans and eider-ducks, especially at their moulting and spring and fall staging sites; all species of raptors, but particularly peregrine falcons, because more precise definition of the zone of protection for them and the degree to which raptors may adapt to various disturbances is required; and caribou, including behavioural and physiological reaction to various disturbances.*

9 Fish

The problem of fish and fish resources is complex because the aquatic data are incomplete for areas that are of critical importance to fish. We also tend to view the problem too narrowly: we are inclined to concentrate on fish rather than on the ecosystems of which they are part. A species-specific approach is undoubtedly necessary but we must not forget that a broader view of the aquatic ecosystem will lead to more effective identification of problem areas, and development of protective measures.

My principal concern for fish is similar to my principal concern for wildlife: we cannot protect every fish, but we must safeguard those areas where fish concentrate and we must avoid fish populations when they are sensitive to disturbance.

1. To ensure that the fish resources of the Mackenzie Valley and Mackenzie Delta are maintained, measures shall be employed to preserve aquatic habitat and to avoid disturbance of fish during critical life stages.

The evidence I have heard tends to fall into three categories: fish protection, monitoring of the aquatic environment, and fisheries management. I shall deal with each of these topics, but first we need to know the characteristics of northern fish if we are to understand the significance of the measures that are necessary to protect them from the impacts of development.

Characteristics of Northern Fish

Because of their specific life cycles and biological characteristics, the species of fish present in the Mackenzie Valley and the Mackenzie Delta are particularly sensitive to man-made disruptions of their aquatic habitat. Northern fish typically have slow growth rates, are large for their species, and reach sexual maturity at a late stage in their development. These factors mean that in most areas there is a large standing stock of the fish, but a low rate of productivity to maintain that stock.

Most northern fish have specific migration routes and limited spawning, overwintering, nursery and feeding areas.

Northern fish can spend their lives entirely in fresh water or in salt water, or move between the two during various stages of their life cycles. Populations of some species, such as the arctic char, spend their lives in fresh water, whereas other populations of the same species migrate to sea. Throughout much of the Arctic, many populations of whitefish and lake trout use productive lakes as substitutes for the sea.

The Mackenzie River, because it originates in warmer latitudes, is more productive and therefore supports more fish species — 34 species have been found there — than most arctic rivers. The Mackenzie Delta and adjacent coastal estuary and lagoons are particularly important to fish: nineteen fresh-water and four marine species are known to use these areas extensively.

Fish can be classified as either spring spawners or fall spawners. The eggs of fall spawners have to survive the rigors of the winter environment; they lie in the gravel from October until break-up the following May or June, when the fry hatch and move to nursery areas. Spring spawners deposit their eggs at break-up and the young emerge within a few weeks. Consequently, there is an important difference in the length of time the eggs of the two groups are vulnerable to environmental disruption.

In the Mackenzie River, fall spawners constitute 62 percent of the fish population, and spring spawners constitute 35 percent. The burbot, or freshwater cod, is the winter spawner in the system. Major spring spawning species are arctic grayling, yellow walleye, northern pike, longnose sucker and flathead chub. The arctic grayling, which is distributed throughout the system, is probably the most sensitive species of spring spawner.

Fall spawners in the Mackenzie system are dominated by the Coreonid (whitefish) class, the humpback, broad and round whitefish, arctic and least cisco, and the inconnu. With the exception of the more extensive lakes, these species have larger populations in the north end of the Mackenzie drainage. Well-defined spawning migrations of the whitefish family take place in the Mackenzie Delta channels and the Arctic Red, Peel, Great Bear and Mountain rivers. Arctic and least cisco live in the sea during much of their lives. Populations of all of these species use the Delta channels and brackish Mackenzie estuary as feeding, nursery, and overwintering areas.

Lake trout occur in significant numbers in the deep lakes of the Mackenzie tributaries and the Delta. They do not appear to be a major species in the flowing waters of the system.

Fish Protection

Principles of Protection

The basis of all fish protection is to safeguard critical aquatic habitat and life stages. In Part Three of this report, I deal with many of the specifics of protection as they relate to the pipeline project, but here I want to define biologically appropriate terms and conditions, and emphasize the two fundamental principles.

2. *Measures to protect fish should focus on important fish populations rather than on scattered individuals.*

3. *Fish protection should be designed to minimize disturbances where and when fish are most sensitive and most numerous, particularly in spawning grounds and overwintering areas, and along migration routes.*

Spawning and rearing areas, overwintering sites and migration routes are probably the most critical habitats for fish in the North. In addition to the physical sites, suitable water quality and food sources are also essential. Habitat areas and parameters are particularly important in the Arctic because of the generally limited ability of fish populations to recover their original levels after a severe environmental disruption has reduced their numbers.

Most northern fish species need spawning grounds that have the correct substrate — usually gravel or cobble — and suitable water temperatures. The gravel must be free of silt so that water can percolate around deposited fish eggs and permit gas exchange with the surrounding water. Clean gravel also provides good substrate for juvenile fish food, and suitable living space. A pipeline project could disrupt spawning and rearing areas by removing the gravel used for spawning or rearing; by changing the water temperature or chemistry conditions in a way that would be harmful to fish; by causing suspended sediment loads in streams to increase, which would induce silt to settle out on spawning beds and to smother eggs; or by polluting streams with toxic fuels or chemicals.

To survive the severe conditions of the Arctic winter, fish must stay in waters that are sufficiently deep that they will not freeze to the bottom. The flow of water into these areas must be monitored and that water must have tolerable chemistry, dissolved oxygen levels and silt loads and must be free of toxicants. The eggs of fall spawning fish must be in clean, well-oxygenated water during their incubation time. Fish or egg overwintering areas could be damaged by the same pipeline activities that could damage spawning and rearing areas, and by ditching or water removal that could cut off the intragravel flow into the overwintering areas.

Any disturbance of river beds that prevents or delays fish from migrating to normal life cycle areas can affect survival. Some species do not feed en route to spawning areas, and any significant delay in the migrating time might leave them with insufficient body energy to move to these areas. Project activities that could disrupt migration routes by creating barriers in rivers and streams include the installation of culverts, river diversion structures or ice bridges, and the lowering of water levels.

Northern fish also have a limited tolerance to changes in water chemistry — that is, to changes in temperature, in the levels of suspended solids, dissolved oxygen, and pH, and in salt content. They also have a limited tolerance to toxic substances, such as methanol, fuels and pipe-coating materials. Increased levels of suspended solids, for example, could be abrasive to fish gill membranes, and could be toxic to some invertebrate fish food and to fish eggs; and increased water temperatures could make important habitat areas unsuitable. And changes in all of these parameters could result from pipeline activities.

Some changes in aquatic environments may not affect the survival of the fish but they may leave the fish either unpalatable or unsafe to eat. A pipeline project could disrupt sport, commercial and domestic fisheries by introducing persistent materials, such as pesticides, PCB's, or heavy metals, into watercourses, where they could be picked up by fish directly or through the food chains, and accumulate in body tissue.

The ecological balance in a particular aquatic system can also be disrupted by reducing certain species, by removing food sources through chemical contamination or siltation, or by introducing a new species into a watershed in which it is not native. Because there are relatively few species in the North, and because food chains are short and the relationships between species are simple, northern populations are particuarly susceptible to disruptions of this kind.

Different fish species vary in their ability to tolerate disturbance. Arctic grayling, arctic char, pacific salmon, lake trout, inconnu, humpback and broad whitefish, and arctic and least cisco, because of their relatively low tolerance to siltation, particularly during spawning, appear to have the least resistance to disturbance. Slow growth and narrow age classes delay recovery. Economically, however, these are the most important species in the domestic, commercial and sport fisheries. Northern pike, walleyes, longnose and white suckers, flathead, chub and burbot have a broad habitat tolerance and relatively wide distribution, and they are, therefore, probably more resistant to the effects of environmental disturbance. The piscivorous or fish-eating species, such as pike, char, inconnu and burbot, would be most susceptible to chemical contamination because many biological contaminants pass up the food chain and concentrate in such predator species.

4. Pipeline construction and other activities should not be allowed at sensitive times near areas used by fish for spawning, rearing, overwintering and migration.

Spawning and rearing areas should be protected from siltation, gravel removal, fuel spills, and from changes in water temperature, water chemistry, and levels of dissolved oxygen.

During the winter, overwintering areas should be protected from any decrease in water level and flow caused by construction or water intake. They should also be protected from excess siltation, chemical pollution, changes in water temperature and decreases in dissolved oxygen levels.

Migration routes and times should not be disrupted by any blockage or diversion of flow, lowering of water level, significant increases in suspended sediment, or spills of fuels or toxic chemicals.

THE USE OF NUMERICAL STANDARDS

Much of the evidence I have heard suggests that it is not enough to state the principles of fish protection: it is often difficult to translate them into specific and workable measures. Numerical standards, it seems, are needed as a guide for all who are concerned with the design, review, construction and operation of the pipeline. However, Arctic Gas and, to a lesser extent, Foothills do not agree. They argued that a competent biologist should make site-specific decisions. I agree in principle with their argument, but I do not think it is practicable for a project of this size. Indeed, a protection program founded entirely on such individual judgments may result in unnecessary delays, and unwarranted confusion and, most important, may fail to protect the fish.

It requires a certain academic naïveté to believe that thousands of site-specific design and construction situations can be evaluated satisfactorily by competent biologists. The principle of numerical standards should, therefore, be vigorously promoted. Such standards will inform design engineers of the criteria they must meet; they will show construction personnel the permissible levels for environmental disruption; and they will indicate to operational personnel the operating specifications that must be followed.

I recognize that, in isolated situations, it may be impractical, and perhaps even harmful to the environment, to comply with the numerical standards. If the Company can demonstrate to the Agency that certain numerical standards should not be expected in a particular situation, the Agency may grant an exception. Nevertheless, the principle of numerical

standards should, I believe, provide the cornerstone of a sound fish protection program.

Suspended Sediment

The construction of the pipeline will cause increased siltation of waterbodies through the direct disruption of the waterbody, or through increased run-off from adjacent land areas. Although concentrations of suspended solids must be extremely high before they cause direct, short-term damage to fish, finely divided material may settle to the bottom and blanket out normal fish food organisms, or they may spoil spawning beds by decreasing the percolation of water through the substrate. If siltation damage to spawning beds or fish food occurs in only one year, recovery of the stream bed can be expected in successive seasons, and the overall damage to fish populations would probably not be great.

To predict the impact of suspended sediment on the aquatic ecosystem requires an awareness of the seasonal variation of sediment loads; what may be tolerable in spring, when natural sediment loads are high, may be unacceptable in the winter, when most northern rivers are relatively clear. Winter construction of a pipeline may, therefore, cause special suspended sediment problems in watercourses.

5. The construction and operation practices of the Company shall be such as to minimize the release of silt into waterbodies frequented by fish. In areas that are important to fish and where silt loads from project activities can be expected to be significant, the Company shall institute silt control measures before construction activities start.

6. Specific standards shall be established by the Agency to measure the natural silt load in watercourses, and to set upper limits for increased silt loads. If silt loads exceed the upper limits, erosion and silt control measures shall be put in place, or existing ones shall be improved to ensure that the critical habitats and life stages of aquatic resources are protected.

GUIDELINES FOR SUSPENDED SEDIMENT STANDARDS

In his final submission, Commission Counsel proposed a turbidity and macroinvertebrate standard for estimating the increase in finely-divided solids in waterbodies and for assessing the effects of any increase on bottom macroinvertebrates in a stream. These standards and the rationale behind them are given extensive treatment in the submission (Commission Counsel, 1976, "Fish Protection: Suspended Sediment Standards"). I endorse the standards proposed by Commission Counsel and I recommend that experts in the Agency and in the Company refer to that document to appreciate the approach I have adopted below. I must emphasize at the outset that these standards and methods of measurement need further refinement. In particular, they have yet to be tested under winter conditions in the North.

7. The standards for suspended sediment should be tested by the Company and the Agency under field conditions in the pipeline areas and should be refined so that acceptable and practicable suspended sediment criteria for monitoring the pipeline project can be developed. If other standards are considered, they should have the following characteristics. They should be quantitative and objective; they should be practical enough to be used and to be enforced in the kinds of conditions that will be encountered by the pipeline project; they should be routinely workable by a small staff that is not highly skilled in scientific sediment load assessment practices; and they should measure both short-term and long-term increases in sediment load.

A standard that sets limits on changes in suspended sediment is necessary to prevent widespread or continued damage to aquatic life. Because it is fairly easy to determine in the field and because the results are known immediately, Commission Counsel recommended that a turbidity standard be adopted.

Before the turbidity standard can be implemented, the following problems may have to be resolved. First, results may vary across the width of a stream river, or from day to day because of wind on lakes. The standards are intended to apply at any point that is the recommended distance from operations. Secondly, the collection of samples will be difficult in winter; it will require well-designed equipment for penetrating the ice and retrieving samples. Finally, if turbidity exceeds the standards, it will be an indication that construction practice is not satisfactory. This situation will be difficult to correct quickly because of the lingering effects of the causes of siltation.

A macroinvertebrate standard assesses the biological effects of an increase in sediment. Because the status of the resident macroinvertebrate community reflects conditions over previous weeks or months, it serves as a continuing, cumulative monitor, and to a large extent it will reflect any problems that are not detected by the infrequent turbidity measurements. Since the diversity of the aquatic community also monitors environmental effects other than siltation, the Agency could use the biological evaluation as an overall check. In questionable cases, findings of the biological survey should take precedence over the physical and chemical surveys.

There are many ways of interpreting ecological data, and Commission Counsel recommended that the Shannon Diversity Index be used because we have experience with it and because it is sensitive, reliable and conducive to use by both professionals and laymen alike. However, two problems may be encountered when implementing the macroinvertebrate standard: it may be difficult to take samples of benthic invertebrates during periods of high discharge in rivers, and it may be difficult to separate benthic invertebrates into individual species.

8. The frequency and locations for suspended sediment sampling in rivers, streams, lakes and ponds shall be as defined by the Agency. The direction of the sampling site from the construction activity shall be that of maximum effect, depending upon currents and wind. A control sample shall be taken in an unaffected part of the same waterbody or, if that is not possible, in a similar, nearby waterbody.

Samples shall be taken frequently enough to provide adequate assessments of the amounts of finely-divided solids generated by construction both during the construction phase and immediately afterwards. In particular, turbidity shall be measured at the time of peak activity and during changing discharge.

9. Turbidity shall be measured in nephelometric turbidity units (NTU), using any reliable, commercially available meter. Procedure for measurement shall follow part 214A of Standard Methods for the Examination of Water and Wastewater, prepared by American Public Health Association et al.

10. The following standard should be used to determine allowable levels of finely-divided solids in water: at the specified distance from operations, turbidity of the water shall not average more than 27 times the natural level during any 8-hour period, or more than 9 times the natural level during any 96-hour period, or more than 3 times the natural level during any 30-day period. (For rationale see Commission Counsel, 1976, "Fish Protection: Suspended Sediment Standards.")

11. Benthic macroinvertebrate samples should be taken in stream riffles using a reliable quantitative device, such as the Surber sampler. The same apparatus shall be used to take both control samples and test samples, and because macroinvertebrate communities may vary seasonally, the samples shall be taken at the same time. The test and control sampling areas must be as similar as possible, particularly with regard to bottom type and velocity of water.

12. The following standard should be used to determine ecological damage: at the specified distance from operations, the Shannon Diversity Index for bottom-living aquatic macroinvertebrates shall not be changed more than 25 percent from the natural value as a result of the addition of finely-divided solids. (For rationale see Commission Counsel, 1976, "Fish Protection: Suspended Sediment Standards.")

13. The suspended sediment standards shall apply during construction activities, and for two years after they have ceased.

14. In the year that starts 12 months after completion of a construction activity, turbidity should not exceed one-half of the levels recommended above and diversity shall not be changed more than the 25 percent recommended above.

Barriers to Fish

During construction and operation of the pipeline, a variety of structures that could become barriers to the normal movement of fish will be placed in watercourses. There will be culverts beneath temporary and permanent roads, dykes and coffer-dams to divert river flows, and ice bridges, wharves and work pads at river crossing sites. These kinds of installations, which are a vital part of any construction program, could prevent or delay fish migrations by constricting the channel and thereby increasing the water velocity, by altering the river regime, or by physically obstructing the migration routes.

15. Installations and activities in waters that are inhabited by fish shall avoid fish-sensitive areas, and shall be designed and scheduled to provide for uninterrupted movement and safe passage of fish. Any structure or stream channel change that may cause blockage to fish, or that may create velocity barriers to fish movements, shall be provided with a fish passage structure or facility approved by the Agency.

16. The Company shall submit to the Agency, for design review, complete plans for dredging, trenching, diversion structures, or road crossings of waterbodies. The plans shall include such matters as: schedules for activities; amounts of spoil material to be removed or placed; designs and methods of construction; data on present flow regime or bathymetry of the waterbody in which work will be done; data on the fish resources that are present in the waterbody at all times of the year; information on how flow regimes or bathymetry of the waterbody will be altered by construction; and an assessment of how the fish species that are present in the system will be affected.

DESIGN GUIDELINES: BARRIERS TO FISH

17. On fish migration routes, bridges with large spans across watercourses shall be used, wherever practicable, instead of culverts.

18. Culverts in watercourses that contain fish shall be of such a size and gradient that the peak water velocity and minimum water depth will not inhibit the passage of migrating fish. The lower ends of culverts in stream beds will be so placed as to eliminate any drop. The applicable standards for fish passage requirements and culvert design shall be as outlined in Guidelines for the Protection of the Fish Resources of the Northwest Territories During Highway Construction and Operation by Dryden and Stein.

19. Subject to the approval of the Agency, designed fords may be used for temporary stream crossings.

20. Winter road ice bridges shall be removed from small watercourses before break-up.

21. Construction and use of temporary coffer-dams, berms and diversion dykes in any watercourse that is frequented by fish shall be done in stages or shall be time-staggered to ensure

that water velocity does not prevent fish passage. Abandoned water diversion structures shall be plugged and stabilized to avoid trapping or stranding fish.

22. If borrow material sites are approved adjacent to or in waterbodies, the Company shall provide levees, berms or other structures to protect fish and fish passage, and to prevent siltation of such waterbodies.

23. Water intakes shall be installed and screened in such a way that the intake will not harm fish. (See Water Withdrawals.)

Underwater Blasting

Some underwater blasting will be necessary in the course of pipeline work. Throughout the hearings, there was frequent comment, particularly in the communities, on the detrimental effects of underwater blasting on fish, muskrat and beaver. Although I am concerned here only with fish, my observations may also apply to aquatic mammals. (I discuss terrestrial blasting operations in the chapter on Terrain Considerations.)

The effects of blasting on fish include direct consequences from the blast, and siltation from the blasted material. Blasting affects the swimbladder, an organ present in most freshwater fish to aid in swimming: the shock waves rupture the bladder, often bursting blood vessels and damaging tissue organs near the bladder. Furthermore, it has been suggested that chemicals present in the water immediately after the explosion may also be detrimental to fish and could disrupt fish migrations.

Factors that determine the extent of damage to fish include water depth, distance from the blast, strength of charge and position, and type of bed. The most serious damage occurs close to a blast site, in gravel-bottom or rock-bottom streams. Silty or muddy stream beds absorb some of the shock waves that are generated by a blast, whereas hard stream beds reflect the shock. Detonations under ice are more damaging to fish than those in open water because ice tends to contain the shock waves.

Blasting could significantly reduce fish populations if it took place in breeding or overwintering areas at times of high fish concentrations. Simultaneous activity in a watercourse could increase the damage to fish populations because it would reduce the number of areas that fish could move to during a blasting operation.

24. Blasting in waterbodies should be avoided near fish-sensitive areas. Where blasting must be carried out, every effort should be made to schedule the activity so that fish concentrations are avoided, especially at critical stages of their life cycle.

25. Blasting shall not be permitted in waterbodies within 1,000 feet of areas in which concentrations of fish eggs are present in the bed, fish are spawning in restricted areas, fish are overwintering in restricted areas, or fish are migrating in concentrated schools.

26. Where a requirement for blasting in a waterbody is identified during design and planning, the Company shall submit to the Agency an application for permission to blast, together with the information needed to assess the potential impact on fish, and a statement of measures to protect the fish during blasting.

Where a requirement for blasting in a waterbody is identified during construction activities, the Company's blasting proposal, its potential impact, and fish protection measures shall be subject to approval by the Agency in the field.

27. Blasting shall be permitted in water that is frequented by fish only if effective measures are taken to protect the fish. Such measures could include adjusting the time of the blast, moving fish and keeping them out of the blast area by means of nets, using blast deflectors (sand bags) or absorbers (air curtains), using charges of minimum size, and detonating charges in sequence with sufficient delay between firings to permit dissipation of the shock wave.

28. Underwater blasting shall conform to the same siltation standards as other in-water pipeline activities. (See Fish: Suspended Sediment.)

29. Underwater blasting shall be prohibited within one mile of fishing sites that are being used by local people and local fishermen.

Monitoring of the Aquatic Environment

In the chapter on Wildlife, I stated that a monitoring program is essential to ensure both the maintenance of populations and the effectiveness of any protective measures that may be adopted as part of a pipeline project. Monitoring of the aquatic environment is particularly important: the aquatic environment is less accessible to observation, and problems are often not evident until they reach intolerable levels. In some cases, postconstruction monitoring will be particularly important. The monitoring of siltation levels, for example, is probably more important after construction than at any other time. Such monitoring may be necessary for several years after construction ends.

30. During the construction and operation of the pipeline the aquatic environment shall be monitored. The Agency, in cooperation with the government agencies responsible for ongoing fish protection, should develop the monitoring program and establish what the responsibilities of the Company will be before, during and after construction.

I recognize that the development of a monitoring program will require a detailed knowledge of local conditions and

project activities. Although I cannot say what form such a program would take, I can suggest aspects of monitoring that may be necessary and appropriate. I have based my guidelines on those contained in Commission Counsel's final submission (Commission Counsel, 1976, "Fish Protection: Monitoring of Aquatic Environment").

Monitoring Guidelines

31. An aquatic environment monitoring program should be divided into three phases — preconstruction, construction and postconstruction — and should incorporate the following observations and factors:

Turbidity should be used to compare postconstruction levels of suspended sediment with preconstruction levels. During construction, turbidity levels downstream from construction should be compared with turbidity levels upstream.

Dissolved oxygen levels should be monitored to ensure adequate oxygen levels in water where fish resources are present. These levels, which are most critical in winter, should be measured in waters that may be disturbed by construction or operation of the project.

Water levels and flows should be monitored where and when water quantities are limited, to ensure that adequate quantities are maintained for fish.

Nutrient levels should be monitored in waste disposal areas to prevent overenrichment of fish habitat or high biological oxygen demand.

Fish and bottom sediment contaminant levels should be monitored as a baseline measure that will warn of any contamination of a fishery resource.

Water temperature should be monitored to ensure that tolerable limits for aquatic resources are maintained, and that water temperature is low enough to maintain adequate oxygen levels.

Gravel removal sites should be inspected before, during and after construction to determine the suitability of the site for removal of material, and to assess conformity with extraction plans, adequacy of restoration of site, and return of site to a stable state.

Chemical water quality parameters should be monitored in locations where pipeline-related activity might create chemical changes in water quality that could adversely affect fish.

Water velocities through culverts and some diversion structures should be monitored to ensure that velocities do not exceed the capabilities of fish migrating upstream.

Use of explosives in water should be checked visually to ensure that local fish populations are not affected by shock waves from blasts.

Pipeline crossing site inspections should involve visual

checks to ensure that erosion control devices are working, and that disturbed areas do return to a stable state.

In addition to general monitoring, a few comprehensive studies may be necessary in certain aquatic environments that are sensitive to environmental disruption, or to the extensive use of resources by man. For example, it may be necessary to establish parameters such as benthos productivity and diversity, and the population dynamics of a domestic fishery resource, and to monitor the abundance of rare species.

Fisheries Management

Man's Use of Fish

In the North, the domestic, commercial and sport fisheries overlap in some areas as each fishery competes for the same species. This overlap will probably increase in the future.

The government's management programs are, for the most part, directed towards the benefit of native people. Accordingly, the harvesting of fish for domestic purposes has precedence over commercial or sport fishery development.

The domestic fishery is traditionally an important source of protein in the Mackenzie Valley and Mackenzie Delta. Native people depend on fish for part of their dietary requirements, and as food for their dogs. The domestic fishery has declined somewhat since the snowmobile replaced dogs in many areas, but the catch is still important as a supplement to other wildlife sources of food.

Since its start in 1945 on Great Slave Lake, commercial fishing has continued uninterrupted in the Mackenzie drainage. Whitefish is the most important species harvested. At the present time the only other commercial operation outside the southern lakes of the system is a small, experimental commercial fishery on the East Channel of the Mackenzie Delta.

Sport fishery for arctic grayling throughout the Mackenzie drainage, and for char and lake trout in the Mackenzie Delta, represents a great tourist potential.

Fisheries and the Pipeline Project

Pipeline construction will make accessible many domestic, commercial and sport fishing locations that were previously isolated. Access will be provided by new roads, the location of construction and operating personnel in remote areas, and an increase in air and water traffic along the route. The increase in sport and commercial fishing activity could affect the ongoing domestic harvest. River traffic, fishing by construction personnel, spills, the location of facilities such as stockpile sites and wharf sites, and the general consequences of constructing the project on fish biology will all have a significant effect on fishing activities.

As I explained earlier, northern fish populations have a limited capacity to recover from unnatural losses. If fishing by pipeline personnel is not regulated, short-term reductions in fish populations along the route may occur. Long-term reductions could result if permanent access routes are opened up, and if fishing is not adequately controlled.

32. *Construction and operation of the pipeline and associated activities shall not interfere with ongoing domestic, commercial or sport fishing activities of the region. Pipeline activities shall not disturb fishing areas or cause changes to water, with the result that fish avoid certain fishing areas. Protection shall be afforded first and foremost to domestic fishing activities and domestic fish resources.*

33. *Unless otherwise approved by the Agency, pipeline-related facilities and activities shall be located at least 1,000 yards from any existing, well-defined domestic, sport or commercial fishery. Where pipeline activities or facilities are within one mile of such a site, the Company shall provide the local people with a description of its planned activities in the area. Any modifications requested by the local people shall be worked out in consultation with representatives from the local people, the Company, and the Agency.*

34. *Where local people and government authorities agree that project access roads are beneficial to local fisheries, they should be left intact when pipeline construction is completed. All other project access shall be blocked and the disturbed areas shall be restored when pipeline use of the access route has ended.*

Throughout the Inquiry, biologists told me that there are insufficient data on fish, particularly the domestic fishery, to develop a comprehensive management program. In my opinion, both the proponent of a major frontier development and the government have an obligation to ensure the continuation of fisheries in the region. The pipeline company has an obligation to show that it has properly researched the impacts of its project on resource harvesting activities.

In order to draw up workable and detailed plans for protecting fishing activities during pipeline construction, specific information is necessary.

35. *To plan for the protection of fisheries, the Company, in cooperation with all agencies responsible for fisheries management and the native organizations, shall compile a catalogue of fishing areas and fishing activities along the route. (See Renewable Resources.) This catalogue should provide a complete listing of all fish species caught in the domestic, commercial and sport fisheries, as well as information on the numbers of fish caught, the time of year and location of catches, the fishing methods used, an approximate estimate of catch per unit of fishing effort, the way fish are used after being caught, and the numbers of people involved in each fishery and the locations of fishing camps.*

36. *Before pipeline activity begins, the Agency shall establish regulations to control the level of fishing activity by Company* personnel during construction, and shall develop programs to monitor changes in fishing activity that result directly or indirectly from the pipeline project.

37. During the pipeline construction period, no sport fishing shall be permitted from pipeline structures or within the pipeline right-of-way. Personnel engaged in pipeline construction, operation or maintenance shall not fish within 1,000 yards of any domestic or commercial fishery, or any area, such as a well-defined fish overwintering region, that is vulnerable to overfishing. Maps and descriptions of prohibited areas shall be posted in pipeline camps, and explained to personnel in worker-orientation programs.

38. The Company shall ensure that all fishery regulations are observed by all persons working on the pipeline project.

10 Northern Conservation Areas

A Northern Conservation Strategy

With the rejection of the Arctic Gas pipeline proposal, there is now an opportunity to plan for land use in the Mackenzie Valley and the Western Arctic without the pressure of imminent, large-scale industrial development. This opportunity should not be lost. Clearly, comprehensive land use planning can only emerge from a negotiated settlement of native claims — indeed, a settlement of native claims is the keystone of land use planning in the North. At the same time, significant natural and cultural resources can be protected by conserving areas of various types. And areas can be conserved in a manner that does not prejudice native claims. In fact, as I explain below, some withdrawals of land may be necessary if claims are not to be prejudiced by industrial development.

Conservation areas should not be selected only from those lands that are of no value to industry. Conservation is itself an important land use and areas should be identified and set aside while the options are still open. In Volume One, I recommended the establishment of a number of conservation areas, including a wilderness park in the Northern Yukon, a whale sanctuary in west Mackenzie Bay and bird sanctuaries in the Mackenzie Delta and the Mackenzie Valley. Planning for these and other conservation areas can and should proceed now.

In the last century, at a time when western lands were wholly under federal jurisdiction, the Government of Canada established the great national parks in the Rocky Mountains. An act to establish Banff National Park was passed by the House of Commons in 1887, during the administration of Sir John A. Macdonald. In the North today, we have the same opportunity to set aside conservation areas in perpetuity.

The possibility of an energy corridor across the Northern Yukon and along the Mackenzie Valley has focused attention on this region and I have recommended that specific areas be set aside to protect the Porcupine caribou herd, the white whales of the Beaufort Sea, migratory waterfowl and raptors.

While I attach great importance to these specific recommendations, I am anxious that there should be adequate planning for all northern conservation areas before proposals for new large-scale frontier projects are advanced.

Evidence presented to the Inquiry indicates the need for a northern conservation strategy — a strategy that recognizes the claims of northern native people, as well as the constitutional situation in the North and the special characteristics of the northern environment. Such a strategy would include not only the setting aside of land and water for scenic, scientific and recreational purposes, but the protection of critical habitat for fish and wildlife, which are essential to the welfare of native people of the North.

1. As part of comprehensive planning in Canada's North, the federal government should develop a northern conservation strategy to protect areas of natural or cultural significance. This strategy should comprise inventories of natural and cultural resources, identification of unique and representative areas, and withdrawal and protection of such areas under appropriate legislation.

2. A northern conservation strategy should be implemented by distinguishing the different types of conservation areas and matching the degree of protection to the nature and importance of the resource. Such conservation areas may include wilderness parks, national parks, national marine parks, national landmarks, wildlife areas, wild rivers, historic water routes, historic land trails, ecological reserves, recreation areas, and archaeological and historic sites.

3. There should be full consultation with native people before lands are withdrawn for any conservation area in the North.

4. As far as possible, the pipeline route shall avoid all areas identified as having natural or cultural significance whether they have been formally withdrawn or not. Where such areas cannot be avoided, the Company shall prepare, for Agency approval, plans for special protection measures to be used during construction, operation and abandonment of the pipeline so that the natural or cultural values of the areas are maintained.

Major Environmental Recommendations (Volume One)

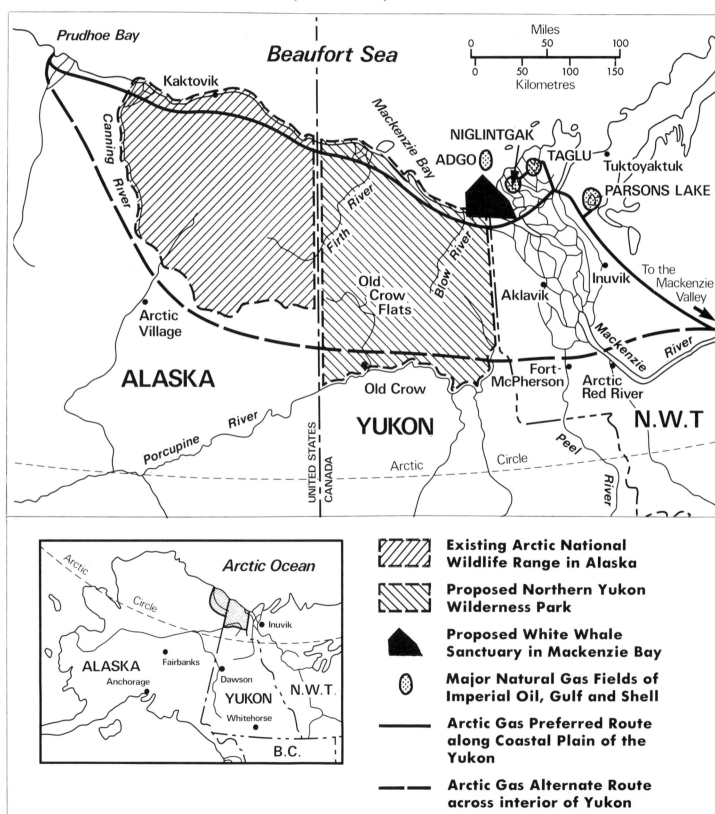

Proposals Made by the United States in Alaska

Since Volume One was released in May of this year, the Government of the United States has made certain proposals for the conservation of lands in Alaska. These proposals give an enhanced timeliness both to the recommendations I made in Volume One for the establishment of conservation areas such as a wilderness park in the Northern Yukon, and to the recommendations I make in this chapter.

In September 1977, the Carter Administration proposed amendments to Bill H.R. 39, called the Alaska National Interest Lands Conservation Act. Those amendments call for some 90 million acres in Alaska to be set aside as conservation lands. This is in addition to the nearly 30 million acres in Alaska that are already dedicated as national parks and wildlife refuges. The President's proposals include designating 2.5 million acres as wild rivers, 45 million acres as new wildlife refuges or expansions to existing wildlife refuges, and 42 million acres as new national parks or expansions to existing national parks. The area to be devoted to conservation lands in Alaska will total 120 million acres — almost one third of the entire state.

In the United States, wilderness is a designation overlaid or superimposed upon those existing conservation areas, such as national parks, wildlife refuges and national forests, that qualify under the Wilderness Act. The Carter Administration has recommended that 43 million acres of existing and proposed conservation lands in Alaska be designated immediately as wilderness. This includes the Arctic National Wildlife Range, which lies entirely in Alaska. The Administration also proposed a non-wilderness addition to the Range that would double its size to about 17 million acres. The proposed Yukon Flats National Wildlife Refuge (in Alaska) — some 8.5 million acres — would be contiguous with the Range on the south. One hundred miles of the Porcupine River west and downstream from the Yukon–Alaska border is also proposed for inclusion in the Wild and Scenic River System.

I cite the United States' initiative in Alaska to illustrate the appropriate dimensions, timeliness and feasibility of a wilderness park in the Northern Yukon and of a broadly based conservation and land reserve program in the Canadian North. In Volume One, I proposed that we should not only establish a wilderness park in the Northern Yukon, but that we should seek to establish an International Wilderness Park, comprising the Northern Yukon and the contiguous area of northeastern Alaska, that is, the Arctic National Wildlife Range. Given the United States' proposal to designate the Arctic National Wildlife Range as wilderness, the establishment of an international park lies within our reach.

Wilderness Protection

Wilderness is a non-renewable resource. If we are to preserve wilderness areas in the Canadian North, we must do so now: the areas available will diminish with each new industrial development on the frontier. Wilderness areas, if they are to be preserved, must be withdrawn from any form of industrial development. That principle must not be compromised.

I have already stated in Volume One the case for the establishment of a wilderness park in the Northern Yukon — a case based upon the most authoritative and exhaustive examination of environmental protection in any region of Canada. But the wilderness does not stop at the boundary between Alaska and the Yukon. In fact, the calving grounds of the Porcupine caribou herd extend well into Alaska, along the coastal plain as far as Camden Bay, 100 miles to the west of the international boundary; the area of concentrated use by staging snow geese and by nesting and moulting waterfowl also extends far into Alaska. So we must cooperate with the Government of the United States. That is why I urged in Volume One:

> If a decision should be made in favour of a pipeline along the Alaska Highway Route, or over any other southerly route across the Yukon Territory, I recommend that any agreement in this regard between Canada and the United States should include provisions to protect the Porcupine caribou herd and the wilderness of the Northern Yukon and Northeastern Alaska. By this agreement, Canada should undertake to establish a wilderness park in the Northern Yukon and the United States should agree to accord wilderness status to its Arctic National Wildlife Range, thus creating a unique international wilderness park in the Arctic. It would be an important symbol of the dedication of our two countries to environmental as well as industrial goals. [p. 50]

An agreement has been reached between our two countries to build a pipeline along the Alaska Highway Route. Now we should work toward an agreement for the establishment of an international wilderness park.

It may be said that means already exist to protect wilderness areas such as the Northern Yukon under the National Parks Act and under the Canada Wildlife Act. Without doubt, these statutes are useful, but they have weaknesses that could undermine the wilderness concept. Under the National Parks Act, permission, leases and permits may be granted for a wide range of activities, many of which are incompatible with the wilderness concept and wilderness values. Within national parks, the area used for intensive visitor activities is normally quite small and most of the park area is reserved in its natural state. But zoning of national park lands can be changed without consulting Parliament.

A cooperative wildlife sanctuary established under the Canada Wildlife Act would also have fundamental limitations with regard to protection of the wilderness. The Act does not provide for exclusion of development. At the discretion of the Minister, permits for various industrial activities may be granted. Furthermore, no conditions attached to a permit could protect the wilderness values of a wildlife sanctuary — the Canada Wildlife Act was never intended for that.

Wilderness and wilderness values are too important to be offered anything less than the protection that only Parliament can confer or withdraw. Our present legislation is not adequate, so our National Parks Act should be amended to provide for a new statutory creation: the wilderness park.

Wilderness protection should be granted to the whale sanctuary in west Mackenzie Bay that I proposed in Volume One. Like the Porcupine caribou herd, the white whales of the Beaufort Sea are an international resource, and the establishment of a whale sanctuary in which development is excluded is the only means to protect the population that calves in Mackenzie Bay. In Volume One, I discussed this proposal at length and I found it possible to limit the boundaries of the proposed sanctuary to waters where no discoveries of gas or oil have yet been made. Thus, if present trends continue, a whale sanctuary can be set aside, and oil and gas activity can be forbidden there without impairing industry's ability to tap the principal sources of petroleum in the Mackenzie Delta and beneath the Beaufort Sea.

The wilderness concept has the potential for wider application in the North; other, as yet undisturbed, areas may also merit such strong legislative protection from the activities of industrial man. The identification and protection of other wilderness areas should be a significant component of the northern conservation strategy that I have recommended.

5. *Lands for the wilderness park in the Northern Yukon should be withdrawn immediately under section 19(c) of the Territorial Lands Act and accorded strict legislative protection through an appropriate amendment to the National Parks Act. Agreement should be sought with the United States regarding the establishment of an international wilderness park in the Northern Yukon and northeastern Alaska.*

6. *Wilderness protection should be afforded the area of west Mackenzie Bay that I proposed be set aside to protect the calving grounds of the white whales.*

7. *In the future, wilderness protection should be provided for appropriate conservation lands in the North, following consultation in this regard with northern governments and northern peoples.*

National Parks

National parks are intended to protect areas that are representative of a broad natural region, including geological, physiographical, geographical, oceanographical and biological features.

Parks Canada has identified 39 terrestrial and nine marine natural regions across Canada and the long-range goal is to identify and protect in national parks at least one area within each of these natural regions. In a policy statement issued in 1972 under the authority of the then Minister, Jean Chrétien, the Department of Indian Affairs and Northern Development said: "At least 30 more National Parks are needed [across Canada] to preserve that which is best in our natural environment" (*Byways and Special Places*, p. 44). The extension of the national parks system to the North should be an essential part of a northern conservation strategy.

Pre-emption by industrial development is a very real threat and may prove an almost insurmountable impediment. It may mean that only smaller or second best areas will be available for park purposes. And it may mean years of effort and negotiation before agreement can be reached. Such land use conflicts have already been encountered in the North: with mining interests in negotiations for Kluane National Park in the Yukon and with hydro-electric development in negotiations for Nahanni National Park, Northwest Territories.

National parks have a valuable role to play in preserving representative natural areas. Some of the natural regions in the North are now represented in three existing national parks — Kluane, Nahanni and Auyuittuuq — and other natural areas of Canadian significance are being studied.

8. *As part of a northern conservation strategy, national parks should be established so that each of the major terrestrial and marine natural regions of the North is represented and protected in Canada's system of national parks.*

Other Conservation Areas

National Heritage Areas

Parks Canada has a mandate to establish types of conservation lands other than national parks. In 1972, Jean Chrétien announced the Byways and Special Places Program, which set out new initiatives to preserve our national heritage. Particularly relevant to the Mackenzie Valley and Western Arctic were proposals for national landmarks, wild rivers, historic waterways and historic land trails. Although considerable planning has taken place, no conservation areas of these types have been established that were not in existence prior to 1972. The Mackenzie Valley and the Western Arctic offer many possibilities for implementing these new initiatives.

National landmarks are intended to protect small, unique natural features. After ten years of deliberation and negotiations, it appears that Canada's first national landmark may be established among the pingos east of the Mackenzie Delta on the Tuktoyaktuk Peninsula. Other unique natural sites should be given appropriate protection as soon as possible before land use conflicts arise.

Parks Canada has made a preliminary survey of 65 wild rivers across Canada, including 22 in the Yukon and Northwest Territories. It is unfortunate, in my view, that this inventory has not been used as a basis for creating a system of protected wild rivers in Canada, similar to the United States National Wild and Scenic Rivers System. Certain proposed national parks may contain outstanding rivers, but in the absence of specific means of protection, important natural waterways may be altered or obstructed without due consideration of their value. The best opportunity to set aside unspoiled rivers in Canada today is in the North.

Conservation Areas of International Importance

Canada is a participant in major cooperative programs — the International Biological Programme (IBP) and its successor, the Man and the Biosphere (MAB) Program — to preserve genetic and biological resources and to study man's relationship to his environment, including measuring the impact of major development projects. Basic to these programs is the establishment of natural conservation areas that can serve both to protect important ecological features and as permanent outdoor laboratories for baseline and comparative studies. For example, under the IBP, which terminated in 1974, a large number of candidate ecological reserves were identified in the Mackenzie Valley and Western Arctic. In 1975, the Minister of Indian Affairs and Northern Development gave his support in principle to the concept of ecological sites in the North, but no sites have yet been established. Action to protect areas identified by the IBP and the MAB Program should be an essential part of a northern conservation strategy.

Wildlife Areas

Provisions for wildlife protection and wildlife sanctuaries are vital to any comprehensive conservation strategy in the North. The idea of sanctuaries is not new: Constance Hunt, in "The Development and Decline of Northern Conservation Reserves," traces the history of the public reserve system and game regulations in the Northwest Territories since 1877.

Today, formerly inaccessible wildlife populations and critical habitat are subject to disturbance and are threatened by the advance of a wide range of frontier developments. The Environmental-Social Program's Wildlife Habitat Inventory and the Biological Report Series prepared for Arctic Gas provide a new foundation on which to build; and there is new legislation, the Canada Wildlife Act. This Act reflects new knowledge about the sensitivity of wildlife to disturbance and the critical role of habitat and life stages. It offers the protection that I said must be afforded the bird sanctuaries I recommended be established in the Mackenzie Delta and Mackenzie Valley. That is, the Canadian Wildlife Service, through the Canada Wildlife Act, can control activities even when the birds are absent, so that the habitat, not just the birds, is protected. Let me add that withdrawal under this legislation will not result in the exclusion of exploration and development; rather, the Act controls activities so that they are compatible with wildlife protection.

Many of the populations of birds and wildlife in the North are international in range. The Canadian Wildlife Service has the mandate and the means under the Migratory Birds Convention Act and the Canada Wildlife Act to fulfil its national and international responsibilities. The Yukon and Northwest Territories are also responsible for preserving game under Territorial Ordinances.

As part of a northern conservation strategy the federal and territorial governments should identify and set aside wildlife conservation areas.

Recreation Areas

Outdoor recreation by local people and tourists is an essential ingredient of northern life, and one that will increase substantially in the future. Development activities in general will assuredly lead to a sharp increase in outdoor recreation in the Mackenzie Valley. With increased access, a growing population and a wider knowledge of the region, will come a need for recreational facilities, such as roadside parks and camping areas. These recreation lands should be identified now before the choice becomes further limited.

Archaeological, Cultural and Historic Sites

A strategy for northern conservation should also include historical, cultural and archaeological sites. Places of cultural significance to the native people are being identified in their claims and, through a negotiated settlement, such places can be protected. It is important, nonetheless, that Parks Canada's program for commemorating persons, places and events of national historic significance should give greater recognition to native history.

Native Claims Aspects

To what extent will a northern conservation strategy bear on native claims? I dealt with this question in Volume One in relation to the proposal to dedicate the Northern Yukon as a wilderness park. I said that such action would not prejudice native claims because preservation of the wilderness and of the caribou herd is plainly in keeping with the desires of the native people. The rights that the native people would enjoy throughout the area covered by the park would have to be negotiated between themselves and the Government of Canada as part of a comprehensive settlement of native claims. These rights would include a core of essential conditions such as hunting, trapping and fishing rights within the park. The people of Old Crow, who live within the boundaries of the proposed park, have already announced their support for the park. So what will the strategy mean elsewhere as far as native claims are concerned?

I do not think withdrawal of conservation lands will prejudice native claims. It is not the withdrawal of conservation lands but rather the activities on these lands under existing or future permits, that prejudices native claims. Withdrawal would protect these lands from incompatible exploratory and industrial activities until a settlement of native claims is reached. The government cannot have a double standard; it cannot refuse to withdraw lands on the grounds that that would prejudice claims, while at the same time grant land use and exploration permits and allow consuming uses of land — alienations that clearly prejudice not only the claims of the native people, but the interest of all Canadians in the preservation of northern lands.

The national parks already established in the North were withdrawn under Section 19 of the Territorial Lands Act, and were later established as reserves for national parks pending the settlement of native claims. They are also subject to native hunting, trapping and fishing rights. This is clearly spelled out in Section 11 of the National Parks Act.

Native people must be guaranteed their hunting, fishing and trapping rights in all conservation lands in the North. As I said, the full extent of their rights to the lands in question must be negotiated between the Government of Canada and the native people; but I go further. I think a northern conservation strategy offers an opportunity to involve native people in the whole conservation lands program in the North.

This involvement should be formalized through a claims settlement, but there is an opportunity for immediate involvement in fish and game management, in compiling inventories of environmental and recreational resources, and in management of wilderness parks, and wildlife and other conservation areas. This would offer native people employment, training in skills that are relevant to the preservation of their northern homeland, and in a livelihood that would allow them to remain in their own communities and regions. There is no reason why management of northern conservation areas by native people should not be an objective of the Parks Canada Program and other conservation lands programs.

9. *When government withdraws conservation lands, it should formally guarantee to the native people that such withdrawals will not prejudice their claims and that no final disposition of these lands will be made until there is a settlement of claims.*

10. *Government agencies that have mandates relative to conservation lands must offer guarantees of traditional hunting, trapping and fishing rights within conservation areas.*

11. *A principal objective of claims negotiations should be the development of joint programs between the Government of Canada and native people for the management of conservation lands and of renewable resources.*

Conclusion

In this chapter, I have urged that the federal government adopt a northern conservation strategy. In so doing, I am simply pulling together federal policy in a number of areas. The policy I have enunciated is not my policy: it is the Government of Canada's policy — and it is opportune to implement that policy in the Mackenzie Valley and the Western Arctic now, before new proposals for industrial development on the frontier come once more to the fore. A northern conservation strategy will not prejudice a settlement of native claims; rather it can, for the reasons I have given, enhance it.

Finally, although a range of proposals are made in this chapter, the area of land they encompass is small when measured against the vastness of the Canadian North, or even when it is measured against comparable proposals made by the Carter Administration for Alaska.

PART THREE

The Project

11 Location, Construction Plan and Scheduling

Location

The first issue I shall address in this discussion of the project is the location of the pipeline right-of-way and its facilities. Throughout the course of the Inquiry, the general routing of the Mackenzie Valley pipeline between the Mackenzie Delta and the Northwest Territories—Alberta border has, for the most part, been taken for granted. But for many people, the proposed locations of the pipeline right-of-way, ancillary facilities and access routes are unacceptable. In particular, the native people have insisted on their right to reserve decision on routing pending settlement of their claims.

Apart from minor differences, the alignments of the mainline, as proposed by Arctic Gas and Foothills, are virtually identical and their potential for impact is, consequently, very similar.

Both pipeline companies have made changes in their original routing and location proposals for a variety of reasons. For example, the first change made by Arctic Gas, which moved the alignment east of Fort Simpson, is an improvement in environmental terms; the fact that the amended route would pass through the proposed Ebbutt Hills International Biological Programme site does not present a major problem. The social concerns, however, are more serious because now there will be a compressor station and a wharf site very close to Fort Simpson. In addition to large-scale amendments, there have been more modest changes. Both companies have modified the locations of river crossings, wharves, stockpile sites, and access roads; and both have introduced the Niglintgak lateral pipeline. Arctic Gas changed the routing of their Parsons Lake lateral pipeline and abandoned many of their communications towers and associated access routes. Foothills have made minor adjustments in pipeline routing north and south of Norman Wells. Most of these changes represent some degree of socio-economic or environmental improvement but much more can obviously be done by further adjustment of the route, the location of facilities and other areas used by the project.

Native people in all of the communities along or near the proposed route have expressed some basic fears about the location of the pipeline and associated facilities in the Mackenzie Valley. These fears are specifically concerned with the location of pipeline lands in relation to the communities themselves, to traditional land use areas and sites of religious importance, and to geographic features of special significance to native people, such as Great Bear River. In response, both pipeline companies have either made changes in location or indicated their willingness to do so. For instance, to avoid the communities of Fort Good Hope, Fort Norman and Wrigley, Arctic Gas proposed to relocate wharves, stockpile sites, access roads and airfields.

To date, such changes have been introduced unilaterally, and there appears to have been no progress towards instituting a review process for resolving conflicts on pipeline routing and location. In fact, there has been little effective communication on this matter between local people, the pipeline companies, government and other interested groups. Nonetheless, the 1972 Pipeline Guidelines state:

> ... where the pipeline construction is planned to be located in proximity to a settlement — particularly a native settlement or localized area subject to intensive use — then the location of construction camps, associated activities and the detailed siting of the pipeline will be decided by government after consultation with the Applicant, and the settlement council, or local government body, or the native organization. [p. 29]

In terms of minor changes, as opposed to major alterations, there is no convincing evidence that the locations chosen for the pipeline and related facilities are the best, either environmentally or from the point of view of land use. Neither pipeline company has responded to criticisms of specific locations raised by various participants, except to say that the present locations are not final. Nor has there been a commitment to any process of route location refinement in final design that will ensure adequate consideration of environmental and land use concerns. Indeed, during the Inquiry little progress was made on a means to ensure that localities of concern are avoided, and that location refinements will move the alignment to areas of less rather than more environmental and socio-economic sensitivity.

1. The government should adopt policies that afford maximum protection for wildlife and fish in the vicinity of the pipeline route, and that preserve as much of the nearby land as possible in its natural state. These policies should apply to nearby governmental and industrial activities in the vicinity as well as to the pipeline project.

The Agency should ensure that the location, construction and operation of the project are consistent with these policies, and are acceptable to local people. In particular, the pipeline project should be modified to avoid interfering with local fishing, trapping and hunting patterns, and to satisfy the environmental concerns identified elsewhere in this report.

2. Routing must not be decided simply in terms of engineering and cost. Proposals relating to the location of the right-of-way and facilities should be progressively refined by a process of successive Company proposals and Agency and public responses that takes all environmental and socio-economic factors into account. (See Project Regulation and Review.)

3. Before the final review phase, the Company shall submit to the Agency for approval the rationale behind the location of its route and facilities in terms of potential impact on birds, mammals and fish and on traditional land use by native people. The Company shall also submit proposals for modifying the route and locations to meet environmental concerns. If requested by the Agency, the Company shall include social, environmental, engineering and cost comparisons of alternative right-of-way and facilities locations. The Company should address such matters as the following:

Adjustment of the pipeline route and locations to avoid conflict with areas designated as present or future conservation lands. (See Northern Conservation Areas.)

Adjustment of the location of compressor stations, and the groups of facilities associated with compressor stations, to avoid the valleys and rivers tributary to the Mackenzie River, and the mouths of those tributaries. If a compressor station cannot be moved, then the associated facilities — wharf, stockpile site, airfield, borrow pits, road, camp, and waste facilities — should be kept away from tributary valleys and rivers and river mouths.

Adjustment of the location of wharves and stockpiles along the Mackenzie River to avoid interference with communities and domestic, commercial and sport fishing sites.

Modification of the location of borrow pits to avoid any borrow resource conflicts. (See Terrain Considerations.)

Adjustment of route and locations and established aircraft flight corridors to meet the concerns outlined in the chapters on Wildlife and Aircraft Control.

Adjustment of the pipeline route to minimize the length of pipe on terrain that is potentially susceptible to frost heave,

thaw settlement, slope stability, buoyancy and erosion. (See Geotechnical Considerations.)

A review of the location of the Mackenzie Valley pipeline and associated facilities in terms of their potential for separate or cumulative environmental impact. Any relocations of the pipeline or other corridor developments that could reduce environmental impact should be included.

Construction Plan and Scheduling

In Chapter 3 of Volume One, I described how the pipeline project North of 60 will challenge the engineering and logistics capabilities of designers and builders. The challenge relates not only to the size and complexity of the project but also to its remote setting, to the arctic climate and terrain, and to those components of the project and its design that lack precedent. There are, for example, the fundamental and unresolved design problems associated with frost heave. These problems illustrate the deficiencies in some aspects of the pipeline proposal and the inadequacy of the information that is available to the Inquiry and to the government — information that provides the basis for an assessment of the precedent-setting or innovative engineering aspects of the project.

The innovations and problems are not confined to design: the construction plans and proposed schedules for the pipeline also involve techniques that lack precedent. Volume One outlined the major issues related to winter construction — snow roads and productivity — and focused primarily on the Northern Yukon. Similar problems will face a pipeline in the Mackenzie Delta and Mackenzie Valley. The environmental, social and economic assessments made by the pipeline companies were predicated on the assumption that the project would, in fact, be built as proposed. However, any substantial modification to the schedule or to the methods of construction will obviously alter those assessments. If a schedule cannot be met and plans have to be changed, each party concerned would respond in a way that reflects its own area of interest, and the result could be *ad hoc* solutions, loss of quality control, and an increase in accidents. Despite original intentions, it might become impossible to protect the environment and the local people.

We must be careful to confirm all of our assumptions and contingent evaluations. With regard to any potential impact of pipeline construction on the environment — namely, the direct disturbance of wildlife, fish and whole ecosystems — a schedule limited to the winter months should have the least impact. This does not mean that there will be no impact during winter construction, nor does it mean that the potential impact of modifications to the construction schedule will automatically be unacceptable in the Mackenzie Valley. For reasons set out in Volume One, an extended summer season or an all-year schedule would be unacceptable in the Northern Yukon; indeed, it was one of the concerns that led to the rejection of the proposed Arctic Gas route across the Northern Yukon. The consequences of a change to summer and winter construction in the Mackenzie Valley would be substantial because, for one thing, an all-weather road would have to be built. In fact, such a change would invalidate nearly all of the planning and assessments presented to this Inquiry.

Although both pipeline companies have indicated their willingness to accommodate delays for environmental reasons, neither company has developed a contingency plan in case of a delay in schedules. No allowance has been made for delays in the delivery of supplies and materials, or for failure in the river transportation system; but most important of all, no allowance has been made for the possibility of any labour problems such as strikes, or even a lack of skilled labour. The most serious potential problems for the northernmost part of the pipeline that could delay the project from the very outset are insufficient snow and a shorter winter season because of a late fall or an early spring (*See Terrain Considerations: Snow Roads*). At the very least, a contingency plan to counter these events would seem to be an essential part of any construction plan.

Delays in construction activities will involve more than additions to the number of men on the line: each man brought in will require extra food, fuel and equipment and this, in turn, will add to the number of aircraft flights. Extra men will most likely be needed towards spring, which means that any extra flight activity might well take place at a time that is critical for some wildlife activities. As well, extra flights will put more pressure on traffic control programs, on airstrips and community airport facilities, and on local operators. At a glance, we can see the cumulative impact that could result from even this incomplete chain of events following a change in the work schedule.

To resist pressures from the Company to take shortcuts or to change its basic plan in any way, the Agency must identify very early any problems or potential trouble spots. The key factor is to avoid the basic problem in the first place through careful construction. planning and scheduling.

One of the unique features of the Mackenzie Valley pipeline project is the need to consider "extraordinary" or non-project occurrences, such as migrating or staging birds at the site of construction activity. These atypical occurrences will restrict construction activities just as much as any of the usual and foreseeable difficulties, such as labour problems, delivery failures, and extended periods of bad weather. While these events can be anticipated and alternative plans prepared, some of the environment-related incidents may not be so amenable to planning. Nonetheless, environmental constraints must be seen as equally important, and must be incorporated into project plans from the very beginning. The pipeline companies' studies, which were submitted as background information to their applications, and the information available through the exhaustive hearings process, have emphasized the possibility that fish, mammals and birds will, in the course of their own natural cycles, preclude use of some land or water areas at certain times for construction of the pipeline or related facilities. The land-based activities of the native people may also raise conflicts.

Every aspect of the Company's plan that might lead to pressure to avoid or ignore some environmental or socio-economic restriction must be scrutinized from the point of view of the need for contingency planning and scheduling for potential spillovers.

4. The Company shall develop a construction schedule that minimizes the adverse impact of the pipeline project on the socio-economic fabric of the region and on the physical and living environment. To this end, the Company shall submit to the Agency for approval a preliminary construction and logistics plan for each spread, and shall demonstrate their technical feasibility and environmental acceptability.

5. As part of its final design submission to the Agency, and before commencing any work other than clearing, the Company shall provide the Agency with a sequential activity analysis in a form that is acceptable to the Agency. The analysis shall consider all construction-related activities, as well as all possible environmental and other constraints, together with the courses of action that will be followed if such constraints do occur.

6. During construction, the Company shall prepare a monthly progress report for each spread or part thereof, as prescribed by the Agency. The report should detail such matters as the construction progress to date on each spread, keyed to an updated sequential activity program; construction delays and proposed methods for overcoming them, including a revised forecast of project scheduling and activities that show how all physical constraints and all stipulations will be met; the physical condition of snow and ice roads; and the need for any actual or planned additions to the work force that is accommodated in construction and other camps.

12 Geotechnical Considerations

General Approach

The design, construction and operation procedures for a refrigerated natural gas pipeline in the North are unprecedented and must be novel, effective and economical under exceptionally adverse conditions. At the same time, we must protect the northern environment from any possible permanent damage. Many of the unprecedented aspects are related to geotechnical matters. The existence of permafrost along the pipeline route makes it necessary to depart from the engineering design and construction procedures commonly used by the pipeline industry. Some of these departures involve the innovations discussed in Chapter Three of Volume One.

Geotechnical considerations have a direct bearing on three areas of concern: engineering feasibility, the need for remedial construction on a threatened portion of the pipeline, and environmentally undesirable effects of geotechnically related activities. I shall deal briefly with each of these areas before turning to specific geotechnical problems.

The feasibility issue which, in Volume One, was central to my discussion on engineering and construction of a buried refrigerated gas pipeline in the North, is important because several aspects — including chilling the gas — lack precedent. For example, the pipe is expected to heave differentially as it passes through several hundred miles of discontinuous permafrost. Arctic Gas have undertaken an extensive laboratory and field research program into the phenomenon of this frost heave, and during the Inquiry, the mechanism and extent of the heave was the subject of much debate among many experts. Nevertheless, fundamental differences of opinion remain.

It cannot be said that a gas pipeline cannot be built and operated along the Mackenzie Valley, however, the limits within which the pipeline must be designed and built to ensure acceptable performances have yet to be determined. Some uncertainties will doubtless still exist at the start of construction, and they may be resolved only by observing the pipeline in operation. A comprehensive overview of such aspects of the work will obviously be required.

1. These geotechnical aspects of the proposed project that lack precedent and experience should be independently reviewed by a board of competent experts appointed by the Agency. The board should consist of three experts, such as a permafrost geologist, a cold regions geotechnical engineer and a gas transmission engineer, with specialist advisers available as required on temporary assignment.

The evidence I have heard shows that, because of lack of precedent, important geotechnical engineering decisions have been reached using empirical formulae derived from laboratory tests and the interpretation of site conditions that are not well-known. Schedules have been established on the basis of assessments of situations that are not well-understood. It is important to determine the sensitivity to error of such decisions. For example, towards the end of the hearings, Arctic Gas disclosed that certain testing equipment was faulty, casting doubt on the accuracy of information about feasibility of deep burial and surcharge as a practical method of controlling frost heave.

2. The Company should establish the sensitivity to error of decisions based on empirical formulae and site conditions and evaluations that are not well-known. Where the basis for decision is found to be sensitive to error, its reliability should be established by the use of thorough cross-checking procedures that are satisfactory to the Agency.

My concern with the second issue — remedial construction — relates primarily to the environmental consequences of emergency repairs to the line. If these repairs have to be carried out during spring thaw or at a time of year when wildlife is sensitive to disturbance, they could cause unacceptable damage. For example, the Applicant, using for the most part statistics for the operation of warm gas lines in areas without permafrost, predicted a probable pipeline breakage frequency of once in ten years. Such statistics, however, do not necessarily apply to the operation of refrigerated gas pipelines in permafrost areas: the actual performance may be better or worse. Clearly, the lack of precedent, together with engineering innovation and the possible environmental consequences of untimely repairs make it desirable to use design and monitoring methods that will reduce risks.

3. The approach to design, construction method and control should be more conservative than is customary in pipeline engineering practice. In particular, the Company should prepare environmental contingency plans to cover a wide range of project conditions that may arise during construction and operation of the pipeline.

Finally, there are several circumstances that, although acceptable from a geotechnical viewpoint, may be environmentally undesirable. For example, the development of the frost bulb around the refrigerated pipe could, without threatening the pipeline, interrupt drainage and cause terrain damage through permafrost degradation; or it could result in the blockage of low winter flows to downstream pools in creeks where fish overwinter. Although not serious with respect to pipeline operation, the consequences could be environmentally significant.

4. In order to minimize geotechnically related environmental disturbance, the Company should, before construction, obtain as much data as possible on surface and subsurface conditions. Because of the size of the project and the remoteness of the area, it is inevitable that much important information on geotechnical design will be discovered only during construction. The pipeline design phase shall, therefore, be considered as part of the construction phase, to be terminated only at the end of construction. The Company shall establish a workable liaison between those responsible for design and those responsible for construction, and shall demonstrate, to the satisfaction of the Agency, that all the engineering and environmental implications of the design concept are being carried through into construction.

5. Bearing in mind the proposed rapid pace of construction, the Company should establish, in cooperation with the Agency, an appropriate and reliable means of carrying out desirable design changes. Such changes would probably be done by a field design staff, with recourse to the main design office for major design changes only.

The need for a well-selected and organized field team for inspection and construction control is obvious. Bearing in mind the considerable number of people required on this team, and the seasonal nature of the construction schedule, it will be difficult to find and keep qualified personnel. As I mentioned earlier, the work must be as error-proof as possible by conservative design, but a reliable system for checking the work is also needed.

6. The Company should establish an educational program to ensure that all geotechnical field personnel fully appreciate the environmental significance of their work.

The first six recommendations are general, and deal with geotechnical problems in an overview fashion. Given below are descriptions and recommendations on the major geotechnical design aspects: frost heave, slope stability and pipe buoyancy.

A great deal of information on major geotechnical issues was brought before this Inquiry and the National Energy Board; nevertheless, much uncertainty still remains about this critical aspect of the project. I intend to review the evidence so that all parties will know, without laborious research into applications, transcripts, evidence and cross-examination, where the issue stands. I have relied to a great extent on the information in Commission Counsel's final argument and on the subsequent work of my staff in reviewing and updating information. They, of course, referred to the National Energy Board transcripts when doing this.

Frost Heave and Thaw Settlement

One of the most important geotechnical design factors examined during the hearings was frost heave in unfrozen ground, that is, the upward movement of a buried pipeline resulting from freezing. To avoid melting the permafrost, the pipeline companies propose to keep the gas flowing through the pipeline at temperatures below the freezing point of water. However, the permafrost is not continuous, and when the chilled pipeline crosses unfrozen ground freezing would be induced in the soil around the buried pipeline. The frost penetration could, under certain circumstances heave the pipeline in these areas.

A buried refrigerated pipeline through discontinuous permafrost is without precedent. The phenomenon of frost heave applies to a significant length of the proposed pipeline and the control of frost heave is therefore central to the feasibility of the proposed pipeline. The evidence given on frost heave and thaw settlement, as they relate to the construction and operation of the proposed pipeline, reveals that uncertainties still exist in four areas: prediction of frost heave and the effectiveness of the preventive and remedial measures; location of the southern limit of refrigeration; confirmation of design assumptions during construction; and monitoring of frost heave after construction. These four considerations are basic to the geotechnical design of the pipeline, and the resolution of any problems they may cause is essential for an engineering design that is environmentally acceptable.

Prediction of Frost Heave and Effectiveness of Preventive and Remedial Measures

A reliable prediction of frost heave is central to the design of effective frost heave control measures. Attempts to predict the magnitude of frost heave must be based on a complete knowledge of the freezing processes involved. As I described in Volume One, a full understanding of these processes does not appear to exist.

To study the frost heave phenomenon, Arctic Gas carried out a series of laboratory tests and a full-scale field test in Calgary. From these tests they derived a set of empirical equations that they believe encompass the signficant parameters governing frost heave. Their study reveals that the growth of ice lenses where frozen and unfrozen ground meet is governed, in part, by the effective stress in the soils at that location. Once a critical effective stress — the shut-off pressure — is reached, the ice lenses will not grow at the frost front, and the problem of heave is considered solved. Because the shut-off pressure varies with soil type, Arctic Gas determined its value for the range of soils likely to be encountered along the route of the pipeline.

Although heave is the central phenomenon, it is differential heave, — that is, the relative heave of adjacent locations with different soil properties — that requires most attention when considering the adverse effects of heave on the pipeline. A parametric study carried out by Arctic Gas indicated that the time to reach the point at which differential heave became critical, that is, at which rupture of the pipe would occur, is a function of length of heave section, and of the uplift resistance of the frozen ground at each end of the heave section. The study indicated that the minimum time to rupture, assuming frost heave is not controlled, ranges from about eight months to several years. Assuming that the empirical method for predicting frost heave and shut-off pressures is valid, the study concluded that increasing the effective stress at the frost front would be an effective technique for keeping differential heave within acceptable limits.

Based on this understanding of the frost heave problem, both Arctic Gas and Foothills proposed two techniques to limit the effects of frost heave: first, surcharge the ground surface with an earthen berm so that the overburden pressure at the frost front below the pipe approaches the shut-off pressure; secondly, bury the pipe deeper so that higher effective pressures are achieved at the frost front. For special circumstances, and as contingency measures, they proposed a number of other techniques: the excavation and replacement of frost susceptible material; the use of insulation around the pipe, along with granular backfill below the insulation; dual pipelines at river crossings so that gas flow can be run alternatively between each pipe; local increase in the temperature of the gas to relieve the stresses from frost heave; localized freezing to accelerate the growth of the frost bulb so that the frost front beneath the pipe penetrates rapidly to a depth where the overburden pressure is close to the shut-off pressure; and use of slip joints or pliant clay around the pipe to reduce pipe stresses where critical differential heave is anticipated.

Arctic Gas concluded from their test data that the maximum shut-off pressure in the field would be in the range of 4,000 to 5,000 pounds per square foot (psf) and the primary mitigative measures would include either deep burial, or a non-erodable surcharge berm with maximum height of about 10 feet or some combination of both measures, to limit the heaving to an amount acceptable from engineering and environmental viewpoints. They also indicated that berm heights of over 11 feet, and burial deeper than 15 feet, were impractical.

Arctic Gas and Foothills said that, before construction, they will identify areas of potential frost heave along the route and decide on specific measures to limit it. For this purpose, they have characterized the potential for frost heaving of a number of terrain types. They also propose to determine the distribution of unfrozen soils along the route by geophysical profiling immediately after right-of-way clearing. Arctic Gas claim that their geophysical profiling has successfully distinguished between frozen and unfrozen ground.

On October 7, 1976, Northern Engineering Services, engineering consultants to Arctic Gas, informed both this Inquiry and the National Energy Board of a previously undetected leak in their laboratory test equipment. This flaw seriously affects the validity of the test results used to predict the shut-off pressures for various soil types. In their evidence, Northern Engineering Services stated that the shut-off pressures may exceed 7,000-10,000 psf, which is significantly higher than their initial estimate.

In February 1977, Arctic Gas filed with the National Energy Board information regarding their plans for controlling frost heave. In this evidence they conceded that, for virtually all soils to be crossed by the refrigerated pipeline, the depth of burial and the height of berm required to control frost heave would exceed practical limits. Moreover, Arctic Gas indicated, for the first time, that frost heave would be a problem where the pipe passes through shallow permaforst.

According to the new plans presented with the foregoing evidence, insulated pipe with heat trace would be used in all overland sections where the ground is unfrozen, or where permafrost is less then 15 feet thick. Heat probes would be used to prevent the build-up of ice lenses where permafrost is 15 feet or more thick. At river crossings in frost susceptible soils, a heavy casing would be placed around the insulated pipe and heating cables would also be used. Foothills, on the other hand, propose to use insulation, with replacement of frost susceptible materials, to control frost heave. There are, however, no experimental or field observations to confirm that Foothills' approach will work.

A review of all available evidence reveals a number of uncertainties and concerns. First, it is apparent that the phenomenon of frost heave is not well-understood, and that a reliable prediction of frost heave magnitude under various terrain conditions is not yet possible. The major redesign of frost heave mitigative measures by Arctic Gas during the hearings reflects this problem. An erroneous prediction resulted in an unsuitable initial design.

The absence of empirical verification of frost heave predictive methods, the lack of information on the behaviour of pipeline insulating materials, and the lack of precedent for frost heave under operating conditions make it difficult to examine the effectiveness of the redesigned mitigative measures, including insulation and heat tracing, proposed by Arctic Gas. There is also some concern about the environmental effect of the extensive overhead electrical transmission system required for heat tracing. However, the criteria for redesign of frost heave mitigative measures focus on the elimination of frost heave in most areas, which appears to be a prudent approach at this time.

Performance of the insulated pipe proposed by Foothills is particularly sensitive to design errors and standards of construction. The design philosophy is to limit the penetration of the frost front to a depth of about 2.5 feet below the insulation, and, where necessary, to replace the frost susceptible soil within this depth with non-frost susceptible material. Should the frost front penetrate beyond this depth and into frost susceptible material, the resulting total and differential heave, because of relatively low overburden pressure and close proximity to the pipe, could be greater than would have been experienced without insulation. The initial performance of such a pipe could be deceptive in that it may take several years for heave problems to develop; once started, however, they could advance rapidly.

To date, insufficient information exists on where critical conditions for differential heave will be encountered in the field. It is uncertain if the worst conditions were understood and allowed for in the analysis. In extreme cases, lack of information could result in increased maintenance over the life of the pipeline, with attendant environmental implications.

Furthermore, no full-scale tests have been carried out to assess the problem of differential heave. The Calgary field tests were conducted in nearly homogeneous soils, and total heave only was measured. Evidence presented at the Inquiry revealed a concern that the developing frost bulb in the prototype would have both strong and weak sections, depending upon the heterogeneity of the surrounding soil, and that any pipe deformations would be concentrated in the weak sections. The concern is apparently unresolved at this time.

Although it is generally agreed that ice lensing and heave can occur in soil already frozen, that is, behind the frost front, as well as in soil as it freezes, experts disagree on whether or not this phenomenon is of engineering significance to the pipeline over the long term. The study of water migration in frozen soils is a new area of research, and the disagreement results in part from a lack of scientific knowledge.

7. Because the issues involved in the geotechnical aspects of the engineering and construction of the pipeline are unprecedented, and because the detailed experience gained by those *associated with the Mackenzie Valley Pipeline is unusually valuable both in itself and as a base for further necessary investigations and studies, the Company and the Agency should make a sincere effort to use the existing expertise. At the same time, the Inquiry has shown the merits of new and independent appraisal, and this should be encouraged throughout the geotechnical design and review process.*

8. The Company should adopt an approach to unprecedented geotechnical issues that will ensure a suitably conservative design. In particular, the design and construction contract arrangements for the project should be flexible enough to permit substantial changes as more understanding is acquired of geotechnical conditions and techniques.

9. Emphasis should be placed now on further theoretical and field investigation into the effectiveness of insulation plus heat tracing in controlling frost heave.

10. The field drilling program and geophysical profiling should be completed before the final design phase. Detailed subsurface investigations should be carried out at locations typical of those where severe differential heave is anticipated.

The Location of the Southern Limit of Refrigeration

The main reason for refrigerating the gas below the freezing point of water is to prevent permafrost regression and associated environmental and thaw-settlement problems. In northern areas where the pipeline passes through predominantly ice-rich permafrost, potential problems caused by thawing of the ground are a more serious consideration than any problems that could arise from frost heave in occasional segments of unfrozen ground. In such areas, the merit of chilling the gas is obvious. In the southern part of the discontinuous permafrost zone, however, the amount of unfrozen material along the pipeline route increases to the point where potential problems from frost heaving are more serious than problems associated with the thawing of permafrost. Therefore, it is necessary to establish a geographic limit for refrigeration that is, in effect, a trade-off between the problems caused by chilling and the problems caused by thawing of permafrost.

A final decision on the location of the limit of chilled gas transmission is difficult to make. During the Inquiry, Arctic Gas changed their southern limit, which meant that the gas temperature would have remained below freezing to a point approximately 50 miles south of the Northwest Territories— Alberta border. Following the discovery of the flaw in their freezing test apparatus, Arctic Gas again moved the southern limit of refrigeration, this time to a point north of Fort Simpson. This change meant that the section south of Fort Simpson would be kept above rather than below freezing, and any permafrost encountered would be thawed. To maintain pipe stability where this thawing occurs, Arctic Gas proposed deep burial of the pipe; and, in critical locations, they proposed supporting the buried pipe on piles fixed in stable material beneath the thawed area.

Foothills reported that their tentative location for the limit of chilling is just southeast of Fort Simpson. Drilling and terrain analysis from this point towards the Alberta border for a distance of approximately 100 miles indicates that one-third of the route is in permafrost. Some of this permafrost can be expected to have high ice content and, therefore, to be thaw unstable. Foothills' consultants, and the National Energy Board have concluded that additional exploration work is necessary before a final design for thaw settlement is prepared.

A review of the evidence indicates to me that neither pipeline company has sufficient field information on which to base a final decision on the best location for a southern limit of chilling. Sufficient information may not be available until construction begins and evidence is obtained from an examination of the trench walls. Furthermore, the two companies have not developed a "trade-off" approach that will mitigate the adverse effects of chilling and not chilling. Although they investigated the problems of chilling, Arctic Gas have not thoroughly investigated the problems resulting from thaw settlement. There is evidence that problems resulting from permafrost thaw could occur over a longer period of time, and hence involve greater maintenance than those problems associated with frost heave. As well, surface ponding caused by settlement could result in thaw conditions more adverse than those predicted. For this reason, a wrong choice for the southern limit of chilling would increase the need for maintenance and thus the environmental impact.

11. Areas where significant thaw settlement and frost heave could occur should be reliably identified by the Company. Before construction, measures for reducing the impact of thaw settlement should be studied in detail and submitted to the Agency for approval. Where necessary to resolve technical problems related to frost heave and thaw settlement, the Company should conduct supporting field tests to the satisfaction of the Agency.

12. Based on detailed field studies, the Company should use conservative design practices to select a tentative southern limit of refrigeration. This limit is a location south of which the need for cooling equipment is considered remote, using thaw settlement designs with a high factor of safety. If necessary a final decision on the location of the limit of chilling should be postponed until construction, when additional detailed soils data will be available.

13. The design of the cooling equipment should be such that the location of the southern limit of gas cooled below 0°C can be modified, depending upon the behaviour of the pipeline when in operation.

Confirmation of Design Assumptions During Construction

Arctic Gas planned to prepare design manuals and tables that will specify the mitigative measures required for site-specific features such as terrain type and line temperature. Because it is impossible to anticipate all terrain conditions, they propose a design-change manual that will be available before construction begins. This manual is intended to cover most of the changes found necessary because actual conditions differ significantly from those anticipated before the start of construction.

As I said earlier, Arctic Gas intended to identify those locations where permafrost is not present by undertaking geophysical profiling shortly after the pipeline right-of-way has been cleared. They also intended to catalogue permafrost and soil conditions adjacent to and along the right-of-way, and to record, on a mile-by-mile basis, geotechnical conditions in the ditchwall. The frequency of recorded observations in the ditch will be determined by the natural variability of conditions and potentially troublesome sections.

Under the schedule proposed by Arctic Gas, the pipeline would be constructed in three winter seasons, each season being three to five months long. During each winter season, they propose to construct a maximum of 450 miles of pipeline in three spreads in the discontinuous permafrost area. Thus, an average of some 3.75 miles of pipeline per day are to be inspected; problem areas will be identified and appropriate design changes implemented by experienced geotechnical inspectors.

With the rapid pace of construction, it may be difficult to ensure that all geotechnical problem areas are detected and adequately dealt with. Even an examination of the ditch walls may not be sufficient. While the mile-by-mile inspection of the ditch will be helpful, it will not indicate the nature of the soil below the bottom of the ditch. The presence of frost susceptible material may not be established during construction. Furthermore, very highly experienced personnel may have difficulty identifying the nature of frozen soils in a trench wall. Finally, it may be difficult to meet the demand for experienced geotechnical inspectors. For these reasons, frozen soils, frost susceptible material, and areas of differential heave and thaw settlement may go undetected.

14. The Company should demonstrate, well in advance of construction, how it proposes to cope with the problem of selecting, organizing and administering construction control and inspection personnel. (See Project Regulation and Review.)

15. The Company should have on site, as the work proceeds, an adequate team of geotechnical personnel with the appropriate experience to make decisions on the need for design modifications or for further investigation. This team should be efficiently organized and have a working arrangement with contractors that will ensure prompt implementation of the correct design modifications.

16. Before final design, the Company should demonstrate to the Agency that its investigations of soil conditions along the route have been sufficiently detailed to permit the preparation of a design that is reliable and that would require a minimum of changes in the field. The design engineers should develop a systematic feedback of data from the geotechnical field inspector's logging during construction to confirm previous exploration of soil conditions and the site-specific design measures.

17. To ensure that there is a satisfactory mechanism for the prompt identification of problem areas and implementation of design changes, an independent review of the field organization for engineering supervision and construction control should be undertaken periodically by the Agency as construction proceeds.

Monitoring of Frost Heave After Construction

Both Arctic Gas and Foothills stated that they will monitor the pipeline in all areas where frost heave may occur, and Arctic Gas will also monitor all areas south of the limit of refrigeration where frozen soils may thaw.

To measure pipe curvature, Arctic Gas intended to use inclinometers or settlement profilers at river crossings, and risers or other conventional survey techniques in overland areas. They also intended to check the pipeline visually at regular intervals and to use aerial photographs. They estimate that extensive monitoring of frost heave would be required over a 400-mile length, although this calculation may now have changed because of their frost heave redesign.

Because most differential heave will normally occur in the initial years of operation, both pipeline companies recognize that frequent monitoring may be required during these years. The proposed methods of pipeline monitoring may not be suitable for the frequency of observation that may be required during the initial year or two of operation. Some sections of the pipeline may require monitoring monthly. Visual inspections and surveying risers are not only time-consuming and potentially difficult in winter months, they may not detect all locations where differential heave is causing significant change in pipe curvature. If monitoring is not effective or if it is not carried out frequently enough, problem areas may develop undetected, or with insufficient lead time to plan permanent remedial measures. Thus emergency situations may arise, with associated environmental problems.

18. The performance of the pipe should be monitored by the Company on a routine basis in accordance with a schedule approved by the Agency. This schedule should allow for frequent inspections during the first years of operation, with the frequency of monitoring reduced thereafter, depending on the observed behaviour.

19. A study of alternate methods for monitoring the performance of the pipeline, particularly those methods that are feasible for frequent observations, should be carried out by the Company to the satisfaction of the Agency. The use of an instrumented "smart pig," a device that can detect changes in pipe curvature at frequent intervals, is an especially promising alternative and should be given a high priority.

20. Because the monitoring program is without precedent, and because it is an important aspect of the project from an engineering and environmental point of view, both the intended procedure and the results of the program should be thoroughly reviewed and approved by the Agency.

Slope Stability

Slope stability problems involve complex geotechnical considerations that were discussed in some detail at the Inquiry. For the purposes of this report, slope failures in permafrost soils are divided into two categories: shallow failures involving thawed soils, and deep-seated failures involving frozen and thawed soils.

Typical of shallow failures are skin flows, which involve movement of the active layer — the zone of soil above the permafrost that freezes and thaws seasonally — over the top of the permafrost. Skin flows occur in many types of terrain and can be caused by even minor disturbances, such as clearing of the right-of-way. They may also occur in the backfill placed above buried pipe in sloping ground. Arctic Gas stated: "While this type of landslide cannot immediately threaten the integrity of the pipeline, it has been studied in considerable detail because, if left unchecked, unsafe conditions may develop after several thaw seasons" (Northern Engineering Services Co. Ltd., *Some Aspects of Natural Slope Stability in Permafrost in Relation to the Applicants' Proposed Pipeline*, 1974, p. 3).

Deep-seated slides involve displacement of a large mass in the form of blocks of relatively intact material. In the Mackenzie Valley, these slides have affected slopes in the range of 100 to 260 feet high, with an overall slope angle after failure of 9.5° to 20°. Such a large slope failure on the pipeline right-of-way would likely lead to breakage of the pipe.

Creep of frozen soils is a form of slope movement not normally categorized as slope failure. It involves the downhill movement of relatively intact material at a very slow rate.

21. In deciding on the pipeline right-of-way alignment and any subsequent changes that may become necessary during construction, the Company shall avoid, wherever possible, areas of questionable slope stability. Before construction, the Company shall demonstrate, to the satisfaction of the Agency, that it has undertaken adequate field surveys of the route to ensure the identification of unstable areas that might be *affected by project activities and that the necessary mitigative measures have been developed.*

A review of the available slope stability information indicates four broad areas of concern: prediction of flow slide activity; behaviour of deep-seated landslides; effect of interference of subsurface drainage; and creep of ice-rich slopes.

Flow Slide Activity

Skin flows will likely be the common form of slope instability to occur along the pipeline right-of-way. Both Arctic Gas and Foothills have stated that the direct geotechnical and environmental implications of skin flow failures are not severe. However, if these failures should occur to a greater degree than anticipated, and if they are left untreated, additional permafrost regression and subsidence may occur and significant erosion could develop as a result of surface run-off.

Arctic Gas stated that "skin flows can occur for a wide variety of reasons but recent research has stressed the dominant influence of thawing in promoting instability" (Canadian Arctic Gas Pipeline Ltd., *Responses to National Energy Board for Additional Information*, Vol. V, No. 4, Q. 8, p. 4). Accordingly, they have developed a method of analysis based upon the theory of thaw-consolidation. This theory is concerned with the development of excess water pressure in the pores of a thawing soil; it considers the rate at which water is produced by thaw with the rate at which water can be squeezed out of the thawed soil. Excess pore water pressures can result in slope failures. For the purpose of analysis, a slope stability equation was developed to permit computation of the factor of safety against sliding. Although Arctic Gas recognizes other mechanisms that also control skin flows, they have not evaluated them in detail.

By using the slope stability equation and the theory behind it, Arctic Gas intend to identify all potential areas of flow, slide or backfill instability. This equation is also basic to the design of the proposed stabilization measures, and if this equation does not correctly predict actual field behaviour, numerous areas of instability may appear unexpectedly. The slope stability equation is based on the thaw-consolidation theory. Although this theory is supported by valid reasoning and laboratory research, there is only one well-documented case history, which is contained in "An Analysis of the Performance of a Warm-Oil Pipeline in Permafrost, Inuvik, N.W.T." by Morgenstern and Nixon. The authors conclude: "Clearly many more well-documented case histories are required for differing soil and thermal conditions to increase the level of confidence in the application of the theory" (p. 208).

Foothills have challenged the approach taken by Arctic Gas. They argue that the natural variability of the parameters required in the thaw-consolidation theory can be so great as to render the theory unreliable and of doubtful practical value. Other witnesses before the Inquiry expressed similar criticisms. Foothills have emphasized field observation and measurement of actual pore pressures, but have not carried out sufficient field work to demonstrate the practicability of their approach.

22. *The Company should conduct detailed field studies on a number of selected flow slides to consider the effect of variation in topography, slide geometry, soil type and cause. The purpose of this work should be to clarify and extend understanding of flow slide mechanisms in relation to the construction and operation of the pipeline.*

23. *The Company should develop a plan for reliably detecting the occurrence of flow slides along and adjacent to the pipeline right-of-way. Monitoring during construction and operation should be carried out by Company experts experienced in the investigation and assessment of slope stability hazards in permafrost terrain.*

The Behaviour of Deep-seated Landslides

The pipeline route crosses several relatively high, steep slopes, usually at river crossings where there is a possibility that a large, deep-seated slope failure may occur. Arctic Gas identify 33 slopes that are higher than 100 feet and have slope angles greater than 9°. They believe that not all 33 slopes are susceptible to deep-seated failure, because other factors that they consider to be necessary for failure are absent.

The stability of these slopes is assessed using the same basic geotechnical techniques and principles employed in non-permafrost areas. Some modification of these principles is required where the ground is completely or partially frozen. A number of the aspects of deep-seated landslides in permafrost areas are not well-understood, and their behaviour is apparently unique to frozen ground. In particular, uncertainty exists about the magnitude of available strength along potential failure surfaces within frozen ground, and the role of potentially high pore pressures at the permafrost base.

There are no well-documented case histories. The only published analysis of such a slide is found in "The Stability of Slopes in Frozen Soil, Mackenzie Valley, N.W.T." by McRoberts and Morgenstern, and it is based on circumstantial evidence about the soil and thermal condition of the materials actually involved in the slide; as well it lacks topographic data and pore pressure measurements. McRoberts and Morgenstern concluded;

> Geomorphological evidence and experience during drilling at a slide on the Mountain River suggest that substantial pore pressures exist within the unfrozen materials beneath the permafrost. Unfortunately attempts to measure these pore pressures have not been successful and data obtained in the future will be of considerable value in this regard. [p. 572]

Although the preliminary studies conducted by Arctic Gas and their consultants indicate that the deep-seated failure mode can be successfully analyzed using the approach indicated, definite conclusions regarding the reliability of the approach must await the collection of more field evidence. If a critical condition is overlooked, either because field data are inadequate, or because the failure mechanisms are not fully understood, the ensuing landslide would lead to engineering and environmental problems. A large landslide, which could occur rapidly and without apparent warning, might result in emergency repairs with attendant environmental damage.

24. *The Company shall investigate and analyze in detail every slope along the right-of-way with a potential for deep-seated instability. Such slopes should be selected conservatively to ensure that potential failure areas have not been overlooked. Because of the lack of detailed investigations of deep-seated landslides involving frozen material, geotechnical investigations to assess the stability of the higher slopes along the route should be more intensive than those normally undertaken for similar situations in non-permafrost areas.*

25. *Because of the lack of precedent in analyzing high, steep slopes involving frozen materials, the design for any protective or remedial measures such as berming should involve a higher safety factor and a generally more conservative design than is usual for non-permafrost areas.*

Effect of Interference of Subsurface Drainage

Where the chilled pipeline crosses slopes in non-permafrost areas, the frost bulb will disrupt the natural subsurface flow of water. It is conceivable that, under some conditions, especially where the pipeline is on a cross slope, the presence of the frost bulb could cause a significant increase in water pressures upslope from the pipeline. Any resultant landslide would tend to occur unexpectedly, and the slide could be large enough to threaten the integrity of the pipe or to cause environmental problems. Emergency measures may also be required, with their attendant environmental problems.

The possibility of slope failures that result from interference with subsurface drainage has not been adequately considered by either pipeline company.

26. *The Company shall design and test the feasibility of methods for relieving subsurface water pressures on the uphill side of the frost bulb. During construction, geotechnical field personnel should be aware of this potential hazard. Evidence of significant subsurface seepage adjacent to the right-of-way should be reported, and protective measures should be implemented as required.*

Creep of Ice-rich Slopes

Although initial theoretical work indicates that, under some circumstances, ice-rich permafrost soils on slopes can creep a significant amount over a number of years, there is little evidence to show whether or not this acutally takes place in the field. It is recognized, however, that the creep would probably be most significant on the steeper slopes or soils that have a relatively high ice content. Creep may thus be an important consideration at only a limited number of locations.

Creep movements, if they do occur, would likely proceed at a relatively slow rate. It is probable, therefore, that suitable field instrumentation could detect such movements at an early stage and suitable remedial measures could be implemented before the pipeline is affected.

Arctic Gas believe that creep would likely not be a significant factor affecting the pipeline; nevertheless, they have proposed a number of methods to overcome the problem if it should occur. In 1975, they initiated a testing program to determine the creep properties of a range of frozen soils. Other studies done previously were reportedly carried out at higher stress levels than would be encountered on the pipeline. The purpose of the testing program is to provide data for "less conservative final designs" (Canadian Arctic Gas Pipeline Ltd. "Written Direct Testimony, Phase 1A, National Energy Board Hearing," Exhibit N-AG-3-81, Sec. 4, p. 12).

The two pipeline companies have not stated how they would identify areas where significant creep might be anticipated. Given the lack of field information on the creep behaviour of ice-rich slopes, it is unlikely that any reliable method to anticipate creep now exists. Arctic Gas have recognized the need for designs to combat slope creep, but they have so far discussed only concepts; and no specific data exist on the effectiveness of these concepts.

27. *The Company's research into the creep of ice-rich slopes should continue until the Agency feels that sufficient information exists to make a confident engineering prediction of those slopes with a potential for significant creep movements.*

28. *A detailed annual inspection of all slopes that may be unstable shall be included in the postconstruction monitoring program. In their monitoring, the Company shall make use of slope instrumentation techniques acceptable to the Agency.*

Pipe Uplift Problems Unrelated to Freezing

The pipeline companies considered two potential causes of pipe uplift not related to chilling of the gas: buoyancy, and pipe stresses that result from the thermal expansion of the pipe and from the high gas pressure.

An analysis of Arctic Gas alignment sheets indicates that a potential buoyancy problem may exist along 44 percent — at most — of the route from Richard's Island to the Alberta border. In non-permafrost terrain, buoyancy problems may occur in rivers, open bodies of water, muskegs, peat swamps and low-lying flat areas that have a high water table. In permafrost terrain, additional buoyancy problems may occur in beaded streams, thermokarst ponds and ice-rich slopes. As identified by Arctic Gas, the three basic conditions under which buoyancy could occur are: open water flotation, for example, water crossings or wherever free water is encountered in the ditch; delayed flotation following natural flooding of a backfilled ditch where there is inadequate resistance to uplift; and pipe flotation following the melting of permafrost in silty or organic soils that have a high ice content.

In their application, Arctic Gas listed seven methods of restraining buoyant pipe; nevertheless, they have stated that, except for open water areas, they will rely as much as possible on deep burial of the pipeline. They intend to make limited use of anchors.

There are basically three consequences of uplift due to buoyancy. Uplift before pipeline start-up will interfere with the schedule; uplift south of the limit of chilling, during operation, may interrupt surface drainage and necessitate the mobilization of a substantial work force and a temporary shut-down of the pipeline; finally, uplift after abandonment would interrupt surface drainage with its attendant environmental problems.

Uplift due to stresses in the pipe, induced by temperature changes and high gas pressure, can occur where the pipe bends, but it is a particular concern at overbends — perpendicular bends in the pipe, such as at the top of a hill. Although a very real problem, the portion of the pipeline likely to be affected is believed to be considerably less than the portion affected by flotation. Uplift from this cause could affect the construction schedule and interrupt surface drainage.

Design of Control Measures

Pipe flotation problems are a well-known difficulty in the pipeline industry. I was told about a portion of the Pointed Mountain Pipeline located in muskeg that floated in the first year after completion of the pipeline: the saddle weights had slipped off the pipe. A group of Canadian experts that included members of my staff visited the Soviet Union in October 1975, and in Northern Russia they observed sections of large diameter pipeline floating with inadequate weights.

The problem of re-installing an uplifted or floating pipe is a serious one, and Arctic Gas have stated that they intend to avoid the problem by taking a conservative design approach; they are depending primarily on burial to control overland buoyancy problems. The selection of design value for the submerged unit weight of the backfill placed over the pipe is a critical aspect of the present design approach. For backfill soils with submerged unit weight in the 20 to 40 pounds per cubic foot range — a range that is common — the size of the backfill mound and its integrity, particularly with regard to erosion of the mounds and slumping of ice-rich backfill, are critical. A design approach vulnerable to change in field conditions may cause frequent pipe flotations in areas where soil conditions differ only moderately from those assumed during design. In view of this, Arctic Gas' safety factor of 1.25 is probably too low.

It is also apparent that some backfill soils will thaw and behave as a thick slurry. This problem may go unrecognized when the soil is in the frozen state. The work Northern Engineering Services carried out for Arctic Gas in August 1974 (*Depth of Overburden Cover over the Pipe and Pipe Anchorage, Technical and Cost Considerations*) is not applicable because it would lead to a result on the unsafe side.

It is important to bear in mind that pipe flotation normally occurs during thaw seasons. This means that, if emergency repairs became necessary, they would have to be carried out during a period that is usually difficult from a logistics and environmental standpoint.

Although the potential for pipe flotation could be severe south of the limit of refrigeration, neither pipeline company has investigated this aspect in any detail. Most of their work has involved the potential for uplift before start-up north of the limit of chilling.

Although uplift and exposure of the pipeline could pose serious engineering problems, in some areas towards the south it may be possible, from an engineering standpoint, to tolerate an uplift condition. However, there may well be unacceptable environmental ramifications if the condition goes unattended for any length of time.

The design of field pipe bends must take into account unprecedented gas pressures and thermal conditions in a large diameter pipe. Faulty pipe bends, if not identified during pressure testing, will likely become evident immediately upon start-up. The risk of problems developing from this source should lessen after start-up.

29. *The Company should conduct detailed drilling and route investigations to identify the location of those areas requiring uplift control measures not related to freezing, and to determine the most suitable design. In particular, uplift due to buoyancy should be taken into account when selecting the southern limit of chilling.*

30. *Greater emphasis should be placed on the depth of pipe buried in areas subject to uplift caused by buoyancy. The cost-benefit approach initiated by Arctic Gas should be expanded to allow for factors such as the cost of design uncertainties, possible effects on schedules and maintenance costs.*

31. *The prudent approach to the design of buoyancy controls and pipe bends is the use of a suitably high factor of safety. The Company should consider the use of a varying safety factor with reference to the reliability and detail of site information, and the local consequences of uplift or buoyancy.*

Design Modification During Construction

The selection and design of buoyancy control measures depends upon site conditions. Decisions will be made well ahead of construction on the measures to be used where buoyancy problems may occur. For example, Arctic Gas have already decided to use a continuous wire-reinforced concrete jacket for the twin 36-inch lines at river crossings.

Despite the additional subsurface investigations to be

carried out along the route prior to detailed design, it is reasonable to expect that some buoyancy problem areas not identified at the design stage will be encountered during construction. Under the proposed construction schedule, such areas would have to be identified by field inspectors, and appropriate design changes implemented.

With the rapid pace of construction, it will be difficult to ensure that all potential areas of pipe buoyancy not identified during design are recognized, and the necessary design changes implemented. Because of the great demand for geotechnical inspectors on this project, they may not be sufficiently experienced to detect, under winter conditions, changes in site conditions significant enough to affect pipe buoyancy and pipe bend design.

32. Because it is desirable to limit the possibilities of pipe uplift, the Company should examine, from the standpoint of buoyancy control, the difficulties associated with field checking and inspection. The Company should demonstrate to the satisfaction of the Agency how it intends to overcome these difficulties. There is a need, for example, to establish local guidelines to assist the inspectors in recognizing and evaluating, under winter conditions, site facts that are conducive to pipe uplift.

Monitoring and Remedial Measures

Even with a proper design approach and effective field control, it is possible that areas with potential buoyancy problems will be overlooked during design and construction.

Significant changes can also occur during operation; for example, erosion and slumping of the backfill mound, and the melting of permafrost south of the limit of refrigeration, could result in buoyancy problems. Because most problems are expected to arise during the initial years of operation, the pipeline companies propose to include in their monitoring program an inspection of all aspects related to buoyancy.

33. The Company should study in detail the engineering and environmental problems that could result from an uplifted or floating pipe, the feasibility of various remedial measures, and the impact of these measures on the environment.

Buoyancy of Pipe Following Abandonment

Both Arctic Gas and Foothills propose to leave the pipe in the ground following abandonment. They have suggested that those portions of the pipe that may become buoyant could be filled with water. This concept has not been studied in detail. In one sense, any buoyancy problems that might develop after abandonment have the greatest potential for adverse impact, because it is not yet decided who will be responsible for remedial actions. Without decisions and agreements in this area, problems may well go unattended.

34. Before start-up of the pipeline, the Company should submit to the Agency a detailed plan on the problems and remedial measures for pipe flotation after abandonment.

35. The Agency and the Company should reach a formal agreement on who will be responsible for any necessary remedial actions after pipeline abandonment, and on how these actions will be funded.

13 Terrain Considerations

Ground Surface Preparation

Terrain disturbance is an inevitable consequence of a construction project such as the proposed pipeline, but this disturbance need not be environmentally unacceptable if adequate mitigative measures are followed. In this and the following sections, I discuss clearing and grading techniques that will reduce environmental damage. Attention is concentrated on the pipeline right-of-way and on access roads to borrow pits, quarries and the sites of facilities associated with the pipeline.

The borrow pits, quarries and the sites of pipeline facilities are themselves not of great concern in this context. By their very nature, these locations will be reshaped and they will, therefore, require major rehabilitation measures that will go well beyond the ameliorative measures required by areas that have been cleared and graded. The pits and quarries will not normally be opened in materials that are erosion- or thaw-sensitive. The sites of facilities can be relocated to some extent to minimize terrain damage, and, in addition, the surface of these sites will be protected by pads of granular fill.

The pipeline right-of-way and the access roads to it are different: they are continuous and they must have smooth, hard, working surfaces throughout their length to permit the transportation of supplies and the operation of specialized mechanical equipment. They will cross areas of sensitive ground and areas with vegetation that are important either as wildlife habitat or as commercial timber. Sometimes such areas can be avoided by changing the alignment of the pipeline, but often other solutions, such as those I discuss in this section, are required.

1. Some disturbance to terrain is inevitable, so the environmental objective during clearing and grading shall be to adapt the methods and schedules of work to minimize disturbance to the vegetation and the ground surface. Particular attention

shall be given to areas in which cuts are required in the crest of slopes, in valley walls and in the banks of rivers and streams.

The first step towards minimizing disturbance is the construction of the pipeline during winter. The many advantages of winter construction are discussed throughout this report, but the principal advantage is that the ground is frozen and snow covered and it is, therefore, able to withstand the passage of heavy traffic without severe damage to vegetation and terrain.

The usual procedure for laying pipe in winter begins with the removal of vegetation and grading to provide a suitable ground surface on which to work. This procedure is unsuitable in the North because of widespread fine-grained and ice-rich soil. There, care must be taken to preserve the lower vegetation and organic mat so that disturbance of the permafrost is kept to a minimum. In this way it is possible to avoid engineering and environmental problems associated with slumping and thermal degradation of the ground surface. Other special procedures, such as snow access roads and snow working surfaces, have been developed to avoid damaging the permafrost. These procedures are essential principles of what Arctic Gas has called arctic construction.

Although the purpose and methods of arctic construction are clear, the specific locations at which it will be used are still a cause of concern. Sensitive terrain occurs all along the proposed route, a fact borne out by the experience of constructing the Mackenzie Highway: problems related to slope stability and erosion occurred, even though special construction methods were used. Because conventional construction methods are simpler and cheaper than the special procedures mentioned above, there will be an understandable tendency for engineers to use them despite sensitive local conditions and therefore, to create environmental problems.

2. All working areas shall be prepared by use of clearing and grading techniques that minimize disturbance to the ground and surface vegetation. Construction plans shall minimize cuts and grading of the ground surface, and the area disturbed shall be the minimum necessary for the execution of the project in a safe manner. Arctic construction techniques, such as snow roads and snow work surfaces over ungraded ground shall be the standard procedure for all construction spreads working North of 60. Conventional procedures that involve grading may be permitted by the Agency for selected stable areas on the basis of site-specific terrain data provided by the Company.

3. Construction of the pipeline at any time of the year other than winter and construction from a gravel-fill work pad shall not be permitted, except when specific approval has been granted by the Agency. The Company shall demonstrate to the satisfaction of the Agency the need for, and the advantages of, such a departure from arctic construction practices.

Clearing

The Forest: Resource, Habitat and Aesthetic Values

Trees must be felled if the pipeline and facilities are to be built, but the loss of wildlife habitat within the project area need not be of major concern, provided certain precautions are taken.

4. Habitat change caused by clearing operations shall be minimized by limiting the extent of clear-cut areas, by avoiding critical habitat areas wherever practicable and by managing the disposal of debris. Particular attention shall be given to protecting fish populations and their habitat from the adverse effects of siltation caused by erosion of cleared areas and by the disposal of debris adjacent to watercourses. Special considerations shall be given to reducing or modifying clearing activities within areas of particular concern to wildlife, such as raptor protection zones. (See Wildlife: Birds.)

Northern forests may be described as patchy, slow growing, and difficult to reach for lumbering. (See Renewable Resources.) Nevertheless, stands of timber of use to local communities may occur on the pipeline lands.

5. Community interests shall be served by avoiding stands of timber that are valuable for local use. If merchantable timber is felled, local communities shall be offered first refusal of it. The timber shall be suitably cut and transported by the Company to easily accessible locations as defined by the Agency in consultation with the communities.

Serious environmental damage can be caused by disturbance of the surface organic layer, particularly on slopes, where the organic layer and a network of plant roots combine very effectively to resist water erosion. In permafrost areas, this protective cover also limits the depth of the active layer (the layer that thaws during summer) and prevents the underlying permafrost from melting, thereby preserving the

stability of the terrain and guarding against a variety of hazardous erosion processes.

6. Because trees are an important element in the aesthetic quality of the landscape or scenery, as well as important in controlling drainage and erosion, stands of undisturbed timber shall be preserved within cleared areas wherever practicable. For example, stands of undisturbed vegetation should be left between cleared areas and waterbodies, and trees should be preserved near buildings and roads, and at campsites, compressor station sites and other facilities.

Clearing Procedures

The clearing procedures proposed by the pipeline companies are expected to be adequate because they resemble present regulated practice in the region, but the scheduling of clearing operations and the use of machines, rather than clearing by hand, are of serious concern. For instance, if the right-of-way is cleared a year or more in advance of construction, there will be a disturbed surface exposed to at least one spring thaw and summer melt. This exposure will be especially critical on slopes where there could be subsidence, slope instability and stream siltation.

7. The period between the beginning of disturbance by clearing and the implementation of erosion control procedures shall be as short as practicable. Where the right-of-way will be cleared a year in advance of construction, temporary erosion control measures should be implemented immediately after clearing, and there should be no clearing of vegetation from river and stream banks, valley walls or erosion-sensitive slopes, except to allow the movement of men and equipment. The clearing of sensitive permafrost areas should be delayed until immediately prior to construction.

8. Only the minimum area essential for the construction of the pipeline or of a particular facility shall be cleared.

9. Trees and shrubs may be cleared either by hand or by machine, depending on the locality. Where it is necessary to maintain an undisturbed organic cover on sensitive soils clearing shall be by hand, unless otherwise approved by the Agency. Clearing by hand may be done at any season, but clearing by machine should be restricted to the winter construction season. It shall not begin until the frost has penetrated deep enough and the snow cover is sufficient to permit use of clearing equipment without adverse effects on terrain. (See Terrain Considerations: Snow Roads.) The shutdown of machine-clearing operations in the spring shall be at the discretion of the Agency.

10. The blades of bulldozers used in clearing shall be equipped with mushroom shoes, except in areas where grading will be allowed. In permafrost areas, bulldozers shall use high-blading techniques to minimize disturbance of the ground surface during clearing operations.

11. Machine clearing shall be discontinued if clean breaks of trees cannot be achieved, or if the number of uprooted trees exceeds the limit deemed environmentally acceptable by the Agency.

12. To minimize drainage and erosion problems, alteration of the ground surface, such as by removal of the organic mat and by levelling of hummocks to facilitate vehicle movement, shall be delayed until construction is about to begin.

13. All cleared trees, brush and other woody material shall be cut so that the stumps are no higher than six inches, measured from the ground on the uphill side. All trees, snags, brush and other woody material resulting from clearing operations should be disposed of by burning, with the exception of survey lines and winter trails, where lopping and scattering will be sufficient. The use of chippers may be authorized by the Agency. The disposal of cleared woody material shall be concurrent with clearing, except where burning would be hazardous, such as in summer, in which case disposal shall be as specified by the Agency.

14. Debris from clearing operations shall be burned on racks or sleds designed for the purpose, on rock surfaces, or in any other area where there is no danger of subsidence because of thawing of permafrost. To minimize the impact on the aquatic environment, burning sites shall be at least 300 feet away from rivers, streams or lakes, except where burning sleds or racks are used.

Snow Roads

Except for preconstruction activity and for the construction of major water crossings and compressor stations, the pipeline companies propose to build the pipeline in winter so that they can move heavy equipment along the right-of-way when the ground is frozen, thereby making all-weather roads unnecessary. All-weather roads are expensive to build and maintain. Moreover, their environmental and social impacts may be greater than those of the pipeline itself because of the increased access into remote areas, permanent effects on land and waters, and the use of gravel, which is a scarce resource in many parts of the North.

To protect the vegetation and the permafrost from heavy traffic, both pipeline companies propose to use snow roads and snow work surfaces. Snow pavements for the pipeline will have to be built to a higher standard than the conventional winter roads that are used in the North. They will be made of snow densely compacted over the naturally frozen, but undisturbed, ground surface. Adjacent to the snow road on the right-of-way there will be a snow work surface along the ditch line; it will be similar to the snow road, but its pavement will not need to be so densely packed because it will have to sustain only a few passes by slow-moving equipment, such as a ditcher.

I described in some detail in Volume One my fundamental concerns about the use of snow roads and snow work pads, but I have no doubt that. once in place, these snow surfaces will work and that they will limit terrain damage and environmental disturbance in permafrost regions. If a pipeline is built in the Mackenzie Valley, the use of snow roads and snow work surfaces in place of conventional, temporary, graded winter roads will be essential. Their use will help to overcome the problems caused by the complex distribution of permafrost in the southern part of the Mackenzie Valley.

15. Snow roads shall be adopted for all construction related to the proposed pipeline North of 60, except where a different mode (for example, a graded winter road) is specifically approved by the Agency.

In theory, the winter construction scheme seems to be an ideal solution to terrain degradation problems. In practice, however, the performance required to minimize terrain degradation from the construction and use of snow roads and snow work surfaces will be difficult to achieve. There are two assumptions underlying the winter construction concept. The first is that the pipeline trench can be backfilled and the right-of-way restored with frozen material in winter, thus preventing thermal degradation and controlling erosion. The second is that the operation and maintenance of the pipeline system can be carried out without permanent road access to the compressor stations and other facilities. These assumptions have yet to be substantiated. (See Location, Construction Plan and Scheduling.)

Scheduling and Sufficiency of Snow

There are two problems related to the construction and operation of snow roads that are different from those related to the possible effects they may have on the terrain, once they are built.

The first is scheduling: can the snow roads be ready early enough and can they be used long enough to enable the season's construction program to be completed on schedule? There is a definite and limited period of time for winter construction, determined on each side by the start of freezing in the fall and thawing temperatures in the spring. If the pipeline company tries to follow a fixed schedule in preparing snow roads, there may be considerable damage to terrain and consequent disruption of construction plans. Schedules must take into account regional and annual variations in climate, snowfall and frost penetration.

Before snow roads can be prepared in the fall, the ground must be frozen deep enough to support heavy vehicles and there must be sufficient snow to protect the surface vegetation. Frost penetration varies from place to place and from year to year. Streams, drainage channels and wet areas will delay road preparation because they feeeze more slowly than the drier, intervening areas. If it is impossible to wait until the frost has gone enough in wet areas to support the movement of vehicles, temporary crossings will have to be built.

Construction activity in the spring will also be of great environmental concern. There will be compelling reasons to try to extend the use of snow roads as long as possible, particularly if the project is running behind schedule. But the shut-down date of a snow road will depend on the onset of spring weather, which varies from year to year. Construction activity must be able to stop at short notice without harm to the environment.

16. The Company shall demonstrate to the satisfaction of the Agency, that its construction schedules based on snow roads and snow work surfaces take into account regional and annual variations in the frost penetration and in the temperatures that are essential for snow road construction and maintenance. The Company shall also tailor its construction plans so that, in the spring, pipeline construction can stop at short notice, before the environment is damaged by the use of deteriorating snow roads.

The second concern is the quantity of snow: in the northernmost parts of the region, particularly in the Mackenzie Delta, early winter snowfalls may not give enough snow to build the road and the work surfaces required by the construction schedule. Snow fences, snow harvesting from lakes, and snow manufacture have all been proposed to supplement the available natural snowfall, but these measures have had only limited testing on a small-scale.

17. For each construction spread year, the Company shall demonstrate to the satisfaction of the Agency the technical feasibility and environmental acceptability of accumulating, harvesting and manufacturing snow, assuming fall weather conditions as defined by the Agency. Some aspects to be considered are the location, method of placement and orientation of snow fences, the anticipated rate of snow accumulation, the uses of the accumulated snow, and the method and time of removal of snow fences; snow harvesting techniques on land and waterbodies, including details of location and of times and means of access to harvest locations; snow manufacturing techniques, including details of quantities of water, locations of water sources, and the times and means of access to those sources; and the impact of snow fencing, harvesting and manufacturing operations on terrain and waterbodies and on wildlife and fish and their habitats.

Overall Plan

To coordinate planning and consultation by both the Company and the Agency, Commission Counsel has suggested that overall plans should be prepared for various aspects of the pipeline work. (See Project Regulation and Review.) Such a plan for the construction and use of snow roads and snow work surfaces would provide an excellent means of tying together some of the logistical, scheduling and technical problems that were raised during the hearings and, at the

same time, it would provide essential background for the recommendations I have made above.

18. Before the final design phase, the Company shall prepare for approval by the Agency an overall plan for all snow roads, snow work surfaces and winter trails that are expected to be used during the construction, operation and abandonment of the proposed pipeline. Subject to the direction of the Agency, the overall plan shall be in cartographic form, and it shall be compatible with the other overall plans requested elsewhere in this report. The Agency may request the Company to resubmit parts of the overall plan that do not meet with its approval. The Company shall undertake to keep the overall plan up to date so that it reflects the latest policies and actions of the Company, the Agency and government.

19. In addition to the requirements of recommendations listed under Scheduling and Sufficiency of Snow above, the overall plan shall specify such items as the general timing and extent of pipeline activities; the location of all snow roads, snow work surfaces and winter trails, and where they cross streams and rivers; the design standards to be applied, including those for stream and river crossings, snow pavement properties, and maximum grades; and the water withdrawal requirements for snow road construction. (See Water Withdrawals.)

20. The overall plan shall be approved by the Agency before site-specific applications are submitted for construction activities.

Site-specific Information

21. The Company shall file with the agency separate site-specific information for the use of snow roads and snow work surfaces for each winter by construction spread, or as specified by the Agency. This information should include such items as the exact location of snow roads, potential water sources, and snow harvesting locations; the methods and equipment to be used for right-of-way preparation (including enhancement of frost penetration), snow harvesting and hauling, snow compaction and ice capping; the date when snow road construction can be expected to begin, the date when it will be required for use, and the flexibility of this date. The information should also detail the nature, number and location of wet areas (including, but not limited to, rivers and streams) that will require special measures during the construction, maintenance or abandonment of a snow road, the methods to be used to cross these areas, and the required crossing dates for each area; the methods and equipment to be used for the construction of ice bridges and the approaches to them; and the methods and equipment to be used to maintain snow roads. The information should include the anticipated date when use of each snow road will be terminated at the end of the winter construction season, and should detail the procedures for terminating their use, for abandoning them and for rehabilitating the areas over which they have passed;

in particular, the procedures for ensuring that snow roads that cross rivers and streams do not interfere with normal break-up and that overland drainage is not blocked or concentrated shall be specified.

Where it is necessary to augment natural snowfall, the site-specific information shall specify the access routes to all water sources and snow harvesting areas; the equipment to be used, and how it will be placed and used so that it does not cause unacceptable terrain damage. Where snow harvesting is planned, the location, dates and methods of harvesting, and the measures to be taken to protect wildlife and fish and to rehabilitate any area so used, especially damaged lake margins, shall be given. Fences to collect snow shall be placed so they do not interfere with wildlife movements and shall be removed by the end of each construction season, unless otherwise approved by the Agency.

Snow Road Guidelines

I have heard a great deal of evidence about snow roads, and I think that it is important to summarize here some of the pertinent guidelines. I do so, of course, in the belief that continued research by the Company and by the Agency will lead to further refinement.

22. Snow road preparation shall not begin until frost has penetrated at least eight inches into the ground and four inches of snow has accumulated on it. However, the Agency may approve plans to accelerate frost penetration and to manufacture or haul snow in advance of its planned use. All types of equipment for the preparation of snow roads and the uses to which they are put shall be approved by the Agency.

23. Snow roads will be maintained to prevent contact between the wheels or tracks of vehicles and the ground surface. Generally, snow roads must have a compacted thickness of 10 inches of snow and a density of at least 0.5 gms per cubic centimeter before traffic other than low ground pressure vehicles will be allowed. In areas of hummocky terrain, the depth of compacted snow will be measured from the crests of the hummocks.

24. Frozen stream crossings shall be made of snow or ice or both. No earth, timber or brush shall form any part of such crossings.

25. An Agency-approved technique or structure for a temporary crossing shall be required for the crossing of any unfrozen stream, both during the preparation of snow roads and during the construction of the pipeline.

26. Access to waterbodies for the purpose of snow harvesting or water removal shall not damage their margins or banks unduly. Cuts should not be allowed, and all fills should be made of snow or ice or both. Terrain damage shall be repaired as soon as practicable. (See Water Withdrawals.)

27. When the snow road pavement begins to deteriorate, the Company shall be ready to terminate its winter construction

activities on a week's notice and shall be prepared to cease using the road on 48 hours' notice.

28. Unless otherwise approved by the Agency, the Company shall remove all material and equipment from the work areas that are serviced by snow roads before the roads deteriorate. If such removal is not practicable, the Company shall store such material and equipment at a location approved by the Agency. Stored material and equipment shall not be moved from such a location without the Agency's approval.

29. All snow roads and temporary winter crossings of streams and rivers shall be removed to the satisfaction of the Agency before spring break-up.

30. In areas where the concentration or diversion of overland flow in spring could result in erosion, snow roads shall be cross-ditched before spring break-up.

31. Terrain damaged during the construction, operation and abandonment of snow roads shall be repaired as soon as practicable.

Drainage and Erosion

Measures to control drainage and erosion are especially important in the construction of a pipeline because, to a large extent, they will ensure the pipeline's uninterrupted service. Such measures, therefore, normally receive careful consideration in the design and maintenance phases of the pipeline. Obviously the construction of a chilled gas pipeline in the North poses special problems because of special geotechnical considerations, such as permafrost and the growth of a frost bulb around the pipe. I think there is ample evidence to show that engineers understand how to protect the pipe: my main concern is not with the safety of the pipeline itself, but with the protection of the environment from adverse effects that may be caused by drainage and erosion.

One of the most important means of mitigating the adverse environmental effects of pipeline construction and operation will be the effective implementation of measures to control drainage and erosion. Terrain damage, obstruction and alteration of watercourses, and siltation must be viewed, not just from the point of view of the pipeline's integrity, but also from the broad perspective of their effects on the physical and living environment. A wash-out on a cut river bank, for example, may not threaten the pipe itself, but it could lead to siltation and thereby threaten important fish-spawning or overwintering habitat.

32. During design, construction, operation and abandonment of the pipeline, measures to control drainage and erosion shall take into account protection of the physical and living environment as well as traditional considerations of design and cost that are associated with the pipeline's safety.

I recognize that the selection and design of measures to control drainage and erosion are complex matters that involve a wide variety of site-specific, physiographic factors. These decisions must, by necessity, be left until late in the design and construction process. Nevertheless, there must be a clear methodology and a timetable for implementing them.

33. The Company and the Agency shall agree on the schedule, the level of detail, and the scale of presentation, review and approval of submissions regarding measures to control drainage and erosion before the final design phase.

I have heard a great deal of evidence on the environmental aspects of drainage and the control of erosion. I summarize this evidence and present my recommendations below under the headings: Surface Drainage and Erosion, and Subsurface Drainage. The next section, Revegetation, deals with a particular mechanism for rehabilitation.

Surface Drainage and Erosion

From our everyday observations, most of us can understand the problems associated with surface drainage and erosion. The ponding of water, the flooding of land because of interference with natural drainage courses, the gullying effect of rainwater on cleared slopes, and the siltation of water-bodies by increased erosion are not uncommon events. On a limited scale, these effects do not cause alarm, but the pipeline and its numerous ancillary facilities will have the potential to disrupt surface drainage on a scale that could lead to unacceptable environmental damage to both land and water.

My concern about surface drainage focuses on three interrelated issues: the approach to the design of the pipeline, the methods of its construction, and the nature of the control methods. I shall deal with each of these issues in turn.

DESIGN APPROACH

The volume of surface run-off dictates to a great extent the measures to control drainage and erosion that must be employed. But the prediction of run-off in the North is not an easy task because of the lack of long-term meteorological data and because of permafrost, which alters the standard coefficients of run-off used by engineers in the South. To surmount these problems, both pipeline companies have devised their own methods to arrive at a general approach and an estimate of the cost of controlling drainage and erosion.

One of the main disputed issues is the selection of criteria to determine surface run-off. My discussion of this topic in the chapter on River and Stream Crossings and the principles I advance there for the selection of the project-flood apply to this problem. This theoretical dispute must be resolved to the satisfaction of the experts involved, but it is apparent that, as with the construction of conventional pipelines elsewhere, the criteria are based almost completely on capital cost and the maintenance cost associated with the pipeline's integrity.

I am not satisfied that environmental concerns have been adequately integrated.

34. The selection of design criteria and the theoretical approach to the design of works to control drainage and erosion shall be on the basis of principles agreed to by the Company and the Agency before final design. In developing such principles, the usual economic considerations that are associated with pipeline integrity shall be augmented to include considerations that are associated with the preservation of the physical and living environment, with emphasis on the elements of the environment that are critical for populations of mammals, birds and fish or are otherwise important from a local land use perspective.

CONSTRUCTION CONSIDERATIONS

Different approaches to the control of drainage and erosion and to the maintenance of surface stability will be required along various sections of the right-of-way, depending on the sensitivity of the terrain and on the degree of ground disturbance. Areas in which arctic construction techniques are used will probably present less serious problems than areas in which conventional winter construction techniques are used because, in the former case, a smaller area of ground will be disturbed — only the ditch line — whereas most of the right-of-way will be disturbed in the latter. However, the consequences of erosion and the difficulty of stopping it, once started, may be much greater in areas of arctic construction techniques because of the sensitive nature of the terrain there.

35. Design and construction plans shall reflect the potential dangers of erosion and the necessity to select sites with minimum slopes. The plans shall show the measures to be taken to minimize disturbance to the ground surface during clearing and construction, particularly in sensitive areas with permafrost and fine-grained soils.

36. Measures to control drainage and erosion shall be implemented as construction proceeds from the first clearing and site preparation through to project completion. In particular, enough stilling ponds, settling basins, sediment traps and other devices shall be installed to ensure that sediment created by construction activities does not adversely affect aquatic habitat.

37. Separate proposals for the control of drainage and erosion along the pipeline right-of-way shall be prepared for areas in which different construction modes are proposed to be used. Proposals shall be prepared for areas of arctic construction, in which the pipeline will be built from a snow road along the right-of-way; areas of conventional winter construction, in which the pipeline will be built from a graded winter road; and areas of summer or fall construction, in which the pipeline will be built from a gravel work pad.

38. Particular attention shall be paid to the maintenance of works to control drainage and erosion at all sites that are used during the construction of the pipeline but that are then closed down and not used during the operation or maintenance of the pipeline. Such sites include, but are not limited to, borrow sites, spoil disposal sites, wharves, stockpile sites, and work pads used during the construction of major river crossings.

SURFACE INSTALLATIONS

The objective in controlling drainage and erosion at all surface installations along the pipeline is to maintain, as far as is practicable, existing natural drainage patterns. Many methods to control drainage and erosion are derived from conventional engineering practice in the construction of highways and piplines, and they can be expected to work along a Mackenzie Valley pipeline if they are conscientiously applied. Extensive research has been devoted to revegetation as a primary method of controlling erosion, and I deal with this aspect in the following section. However, other methods will also be required to maintain drainage and to prevent erosion especially during and after construction of the pipeline and before revegetation is effective.

39. *To avoid the adverse environmental effects of ponding water and of mechanical or thermal erosion that may be caused by channelized overland flow, natural drainage patterns shall be maintained, so far as practicable, in all aspects of the proposed construction.*

40. *Structures to control drainage and erosion shall be designed not only to complement the stabilizing effect of revegetation, but also to achieve the required control unaided by new vegetation. These structures shall be kept in good repair until their function has been completely taken over by vegetation.*

Recent experience during construction of the Mackenzie Highway northwest of Fort Simpson and around Inuvik has provided examples of methods to control surface drainage and erosion in northern conditions that are applicable to the pipeline and its ancillary facilities. Concern for the environment led to the use of fill over sensitive soils, the avoidance of ditch excavation for road drainage, the use of ditch blocks to prevent water from flowing parallel to the road berm, and the use of non-erosive blankets and of ditch checks to prevent erosion. In addition, the use of vehicles away from prepared gravel surfaces was strictly controlled and kept to a minimum to avoid the disruption of drainage on sensitive soils and permafrost.

These and similar methods must be used during construction of the pipeline. Probably the best way to handle surface run-off caused by the spring melt or by summer storms is to guide the water across the right-of-way by low diversion dykes that have breaks in the backfill mound over the ditch. In addition, the sides of the diversion dykes, the backfill mound, and the floors of the mound breaks will have to be specially treated to inhibit the erosive action of running water. This treatment will be supplemented with baffles and diverters to break up and disperse any concentrated flow of water before it drains onto undisturbed land off the right-of-way.

Gravel pads for such facilities as compressor stations, stockpile sites and airfields must be given special consideration. The areal extent of these installations will cause some disruption of surface drainage and may lead to ponding, thermokarst failures and erosion, each of which would have its effects on the local environment. Drainage from such pads may contain considerable quantities of fine sediment, and it must be prevented from reaching any waterbodies. If there is any risk that this drainage contains toxic chemicals, such as fuel or other petroleum products, the problems will be greatly aggravated. Permanent gravel roads present similar problems.

Pipelines and facilities in the northern part of the Mackenzie Delta will be subject to flooding either by storm surges or by ice jams during spring break-up. This danger, of course, will be of particular concern in the design of gas plants and feeder lines, and in any proposal, such as that put forward by Foothills, that requires an extensive gravel work pad for construction purposes. Because all above-ground structures in the Delta area, including structures to control drainage and erosion, will have to withstand the damaging effects of waves and ice jams, there will have to be extensive use there of gravel and riprap. This demand in itself could have a considerable impact through increased use of borrow pits, of blasting and of the necessity for long roads to acceptable borrow sites.

41. *Surface drainage shall be provided across the backfill mound of the ditch, the surcharge berm and the gravel work pad along the right-of-way and elsewhere for roads, airstrips and similar structures according to criteria approved by the Agency.*

42. *Permanent project roads and temporary roads that are to be in place during the summer shall incorporate the best design standards for the control of drainage and erosion practised in northern highway construction. In particular, enough through-grade culverts or bridges shall be installed to allow overland drainage and fish to move freely. (See Fish.) Each culvert should be equipped with a ditch block or diversion structure to minimize the flow of water along the road berms, and ditches shall incorporate measures to prevent erosion.*

43. *Plans shall be presented for the design and installation of measures to control erosion at all stream crossings designated by the Agency. In particular, plans will be required for all crossings of major rivers during summer construction.*

44. *Enough stilling ponds, settling basins, sediment traps or other devices shall be installed to ensure that sediments, particularly silt particles, in water flowing from the right-of-way or from facilities do not adversely effect the surrounding terrain or waterbodies. Particular attention shall be paid to the* prevention of erosion on the banks of rivers and streams, valley slopes, cut-slopes, and in cuts along the right-of-way.

45. All drainage water that contains petroleum products or other chemicals shall be trapped, contained and disposed of according to the provisions outlined in the chapter entitled Management of Fuels and Hazardous Substances.

46. The structures to control drainage and erosion shall be carefully maintained and observed each year as part of the procedure for patrolling the operating pipeline. The Company shall be responsible for constructing and maintaining devices to control drainage and prevent erosion on all lands that have been disturbed during the construction of the pipeline, including not only lands under lease by the Company, but also lands not under lease, such as borrow sites or stockpiles. In some instances, the Company's responsibility may extend to land adjacent to the land under its care, even though this land was not directly disturbed during the construction or operation of the pipeline.

47. Drainage and erosion control devices shall be designed and constructed in a manner that will facilitate travel along the right-of-way. These devices must not be rendered ineffective by the passage of operation and maintenance vehicles.

48. All drainage ways and control structures shall be designed and maintained in a manner that will accommodate any changes in ground level that might be caused by frost heave, growth of the frost bulb, thawing of the ground or surface subsidence along the right-of-way. Allowance shall also be made for disruption of drainage patterns by the growth of stream icings and surface icings along the right-of-way.

Subsurface Drainage

The problems associated with subsurface drainage for a refrigerated gas pipeline remain controversial, and because a technical solution is lacking, they give rise to a number of environmental concerns.

The frozen ground around a buried refrigerated gas pipeline will create an underground barrier along the length of each section of refrigerated pipe that passes through previously unfrozen ground. This barrier will block the movement of shallow subsurface water across the pipeline's route. Ponds or surface icings might be created, or water might begin to move along or parallel to the pipe. Such movement of groundwater on sloping terrain could lead to erosion or to slope instability and, at certain places, it could create problems related to pipe buoyancy. In addition, many rivers and streams have flow within their granular beds. When the pipeline passes beneath such watercourses, the frost bulb created by the chilled pipe could block or divert flow in the streambed. Where streams freeze to the bottom, this streambed flow of water may be vital to the survival of fish that overwinter in the stream's deeper pools.

49. Before the final design phase, the Company shall demonstrate to the satisfaction of the Agency that the frost bulb created by a buried refrigerated pipeline will not create adverse effects on drainage or on terrain, waterbodies or aquatic habitat. Documentation shall include theory, site-specific appraisals and tests, construction techniques, and plans and procedures for operation, maintenance and monitoring. Particular attention shall be given to the maintenance of subsurface flows that may be essential to aquatic resources in winter.

Revegetation

Vegetative cover, with its underlying organic mat and network of roots, plays a vital role in terrain stability and hence in the control of drainage and erosion. In permafrost areas where soils are fine-textured and ice-rich, disturbance of the vegetative cover can cause thawing and lead to problems of instability, such as subsidence and slumping. In both permafrost and non-permafrost areas, the plant cover prevents wind erosion and various kinds of water erosion. Therefore, the maintenance of plant cover is a key to the mitigation of terrain damage and related impacts such as silted watercourses.

Erosion of disturbed surfaces can be prevented by revegetation, but only in conjunction with the non-biological measures to stabilize the surface that I have described in the preceding section. Permafrost degradation cannot be prevented in the short term by newly established vegetation. Other means must be used.

50. Revegetation shall be planned and implemented as a complement to non-biological measures to control drainage and erosion.

The objective of a revegetation program is to control erosion by promoting the re-establishment of plant communities natural to the area. There are, however, fundamental differences between the proposals of the two pipeline companies. Arctic Gas propose to depend primarily on agronomic varieties of grasses to provide the initial ground cover, and on shrub cuttings to revegetate slopes. Native species have only a limited and secondary role in this plan. Foothills, on the other hand, propose to use only native species in their revegetation programs, and to rely to a greater extent than Arctic Gas on vegetative methods of erosion control, including cuttings. In neither case is the effectiveness of large-scale revegetation programs on the right-of-way and at abandoned borrow areas, stockpile sites and other disturbed areas fully proved.

51. The Company shall revegetate all lands disturbed by the construction, operation, and maintenance of the pipeline, first, to control erosion and its environmental impacts, and secondly, to re-establish native plant communities and to restore aesthetic values.

52. *Before the final design phase, the Company shall submit for Agency approval a general plan for implementing the revegetation program on all lands disturbed by the project. Evidence on the effectiveness of the revegetation program to control erosion, together with criteria and a schedule for evaluating the effectiveness of the revegetation program, shall be included in the plan. The use of native grasses, shrubs and naturalized varieties of introduced grasses is encouraged. The plan shall specify the various types and conditions of terrain to be revegetated and shall incorporate the vegetative methods and schedules, the types and mix of seeds, the types and quantities of fertilizers, and the types of equipment to be used. The revegetation plan shall also describe how the procedures, seed mixes and fertilizers will be adjusted to accommodate changes in topography, soil and drainage. Information shall also be provided on the source of supply of the plant material required for revegetation, on manpower and aircraft requirements for these plantings, and on support camp locations, timing, and potential conflicts with wildlife populations.*

Revegetation plans shall include measures to be implemented following forest fires on lands under permit to the Company. (See Terrain Considerations: Forest Fire Prevention and Suppression.)

53. *The Company shall ensure that revegetation, together with the necessary clean-up, regrading, and preparation of drainage and erosion control structures, is completed promptly after the termination of pipeline construction activity or other use of land.*

The speedy establishment of a continuous cover of new vegetation along the right-of-way and in other disturbed areas is the best long-term protection against the adverse effects of erosion and sedimentation. However, it may be some years before the vegetation cover is sufficiently thick and continuous to provide this protection. The success of a revegetation program depends on a stable soil surface. Although there have been some small-scale tests, neither of the pipeline companies has demonstrated that a stable surface for revegetation can be achieved everywhere, especially on slopes or in cuts through ice-rich soils. It appears that a large-scale test of any proposed revegetation procedure should be carried out on slopes in an area that has a high potential for erosion.

54. *Before the final design phase, the Company shall demonstrate to the Agency, by means of approved field tests in the project area, the suitability of its proposed revegetation procedures for the control of erosion on slopes and in cuts through ice-rich permafrost soils.*

Because the initial revegetation program will not at once establish a complete vegetation cover, follow-up programs will be required. These programs will take place primarily in the summer, and they may possibly disturb wildlife populations. In any adjustments to the revegetation program because of such conflicts, or for any other reason, priorities should be established to protect the areas that are most susceptible to erosion.

55. *In all revegetation programs, priority shall be given to the areas that are most susceptible to erosion. Where there may be conflicts between revegetation activities and the disturbance of wildlife, the Company shall prepare for Agency approval special techniques to minimize such disturbance.*

56. *As an integral part of its revegetation program, the Company shall monitor the success of the initial revegetation program and shall repeat the measures required for revegetation until they are successful.*

57. *The Company shall monitor, as part of its construction, operation and maintenance program, the success of its revegetation program. To limit the long-term persistence of non-native species along the right-of-way and to encourage the re-establishment of native plant species, supplementary seedings will be limited to those that are required to control erosion; they will not be allowed solely for aesthetic reasons.*

Forest Fire Prevention and Suppression

In the Mackenzie Valley where forest fires are common, a cross-country construction project such as the pipeline will inevitably become involved with forest fires and their control. My concerns focus on environmental impacts during and after a fire, especially with respect to thermal disturbance of permafrost areas, to slope stability and drainage, and to the destruction of critical wildlife habitat; and on the people, especially with respect to indirect impact of fires on renewable resource harvesting.

There are two main issues — fire prevention and fire suppression — and a corollary issue — the restoration of areas after a fire. Let me deal with each in turn.

Fire prevention during the construction and operation of a pipeline is, in general, the application of technical procedures and the control of employees in a manner that is good practice anywhere. Most of these procedures are routine and do not warrant extensive discussion here. However, the scale of the pipeline project and the nature of its activities, which will be scattered along a corridor through remote and uninhabited areas, parts of which comprise critical wildlife habitat, will add to the normal problems of controlling activities and of educating workers in the use of preventive measures. There is also the very real possibility that some summer construction or maintenance activities will have to be curtailed or delayed when the risk of fire is high. The greatly increased risk of fire during summer must be recognized in all construction planning.

Fire suppression must consider the possibility that forest fires may be caused by project activities, either through carelessness or accidents, such as a ruptured line, or by natural or other causes not related to the pipeline. Obviously fires, whatever their cause, must be suppressed if the pipeline and its facilities are threatened, yet the matter seems to have received less than adequate attention by the pipeline companies. I am concerned by the lack of agreed procedures for the suppression and control of fires, because hasty and improvised measures, such as bulldozing fire-guards (a common approach in the South), can cause extensive environmental damage in permafrost areas.

The restoration of burnt areas, particularly those underlaid by ice-rich permafrost, also concerns me. Fire can reduce the insulating effect of the surface cover and lead to terrain instability; increased erosion could lead to problems of siltation in adjacent waterbodies; and, of course, the pipeline itself could be threatened, in which case extraordinary corrective measures might be, without careful planning, the cause of serious consequences to the environment.

The proposals made by the pipeline companies for fire prevention and suppression do not deal adequately with these issues. The consequences of forest fires go well beyond the project to involve government, local people and local industries. Clearly, there is a need here for a comprehensive and coordinated plan to deal with such fires. The following recommendations, developed from the evidence before me, should serve as the basis for such planning, at least in the area affected by the pipeline.

58. *Before the commencement of any construction activity related to the pipeline, the Company shall submit for approval by the Agency a plan for the prevention, detection and suppression of forest fires that are related to or that may affect the construction and operation of the pipeline. This plan should be developed in collaboration with the Northwest Lands and Forests Service and, where applicable, with the Yukon Forest Service. Because wildlife is of greater value as a resource than timber in the North, the primary environmental object of the plan should be the protection of wildlife habitat, not timber-harvesting interests.*

The plan shall detail fire prevention measures, such as employee education and training; operation and maintenance of equipment; conduct of all pipeline activities associated with burning to minimize fire hazards, with special attention given to preventive measures in summer and winter; and restriction of personnel and curtailment of activities during periods of high risk.

The plan shall detail fire suppression measures, such as fire detection and reporting procedures that take into account existing practices in the North; placement of the necessary equipment and the availability of properly trained teams for fighting fires at construction sites, camps, stockpile areas and all lands adjacent to the pipeline right-of-way; and availability of on-site personnel of both the Company and its contractors to fight fires, if required.

59. *The Company shall keep the fire prevention and suppression plan up to date to reflect conditions along the right-of-way, changes in government operations and procedures, and the success or failure of fire prevention and suppression methods that have been applied on the project or elsewhere.*

60. *In conjunction with the fire prevention and suppression plan, the Company shall prepare measures designed to protect particularly sensitive components of lands under permit to the Company from degradation following a fire. (See Terrain Considerations: Revegetation.)*

Blasting

Blasting is fundamental to construction of any pipeline, and the Mackenzie Valley pipeline will be no exception. Blasting will be extensive and will occur in all seasons for a variety of activities that include quarrying, construction of facilities and river crossings, preparation of the right-of-way and excavation of parts of the pipeline trench. The variability of terrain conditions and the need to make decisions in the field combine to make certain that blasting will occur at unanticipated places at unforeseen times. All blasting has the potential for causing unacceptable disturbance to terrain, wildlife and fish.

Existing standards, which mainly relate to aspects of engineering and human safety, already exist for blasting, and they will certainly apply to the extensive construction operations that have been described to the Inquiry. However, if we are to protect the northern wildlife and fish, then environmental standards are needed for blasting, too. The definition of most of these standards will follow naturally from the sensitivities that I have described in the chapters on Wildlife and Fish and the use of these resources by native people. I have offered specific recommendations for fish, many of which apply equally to aquatic mammals, such as muskrats, beavers and whales. In this section, I expand the subject to include wildlife and to human use of wildlife resources.

My primary concern is that blasting will disturb wildlife — particularly raptors, waterfowl and whales — during the sensitive periods of their life cycles when they are concentrated in certain areas, and that it will disturb aquatic furbearers. Destruction of habitat is also involved.

61. *The adverse effects of blasting on wildlife shall be kept to a minimum, either by scheduling blasting when vulnerable species are not in the area or by controlling the frequency and level of the blast.*

62. *The Company shall confine all of its blasting operations to lands covered by permit from the Agency.*

Throughout the North, the native people are concerned over the effects of blasting on wildlife because of their past experience with the petroleum industry's seismic operations. At the community hearings, the Inquiry heard many complaints about the adverse effects of this blasting. The native people fear that blasting activities associated with the pipeline will further ruin the land and upset the natural conditions for their traditional pursuits.

63. *In planning any blasting activities, the Company shall take into account traditional pursuits of the native people. This consideration shall not be limited to areas in which people hunt and trap, but it shall also include consideration of harvested species during periods when the animals are concentrated or are otherwise sensitive to disturbance.*

With these broad principles in mind, I propose the following recommendations to mitigate the adverse effects of blasting on wildlife, fish, birds and the traditional use of the land by native people.

Overall Plan

64. *Before the final design stage and before any site-specific approvals are granted, the Company shall prepare for approval by the Agency an overall plan for blasting during construction of the pipeline. The form and content of the plan shall be subject to the direction of the Agency, but generally it should outline the Company's proposals to minimize adverse effects of blasting on the environment. The overall plan should indicate such items as: the approximate locations, dates, charge sizes and duration of blasting activities; general land use in the surrounding area, particularly as it may be related to wildlife and to traditional use by local people; methods and procedures that will be used to prevent damage, defacement or destruction of the landscape and waterbodies by eliminating the scatter of blasted material beyond the immediate working area; procedures to minimize shock or instantaneous peak noise levels that may be disruptive to local people, wildlife and fish; and plans to train personnel (who must be qualified to carry out blasting work under existing regulations) in the special environmental impacts that blasting may have and in the mitigative measures that are to be employed in the field. The Company shall undertake to keep the overall plan for blasting up to date and to reflect the latest policies and actions of the Company, the Agency and government.*

65. *The overall plan for blasting shall be approved by the Agency before the Company submits any site-specific construction plans that involve blasting.*

Site-specific Information

Although site-specific applications for blasting *per se* may not be required by the Agency, the Company will have to submit information on blasting as part of the other site-specific applications required elsewhere in this report.

66. *Details on blasting locations, dates, charge size, duration and environmental procedures shall be submitted to the Agency as part of the site-specific construction plans.*

Blasting and Traditional Activities

Land use by northern native people is extensive, and it should not be unduly interrupted, altered or prevented by blasting activities. It is the Company's responsibility to develop a blasting schedule and a program of local communications to ameliorate this problem to the satisfaction of the Agency.

67. *The Company shall notify local people at least one month in advance of any blasting operations planned for areas that are used by the people. Where unforeseen circumstances make such notice impossible, the Company shall notify local people as soon as possible and, in any event, at least 48 hours in advance of actual blasting.*

68. *If a blasting operation in any way puts at risk a camp, trap line or any other aspect of the local people's land-based activity, the Agency shall prohibit it or shall prevent it from taking place until adequate compensation is made.*

Blasting and Wildlife and Fish

69. *Blasting operations shall not be permitted within 1,000 feet of rivers, lakes or streams that are frequented by fish or aquatic mammals without site-specific approval from the Agency. Therefore, the Company must apply to the Agency for permission to blast any site that is within 1,000 feet of a waterbody and demonstrate either that fish and aquatic mammals are not present, or that the proposed blasting activity will not have significantly adverse effects on the fish and mammal populations, fish-spawning beds and overwintering areas, bank stability, silt load, and other components on the specific waterbody.*

70. *The Company shall limit and otherwise appropriately control its blasting activities at times and in areas that are important for wildlife. Unless otherwise approved by the Agency, the following recommendations shall apply to protect particular wildlife species.*

Blasting activity within raptor protection zones shall be prohibited during sensitive periods and at other times, if blasting would damage the nest site. (See Wildlife: Birds.)

Blasting activity in areas used by concentrations of nesting, moulting or staging waterfowl shall be prohibited or severely constrained to limit disturbance so that the birds' normal activities are not interrupted in any way. As a general guideline, blasting within five miles of waterfowl concentration areas shall be considered to be potentially disturbing. (See Wildlife: Birds.)

Blasting activity shall not occur within one mile of marine or estuarine waters when they are being used by schools of migrating, calving or nursing white whales. (See Wildlife: Mammals.)

Blasting activity shall be prohibited in any location where it might disturb or alarm migrating, calving or nursing caribou or Dall's sheep or any herd or band of either animal. As a general guideline, any blasting within five miles of concentrations of these species shall be considered to be potentially disturbing. (See Wildlife: Mammals.)

Blasting activity in habitat populated by aquatic furbearers shall be conducted in a manner that assures the continued well-being of the local populations of furbearing species and the continued harvest of these populations by native people. (See Wildlife: Mammals.)

Borrow Operations

In the North, borrow pits are generally of two kinds: pits in upland areas and pits in river channels. Both kinds were discussed extensively at the Inquiry. In his final submission, Commission Counsel dealt at great length with borrow operations in river channels, largely because Arctic Gas proposed to mine gravel from rivers in the Northern Yukon. Borrow pits in river channels are not a cause of concern in the Mackenzie Valley: their use was prohibited in the guidelines prepared by Dryden and Stein (1975) for construction and operation of the Mackenzie Highway, and those guidelines have become generally accepted practice. The discussion that follows focuses, therefore, on upland pits.

In general, there should not be any serious shortages of borrow materials, but because they are unevenly distributed over the landscape, in terms of quantity and quality, there could be local shortages. And such local shortages could be exacerbated by competing demands from community development, for construction of the Mackenzie and Dempster highways, and from such things as petroleum exploration and development in the Mackenzie Delta and Mackenzie Valley.

The development and operation of borrow pits and quarries must, by their very nature, disturb terrain and they may also have secondary, but severe, impacts on waterbodies, aquatic organisms, mammals and birds. An enormous amount of borrow material from a large number of pits will be needed if the pipeline is to be built: this cannot be avoided. It will not be possible, therefore, to eliminate all impacts on the land and the environment. But if the pits are properly developed and operated, these impacts can be controlled and kept to an acceptable level.

71. The Company shall select, develop, operate, close and restore all pits and quarries in a way that minimizes disturbance to land and the environment and that minimizes the amount of land used and the amount of materials extracted.

Impacts of borrow operations depend on the local terrain and biota and on the proximity of the pit to communities or other developments. Terms and conditions for borrow operations should, therefore, be designed to meet particular concerns about individual pits and their operation. Unfortunately, site-specific recommendations of this kind cannot be made now because neither pipeline company has made a final decision on which pits to use and on how they should be developed and operated. As a result, my recommendations take the form of advice for those persons who will be responsible for developing and reviewing site-specific plans.

Overall Plan

Because many decisions still have to be made with regard to borrow pits and their operation, an overall plan, similar to those I have described elsewhere in this report, will be needed. This plan will enable the Agency to review borrow pit operations in the context of overall project activities, to make proper environmental assessments and to request site-specifc ameliorative measures.

72. Before the final design phase, the Company shall prepare for approval by the Agency an overall plan for borrow operations. Subject to the direction of the Agency, the overall plan shall, as far as possible, be in cartographic form and it shall be compatible with the other overall plans requested elsewhere in this report. The Agency may request the Company to resubmit parts of this overall plan that do not meet with its approval. The Company shall undertake to keep the overall plan up to date so that it reflects the latest policies and actions of the Company, the Agency and the government.

73. The overall plan shall list all the sources of borrow material proposed for use, the quantities and grades that will be taken from each source, the time of year that the sites will be worked, the general purpose, timing and point of use of the materials removed, and the plans for access, development, closure, restoration and abandonment of borrow sites. In addition the overall plan, shall include such items as the mitigative measures that will be used to control the adverse effects on the physical and living environment, and non-pipeline requirements for borrow materials in the project area.

74. The overall plan shall be approved by the Agency before site-specific applications are submitted for use of borrow pits.

Site-Specific Applications

The Department of Indian Affairs and Northern Development is at present revising the Territorial Quarrying Regulations that govern the opening and operation of pits and quarries in the Northwest and Yukon Territories. The stipulations made by Dryden and Stein (1975) that relate to the operation of borrow pits for the Mackenzie Highway have become generally accepted practice. And the Department of the Environment, Fisheries and Marine Service has also developed guidelines to control borrow pit operations, such as *Guidelines Concerning Applications to Remove Gravel From or Adjacent to Streams Frequented by Fish.* These documents, together with our extensive experience with northern borrow operations, provide a solid basis for the implementation of practicable, site-specific terms and conditions. There are, however, a number of points that need to be dealt with in the context of the very large scale that will apply to borrow operations on the pipeline project.

The pipeline project will require large volumes of borrow materials and a wide range of those materials. To ensure that the most appropriate sources are exploited, an exhaustive search and categorization of borrow sources is necessary. Some geotechnically suitable and conveniently located sources may not be acceptable from an environmental standpoint. Other sources may be inappropriate because they conflict with the needs of communities in the region. In many cases, trade-offs will be necessary to ensure that sufficient high-quality borrow material is left for future developments in the Mackenzie Valley and Western Arctic. To enable the Agency to judge if the Company's pit operations are the best possible, in terms of local needs and conditions, site-specific plans for borrow extraction must be submitted for review.

75. *The Company shall file with the Agency a separate site-specific application for permission to open and develop each borrow pit or quarry necessary for the construction of the pipeline and associated facilities. Each application shall be accompanied by a site plan, a mining or extraction plan and sufficient geotechnical and other information so as to demonstrate clearly the viability of the proposed borrow pit development. In particular, the Company shall carry out sufficient geotechnical investigations in the area to ensure, to the satisfaction of the Agency, that the borrow site it has chosen is the most appropriate for the purposes intended.*

The site-specific application should include details on such matters as the borrow source area; the thickness, quantity and grade of materials; test pit and bore hole data; the placement of the pit and its boundaries with estimates of the quantities and grades proposed to be used and to be left behind; the occurrence of permafrost, ground ice and ground water, and the location of the water table. The applications should also give details of the machinery the Company proposes to use; the timing of the various operations; the details of any processing operations that may be used; details of access to the pit, and from the pit to the point of use of the material; plans to control drainage, erosion and sedimentation during operations; the final form of the pit or quarry; restoration proposals, including spoil disposal, and revegetation; and any other information requested by the Agency.

Guidelines for Borrow Operations

The following nine recommendations apply to all proposed pits and quarries. They are followed by recommendations that apply to operations in river channels and flood plains.

76. *Wherever possible, existing borrow sites shall be used in preference to the opening of new sites.*

77. *In developing access to borrow sites, the Company shall use existing roads, trails or cutlines wherever possible. Temporary access roads shall be constructed of packed snow or ice. (See Terrain Considerations: Snow Roads.) An all-weather, gravel access road with culverts shall be provided to any pit designated for summer operation or for continued use during the operations phase of the pipeline.*

78. *The Company shall operate its borrow sites in accordance with the principles detailed in "General Criteria For Gravel Borrow Pits in Upland Areas" and in "General Criteria for Quarry Sites" (Canadian Arctic Gas Pipeline Limited, Responses to Pipeline Application Assessment Group, Requests for Supplementary Information, Appendix A, pp. 45-49 and 59-62).*

79. *Deposits of high ice-content material, of material covered with high ice-content overburden or of borrow material overlying high ice-content silts and clays shall be used only if no other material is available.*

80. *Where processing of borrow materials is necessary, it shall be done in an environmentally responsible manner either in the borrow area or at the site of use of the material. Where processing at these sites is not possible, it shall be done at sites approved by the Agency.*

81. *To protect the physical and living environment borrow sites shall be selected, operated and restored in locations and in a manner that complies with the recommendations in Part II of this report.*

82. *Unless otherwise approved by the Agency, buffer zones of not less than 300 feet shall be left between all waterbodies and the perimeters of pits and quarries; buffer zones of not less than 100 feet shall be left between all public roads and the perimeters of pits and quarries.*

83. *When closing or abandoning borrow sites, the Company shall promptly stabilize and rehabilitate the area and all access roads so that the pit is not left in a derelict state. The rehabilitation of any pit or quarry shall not unduly hinder other parties from re-opening the sites for future use. Any part of a closed borrow pit or quarry where waste material other than spoil or slash has been buried shall be permanently marked.*

84. *Borrow pits and quarries shall be opened and used in a way that permits archaeological surveys to be carried out during all stages of development.*

BORROW OPERATIONS IN RIVER CHANNELS AND FLOOD PLAINS

Special concerns arise over the proposals to extract gravel from the channel zones and flood plains of some rivers and streams. (The terms "channel zone" and "flood plain" are defined in the chapter River and Stream Crossings.) Borrow operations in such areas pose threats to aquatic resources and river regime stability. From a fisheries viewpoint, watercourses, particularly the channel zone, are a highly undesirable source of gravel because that gravel is important for spawning beds and as habitat.

85. The Company shall not open any borrow pits in river channel zones in the Northwest Territories.

86. Where a borrow site is opened in a flood plain, dykes and river training works shall be constructed to ensure that the pit does not become connected with the river and to prevent the river from changing its course through the pit. A 300-foot wide buffer zone of undisturbed flood plain terrain shall be left between the channel zone and the pit.

87. Because flood plains are occasionally inundated, future water levels shall be taken into account in planning the rehabilitation of abandoned pits on flood plains.

14 River and Stream Crossings

The crucial importance of stream crossings from social, environmental and technical points of view was highlighted by expert and lay witnesses throughout the Inquiry hearings. I was told that several technically favourable sites proposed for crossings are a threat to fish, are near areas traditionally used by local people, are near some important archaeological sites or would disturb local environmental or socio-economic values.

To a great extent, the choice of the pipeline route will be governed by the location of favourable (or least unfavourable) stream crossing sites. The objectives in selecting a stream crossing site are similar to those of route selection that I have described earlier, namely to choose a safe and economical pipeline route that will have minimal social and environmental impact. However, the technical considerations involved in the selection of sites for river crossings are different from those that involve the rest of the route. The main technical points that I have heard about include the stability of the valley wall, of river bank slopes, and of the river bed, water levels, floods, scour depth, and river ice phenomena. And, as I have said in Volume One and in the chapter on The Physical Environment, river valleys are not only important to fish populations, and to fish harvesting, they are also biologically more productive than the surrounding terrain. The social importance of river crossings is evident from the native peoples' traditionally high dependence on fishing, on trapping beaver, muskrat and other aquatic furbearers, and on rivers for travel routes.

The choice of sites for river crossings must be made with regard to severe technical constraints as well as many important environmental and socio-economic concerns. The possibility of conflict in such choices is great, and these choices will be among the most troublesome along the entire route.

1. A special review process for the selection of sites for river crossings and their design, construction and monitoring should be established within the framework of the Agency.

The design of river crossings is not regulated by a specific design code, and the general pipeline design code, Canadian Standards Association (CSA) code Z-184-1975, does not touch upon the hydrological aspects of crossing design. It is obvious from the evidence that considerable controversy exists concerning these hydrological design criteria. For example, some of the criteria proposed by the pipeline companies differ significantly from those imposed on the trans-Alaska pipeline, and I have heard vigorous objections to the imposition of the stringent criteria used in Alaska. There is, however, general agreement that specific hydrological design criteria can be and should be drawn up.

2. A design and construction code dealing with the engineering, environmental and local land use criteria for stream crossings should be developed immediately in consultation with the Company.

Development of this code will involve experts from widely differing backgrounds. Geotechnical and pipeline engineers will provide the detailed project requirements; biologists and land use specialists will underline the issues that relate to the physical and living environment. A useful starting point in this task will be the hydrological information contained in the evidence, cross-examination and final arguments before this Inquiry. Commission Counsel's final argument is particularly useful. Therefore, I present below a compendium of the information available to me under five main headings: definitions, design flows and levels, design criteria, construction, and monitoring. Before these guidelines are incorporated into a code, they should be reviewed and expanded by the broadly based group of experts I have just mentioned.

Definitions

Fundamental to any discussion — particularly one involving several disciplines — is a common understanding of technical terms. It became apparent early in the discussion of river and stream crossings at the Inquiry that there were different understandings of basic terminology. Furthermore, in the technical literature the use of certain terms related to hydrology and fluvial land forms is not consistent. To provide clear regulations, some clarification of these terms is required. I have, therefore, assembled definitions of the fluvial terms that are used in this report and I present them here — although some of them are used mainly in connection with matters other than stream crossings.

Watercourses

Strictly speaking, any identifiable trace of concentrated run-off water can be called a stream. Pipeline construction, however, involves at least four levels of effort in crossing streams, and it is useful to tie regulations to these four levels. The Company should not, of course, be in a position to define these four classifications for regulatory purposes.

At the lowest level, there are small intermittent drainage courses, which require the provision of berm breaks. However,these drainage courses do not involve the pipe itself and they are, therefore, considered to be problems of drainage and erosion control. The remaining three levels involve some type of stream-crossing design. The second level comprises small streams for which ordinary crossing designs should be adequate. Crossings of streams in the third level are likely to require site-specific designs and procedures. All crossings within the first three levels are usually carried out as part of the main pipeline construction by the spread contractor. The fourth level comprises the large streams: these crossings may be built under separate contract and possibly before the main pipeline itself is laid in that area.

The reason for classifying streams along the proposed route is to ensure that the Company will undertake appropriate hydrological and biological studies and will evolve design and construction procedures that do not damage the stream. The definitions presented below are intended to serve as a basis for specifying the extent of the studies that will have to be undertaken before a stream is approached and the procedures that will have to be followed to obtain a permit to proceed with construction across it.

3. *The Company and the Agency should use the following definitions of watercourses in river engineering design.*

Watercourse: *a comprehensive term for any identifiable trace made by concentrated run-off water on the earth's surface.*

Drainage course: *any watercourse smaller than a stream (as defined below) for which drainage and erosion control procedures are obviously necessary, but which do not require hydrological or biological work beyond initial identification through mapping and field work.*

Stream (also river or creek): *any watercourse that seasonally offers habitat suitable for fish or that has an average width of channel greater than three feet or that carries perennial flows of water in excess of 0.05 cubic feet per second or that has a drainage basin greater than one square mile. For*

pipeline construction purposes, streams require hydrological and biological study. The groups of designated streams and designated major rivers are introduced to subdivide further the streams and rivers.

Designated stream (*also designated river*): *any stream or river for which site-specific crossing designs and procedures are required by the Agency. The following streams will be included in this category: streams with drainage areas greater than 10 square miles; streams with the potential for significant channel shift and scour at the crossing site; streams that support significant fish populations at some time of the year near the crossing site; and streams the crossing of which may involve significant technical or environmental hazards.*

Designated major river: *any river that will probably be crossed under a separate construction contract or that will be crossed at a time significantly different from the main pipeline construction there. This category includes Great Bear River, Peel River and Mackenzie River.*

4. *Before the submission of the preliminary river crossing design, the Agency (in consultation with the Company) should prepare a complete listing of all designated streams and all designated major rivers to serve as a reference in design review.*

Fluvial Landforms

5. *The Company and the Agency should use the following definitions of valley components in river engineering planning.*

Stream channel zone (*also river channel zone*): *it is generally the smaller of the following two areas: the area between the top of distinct stream banks or between distinct trim-lines of forest or tundra vegetation; or the area of the stream channel that is covered by flowing water at least once in two years over a long-term average. In the case of braided streams, which are characterized by multiple, laterally unstable channels, the channel zone includes the entire braided zone.*

Flood plain: *a low-lying area adjoining a stream channel that is underlain by alluvial (river-deposited) materials and subject to flooding at least once in 100 years over a long-term average.*

Terrace: *an area that was a flood plain at some earlier period in geological time but that is now relatively higher than the stream and therefore not subject to flooding or that is subject to only very infrequent and minor flooding.*

Design Flows and Levels

A basic consideration for the design of a project related to a natural waterbody is the establishment of the worst conditions that the project will have to withstand over its useful life. Except in the case of major civil works, such as large dams or dyking projects, the worst conditions that are assumed are always well below the worst field conditions that can be expected to occur. This fact implies that some risk is accepted. Generally speaking, there are three aspects to such risk: cost, safety and environment.

The Company will handle problems related to cost, but it is widely accepted that the Agency should state the general criteria regarding safety and environment. The primary reason for presenting engineering evidence before the Inquiry was to discuss the environmental consequences of any failure of the pipeline and subsequent repair operations. In setting the criteria for risk, we must remember that the stiffer the criteria, the larger the engineering structure is likely to be and the greater the initial impact on the environment. In the long run, it may be environmentally preferable to accept the risk of occasional failures in return for less initial disturbance. The converse could also be true, depending on the magnitude of the initial disturbance and the cumulative disturbance associated with maintenance and repair.

In any event, one of the basic determinations to be made is the design flow at pipeline-crossing sites. Other flow criteria to be determined include the maximum flows to be expected during the period when the crossing is to be built, design flows for road crossings (culverts or bridges), design flows for gravel mining in channel zones and on flood plains, and drainage design flows. In situations that may involve severe ice jams, fluctuating lake levels, and tides or storm surges in coastal areas, water levels rather than flows will have to be evaluated.

To ensure conservative design and to reduce potentially adverse environmental impact, there must be uniform design flow and design level criteria. However, there is little information about streamflow and water levels from the northern part of the region the pipeline will cross. Meteorological observations are more abundant, so it seems reasonable to adopt a meteorologically based design flood criterion (standard project flood).

6. Pipeline crossings of all designated rivers shall be designed to withstand standard project flood conditions. The standard project flood is a stream flow estimate based on the assumption that the most severe storm or other meteorological condition that may reasonably be considered as characteristic of the specific region is occurring (Beard, 1975). The largest flood that is considered physically possible, if all flood-producing factors were to combine, is the probable maximum flood. It is roughly twice the standard project flood under normal circumstances.

7. Design water levels that take into account ice jamming, storm surges or any other meteorological or hydrological phenomena affecting the design of the designated stream crossings shall be at least as conservative as the standard project flood. The most severe meteorological or hydrological conditions that may reasonably be considered as characteristic of the general region have to be assumed in determining such design levels, and this estimate is generally achieved by imagining that the most severe conditions ever observed anywhere in the region may possibly occur at the site of interest.

8. Design flows and levels for all other (that is, non-designated) stream crossings shall be selected so that they bear the same degree of risk as the standard project flood; however, in these cases individual standard project floods do not need to be determined.

9. Permanent stream crossings by access roads shall be designed to withstand a 1-in-50 year condition of flow or water levels. Temporary facilities, such as work pads in rivers, perimeter dykes of gravel-mining operations in channel zones, and coffer-dams are to be designed on the basis of the probability of levels that are appropriate to the work in question, bearing in mind the siting, timing and anticipated life of the structure concerned.

Return periods, such as the 1-in-50 years floods may be difficult to determine accurately with the data that is at present available, but the intention here is that these return periods should be used as rough guides in applying engineering judgment. The design flows for culverts along the Mackenzie Highway, for example, are based on 50-year flood return periods besides having to meet several requirements for the passage of fish, that are often more stringent. With time, the data base for final design will be much better, and the specified return periods can then be evaluated more precisely.

10. In addition to design flow specifications, structures shall also meet hydraulic criteria for fish passage. (See Fish.)

11. Before the final design phase, the Company shall submit to the Agency the supporting data and computations that have been used to determine design flows and levels.

Design Criteria

Generally, the design for a river crossing incorporates criteria for avoiding or reducing environmental impact. These criteria should be adjusted to reduce the possibility of a failure of the crossing, for that would lead to environmental disruptions and to the need for emergency repairs. The criteria I propose below are related to the location of crossings, location of sag bends, river training works, groundwater flow, overhead crossings, buoyancy control, scour computations, and dual crossings. All of what is said below about these criteria is intended to serve as the basis for discussion among the parties concerned.

Location of Crossings

Some of the most difficult geotechnical problems in pipeline design are caused by stream crossings and, to a considerable degree, the alignment of the right-of-way is governed by the availability of suitable sites for stream crossings. An associated problem, which I discuss in the chapter entitled Geotechnical Considerations, is to maintain the stability of river banks or valley wall slopes. Other problems that I deal with here are more directly related to rivers.

12. In the selection of sites for crossing rivers and river valleys, sites that are unsuitable for technical, environmental or land use reasons shall be avoided. The selection of these sites should precede final selection of the pipeline route.

13. Crossings shall be carefully sited in reaches of rivers in which the stream flow is reasonably stable and straight. Crossings of flood plains and channel zones shall be as short as practicable.

14. A site-by-site evaluation shall be undertaken to determine the approach to be adopted at sites where highway and pipeline crossings are close together. Safety, aesthetics and geotechnical problems tend to favour wide separation but, in some locations, close spacing could minimize the impact of these crossings on fisheries and facilitate future maintenance.

Location of Sag Bends

A buried pipeline that must cross an obstacle, such as a river or a valley, is designed with what the industry calls overbends and sag bends to permit the pipe to run under the obstacle. A typical river crossing involves two of each: the first overbend directs the pipe from the horizontal down the slope of the river bank, then a sag bend enables the pipe to pass horizontally under the obstacle, the second sag bend turns the pipe up the bank, and the second overbend enables the pipe to continue horizontally, as before.

If a river to be crossed flows in a single, well-defined and stable channel, the sag bends are located a relatively short distance landward of the river banks, thus allowing for minor bank erosion and channel shifts during the life of the pipeline. But the problem is not so easily solved when crossing wide, braided channels or channels that migrate at significant rates across a flood plain. There the designer has two options: he can either locate the sag bends outside the present and potential future channel zone, burying the pipeline deeply all across these channel zones, or he can squeeze the channel zone with river training works and build only a short river crossing. The environmental effects of the two alternatives differ because the first involves considerably more initial work, but less permanent interference with the river, than the second. From an environmental point of view, the first alternative — placing the sag bends well outside the present or any future channel zone — is usually preferable because it reduces the risk of having to undertake major repair or maintenance work.

15. The sag bends of all designated stream crossings shall be located far enough beyond the channel zone to ensure that they will still be a safe distance outside the channel zone after 50 years of natural, unimpeded migration of the channel zone. The Agency may waive this requirement if deep burial beyond the channel zone will do more damage than the construction of the river training works that will be needed to avoid deep burial, if channel zone migration cannot be predicted, or if it would be economically unreasonable.

River Training Works

River training works are structures that are used in a variety of circumstances to alter the direction of river flow or to contain it within a particular location. For instance, by the use of river training works, the channel zone of a river can be narrowed to reduce permanently the length of river crossings, or it can be confined temporarily to make room for a borrow operation in the channel zone. River training works can also be used to arrest the normal process of the migration of channel meanders to provide a stable river-crossing site, and they can be built on the flood plain to prevent future meander cut-offs or other channel changes.

Besides the aesthetic considerations involved in despoiling a natural river, training works may interfere considerably with a river by obstructing the passage of fish or causing siltation. Moreover, they require continual maintenance, and many of them can fail, thereby magnifying detrimental environmental effects.

16. Permanent river training works in the channel zone shall be avoided wherever practicable. Where training works are necessary to prevent a river from flowing along the right-of-way of the pipeline or from entering a gravel pit on the flood plain, or to prevent cut-offs or avulsions, they shall be located on flood plains rather than in channel zones.

Groundwater Flow

There is a certain amount of groundwater flow in the materials below most rivers and their flood plains. The quantity of water involved is normally very small compared with the river flow but, in the case of rivers that have little or no flow during certain parts of the year, it may have biological significance. In many parts of the North, rivers freeze to the bottom in shallow places, thus severely restricting or stopping normal channel flow. Under such circumstances, groundwater flow may maintain pools of water in the deep parts of the river or it may emerge as springs at certain locations along the channel. These groundwater-fed areas can be crucial for overwintering fish and eggs (see Fish). If a chilled gas pipeline is buried in alluvial materials, the groundwater flow needs to be maintained.

The effects on groundwater of various construction techniques for crossing rivers and the possibility of obstruction by a frost bulb below a stream are matters for serious concern (see Geotechnical Considerations). These problems are not yet adequately understood. Whether or not there may be a problem with the groundwater flow at a river crossing cannot be known definitely without site-specific knowledge of river and groundwater flow during winter over a number of years, the aquatic ecosystem, and the design for the crossing. This same detailed knowledge is also necessary before mitigative measures can be prepared.

17. *Design proposals for all designated stream crossings (and for any other crossings as required by the Agency) shall be accompanied by conclusive evidence that the maintenance of winter groundwater flow in the general area of the crossing is not of environmental importance or that the maintenance of such flow is of environmental importance but that the installation of a crossing without special mitigative measures will not have adverse environmental effects. Where special protection measures are known to be needed or where there is no conclusive demonstration that they are not needed, the crossing design shall incorporate measures that ensure continued winter groundwater and channel flow across the installation to provide adequate protection for fish populations and the aquatic ecosystem that supports them.*

18. *The Company shall build a test stream crossing at a typical site that has little or no winter channel flow but that does have significant groundwater flow. This test installation should show that the structures can be installed without significantly increasing the environmental impact of the construction process. The test shall demonstrate the effectiveness of the crossing design to maintain a flow of water around the pipeline to points downstream similar to the flow that would occur naturally; normal physical characteristics of water quality, such as suspended sediment, dissolved oxygen, and* temperature; normal chemical characteristics of water quality, such as pH, conductivity and colour; and normal invertebrate and fish communities including eggs in the overwintering areas downstream from the crossing.

Overhead Crossings

Generally speaking, pipeline designers are reluctant to use overhead crossings — even though they provide a technically feasible alternative for crossing most streams — because they introduce construction and maintenance problems that are quite different from those found along the rest of the buried line. Overhead crossings are not part of either of the pipeline companies' proposals for the main pipeline. Nonetheless, there are at least four reasons why they may be environmentally preferable to buried crossings at certain sites. Such structures would avoid the problems of slope stability and erosion in narrow, deep valleys, difficult scour problems in rivers, frost bulbs that might interfere with groundwater flow, and frost heave.

19. *Where preliminary design review indicates that a buried crossing would involve major unresolved environmental concerns, the Agency should instruct the Company to prepare a comparison of the buried crossing with an overhead crossing and to justify its choice of the mode of crossing in both engineering and environmental terms.*

Buoyancy Control

Buoyancy control at river crossings involves standard procedures that are not expected to cause direct environmental concern. However, if the techniques used to control buoyancy prove inadequate — a concern of particular importance with regard to the periodically innundated flood plain — then the pipe will float and will have to be repaired. If these repairs are necessary in sensitive locations or at sensitive times, then the possibility of environmental damage is greatly increased.

20. *Buoyancy control weights shall be required at river crossings for the entire length of pipe that, under design flow conditions, would be submerged.*

Another buoyancy control problem, although not one that exclusively concerns river crossings, is the tendency of saddle weights (concrete blocks that straddle the pipe) to slip off. This slippage may be caused by their having been incorrectly installed, but the problem seems to be particularly acute in muskeg areas, where there is insufficient lateral resistance in the soil to keep the weights stable over the pipe.

21. *Where weights are used for buoyancy control, techniques shall be used to ensure that the weights will not slip off the pipe. Where saddle weights are used, the Company shall demonstrate to the satisfaction of the Agency that the construction procedures used will ensure proper centring of the weights and that, after backfilling, the soils will have* *sufficient lateral resistance to prevent movement of the weights.*

Scour Computations

A considerable amount of evidence was presented to the Inquiry about the unusual and poorly understood phenomenon of the scouring of river beds by ice along the proposed pipeline routes. Scouring occurs under massive ice jams, such as those observed upstream from Point Separation on the Mackenzie River. Related problems include the migration of very deep and not well-understood scour holes that occur in the Mackenzie Delta and scouring associated with spring run-off that flows over and beneath icings. In addition to scouring by run-off, up-ended cakes of ice can scour or gouge the river bed during the break-up period. These kinds of scouring could threaten the integrity of the pipe and cause engineering problems that would have significant environmental consequences.

22. At the request of the Agency, the Company shall submit the data and computations it has used to calculate scour and the general degradation of the river bed at stream crossings. In general, the security of all crossings shall be assured to a level of risk comparable to that of the standard project design flood.

Dual Crossings

At certain times of the year, such as at freeze-up and break-up and during spring flood, it would be impossible to repair pipeline failures at some of the larger rivers. These are, however, the times at which failures are most likely to occur, because then various fluvial processes, such as scouring and bank erosion, are most active.

Although Arctic Gas proposed dual crossings for economic reasons, they may also have an environmental advantage: with dual crossings, repairs in the river or on river banks would not need to be done on an immediate or contingency basis, but they could be scheduled in an orderly way, and due allowance made for environmental protection. Of course, the chance of major environmental degradation caused by emergency repairs at an unsuitable time at any particular single crossing has to be weighed against the detrimental effect of building two pipelines there rather than just one.

23. The Company, in submitting preliminary designs to the Agency for each designated major river crossing, shall explain the reasons, including environmental considerations, that were involved in deciding whether to use a single or a dual crossing. The Agency may extend this requirement to crossings of other large rivers. The preliminary design for any dual crossing shall include the approaches to it as well as the crossing itself.

24. If the project involves long sections of dual pipeline, an adequate number of cross-overs or connections between the

two pipes should be installed during construction to increase flexibility in the scheduling of repairs.

Construction

The problems that are encountered in carrying a buried pipeline under rivers and the techniques used to overcome these problems set the construction of stream crossings distinctly apart from the rest of the pipeline construction. Although river crossings amount to only a small fraction of total pipeline construction, they are a major factor in terms of potential environmental impact.

Timing of Construction

Most of the pipeline will be built during winter, but the construction of the major river crossings is scheduled for summer. In permafrost areas with ice-rich soils, summer construction activities on the approaches to the river crossings could cause problems of terrain instability, erosion and siltation.

The construction of a large river crossing, whether in summer or winter, involves a fairly rigid sequence of different activities, of which the most important are discussed in subsequent sections. These engineering requirements must also be scheduled to accommodate seasons of environmental sensitivity and of land use activity by local people. My concern is that, even with the best of intentions on the part of the Company, unforeseen delays, which are common in any level of construction, combined with very rigid overall deadlines, could disrupt any schedule that was organized, in the first place, to take environmental considerations into account. Unforeseen delays are even more likely in the North than in more temperate latitudes.

25. The Company shall prepare detailed schedules for all construction work associated with crossings of designated streams and shall submit evidence to show that the schedule is realistic and contains adequate allowances for contingencies. In particular, the Company shall show that the proposed schedule for construction and its logistics does not unduly interfere with significant biological resources or with traditional hunting and fishing activities.

26. On request from the Agency, the Company shall draw up construction plans for the crossing of selected designated streams at times other than in winter, and it shall evaluate these plans for feasibility, cost and environmental impact. These plans shall be implemented if so requested by the Agency.

27. Summer construction of river training works shall be avoided unless all necessary materials and equipment can be brought to the site without damage to sensitive terrain.

28. The work pads and approaches to river crossings to be

constructed during summer shall be built in winter unless the Company can demonstrate that summer construction is more desirable at a particular site.

Installation of the Pipe

The various methods of installing a pipeline below a stream bed give rise to a number of closely related concerns. Easiest to cross are streams that dry up during winter, particularly if the excavation for the pipe ditch does not encounter taliks (unfrozen zones) below the channel. Such crossings can be carried out as part of the normal pipe-laying procedure. However, if the ditch intersects taliks, they will complicate construction. Any excavation through them will fill with water, which will then freeze rapidly.

In the chapter on Fish, I have outlined the environmental problems that are involved in winter crossings of streams that carry limited flows and contain overwintering fish or eggs. It may be impossible to predict which streams will be flowing, particularly because there may be marked differences from year to year. Nevertheless, crossings must be installed without interrupting stream flow and without damaging downstream reaches of the river by increased sedimentation.

29. The Company shall endeavour to make or have available periodic observations of winter flow over at least two years for all designated stream crossings before the completion of final design.

30. To minimize the adverse effects of sedimentation and the interruption of stream and groundwater flow, the time between the excavation of the ditch and backfilling it shall be kept to a minimum.

31. All winter construction across watercourses that contain overwintering fish or that have fall spawning areas downstream, which could possibly be affected by the construction, is to be done under dry conditions. These conditions may be achieved by waiting for the stream to dry up, by diverting the stream, or by staging construction through the use of coffer-dams. Water flow, including flow through the gravel under the stream bed, shall be maintained to any areas where there are fish or eggs overwintering, and siltation shall be controlled to the levels outlined in the chapter on Fish.

Much of the material excavated from the ditches at stream crossings will be used as backfill, but any material that is left over must be disposed of in a manner that does not interfere with the stream. The proposed summer crossings of large rivers may create problems of spoil disposal. The excavation by dredge that has been proposed for crossing large channels will primarily involve the removal of sand and silt. The discharge of these materials into the river downstream leads to two basic concerns: an increase in the sediment load of the river and obstruction of the river. The excavation of a ditch by dragline provides much less flexibility in the disposal of spoil than dredging, and the obstruction of the river channel by this

method could be a concern. Spoil from both dragline and dredge operations can be disposed of on land or by barging it to suitable dump sites. Selection of the method to be used should involve a careful review of local environmental factors.

32. Ditch plugs shall be left in place on both sides of a stream crossing until the last possible moment to ensure that little or no flow from the ditch can enter the stream and that no stream flow can enter the ditch.

33. The interference with aquifers below channels that are dry in winter shall be minimized. In particular, the Company shall avoid plugging aquifers with silt or contaminating the groundwater in a significant way. The construction time of crossings that might interfere with such aquifers shall be made as short as possible.

34. The ditch across the stream shall be backfilled with material from the channel bed unless otherwise approved by the Agency.

35. As part of the planning for crossings to be built in summer and for any other crossings that are not built in dry conditions, the Company shall, at the request of the Agency, evaluate alternative schemes for excavation and spoil disposal from an engineering and environmental point of view. If it is proposed to dispose of spoil in the river channel, the Company must show that such disposal will not increase the channel velocity enough to interfere with navigation or with fish migration and that it will not lead to an increase in suspended sediment that may be hazardous to fish. (See Fish.)

36. Blasting should conform to the recommendations listed in the chapter on Fish: Underwater Blasting and in Terrain Considerations: Blasting.

Work Pads and Berms in Channel Zones

At rivers to be crossed in summer, the pipe should be assembled into segments of several hundred feet on a work pad, then pulled across the river. This operation can be done in stages, depending on the size of the work pad and on the width of the crossing. Depending on the topography of the valley, the work pad may be built on a flood plain beside the channel, which is the preferred location, but it may have to be built in the channel zone itself, where it might interfere with stream flow or might get washed away during a flood. If the river erodes part of a work pad, it may cause siltation problems that may be more or less serious, depending on the materials that have been used in constructing the work pad.

Similar problems can arise if the channel or parts of it are dyked off by a coffer-dam to permit pipe laying in dry conditions. An obstruction in the channel will increase the velocity and erosive power of the remaining flow, which could interfere directly with navigation or with fish migration, and it could also cause erosion of the channel bed and of the banks.

37. *The size of work pads or of the dyked areas in the channel shall be limited at any one time so they will not interfere with navigation or with fish migration and will not cause significant erosion at the design flood condition.*

38. *In general, a work pad or a dyked area should not occupy more than two-fifths of the width of the channel zone.*

39. *Any borrow or spoil materials that are left in the river after the removal of a work pad and any other materials that the river may erode shall not alter the morphology of the channel, bank or river bed in a way that may be detrimental to fish or wildlife or to any other use of the watercourse.*

Sedimentation

Many of the concerns related to fish and fisheries have to do with the possibly harmful introduction of sediment into streams. The effects of suspended sediment on stream biota are complex and by no means fully understood. It is, therefore, difficult to state in simple terms what may be harmful to fish and what may not. Whether or not a certain sediment concentration is harmful depends on where and when it occurs. The introduction of fine sediments (silt and sand) into a stream is, however, likely to be harmful — certainly it will not be beneficial — so it should be avoided so far as practicable.

If concentrations of suspended sediment are kept within the natural range typical for the stream site, the time of the year, and the prevailing discharge, no harmful effects are likely to result. Discharge is particularly important because naturally high concentrations of sediment are associated with flood discharges that rapidly wash the sediment down the channel without significant deposition. A similarly high concentration of sediment during a period of normal or low discharge would settle out on the stream bed with environmentally unacceptable consequences.

Many of the recommendations in this section and in other sections of this report that deal with river crossings have the control of sedimentation as their main objective. Further recommendations relating to suspended sediment occur throughout the chapter on Fish.

Restoration of River Beds and Banks

The ditch across a stream channel is normally backfilled with the materials that were previously excavated from it. If the backfill is made to correspond roughly to the original shape of the stream bed, the stream will regrade its bed during the next flood. There is little potential here for significant long-term effects, apart from the initial impacts caused by construction work, which I have discussed above. Fills placed on top of streambeds for work pads, ramps and so forth, must be removed, but their removal generally has little potential for long-term effects on the environment as long as the work is done properly.

The restoration of river banks may have effects in the longer term. Poor restoration is unaesthetic and it could lead

to slides of earth into the river and associated siltation, or the river might break through a cut bank to find a new course. Rivers with broad flood plains and river channels in deltas are normally contained by natural levees. Such levees tend to be very resistant to erosion and are rarely breached by flood flows, although they may be frequently submerged. All of the distributaries in the Mackenzie Delta have such levees associated with them and it is particularly important that they be properly restored at all pipeline crossings.

If the river bank material is ice-rich, a cut into it that is left exposed could initiate a lengthy cycle of thaw erosion. The proposed method for dealing with such cuts is to backfill them with native material, then to blanket them with select backfill to prevent gullying and thaw erosion. If the installation of the river crossing has reduced the resistance of the river bank to erosion, riprap or other measures to control bank erosion, such as gabions and spurs, must be used. My concerns for these problems have been discussed above under the heading River Training Works. The pipeline will frequently approach streams through a cut in the bank, and the cut will naturally attract run-off water. Many river banks are too steep to be restored to their original shape and, unless properly protected, these cuts will develop into deeply scoured gullies and the pipe may become exposed. The Kotaneelee River crossing of the Pointed Mountain pipeline, in the southwestern part of the Northwest Territories, was cited at the Inquiry as an example of this sequence of events.

The danger of erosion to steep river banks and valley walls is one of the most important and most frequently stated environmental concerns related to the proposed pipeline project. The means of preventing such erosion are well-known: they include granular backfills and blankets, insulation, revegetation, and diversion of storm run-off away from the pipeline right-of-way (see Terrain Considerations: Drainage and Erosion Control). These measures are relatively expensive and they are not, therefore, always applied. The problems at river banks are not intrinsically different from those on any other slope.

40. *On the completion of pipeline construction across a stream, the stream bed must be restored to its original shape using native or closely similar materials. On request, the Agency may relieve the Company from this requirement if the Company can show that the stream in question is sufficiently active to ensure restoration of its bed during the first freshet following construction, and that it will not interfere with the biological resources of the stream.*

41. *Stream banks are to be restored as close to their original shape as drainage and slope stability will permit. The restored banks must be as erosion-resistant as the natural banks immediately upstream and downstream from the crossing.*

Monitoring

Although a river crossing is designed to withstand changes in flow and the position of the channel, and to avoid disturbing the natural processes of fluvial evolution, not all changes can be predicted accurately in advance. Prediction of the behaviour of rivers in the North is particularly uncertain because it involves processes that are not encountered elsewhere, such as the formation of icings and the thermal erosion of ice-rich soil along the banks. Although catastrophic changes must be dealt with as contingencies, slower changes can be monitored by repeated measurements that will provide a basis for the planning of countermeasures. Changes that are seasonal or cyclical, as well as those that are progressive, must be monitored. Parameters to be recorded include the rate of channel shift, changes in channel depth relative to the position of the pipe (scour depth), ice jams and their effects, river icings and subchannel flow in streams that have low winter flow, changes in suspended sediment, and pipe movements caused by buoyancy and frost heave.

41. *A monitoring plan and schedule shall be submitted to the Agency for approval with the final design for each designated river crossing. Site-specific adjustments to the plan may be submitted up to the time the pipe is commissioned. During operation of the pipeline, the appropriate governmental body may carry out or instruct the Company to carry out additional monitoring at particular river crossing sites.*

42. *The following components should be part of the monitoring program. Vertical stereoscopic aerial photographs at an appropriate scale should be taken once a year or, for any crossing of a stream that shows significant past channel migration or bank erosion, more frequently. Channel soundings should be made once a year in designated major stream crossings that have mobile beds or are subject to scour; the soundings should extend over a channel reach of about ten channel widths, both upstream and downstream from the pipeline. Soundings and other observations should be made at crossings where major ice jams occur; as soon as possible after each ice jam has formed, the crossing site should be sounded for scour holes; a procedure for detecting scour depth beneath ice jams should be developed. Water flow and levels should be measured during winter at crossings where low water flow or the flow of groundwater is important to overwintering fish; these measurements could include water yield of springs, piezometric measurements of groundwater and observations on icings. Suspended sediment concentrations should be observed as outlined in Fish. The position of the pipe relative to an established datum should be measured at crossings where any freezing of the soil around the chilled pipe could encounter frost-susceptible soils.*

43. *The Company may request permission to drop its monitoring program at any crossing for which there is enough evidence to show that a reduced monitoring program is not likely to lead to engineering and environmental problems.*

15 Water Withdrawals

There are many practical administrative problems associated with water resource management. One of these is the withdrawal of water. Quite early in the hearings, it became apparent that water withdrawals during construction and operation of the pipeline could have substantial environmental and socio-economic consequences.

Construction of the pipeline will require hundreds of millions of gallons of water. And water requirements for the operation and maintenance of the pipeline, while substantially less, will still be significant. Although there are large volumes of water along most of the proposed corridor, there will be localized shortages and conflicts with other, competing uses. The shortages may affect fish and fisheries, and they will be accentuated by the scheduling of major parts of the construction work during winter, when stream flows and water levels are at their lowest. There will inevitably be competing demands for water between the project on the one hand and elements of the local environment on the other. There will be a host of other major and minor considerations, ranging from other human demands on a water resource, concerns over waterfowl and aquatic furbearers, to recreation and aesthetics. The effect of many other project-related activities on waterbodies must also be considered. I have discussed elsewhere wastewater, river crossings, and spills, all of which overlap considerations related to water withdrawal. All of these considerations should be taken together to form a comprehensive water resource management scheme.

The water resources of the Northern Yukon were of particular concern to many witnesses before the Inquiry. My recommendation against a pipeline across that region was partly based on this concern, particularly because of localized water shortages and the effects of low water flows on overwintering fish. The problems of water withdrawals elsewhere along the pipeline route warrant careful attention. Water will be required to test the pipeline hydrostatically, for camps, and for the construction of snow and ice roads, particularly along the northern part of the route where snowfall is low. But whatever may be the project's needs, the constraints imposed by the competing uses of the living environment must be considered. These constraints go beyond the obvious limitations of supply, with which engineers and contractors are familiar, to encompass the less obvious, but equally important, requirements for fish protection, habitat maintenance and aesthetics.

1. The objective in regulating water withdrawal shall be to control the location and time of withdrawal, the volume removed, and associated activities so that they will not adversely affect: other industrial, or domestic or recreational uses of the water; transportation on, or access to, the waterbody; trapping or fishing in or near it by local people; populations of fish and and other aquatic biota in the waterbody; and waterfowl or wildlife that use the waterbody or its margins.

The need to regulate water use is recognized in existing legislation such as the Inland Waters Act and the Fisheries Act. However, it may be that the proposed pipeline, because of its scale, may require measures not considered in the existing statutes. The project will involve hundreds of withdrawal sites and hundreds of millions of gallons of water, all within a very short period of time. Each water withdrawal activity will be linked to the next by very pressing schedules for project design, construction, operation and abandonment. The sites will be spread over an extensive area; the volumes used at some sites will be small but at others very large. Each withdrawal will have broad implications on project activities, on regional environment in general and on local water sources in particular; applications cannot, therefore, be considered in isolation.

The cumulative effect on the environment of all the water withdrawals could well be greater than the sum of the individual withdrawals. So, in planning and regulating the project, we must take a regional overview, as well as look at site-specific details.

2. The Company's water withdrawal schemes shall be comprehensive by considering the immediate and cumulative environmental impact of all aspects of the preconstruction,

construction, operation, maintenance and abandonment phases of the proposed pipeline.

Overall Plan

We have available some outstanding environmental studies that relate to water withdrawal but this work has not been brought together to give a comprehensive overview of the nature and scope of water withdrawals and their possible effects. It is essential that the concerns emphasized in the chapters on fish and the physical environment be considered together with such requirements of the project as pipe testing, snow roads, camps, and river crossings so that their relation to the problems of water withdrawal is clear to everyone involved with the design and approval of plans.

Overall plans have been recommended for various aspects of pipeline construction and operation. Because of the interrelationship between water withdrawals and the other uses of water resources, these plans must all be concisely keyed to each other. This could not be done during the Inquiry hearings, but it seems to me that it will have to be carried out before the government or other interested parties will be able to provide meaningful direction or comment. An overall plan is a means by which the views of experts and specialists in all fields can be incorporated into the planning and review process. I therefore endorse the approach taken by Commission Counsel in his final argument that, as in the case of all other aspects of the management of water resources, there should be an overall plan as well as site-specific applications.

3. Before the final design phase, the Company shall prepare for approval by the Agency an overall plan for the water withdrawals for all construction activities and all permanent facilities over the life of the pipeline up to and including its abandonment. Subject to the direction of the Agency, the overall plan shall, as far as possible, be in cartographic form, shall be presented by drainage basin (or a part thereof) as designated by the Agency, and shall take into account, by means of overlays or other graphic techniques at the same scale or by notations, the other overall plans requested elsewhere in this report. The Agency may request the Company to resubmit parts of this overall plan if, for any reason, they do not meet with its approval. The Company shall undertake to keep the overall plan up to date so that it reflects the latest policies and actions of the Company, the Agency and government.

4. The overall plan shall specify such items as the general timing and the extent of pipeline-related activities; the source of all water to be used and the proposed method of its withdrawal, means of transportation, storage, treatment and use; the anticipated volume and the rates and periods of withdrawal; the general physical and biological characteristics and the domestic or commercial uses of the water source; and other details the Agency may require, such as alternative withdrawal sites and plans.

5. The overall plan shall be approved by the Agency before site-specific applications are submitted for water withdrawals.

Site-specific Applications

6. The Company shall file with the Agency a separate site-specific application for each water withdrawal, regardless of its rate or duration. Each of these applications shall be keyed to the overall plan. For administrative purposes, such individual applications may be group-filed by each spread year, except when they are not related to any specific spread location. In this event, they shall be filed on an individual basis.

7. In all circumstances, the Company shall supply to the Agency all information that is required or requested regarding the potential effect of a water withdrawal on the environment, particularly as it relates to fish or to the use of a waterbody by other people for domestic or other purposes. In particular, each application shall outline the need for water and shall specify such items as the source of the water and the location of its use; the maximum rates of withdrawal; the total volume to be withdrawn or, in the case of a continuing withdrawal, the volume per unit of time; the design details of the means of taking, transporting and treating the water; the particular environmental and land use characteristics of the water supply source (including its use by fish, wildlife, trappers, fishermen or by any people for recreational, professional or other uses) on which the Company's assessment of the site and of the effects of the proposed withdrawal are based; the proposed methods for and the times of monitoring water withdrawals and their effects on the environment; and other details as requested by the Agency.

The application shall predict the physical changes to the waterbody that may result from the withdrawal. In the case of watercourses, this will include the percentage decrease in flow rate, water depth and water level; and, for winter withdrawals when fish or eggs are present downstream, the changes in depth and area of pools during minimum flow and maximum ice cover. For lakes, it will include the percentage decrease in the water volume, the maximum water drawdown anticipated, and the length of time the waterbody will take to recover its natural level.

8. Applications that are approved shall be valid for only the quantities, locations and periods of withdrawal specified. If the conditions are altered in any way that would increase or change the location of the impact, the Company shall submit an amended application for approval.

Design Guidelines

Many principles of design and operation were placed before me in evidence that will assist the government and the Company in the preparation and execution of their plans. I have asked my staff to develop guidelines from this evidence, and I commend them, together with the recommendations I have made elsewhere in this report, to everyone concerned, as a common starting point in the development of a comprehensive approach to water withdrawals.

9. *All water withdrawals shall be made only in accordance with site-specific plans prepared by the Company, signed and sealed by a professional engineer and approved by the Agency.*

10. *To protect the physical and living environment, the design of all water withdrawal facilities shall be in accordance with the following parameters:*

a) *Water shall not be removed from a waterbody frequented by fish, waterfowl, or aquatic furbearers, unless the Company has demonstrated that this withdrawal will not be detrimental to the fish, waterfowl or aquatic furbearer populations and resources in and around the waterbody, either at the time of removal or at any subsequent time. If the Company submits that a waterbody is not frequented by fish, it must be able to demonstrate that claim to the satisfaction of the Agency.*

b) *No water intake shall be located within 1,000 feet of fish spawning or overwintering areas that have well-defined boundaries. Water removal from large waterbodies that have scattered fish overwintering and spawning areas shall be permitted, if proper screening and approved velocities are maintained.*

c) *Water removal shall not exceed 10 percent of the minimum quantity of water in the waterbody during the period of removal. In any case, water shall not be removed from any lake that contains fish, unless it is deeper than 12 feet, or from any flowing waterway that contains fish, if removal would reduce velocity below 75 percent of the normal flow or to a depth of less than 0.6 feet. In all waterways that contain overwintering fish, the flow rate shall be maintained at least at the natural median monthly minimum flow level between November and April. The monthly minimum flow calculation shall be based on the flow normally expected in streams during nine out of 10 years in each of the winter months.*

d) *Water removal shall not cause siltation or turbidity in excess of the standards set out in Fish.*

e) *Intake structures shall be located and designed so that the maximum inlet velocity is one foot per second or a velocity that is demonstrated to avoid interference with indigenous fish populations, assuming a worst-case situation with ice accumulation on the screen and in the water. Where it is necessary to avoid adverse effects to migrating juvenile fish, intakes shall be recessed into stream banks.*

f) *Stationary intakes shall conform to the specifications outlined in "Intake Screen Guidelines (1972)," prepared by the Fisheries and Marine Service (Vancouver), Department of the Environment.*

g) *Movable intakes shall be assessed and approved on an individual basis, but they should meet specifications that are comparable to those for stationary intakes.*

11. *The design of water withdrawal facilities shall include measures to be taken during use and upon abandonment to stabilize the approaches to the source so that soil creep and erosion will not occur.*

12. *Where permanently submerged water withdrawal structures are used, the Company shall arrange to have a government agency inspect the structure on site before it is installed.*

13. *The Company shall design all water-related systems for construction activities, camps or permanent facilities to incorporate practices and equipment that will minimize the use of water. This practice will be particularly important in areas that are ecologically sensitive or that are without an abundant water supply.*

Operating Considerations

14. *An individual qualified to supervise water withdrawal operations shall be at the withdrawal site at all times during withdrawals of water that will be used for industrial and related operations during pipeline construction and testing (for example, pipe testing, ditch flooding, and snow road construction).*

15. *An individual qualified to supervise water withdrawal shall be a person who has been so designated by the Company and approved by the Agency and who has a demonstrated knowledge of the critical biological features of the water supply source, including the habitat features that must be protected and the presence and movement of fish; the design and operation of the water withdrawal facility; and safety.*

16. *The individual qualified to supervise water withdrawal shall be given authority by the Company to stop all water withdrawals, should he be asked to do so on site by the Agency's representative or should he deem it necessary on the basis of his own judgment.*

17. *If an intake impairs fish habitat or interferes with fish movements, directly or indirectly, it shall be shut down and either redesigned or moved to a more suitable location that has been approved by the Agency.*

18. *If the minimum flow or depth in the watercourse or lake is approached during water withdrawal, the extraction of water shall be reduced until a safe water level has been restored.*

19. *Upon abandonment of a water withdrawal facility, or when such a facility will not be used for an extended period of time, as determined by the Agency, the Company shall remove the intake and all related equipment and structures from the water.*

16 Waste Management

The collection, handling, treatment and disposal of wastes are not issues that attract much public attention during the review of a huge project such as the proposed pipeline. They are regarded by most people as matters of routine. However, the evidence now before me demonstrates that explicit directions must be given to avoid unnecessary problems that may arise through misunderstanding rather than from conflicting objectives.

1. Waste from construction camps and permanent facilities associated with the pipeline must be collected, treated and discharged in a manner that will eliminate any hazard to public health, avoid the creation of a nuisance, maintain the quality of the environment, and protect the indigenous flora and fauna.

Everybody will agree with this recommendation, but problems will arise as the Agency tries to quantify, and as the Company strives to meet, these broad objectives.

The northern environment poses special problems for waste management engineers. For example, the prolonged cold inhibits biological degradation of waste and extends the survival period for many pathogenic organisms. Natural dissolved oxygen levels in northern watercourses are often very low, so that the introduction of project-related wastewater (which consumes dissolved oxygen during its decomposition) may locally reduce the oxygen to a level below that necessary to sustain aquatic organisms. The attraction of wildlife to domestic solid waste is a matter of particular concern.

In the North today, there are relatively few major sources of pollution: the rivers, lakes and streams are among the cleanest in North America, and the land has not yet been much altered by man. These qualities are, in themselves, worth preserving, but in attempting to preserve them, we must be realistic, particularly in view of the limited duration of most pipeline activities. There are limits to environmental control: we cannot protect every blade of grass. We cannot guarantee that there will be no losses to fish and wildlife populations.

On the other hand, we must work with the environment as much as possible to reduce total impact. For example, if waste were allowed to be disposed of without the use of elaborate treatment facilities, its short-term impact could be great, but its long-term impact might be less than the total environmental consequences that would result from the fabrication, construction and abandonment of such facilities. We must understand the costs and limits of practicable technology and we must know what is the environment's natural assimilative capacity. For example, some of the large waterbodies in the North, particularly the Mackenzie River, can assimilate substantial quantities of domestic wastewater without environmental harm. Prudent use of such assimilative capacity, particularly on a temporary basis, may be good environmental management.

Waste Management Plans

For a realistic and comprehensive approach to the management of waste produced by the pipeline project, there must be, at the outset, agreement between the Company and the Agency about the nature and extent of the subject. The preliminary nature of the waste management proposals that were put before the Inquiry makes it impossible, at this stage, to piece together an overall picture. However, it is important to say something about the relation of the locations, volumes, and periods of discharge of all wastes — liquid and solid — to other aspects of the project, especially if they may have a cumulative or compounding effect on the receiving environment. Sources of water and the points at which pipe test liquids are discharged should be considered, as well as environmental constraints, such as the natural characteristics and fluctuations of dissolved oxygen levels in waterbodies, permafrost soils, fish spawning and overwintering areas, and the use of water, land and renewable resources by people. In this way, the problems posed by waste disposal may be seen from the overall perspectives of both the project and the local environment.

Consequently, I endorse the approach taken in the submission of Commission Counsel in his final argument, which requires the Company to develop an overall waste management plan before submitting site-specific applications. Commission Counsel's proposals, which I present here in a slightly revised form, should be adopted.

Overall Plan

2. Before the final design phase, the Company shall prepare for approval by the Agency an overall plan for the disposal of wastewater and solid waste from all construction activities and from all permanent facilities related to the pipeline project, up to and including abandonment. Subject to the direction of the Agency, the overall plan shall, as far as possible, be in cartographic form, shall be presented by drainage basin (or a part thereof) as designated by the Agency, and shall take into account, by means of overlays or other graphic techniques at the same scale or by notations, the other overall plans requested elsewhere in this document. The Agency may request the Company to resubmit parts of this overall plan if, for any reason, they do not meet with its approval; the Company shall undertake to keep the overall plan up to date so that it reflects the latest policies and actions of the Company, the Agency and government.

3. The overall plan shall specify such items as the general timing and the extent of pipeline-related activities; the points of generation and disposal of waste; the proposed methods of collection, storage, treatment and disposal of all waste; the anticipated volumes, the physical, chemical and biological characteristics, and the periods of discharge of all waste; the general physical and biological characteristics of the environment in the vicinity of any waste discharge sites; the location of any communities or camps in the vicinity of the proposed activity, with a description of the use they make of the waters and lands that may be affected by the waste disposal actions of the Company; and other details the Agency may require, such as alternative waste disposal sites and plans.

4. The overall plan shall be approved by the Agency before site-specific applications are submitted for wastewater discharge.

Site-specific Applications

5. The Company shall file with the Agency a separate site-specific application for each discharge site of solid and liquid waste, regardless of the quality, rate or duration of the discharge. Each of these applications shall be keyed to the overall plan. For administrative purposes, such individual applications may be group-filed by each spread year except when they are not related to any specific spread location. In this event, they shall be filed on the basis of the activity or the geographical area involved.

6. Each application shall specify such items as the normal and maximum population of all facilities at which domestic waste will be generated; the complete design parameters of the facility proposed to dispose of waste, including a documented estimate of the quantity, its chemical, physical and biological characteristics, and the location, method and periods of discharge; the design and operating considerations for handling upset conditions such as surge flows, hydraulic overloading, equipment failures and the collapse of biological processes; the particular physical characteristics of the receiving environment, its use by fish and wildlife species and by hunters, trappers or anyone else for recreational, professional or other use, together with the Company's assessment of the degree of treatment that is needed at a particular discharge site; and the proposed methods and times both for the monitoring of receiving lands and waters, and for their rehabilitation after the discharge has stopped.

7. The Company must be able to satisfy the Agency that the collection and treatment processes will be performed to the standards specified under the prevailing field conditions.

8. The Agency must approve an application before any on-site construction begins. Approved applications shall be valid for only the quantities, qualities, locations and periods of discharge specified. If the conditions are altered in any way that would increase or change the location of the impact, the Company shall submit an amended application for approval.

9. The Company shall supply to the Agency all information that may be required and requested regarding the effect of any waste discharge on the environment.

Wastewater

The primary purpose of any scheme to manage wastewater is the establishment and maintenance of effluent standards that will achieve the objectives I set forth in my first recommendation. This task is not as straightforward as it may at first seem, and it could lead to misunderstanding among all the parties that will be involved in the construction and regulation of a pipeline.

The Application of Standards

It is worthwhile to place the subject of wastewater treatment in perspective so that we can understand the application of relevant standards in the North. Everyone agrees that it is important to treat sewage to protect the environment. In urban and industrial areas, where most of us live, the volume of wastewater is greater than the local environment can absorb. Thus, treatment of sewage is desirable — if not essential — to our well-being.

Most wastewater technology and programs tend to focus on the urban and industrial problems we face in the South. This perspective is often transferred to the treatment of wastewater problems in frontier regions. Furthermore, we all tend to feel satisfied with forms of technological responses that result in measurable improvements. But is this the right approach in the North? Is there an entrenched administrative approach here, an approach that is strengthened by urban-industrial attitudes, that views with suspicion any softening of southern regulations in the northern context?

Presumably there are economic, technical and administrative limits to environmental protection programs. Are we not, then, obliged to define our concerns on the basis of the actual priorities of the northern environment rather than on the basis of the problems and the technology applied in other parts of the nation? Are not other fresh water issues more important in the North than elaborate sewage treatment? Is it not, for example, more important to eliminate barriers to fish by installing more bridges and larger culverts, to reduce the problems of siltation by using more elaborate devices to control erosion, or to institute comprehensive procedures to prevent and control toxic substances?

I am dismayed by the huge amounts of money and effort that have been spent on sewage treatment in connection with the Alyeska pipeline. Many of the secondary treatment plants did not meet their design specifications, and often the effluent produced by secondary treatment was only slightly better than it was after primary treatment. The Alyeska Pipeline Service Company did not, therefore, achieve the environmental benefits of secondary treatment, yet they poured hundreds of thousands of dollars into the effort. The friction that resulted between the surveillance and administrative authorities seems to me to have been far out of proportion to the importance of the subject. In considering the Alaskan experience, we must look not only at the reasons why the secondary treatment plants failed to operate properly, but also at the justification for these plants in the first place.

Commission Counsel said that "procedures to minimize the adverse effects of waste disposal on the receiving environment are not ... well understood" (Commission Counsel, 1976, "Construction Services and Activities: Wastewater and Sewage: Camps and Facilities," p. 1). Archie Pick, of the Environmental Protection Service, Department of the Environment in Edmonton, after reviewing the argument, disagreed:

> The aspect that is not well understood is a method of rational analysis to determine the level of treatment efficiency required in each site-specific case. The gap is more in the ability to interpret the receiving environment and its limitations and the time required to do so, rather than with the waste treatment systems available. In fact, it is this gap that has led most jurisdictions to adopt a strategy similar to "Best Practicable Technology," which is based on a concept of incremental improvement rather than doing nothing because rational engineering analysis is not fully available. The difficult part of the concept is to define technology that is "practicable." Practicability infers that the system is available, proven and does not create an unnecessary economic or technological hardship....
>
> Conceptually I do not object to the need to consider the

assimilative capability of the receiving environment; however, the difficulty that has been experienced in arriving at waste treatment requirement this way should be recognized. I challenge the second statement [in Commission Counsel's submission] which states that "it would be irresponsible to lay down blanket-type effluent standards that ignore the influent characteristics and the site-specific characteristics of the receiving environment." It has been the cumulative experience of pollution control agencies that attempts to regulate on a site-by-site basis lead to interminable delay and a failure to achieve pollution abatement goals.

> In effect, I am saying that the assimilative approach, while scientifically desirable, is virtually unworkable from an administrative perspective. I believe such a requirement would ensure that no decisions of consequence could be reached until after a pipeline was completed. With the large number of sites involved, the Agency would become bogged down in rhetoric and alternatives. [Pick, personal communication, June 28, 1977]

I am persuaded that these are vital points: we must specify standards that are attainable with practicable technology, as suggested by Mr. Pick, and be prepared to specify the standards without the extensive site-specific analyses necessary to define scientifically the assimilative capacity of the local environment. In doing so, we must recognize the temporary nature of most of the discharges associated with the project and the time constraints that all parties will have to meet during the design and construction periods.

I have heard evidence on the problems of managing the wastewater associated with the Alyeska pipeline. There, the high cost of treatment, and the design and operating problems encountered seem to be tied, in part, to the nature of wastewater produced by the camps: it is several times more concentrated than that produced by cities and towns. The standards applied, however, often do not take this fact into account.

The pipeline companies initially told me that they would provide secondary treatment for all wastes from large camps, and the quality of the effluent from them would have been close to the standard specified in *Guidelines for Effluent Quality and Wastewater Treatment at Federal Establishments* and in *Recommended Environmental Standards for the Design and Construction of a Mackenzie Valley Gas Pipeline*, both published by the Environmental Protection Service, Department of the Environment. However, the companies later modified their statements and suggested a lower quality of effluent. The National Energy Board has rejected this modification and said that the standards set out in the federal guidelines must be met.

I think that, in our efforts to protect the environment, we must be careful that we do not lose sight of our overall objectives and of the limits of practicable technology. The federal guidelines were intended as an example, and they are, therefore, equal to, or more stringent than, the established standards or requirements of any other federal or provincial regulatory agency. I am advised that the effluent limits set out in the guidelines are based on the quality of municipal effluent attainable with well-operated, standard secondary treatment technology, which is considered to be the best practicable technology. This technology is considered to remove at least 85 percent of suspended solids and five-day biological oxygen demand (BOD). For domestic wastewater at the federal establishments for which these guidelines are intended, the specific effluent limits are, therefore, 20 milligrams per litre (mg/l) BOD and 25 mg/l suspended solids.

However, if we recognize that camp wastewater will be several times stronger than municipal wastewater, it is obvious that a practicable reduction by 85 percent of camp wastewater will yield an effluent that exceeds the limits specified in the federal guidelines. If the numerical limits of the guidelines are applied, we shall, in fact, be asking the Company to reduce its wastes by over 96 percent — and that is not practicable. In most instances, it would place an unnecessary burden on the Company and its enforcement would cause considerable difficulty for the Agency. Quite simply, such an approach to the problem will be unmanageable.

James J. Cameron of the Northern Technology Centre, Department of the Environment, in Edmonton has written the Inquiry on this subject.

I do not believe the *Guidelines for Effluent Quality and Wastewater Treatment at Federal Establishments* (EPS-1-EC-76-1) have direct application in these circumstances. I agree that the wastewater management requirements should be site-specific to allow flexibility in engineering and administration and tailoring to the characteristics and uses of the receiving environment. Domestic wastewater effluent quality requirements should be cognizant of the present and future very low population densities, and industrial and agricultural activities within northern watersheds. However, wastewater disposal must not adversely affect the local environment. Northern effluent guidelines *must* consider the relatively long survival time of pathogenic organisms in cold environments and the resulting potential health hazard which is enhanced by the use of receiving waters by local people in their extensive land use activities.

Unfortunately, it is generally impracticable to assess scientifically and to define clearly the assimilative capacity and public health requirements and to administer strict receiving water quality regulations. This is particularly true in the northern environment, which is less studied and understood, and where there are few relevant precedents. Also, the transient nature of this project's activities negates incremental response. Therefore, I believe that it is prudent to present a precise, conservative, yet rational *general* effluent standard. However, these should not be based on the Federal Establishment Guidelines. Rather, their intention of a well-operated secondary treatment system should be applied to the characteristically concentrated nature of the camp wastewater.

Effluent BOD from normal camps is expected to be approximately 600 mg/l. Higher values would be produced where kitchen wastes and grease are not segregated or where water conservation measures are implemented. In contrast, the BOD of domestic type effluents from normal municipalities is generally less than 200 mg/l. The higher strength wastewater is relatively easier to treat and normal secondary treatment technology can achieve a 90 percent reduction in BOD. I understand that on this latter point there is precedent in the Great Lakes regulations for ships. In these circumstances, a strong waste with BOD of 500 mg/l is anticipated and the effluent guidelines specify a maximum effluent BOD of 50 mg/l.

If this "best practicable technology" concept is followed, then maximum effluent requirements for BOD of 60 mg/l and suspended solids of 75 mg/l with a minimum of 90 percent removal and fecal coliform count less than 400 per 100 ml would be appropriate. If such a reasonable general effluent guideline were presented, I believe that it would be adopted without dispute for the majority of camp locations. Indeed, to standardize the design and to show good corporate citizenship and leadership, the pipeline company may choose to adopt these at all but the small, temporary camps, even though such standards were not required on environmental grounds. In those instances where the receiving environment could not readily assimilate such a loading, then flow management lagoons to prevent discharge during critical times of the year will probably be the most economical and environmentally sound solution. [Cameron, personal communication, July 15, 1977]

Effluent and Disposal Standards

Before giving my recommendations, I want to dispel any misunderstanding that may arise from my general conclusion that, although the same principles of waste treatment should be applied to the pipeline project as would be applied to a federal establishment in southern Canada, less stringent numerical standards should be used. This conclusion does not contradict my general view that ambient water quality standards, which I proposed in The Physical Environment: Water, should be maintained. The temporary nature of most discharges, the design and location of camp facilities and the natural assimilative capacity of waterbodies will help to limit most of the adverse impacts on water quality. Of course, if there is any danger of overtaxing the natural assimilative capacity of waterbodies, higher effluent standards can be provided or the discharge may be held until it can be released without harm. My point here is that we must not try to apply standards that we know from the outset are virtually unattainable.

In the chapter on The Physical Environment, I said that wetlands should be accorded the same level of protection as other elements of the landscape. Thus, although I recognize that the Company may, in some circumstances, use wetlands to receive sewage effluent, the quality of the effluent that may be discharged into swamps must be strictly controlled, as outlined below. The value of wetlands, in this context, lies in their capacity to hold water and as habitat for aquatic and other wildlife species. Their value as habitat would not be decreased — in some cases, it could be enhanced — by the addition of nutrients. Also, if wetlands are used as natural sewage lagoons, there will be no need to dig artificial lagoons, which would remain, after they were abandoned, as scars on the landscape. My recommendations aim to prevent the abuse of all northern lands and waterbodies and to ensure the continued viability of their ecosystems.

Obviously a balance must be struck that will ensure the attainment of our objectives in a practicable way under the field and administrative conditions of the project. I have asked my staff to pursue this issue. They have received useful information from the Environmental Protection Service, Department of the Environment, in Edmonton, on which I have relied, in part, in writing the foregoing paragraphs and in what follows.

10. The Minimum Effluent Standards for all facilities shall be based on primary treatment, which shall consist of the removal of settleable, floatable and suspended solids and grease and of appropriate disinfection to ensure that public health standards are met. Primary treatment could be accomplished by screening, grit removal, pre-aeration and primary sedimentation, with surface skimming to reduce grease and floatable solids.

11. The General Wastewater Treatment Requirements that are applicable to major construction camps and to permanent facilities that discharge into environments that have a relatively limited assimilative capacity shall be based on the best practicable technology and on the capabilities of a well-operated secondary treatment technology. In view of the relatively high concentration of camp wastewater, the effluent may have a maximum BOD of 60 mg/l and suspended solids of 75 mg/l, but the maximum must not exceed 10 percent of the influent values and the fecal coliform count must be less than 400 per 100 millilitre (ml). The Agency may specify more or less stringent effluent standards in view of the volume of effluent, its quality, the timing of its discharge or because of other developments in the area and the nature and uses of the particular receiving environment.

12. Unless otherwise noted by the Agency, any application to dispose of effluent in a way that deviates from the General Wastewater Treatment Requirements shall be supported by site-specific information.

13. The discharge of an effluent without disinfection shall be permitted only when it has been proved beyond reasonable doubt that it poses no threat to public health. The Company may be required to institute higher standards of treatment on a site-specific basis to ensure that the effluent is adequately disinfected.

14. The use of chlorine as a disinfectant is discouraged, but where it is used the Company shall demonstrate that the chlorinated effluent is not toxic to aquatic organisms.

15. The wastewater effluent shall be discharged only into a receiving environment that can assimilate the residual pollutants. Outfall works shall be designed to disperse the effluent. Particular attention shall be given to the protection of waterbodies from excessive organic loading during periods of ice cover or low water levels and to preventing discharges into waterbodies that are quiescent or that could become thermally stratified, thereby causing localized concentrations of effluent.

16. Unless otherwise demonstrated as environmentally acceptable, swamps, bogs or fens shall not be used to receive treated effluent for more than five years, and they shall be of sufficient size to allow approximately 120 square yards per contributing man-year. The disposal of treated effluent should, if possible, be into swamps, bogs and fens that have sub-pools that maintain flow throughout the year (Hartland-Rowe and Wright, 1974). All swamp, bog or fen areas used for effluent disposal shall be clearly posted to alert trappers and others that sewage effluent is present.

17. All solids and sludges in, or resulting from, the treatment of wastewater or sewage shall be handled and disposed of in a manner approved by the Agency and consistent with its requirements for solid waste disposal as detailed in Waste Management: Solid Waste.

18. To ensure proper operation of all treatment facilities, a qualified operator or other designated individual shall attend all wastewater and sewage operations at such times as the Agency may designate. The Agency must approve the training program and qualifications of such an operator or individual.

Sampling and Records

19. The procedures for effluent sampling and analysis shall be in accordance with the latest edition of Standard Methods for the Examination of Water and Wastewater (American Public Health Association, 1974).

20. During periods of effluent discharge, composite samples shall be taken and analysed daily or as otherwise specified by the Agency for BOD and suspended solids to ensure that the specified standards are not being violated. Referee samples shall be taken at times specified by the Agency and analysed by personnel approved by the Agency. The results shall be incorporated into the plant records.

21. The Company shall conduct additional tests, such as fecal coliform tests, chlorine residual tests (when chlorine is used as a disinfectant in the effluent stream), and nutrient, chemical oxygen demand (COD), total organic carbon (TOC), and other tests, as the Agency may require to measure the impact of the effluent on the receiving environment.

22. If an effluent is discharged directly or indirectly into any stream, the Company shall sample the water both above and below the discharge point. These samples shall be taken at the same time as effluent samples, or as otherwise directed by the Agency, and they shall be analysed for BOD, suspended solids, total coliforms, chlorine residual and other parameters, as the Agency may specify. The results shall be incorporated into the plant records. Sampling points shall be established as outlined in the chapter on Fish or as otherwise directed by the Agency.

23. For both composite and grab samples taken at wastewater treatment sites, the arithmetic mean for any consecutive 30-day period should not exceed the limits specified; in accounting for minor disturbance to plant operations, the seven-day arithmetic mean shall not exceed 150 percent of the limits specified. If the effluent does not meet these limits, the treatment system shall be declared deficient, and the Company shall immediately take corrective measures that are acceptable to the Agency.

24. Adequate records and reports of the wastewater treatment operation shall be maintained on site in a form approved by the Agency. They shall indicate the characteristics of the raw waste; the amount of waste treated, chemicals used and sludge produced; final deposition of sludge; effluent quality; maintenance done; and characteristics of the receiving environment. During pipeline construction, a copy of all records, duly certified by the operator and camp superintendent, shall be forwarded to the Agency at the end of each month. During operation of the pipeline, these records shall be made available upon request.

Design Guidelines

The terms and conditions I have outlined above to deal with plans for wastewater management and with effluent standards should provide the basis for the preparation, implementation and assessment of comprehensive measures for the management of wastewater. However, further guidelines may be needed to clarify various details. To assist the Company and the Agency, I include below guidelines taken from Commission Counsel's final argument, revised to accommodate the views of participants, and others.

I must emphasize that the objectives of wastewater treatment will be best met by having a plant design that is appropriate to the type of waste expected from camps and by ensuring that the system is operated well. The quality of operation is of paramount importance because excellence of design cannot fully compensate for a poor operator. A good operator, on the other hand, can often compensate for minor shortcomings in design.

QUALIFIED OPERATOR

25. A qualified operator for the wastewater and sewage operations shall be on site at all times when construction and related operations exceed 200 man-days at one location; one day a week, with a minimum of two visits per site, when construction and related operations are less than 200 man-days at one location; and as required at permanent facilities on the operating pipeline to perform normal maintenance and repairs, except that there shall be a minimum of two visits a year (one of which shall be in winter) or once every 200 occupied man-days.

26. A qualified operator shall have successfully completed a training program approved by the Agency. The operator training program being developed by the Water Pollution Control Directorate, Environmental Protection Service, Department of the Environment, and the guidelines for the classification of treatment facilities and certification of personnel developed by the Committee on Training and Certification, Federation of Associations on the Canadian Environment, should be used in developing a program to train operators for work on the pipeline project. Qualified operators should have a demonstrated knowledge of wastewater treatment processes; wastewater sampling procedures; wastewater tests, such as those for BOD, COD, suspended solids, pH, dissolved oxygen, and chlorine residual; interpretation and application of laboratory results; equipment operations, basic repairs and preventive maintenance; basic public health practices; and safety. In particular, the operator must be able to deal with start-up and upset conditions such as surges and the collapse of biological processes.

27. At locations where a full-time qualified operator is not required, one individual shall be designated to ensure the safe and proper functioning of all wastewater and sewage systems. That designated individual shall have a demonstrated knowledge of wastewater sampling procedures; steps to be taken to deal with start-up and upset conditions such as surges and the collapse of biological processes; equipment operations, basic repairs and preventive maintenance; testing and reporting responsibilities; basic public health practices; and safety.

DESIGN

28. Before disposal, all wastewater and sewage shall be collected and treated in accordance with detailed site-specific plans prepared by the Company, signed and sealed by a professional engineer and approved by the Agency.

29. Each wastewater and sewage treatment system shall be designed to handle maximum possible peak flows and surges, plus 20 percent, to minimize the chances of hydraulic overloading of the system. The use of flow equalization systems shall be mandatory for all mechanical treatment plants. Continuously recording flow meters shall be included at the effluent points of all treatment facilities. Biological treatment plants at facilities that experience wide variations in population should use parallel treatment plants to ensure that organic and hydraulic loading are within the acceptable range for optimum treatment.

30. To ensure proper operation of the facility, all treatment plants shall include a laboratory adequately equipped to make the routine influent and effluent analyses.

31. All continuous-flow wastewater treatment facilities that depend upon the operation of mechanical equipment shall have temporary emergency storage ponds or tanks with a capacity sufficient for a 10-day flow of untreated effluent.

Pump facilities to return such stored waste to the treatment facilities shall be provided.

32. All domestic water and sewage systems used in camps or in permanent facilities shall be evaluated so that practices and equipment may be incorporated to minimize the use of water and thus to reduce the volume of wastewater produced. This evaluation will be particularly important in environmentally sensitive areas and in locations without abundant water.

These design considerations are based on the use of conventional systems of water supply and sewage collection and they should be applied accordingly. Where the Company uses a system to conserve water, as it is actively encouraged to do, the Agency should give special consideration to proposals for the adjustment of specific effluent quality limits and to the disposal of any special effluents, such as concentrated sludges and grey water.

33. Sufficient spare parts and equipment shall be stocked in appropriate locations to provide for the timely maintenance of wastewater treatment and disposal systems.

LAGOONS

34. Lagoons for wastewater and sewage treatment shall be designed for a minimum retention period of one year under the worst case of infiltrated water conditions and with maximum population, plus 20 percent, to account for unforeseen variations and to ensure, as far as possible, that hydraulic overloading will not occur. The Company shall limit discharge from lagoons during critical periods of the year, such as the period of ice-cover, to ensure compliance with the criteria for the quality of the receiving water. (See The Physical Environment.)

35. Lagoons shall include a separate primary cell. The sludge shall be cleaned out of it as often as required for good operation and disposed of in a manner approved by the Agency and consistent with the requirements as specified in Waste Management: Solid Waste.

36. All plans for sewage lagoons shall be accompanied by detailed, site-specific, geotechnical and thermal (permafrost) analyses. The materials to be used for waste-impounding embankments, their source, permeability and stability shall be specified. Measures to control seepage shall be described.

37. Natural waterbodies shall not be used as lagoons unless the Company can demonstrate the site-specific benefits of such a practice.

38. Unless otherwise approved by the Agency, sewage lagoons shall not be located within 1,000 feet of any waterbody that supports fish, that is a source of water supply or that is used by local people for hunting, trapping, fishing or for recreational purposes.

39. When submissions are made for the initial authorizations to work, the Company shall submit for approval specific details of the measures that will be taken when each lagoon or wastewater retention pit is to be abandoned. Upon termination of use, lagoon storage facilities shall be maintained for a minimum of one year or until the water quality has sufficiently recovered to permit the discharge of its total contents into the receiving environment. The topography of the lagoon area shall be restored to be compatible with the surrounding terrain and it shall be revegetated. Abandoned lagoons shall be posted.

INDUSTRIAL WASTE

40. Wastewater and sewage from non-domestic operations associated with the pipeline shall be discharged into sanitary sewers only if they do not interfere with the treatment process. Subject to site-specific approvals by the Agency, the wastes should comply with the guidelines given below. Industrial effluents shall not be diluted to comply with these maximum levels.

a) The temperature of industrial waste discharge shall not disrupt the treatment process or the receiving environment.

b) The industrial waste flow shall not exceed twice the designed average daily flow.

c) The pH of the industrial waste shall be between 5.5 and 9.5.

d) Organic and other industrial waste concentrations shall not overload the treatment system.

e) Toxic materials discharged into sanitary sewers shall not exceed the following levels (expressed in mg/l):

Cadmium	3
Chromium	3
Copper	3
Cyanide as HCN	2
Lead	3
Mercury	0.005
Nickel	3
Phenolic compounds	1
Zinc	3

Pretreatment to reduce toxic materials to this level will result in sludges, the disposal of which must be described to and approved by the Agency.

f) Flammable or explosive materials shall not be discharged into sanitary sewer systems but shall be contained and treated as hazardous materials.

g) Animal or vegetable fats or oils shall be limited to 150 mg/l; mineral oil effluent levels shall not exceed 15 mg/l.

h) Substances emitting hazardous or noxious gases, such as hydrogen sulphide, carbon monoxide and ammonia, shall not be discharged into the sanitary system.

i) Wastes containing dissolved salts in excess of 1,500 mg/l shall be pretreated before discharge.

j) The discharge of radioactive materials into sanitary sewer systems shall be prohibited.

Solid Waste

The particular nature of both the proposed pipeline project and the northern environment make it difficult to use a standard approach to meet objectives for the management of solid wastes, such as domestic garbage, and industrial non-combustible refuse. Here again, permafrost, low temperature and remoteness severely limit and, in many cases, preclude the use of conventional southern techniques for the handling and disposal of solid waste.

During the construction of the pipeline, large volumes of various kinds of solid waste will be produced during a short period from centres of activity that are spread over a vast area. Wildlife, particularly bears, foxes and rodents, will be attracted to the organic waste, unless it is properly handled and treated. The disposal of excavated soil and rock will also pose special problems. Much of it will have high ice content, thereby inducing erosion and siltation.

The pipeline companies have said that combustible wastes from camps and facilities will be incinerated and that non-combustible wastes will be stockpiled until they can be taken to previously designated areas or can be buried. In areas without permafrost, the companies have said that they will use sanitary landfill. Scrap metal and machinery will be stockpiled in designated areas approved by the Agency or will be returned to the South. Site-specific details for this plan are lacking, and the need for the overall plan that I have recommended is obvious. However, of all the problems related to solid wastes, the attraction of wildlife to domestic waste is, in my opinion, the most important. It is a common problem throughout the North and the South, and the only sure solution to it seems to be incineration.

I commend to government, the Agency and the Company the following set of guidelines relating to all aspects of solid waste management.

Waste Guidelines

WASTE HANDLING: GENERAL

41. *The Company shall adhere to the* Code of Good Practice for Handling Solid Waste at Federal Establishments *(Environmental Protection Service, Department of the Environment), unless it can demonstrate to the Agency that other practices are preferable.*

42. *All domestic solid waste produced along the right-of-way or anywhere away from a camp or permanent facility shall be incinerated daily on location or stored in tight, animal-proof containers for regular shipment to the nearest approved disposal facility.*

43. *Scrap metal, oil drums, discarded equipment and other non-flammable wastes shall be stored temporarily in designated areas. The volume of these wastes shall be reduced by compaction, and the material shall be transported to previously designated and approved disposal or storage sites, unless the Company can demonstrate that other methods of handling them are preferable.*

44. *Sludges from sewage or from the treatment of water shall be handled at each location according to methods developed by the Company and approved by the Agency. The preferred method of disposal is incineration.*

INCINERATION

45. *All combustible wastes shall be incinerated in an approved incinerator, unless the Company can demonstrate, on a site-specific basis, that other means of disposing of these wastes are preferable and will not attract wildlife.*

46. *Open incineration shall be prohibited except with prior authorization of the Agency.*

47. *Unless otherwise approved by the Agency, emissions from incinerators shall meet the standards prescribed in* Air Pollution Emissions and Control Technology, Packaged Incinerators *(McColgan, 1976).*

DISPOSAL SITES

48. *To avoid nuisance and the contamination of streams, lakes or groundwater, solid waste disposal sites shall be located at least 1,000 feet away from watercourses, human settlements or camp sites, unless otherwise approved by the Agency.*

49. *Solid waste disposal sites shall be managed in accordance with the* Code of Good Practice on Dump Closing or Conversion to Sanitary Landfill at Federal Establishments *(Environmental Protection Service, Department of the Environment), unless the Company can demonstrate to the satisfaction of the Agency that other practices are preferable.*

50. *If borrow pits are to be later used as solid waste disposal sites, they must be so described on the application to use materials from them and shall be approved as such by the Agency.*

51. *Hazardous or toxic wastes, as defined in* Management of Fuels and Hazardous Substances, *shall be excluded from normal landfills, unless specifically approved by the Agency.*

52. *Storage areas and disposal sites shall be adequately fenced to prevent or restrict, so far as practicable, access by scavengers, such as bears, foxes, wolves and wolverines, and to contain wind-blown rubbish.*

53. *Upon completion of disposal operations at a particular site, the Company shall grade and revegetate the area in keeping with local topography and drainage characteristics, and it shall post permanent signs to indicate the extent of the abandoned site and its dates of use.*

WASTE DISPOSAL: CLEARING AND EXCAVATED MATERIALS

54. *Trees and shrubs made waste by clearing or cutting shall be burned or chipped. (See Terrain Considerations.)*

55. *An undisturbed area of natural vegetation at least 300 feet wide shall be left between any disposal site that contains waste soil or excavated material and any waterbody or public right-of-way.*

56. *Waste soil, rock and other materials resulting from construction, operation or maintenance activities shall not be deposited in any waterbody, ice-covered or not, unless specifically approved by the Agency.*

57. *Waste soil from the pipeline trench or other excavations, stumps and other excavated residue should be deposited in designated borrow pits. Waste soil may be spread over the right-of-way or other approved sites, if the Company can demonstrate that this means of disposal will not cause siltation of adjacent waterbodies or interefere with natural drainage, local vegetation or any local program of revegetation. To reduce the risk of erosion and siltation, the waste excavated material shall be spread out in layers not greater than six inches thick and on slopes not greater than three degrees, unless otherwise approved by the Agency.*

58. *Small amounts of waste organic material, such as peat, may be spread on cleared areas, provided it is spread in layers not exceeding six inches thick and is covered with soil or rendered harmless as a fire hazard in some other way approved by the Agency.*

59. *If the amount of waste soil exceeds the capacity of the designated borrow pits and of the right-of-way, the soil may be disposed of in spoil mounds. The Company shall prepare plans for spoil mounds on a site-specific basis and include such details as clearing and stripping of topsoil at the site; topography and drainage before and after disposal occurs; nature of the substrata; properties of the soils or other excavated material to be disposed of at the site; height, side slopes and drainage features of the spoil mound; and measures for rehabilitation of the area, including grading and revegetation.*

60. *Disposal of unstable, ice-rich excavated material shall be completed before it has deteriorated by thawing.*

61. *Unstable, ice-rich excavated material shall be disposed of only in designated borrow pits or as otherwise approved by the Agency. The rehabilitation and revegetation of designated borrow pits shall be carried out in such a way that the areas will be stabilized.*

Hazardous and Toxic Wastes

I heard evidence about the problems of handling, storing, transporting and disposing of hazardous and toxic substances. In the chapter entitled Management of Fuels and Hazardous Substances, which contains a full definition of these substances, I discuss specific aspects of these problems. In this section, I want to cover the problems of disposing of these wastes.

Procedures

No comprehensive approach to the disposal of such wastes was presented to the Inquiry. The problem involves a wide variety of waste products and many special procedures and approvals. The Environmental Protection Service has prepared a comprehensive description of hazardous and toxic wastes, and I recommend its use in disposing of such wastes produced by activities related to the proposed pipeline.

62. *All hazardous and toxic wastes associated with the project shall be handled in compliance with the Code of Good Practice for Management of Hazardous and Toxic Wastes at Federal Establishments (Environmental Protection Service, Department of the Environment, 1977).*

63. *Substances used on the project shall be selected, so far as practicable, according to their least toxicity and persistence of their waste products in the living environment.*

64. *Hazardous and toxic wastes shall be listed and especially noted in the overall and site-specific plans. Each application to the Agency for a permit or approval for any purpose shall specify the use of any or all hazardous and toxic wastes associated with the activities included in the application. Information will include details such as the name, properties and use of each substance; the volume or weight of waste; the toxicity of each substance (if known); the proposed method of packaging, transporting, transforming and stowing of waste; and the proposed method of disposal.*

65. *Radioactive materials shall be handled, stored, transported and disposed of according to the latest government regulations and according to specific plans developed by the Company and approved by the Agency.*

17 Management of Fuels and Hazardous Substances

There is a great tendency to underestimate the magnitude of the problems associated with the storage and handling of fuels and hazardous substances that will be used during construction and operation of a natural gas pipeline. From the evidence before me, it appears that the pipeline companies have not given this problem the kind of consideration that it warrants. This causes me some concern, because casual handling of these substances could pose extremely serious risks to the northern environment.

The problem centres on the storage and handling of the various fuels that will be transported in bulk to power the machines necessary to build the pipeline and to support the enormous infrastructure necessary to feed the construction process. But it also involves other substances, such as lubricants, solvents, alcohols, paints and a host of other chemicals in a variety of forms. Moreover, if methanol is the antifreeze in the water mixture used to test the pipeline under pressure when it is completed, large quantities of it will have to be transported north and stored there. The specific problems associated with the use of methanol in testing the pipeline are dealt with in the chapter entitled Pipe Testing.

Hazardous and toxic substances are defined in the Environmental Protection Service's publication *Code of Good Practice for Management of Hazardous and Toxic Wastes at Federal Establishments*, to include any product or substance that is or contains a poisonous, toxic, inflammable, explosive or corrosive product or any substance of a similar nature that, upon release or escape to the environment, may cause or may contribute to a harmful effect on the environment and on human health and safety. Liquid and solid municipal wastes, non-toxic and non-hazardous commercial and industrial solid waste, and construction debris, are not included in this definition. They are dealt with in the chapter entitled Waste Management.

The management of fuels and hazardous substances involves two aspects that must be addressed properly from the outset: first, to avoid spills by careful and comprehensive planning and, secondly, to minimize environmental damage caused by spills by putting effective contingency plans into action. I wish to emphasize these two issues in this chapter.

Arctic Gas estimated in their application that they would use about 100 million Imperial gallons of fuel and methanol during the construction of the proposed pipeline. Foothills would use quantities of the same order of magnitude. In addition, both companies would use large quantities of other hazardous and toxic substances that could cause substantial damage if they escaped into the environment.

The transportation of fuel and other hazardous substances, whether by rail, air, road, barge or ocean-going ships, and their storage will use both existing and new facilities owned by the Company itself and by non-Company interests. A variety of standards and types of equipment will be used: for example, small volumes of fuel (up to about 1,500 barrels) will be stored in bladder tanks; but steel tanks may be used instead of, or in combination with, bladder tanks for larger quantities (up to about 5,000 barrels). Final selection of tank type will depend on several factors, including volume, length of storage time, and availability of land. Vehicles will transport fuels and other substances from the bulk storage areas to worksites located throughout the project area. During the operation of the pipeline, fuels will be stored at facilities along the right-of-way.

I have heard a great deal of evidence about the threat posed by spills of fuels and other hazardous substances during the construction and operation of a pipeline. Many expert witnesses at the formal hearings testified on environmental aspects of the project, and many people at the community hearings predicted major damage to waterfowl, aquatic mammals, fish and the native people's traditional pursuits, if spills occur. This threat is real, particularly if a spill occurs in the Delta or along the Arctic coast.

The evidence from the hearings, the technical literature and actual world experience show that oil and chemicals, once spilled in water, cannot effectively be cleaned up unless exceptionally calm, temperate conditions prevail at the time of the accident. These conditions are very seldom present in the North. As I emphasized in Volume One, the evidence demonstrates that we do not have the technical ability to clean up major spills in arctic conditions. Every effort must, therefore, be made to avoid spills.

Fuel spills occurred during the construction of the Alyeska oil pipeline. Gilbert Zemansky, who was engaged in monitoring its construction, informed the Inquiry that there were at least three major oil spills: in 1974, a seam on a bladder tank at the Toolik camp site burst and spilled more than 100,000 gallons; between February 1975 and spring 1976, chronic leakages in buried fuel lines at the Galbraith camp site lost between 100,000 and 600,000 gallons; a similar situation was reported at the Prospect camp site, where over 40,000 gallons leaked into the environment (Zemansky, 1976).

I said in Volume One that the extremely large volume of petrochemicals that must be moved and stored during pipeline construction will make spills inevitable, despite the best planning. This issue was given special consideration in the Pipeline Guidelines, yet the plans the pipeline companies laid before the Inquiry were vague on the subject of what must be done to prevent spills. Some attention has been given to contingency plans, but they are still in the most rudimentary stage of development and they do not answer the problem.

The Limitations of Spill Control

I have heard a good deal of evidence on the need for thorough contingency planning. But such planning is for the purpose of developing an emergency response to an environmental hazard that has already become reality. I have heard very little evidence on spill prevention, despite the fact that is the means — indeed, the only means — to a successful resolution of the risks associated with the use of fuels and hazardous substances on the pipeline project.

It must be clearly understood by everyone who may be concerned with the construction, operation and regulation of a gas pipeline, that petrochemical spills will occur, that the technology for dealing with petrochemical spills is in its infancy, and that, as a consequence, some level of damage to the environment will result.

We know from experience in more temperate regions that, once a spill has occurred, the clean-up operation is very difficult, if not impossible. In the North, the problems of clean-up are far worse. Remoteness and the great distances between centres of activity and supply will seriously affect the efficiency of any clean-up operation. These distances will complicate communications, delivery of clean-up supplies, the feeding and housing of clean-up crews, and the repair and servicing of clean-up equipment, and these problems are only a beginning of the difficulties.

The deployment of men and equipment in low temperatures, through broken and moving ice, in stormy seas, darkness and permafrost conditions may be difficult to the point of impossibility. In winter, fuel and chemicals will run under the ice or, if spilled on the ice, will leak through cracks and between blocks and fissures. An ocean or river current (the Mackenzie River averages approximately three miles per hour) will disperse a spill over a considerable distance in a short period of time. Booms to contain spills are relatively inefficient in currents, waves and ice. Many northern rivers, including the Mackenzie River, are subject to flash floods in summer: after a heavy rain, perhaps far upstream, the river rises quickly with an attendant increase in current velocity. Water levels fall rapidly after a flash flood, and in such circumstances a spill might be widely spread over soft mud on the river's banks. These areas, the tidal flats of the Beaufort Sea, and the low, marshy terrain of the Mackenzie Delta would be difficult or impossible to clean up.

Barges will carry tens of millions of gallons of fuel oil during the short shipping season on the river, the equipment available will be used intensively, and in places there will be transfer operations in fast currents, poor weather conditions and darkness. The barges now used on the Mackenzie River to transport fuel vary in design, age, size, equipment and in the lay-out of their piping and pumping systems. These variations create a further potential for accidents, and the likelihood of spills will be still further increased if inexperienced personnel have charge of equipment to transfer cargo.

There is the very real possibility that the huge cost that would be incurred in the clean-up of a remote area would be used as an argument for leaving the area to recover naturally. This has happened elsewhere. But, in the North, natural recovery is extremely slow and, therefore, the impact of oil pollution on northern species and northern ecosystems is likely to be more devastating than in more temperate climates.

Risks to the Environment

There have been several studies of the effects of oil and chemical spills on the environment. Conclusions differ widely, and many of the mechanisms involved in chemical and oil toxicity are not understood. Petrochemical spills may involve different compounds, and the threat of pollution may come from the slick itself or from the toxic effects of petroleum fractions or chemicals. In an aquatic environment, some hydrocarbons and chemicals will float to the water surface, others will settle to the bottom; some are soluble, and many volatile components of the spill will evaporate.

In Volume One, I outlined the general impacts that might result from the spill of fuels in the North. The most visible effects of a spill on wildlife will be seen on sea-birds and waterfowl. Oil will mat the feathers so they can no longer function for flight, water repellency or insulation, and the birds affected generally die by drowning or from exposure. Birds are also harmed by the toxic effects of oil when they ingest it by preening oil-stained feathers. The enormous flocks of the migratory birds that use the Mackenzie Valley and

Western Arctic are vulnerable to this disaster. The threat is not confined to spills that occur during the summer, when the birds are present in the region. A spill in winter would probably persist and affect the environment used by these birds for many years.

There is conflicting evidence on the effects of oil on marine and aquatic mammals. Contamination of restricted areas, such as whale calving waters, seal haul-out sites, and muskrat and beaver ponds, could have a serious impact on the populations that use these locations. Polar bears could also be affected.

Effects on aquatic organisms are generally more subtle, and might not be visible to the casual observer. Aquatic organisms may be killed directly by coating and asphyxiation, by contact poisoning or by exposure to water-soluble toxic components of the spill. Juvenile forms are generally more sensitive and vulnerable than adults. The higher species in a food chain may be affected by destruction of their food resources lower down the chain. The ingestion of sub-lethal amounts of oil or of oil products into aquatic organisms can result in reduced resistance to infection and other stresses, the destruction of the food value of fishery resources, and the incorporation of carcinogens into the marine food chain and into fish used for food by the local people.

Oil can kill salt-marsh grasses, seaweeds and freshwater vegetation, leading to a loss of food and habitat for wildlife and aquatic organisms and, if extensive enough, to the erosion of sediments normally held in place by the roots of these plants. Once contaminated, vegetation is extremely difficult to clean. It generally takes two, three or more years in temperate regions for heavily oiled vegetation to recover its former productivity.

The threat to the aquatic environment comes not only from fuels, but also from a host of other hazardous and toxic substances that will be used on the pipeline. Substances such as the wide variety of lubricants necessary on the project and chlorine, which is used to treat drinking water and waste-water, could present a threat to the aquatic environment if they are not carefully handled.

In addition to the biological effects of petrochemical pollution, there are many non-biological effects that should also be considered because they could have an economic or aesthetic impact on an area. Boats, wharfs and fishing gear might be fouled. The recreational possibilities and the tourist industry in a spill area might be seriously affected for a long period of time. Water supplies could be contaminated, and specific-status land areas, such as parks, ecological reserves and lands and waters used by native peoples in their traditional pursuits, could be spoiled.

Implications

The problem of oil spills during the construction of a gas pipeline is important because of the very large amounts of fuel and chemicals involved and because the means to control spills in northern waters are inadequate. The prospect of other petroleum-related developments in the region makes the threat of long-term adverse effects on the environment all the more serious.

Granted, government and industry are now spending millions of dollars on research that focuses primarily on clean-up technology for oil spills. It is urgent and vital work, but we must never forget that, in the design, construction and regulation of a pipeline, the emphasis must always be on prevention.

A Management Plan

Commitment to a Plan

The plans for fuel storage and handling and for spill prevention and control that the pipeline companies presented to the Inquiry are, at best, rudimentary. A great deal more work will be required to produce plans that are acceptable.

The drilling program in the Beaufort Sea has given some impetus to improving the state-of-the-art, with particular emphasis on clean-up measures to be taken in arctic marine environments. Since the Inquiry hearings ended in November 1976, an intergovernmental task force has developed contingency plans for a major oil spill in the Beaufort Sea, and the Department of the Environment has drafted contingency planning guidelines for spills from oil and gas pipelines.

These plans, however, are mainly concerned with the organizational aspects of a response to an oil spill: the prevention of spills seems to be receiving less attention. I think my most effective contribution is to specify preventive measures that should be imposed on the pipeline project, because prevention offers the best means of protecting the environment.

Because so few regulations to prevent spills are now in force, and because the work of the pipeline companies on this subject is inadequate, despite the specific requirements of the Pipeline Guidelines, I deem the following recommendations to be essential from the commencement of the project.

Overall Plan

To deal adequately with the handling, storage and clean-up of fuels and hazardous substances that may be spilled, the Company and the Agency must come to terms with a host of complex and interrelated considerations of engineering design, construction and operating measures, environmental disciplines and socio-economic factors. A comprehensive approach of this nature goes far beyond the pipeline companies' present submissions. The Company and the Agency must agree on an overall plan that will specify precisely the approach to be taken at each stage of the design, construction and operation of the pipeline and its related facilities.

1. *Before the final design phase, the Company shall prepare for approval by the Agency an overall plan for the transportation, transferral, storage, use and disposal of fuels and other hazardous substances that will be used during the construction, operation and abandonment of the pipeline and all related facilities used by the Company. The overall plan shall emphasize the need to prevent spills and to control fuels and hazardous substances. It shall demonstrate that facilities and handling equipment will be designed, and personnel will be trained, to minimize the risk of spills. It shall also demonstrate that, during construction and operation of the pipeline, products will be transported, transferred, stored, used and disposed of in ways that will most effectively protect the environment; and that there will be effective contingency plans and trained personnel available to deal with spills that do occur, both at the site of the spill and in other areas that may be affected. The overall plan shall outline training programs for Company personnel who handle hazardous or toxic materials.*

Subject to the direction of the Agency, the overall plan shall, as far as possible, be in cartographic form, and shall take into account, by means of overlays or other graphic techniques at the same scale or by notations, the other overall plans requested elsewhere in this report. The Agency may request the Company to resubmit parts of this plan if, for any reason, they do not meet with its approval. The Company shall undertake to keep the overall plan up to date so that it reflects the latest policies and actions of the Company, the Agency and government.

2. *The overall plan shall specify the physical and biological aspects of the environment that must be protected to safeguard the living resources along the pipeline corridor from possible spills of fuels or hazardous substances. It should show, for example, waterfowl and sea-bird concentration areas, habitat for rare and endangered species, and fish spawning and overwintering areas along the pipeline corridor and transportation routes. It should also show locations of communities and of hunting and fishing areas and camps; locations and times of use of all domestic, commercial and sports fishing sites; locations and boundaries of all existing and proposed parks, International Biological Programme sites, bird sanctuaries and other ecological reserves; locations of archaeological or historic sites; locations of all harbours for small craft or areas in which they are used, docks and landing sites for marine vessels, and designated landing and take-off areas for floatplanes; and locations of water intakes for temporary and permanent domestic and industrial use, as well as those used for pipeline construction.*

In addition, the overall plan shall indicate general locations and periods of use of all transportation routes and storage areas for petrochemical and hazardous and toxic substances, and the volumes of these materials to be moved along various routes and stored at the various locations by season. An outline indicating the inspection and construction requirements for all transportation systems and transfer and storage facilities, whether they are owned by the Company or not, should be provided.

The overall plan shall also list all hazardous and toxic substances to be used, and provide details of the name, properties and use of each substance, the volume, the toxicity data (if available), the proposed method of packing, transporting, transferring and stowing for each substance, and the proposed method of disposing of it.

3. *The overall plan shall be approved by the Agency before site-specific applications are submitted for facilities at which fuels or hazardous substances will be handled, used or stored.*

Site-specific Information

4. *The Company shall file with the Agency, as part of its site-specific applications for construction and operation of project facilities, site-specific information relating to the transportation, use and storage of fuels and other hazardous substances. This information shall include designs for fuel and chemical storage facilities, transfer equipment, and transportation vessels and vehicles owned or used by the Company. Site-specific information for storage facilities shall include a summary of the physical and biological environmental conditions in the area surrounding the installations; a complete set of detailed engineering drawings; a complete set of operating standards, including volume through-puts, number of operating personnel, period of use, expected life of the installation, abandonment criteria, environmental protection criteria and environmental restoration plans. Site-specific information shall also include an operation procedure manual for each spread and for each transfer depot and storage facility.*

Site-specific information shall detail specific contingency plans for each spread and for accidents that could occur along transportation routes, as well as specific measures to maximize the chances of cleaning up spills on land rather than on water. To handle spills that do escape into watercourses, plans shall be developed that give first protection to areas important to aquatic birds, fish, marine mammals and human use.

The Agency must approve the location and extent of the areas in which spilled liquids and contaminated materials, such as earth, natural and synthetic absorbants and driftwood, are deposited.

The preparation of the overall plan and of the site-specific information necessary for the submission of site-specific applications will be major undertakings and will require the detailed specification of designs and procedures and a comprehensive understanding of a wide range of biological and socio-economic factors. The responsibility for preparing the information clearly lies with the Company, but the Agency will also have a major task in assessing the plan.

Spill Prevention

To assist in the preparation of a sound spill prevention program, I have developed a comprehensive set of recommendations based on the final submission of Commission Counsel and the information provided by other participants at the Inquiry.

In making these recommendations, I endorse the use of very specific numerical values. It has been argued that this approach is too restrictive and that, instead, a best judgment based on site-specific features by professionals should be made at each location. I reject that approach because, in view of the scale of the project and the time involved, it is simply not practical. In my opinion, the most practical approach for the pipeline project is the adoption of standards that are easily understood by all concerned: the designer, the executive, the inspector, the biologist and the transportation and pipeline contractors. Cases that require special attention can, of course, be dealt with on an individual basis. If the specified recommendations are unsuitable in a particular case, the Company must document the situation and clearly specify alternative measures, which the Agency can then assess and approve or reject. So far as the Company is concerned, this procedure will involve about the same work that would be required for a best judgment by professionals. The difference is that specific requirements support a general standard, and best judgments, by themselves, may not.

The recommendations read like a safety program, and with good reason. Personnel must be continuously trained and supervised to ensure that they are following sound practice to prevent oil spills. The location, design and construction of facilities must be carried out to minimize environmental damage if a spill does occur. The correct operation of storage facilities is a matter of particular importance, and they must be continuously checked to ensure that they are in good order.

Design Guidelines for Spill Prevention

TANKFARMS

5. Reinforced concrete or earthen dykes for spill containment shall surround all above-ground tanks. The minimum dyke heights shall be either two feet for concrete dykes, three feet for earthen dykes, or as calculated as follows, whichever is greater: the capacity of the largest tank (in cubic feet) plus 10 percent of the capacity of all other tanks (in cubic feet) divided by the effective tankfarm area (in square feet), plus

one foot. The effective tankfarm area equals the entire area that is surrounded by dykes, less the area occupied by all tanks except the largest tank.

6. The dyked area of permanent tankfarms shall be rendered virtually leak-proof by ensuring that the maximum percolation rate in the soils is no more than 5×10^{-6} cm/sec. This protection may be achieved by locating the tankfarms in areas that have suitable natural soils, or by importing or preparing suitable soils and lining the tankfarm area with them. These soils shall be protected with a minimum cover of 10 inches of gravel to prevent physical damage to the soil below.

7. The dyked area of temporary tankfarms shall conform to the soil percolation rate requirement specified for permanent tankfarms. This criterion may be met in the same manner or by the use of oil-resistant membranes manufactured for the purpose, such as those made from polyvinyl chloride (PVC) or urethane. These membranes shall be protected against mechanical damage by a 6-inch layer of sand above and below them. Because PVC membranes become brittle at temperatures below 0°C, they should not be used if in contact with frozen ground. Urethane membranes do not last long and should not be used in installations that will exist for longer than two years.

8. Tankfarms shall not be built on permafrost unless the permafrost is insulated from the tanks and other structures to ensure that the contents of the tanks and the structures do not cause melting; and unless soil test results demonstrate that the permafrost will support the loads placed upon it without settlement or movement.

UNDERGROUND STEEL STORAGE TANKS

9. Underground tanks shall be constructed according to the specifications given in Underwriters' Laboratories of Canada Standard S603 and/or Standard S603.1.

10. Underground tanks should not be installed in areas of permafrost.

11. Underground tanks shall be surrounded with a minimum of one foot of clean sand, shall be buried a minimum depth of three feet and, in areas where traffic passes over them, they shall be covered with reinforced concrete slabs.

12. Permanent underground tanks shall be protected from corrosion by the use of anodes. Points shall be installed for anode testing.

ABOVE-GROUND STORAGE TANKS

13. Above-ground shop-fabricated tanks shall be constructed according to the specifications given in Underwriters' Laboratories of Canada Standard S601. Above-ground field-fabricated tanks shall be constructed according to the specifications given in American Petroleum Institute Standard 650.

14. The Company shall prepare a proposal for approval by the Agency for all steel and welding specifications to be used with metal tanks. One area to be considered is protection against the brittle fracture of steel by specifications of a Charpy-Vee Notch impact requirement.

15. Bladder tanks shall be used for temporary storage only. They shall meet the standards of the Underwriters' Laboratories of Canada or government specifications for their intended use. They shall not be used where atmospheric temperatures may go below the minimum temperature for usage recommended by the manufacturer. The tanks shall be installed on a bed of sand at least one foot thick.

STORAGE IN FLOATING VESSELS

16. Storage of fuels and petrochemicals in vessels used for transportation or in any other floating vessel shall be subject to the specific approval of the Agency.

17. The use of floating storage shall be prohibited in ice, unless the barges or vessels are fully protected from moving, floating ice and from being held in the ice, either in a river or at sea. However, special consideration may be given in specific instances to ice-strengthened barges or vessels that are designed for the purpose and that have adequate mooring and docks of sufficient strength to support the loads involved.

18. The use of barges for storage in waters that have a current shall be avoided. If the current exceeds three knots, the use of floating equipment for storage purposes shall be prohibited, except when waiting a reasonable period (about three days) to be unloaded.

19. Barges or vessels may be used for storage in waters provided that the prohibitions on ice and current outlined above are met. The storage barge or vessel shall be surrounded by a floating containment boom, and its mooring arrangements shall be checked and recorded every 12 hours.

20. Daily recordings and reconciliations of cargo tank ullages shall be carried out on all barges or vessels used for floating storage.

21. All dyking requirements for fixed-tank storage shall apply to floating equipment that is used for storage on land.

22. As the bottom structure of most barges is not designed to support the weight of full fuel tanks when they are out of the water, the underside shall be shored up in a manner approved by the Agency for the specific vessel used. Care shall be taken to ensure that the shorings take up the load at the major structural member and not at unsupported panels of plating.

DRUM STORAGE AREAS

23. Storage areas for drums (full or empty) shall comprise a concrete slab or some other impermeable ground cover (such as a steel plate) that is graded so that all leakages collect in one area. The storage areas shall drain toward a sump and, in the case of petroleum storage, to an oil separator.

PIPELINES AND FITTINGS

24. All pipelines connecting to barges, vessels and petrochemical facilities shall be of steel or a steel alloy that is suitable for the purpose; all joints shall be welded or weld-flanged to the required pressure rating.

25. Valves and other pipeline fittings shall be made of forged or cast steel alloys that are suitable for northern temperatures. Valves and fittings used inside vessels or barges may be of cast iron.

LOCATION OF STORAGE FACILITIES AND ROUTING OF PETROCHEMICAL TRANSPORT

26. Sites for the bulk storage of petrochemicals shall not be within three-quarters of a mile of areas where waterfowl concentrate or within 1,000 feet of any waterbody, unless otherwise approved by the Agency.

27. Because of the environmental sensitivity of the Delta, its low topography and its susceptibility to storm surges and floods, every effort shall be made to avoid the risk of an accidental spill. The Agency shall, therefore, institute special measures for storage facilities located there. These include limiting the size of storage facilities (generally, the maximum tank size should be approximately 125,000 gallons, which is equal to about one-quarter of a barge load); restricting the location of storage tankfarms to stable, high, "Old Delta" ground; and permitting drawdown from only one tank at a time, with all other tanks kept locked.

28. Fuel loading and discharge terminals shall be located downstream from loading and discharge berths for general cargo to reduce risks of explosion or fire.

29. Bulk storage and handling sites shall have a maximum surface slope of two percent. (The velocity of drainage on such a slope is generally slow enough so that run-off can be controlled.)

30. Petrochemical transport shall be along designated and approved routes. Waterborne petrochemical transport should not be routed through large areas of waterfowl concentrations nor through ecological preserves. Routes should avoid areas of waterfowl concentration by at least three-quarters of a mile. Considerable research and field work will be required to establish a complete inventory and evaluation of wildlife resources and the sites of human habitation to be avoided by such transportation routes. Navigation hazards, the practicability of landing, and wharf sites must also be considered.

31. Fuel and bulk chemical cargo movements on a river or in the Beaufort Sea should not begin until the ice conditions, water level and current will not hamper activities to contain or clean up an accidental spill (this date may vary from year to year). Fuel and bulk chemical cargo movements on a river should be suspended if there is a rapid change in the water level or current. All fuel and bulk chemical cargo movements should be completed before vessels and barges are in danger of being caught by freeze-up (this date may vary from year to year).

32. If, after approval, the Agency finds that any of the procedures for petrochemical transportation, tranfer, storage or waste disposal do not adequately protect the environment, they shall be altered. This may require the re-routing of supplies, the relocation of storage facilities, or the redesigning of transfer and disposal equipment.

MARINE TRANSPORTATION FACILITIES

33. All ships or barges used to carry petrochemical products in bulk for the pipeline project shall be classed by a recognized international marine classification society, such as the American Bureau of Shipping or Lloyd's Register of Shipping, or approved by the Canadian Coast Guard's Ship Safety Branch. New vessels shall be built to the relevant institution's rules and constructed under its supervision.

34. Cargo tanks shall be subdivided according to the requirements of the Canada Shipping Act, "Oil Pollution Prevention Regulations, Amendment," dated September 6, 1973.

35. Operation, construction and outfit of vessels shall be to the requirements of the Canada Shipping Act, "Load Line Regulations."

36. At present it is standard practice for fuel barges to carry deck cargos, but in many instances, fittings and arrangements to prevent spills are incompatible with the carriage of deck cargo. The Company shall submit for approval the modification that will have to be made to existing barges, and the designs that will be required for new equipment.

PETROCHEMICAL TRANSFER: MARINE OPERATIONS

37. To contain spills that occur during transfer operations, a spill-guard shall be fitted around the perimeter of the decks of barges or tankers. A 12-inch-high spill-guard is usually adequate, but the spill-guard shall be higher if the deck is cambered or if the ship usually operates with trim. Spill-guards must have drain openings to prevent the accumulation of rainwater or spray when underway. These openings shall be provided with plugs that must be fitted during transfer operations. A strip of deck outside the spill-guard shall be painted white to allow easy visual identification of a flow of liquids over the side.

38. To contain minor spills within an area smaller than the whole deck, other spill-guards shall be fitted around the "make-break" connections, tank vents and hose stowage racks.

39. As far as practical, loading and discharge manifolds, cargo tank vents, flow meters, level gauges and pump controls shall be grouped together to aid surveillance during transfer operations.

40. At the loading and discharge manifolds, whether on marine vessels or on land, bolted flanges or quick-operating, flange-type connections shall be used. The manifolds shall be fitted with spill-guards of sufficient capacity to contain the amount of liquid that would be spilled from a manifold connection and equal to the flow through it during the time taken to stop the flow in an emergency. The capacity shall be determined by the design shut-down time. In no case shall a manifold be installed that hangs clear over water or land.

41. A positive means of draining the manifold and hose lines shall be provided with a recirculating pump connection that enables the discharge pump to deliver the liquid product back to the ship's tank, instead of to the shore facility, during discharge operations. Test cocks shall also be fitted so that operators can verify that the lines have been purged before disconnecting the hoses.

42. The complete deck area, and all areas where operations may have to be carried out in darkness, shall be adequately lighted. In internal spaces, such as pump rooms, the minimum level of illumination shall be 15 footcandles, at exterior deck at manifolds and pump controls, 10 footcandles, and for the entire exterior deck other than above, five footcandles.

43. To prevent spills and for general safety, the following precautions against fire must be taken. All electrical devices shall be suitable for use in an explosive atmosphere. All cargo tank vents shall have flash screens. A foam firefighting system shall be permanently installed on the deck. It shall be capable of supplying foam to any part of a deck and, to ensure that enough foam is available, it shall have the capacity to produce 0.11 Imperial gallons per square foot of deck per minute for a total of 20 minutes. (Further requirements are contained in the "Fire Detection and Extinguishing Equipment Regulations" of the Canda Shipping Act.) Spaces below deck, in which fires often start, shall be protected by an automatic carbon dioxide or similar flooding system. This system shall automatically shut off all ventilation to the affected space in the event of fire. Adequate dry chemical fire extinguishers shall also be provided, and large "No smoking" signs in languages or in symbols that are understood by everyone on the site shall be displayed at the gangway, the manifold and at any other locations that may be necessary.

44. To soak up any minor spillage caught within the spill-guard, an appropriate quantity of natural or a commercial absorbant material, an empty oil drum, plastic garbage bags, shovels, rakes, brooms, rubber gloves and boots shall be kept on the vessel. They shall be stowed in a convenient water-tight and secure locker on the deck.

There are no established transfer procedures defined by regulations, but there can be no substitute for conscientious, well-trained personnel, who will take the necessary precautions. Cutting corners to save time or effort invariably increases the chances and severity of an accident. Continuous training and close supervision of work procedures are always necessary.

The following rules shall be incorporated into work procedures to reduce the possibility of spillage and to mitigate the effects of any spills that may occur.

45. At all times during the loading or discharge of liquid products, suitably trained and qualified personnel shall stand by at both the receiving and discharge points. For tanks 1,000 feet from the unloading site, the cargo discharge point on the vessel, the receiving point on land, and the receiving point at the tankfarm shall all be manned (three persons). All personnel shall be fluent in the same language and be equipped with two-way radios for good communication and coordination. A supervisor employed by the Company shall be present and responsible for overseeing the entire operation.

46. Berth operators and crew at marine facilities shall be trained and competent in all vessel and transfer operations including vessel mooring procedures; transfer connection procedures; shoreside and vessel cargo flow routing, loading phases and system timing details; methods for adapting to the different mooring and cargo transfer situations that may be expected at the mooring berth or elsewhere at the terminal; prescribed operating procedures for a particular berth; and emergency and contingency procedures and plans for the particular berth or terminal.

47. During operations that involve the transfer of a liquid product to or from a vessel, all plugs in the spill-guards shall be in place. If there is heavy precipitation, it may be necessary to drain any accumulation of water by removing these plugs: if so, the transfer operation shall be stopped while the plugs are not in place. Transfer of a liquid product shall not be carried out if more than one inch of water is contained within the spill-guards.

48. When topping off the receiving facility, the rate of flow of the liquid product shall be reduced. Before disconnecting the hoses, care shall be taken to purge the lines and to verify that they are purged before the connection is broken.

49. Fire prevention regulations, such as "No Smoking" rules, shall be strictly enforced, and adequate fire extinguishers shall be available near the transfer location. Personnel shall be trained in the techniques of fighting petrochemical or hazardous substance fires.

50. Liquid products shall not be transferred to or from waterborne transport when visibility is restricted.

51. In fast-flowing rivers, particular attention shall be paid to the mooring arrangements of barges. Mooring lines shall be of adequate strength for the size of the vessel, and four lines should be employed, two forward and two aft. All lines shall use separate cleats or bollards, both on the ship and on the shore. The mooring arrangements shall be checked regularly (preferably at least once every hour) by a watchman.

52. In tidal waters, or in waters such as lakes that do not have appreciable currents, all fuel-transporation equipment shall be surrounded by a floating containment boom during the transfer of a liquid product. This boom could be carried by the vessel, but it should normally be stored at the wharf.

53. To keep all transfer systems in good order, a detailed preventive maintenance schedule shall be implemented. Pumps and valves shall be opened for inspection once every 12 months, preferably at the start of each season. Hoses shall be visually inspected for damage before each use and, once every 12 months, preferably at the start of each season, they shall be hydraulically tested to a pressure equal to one and one-half times their maximum working pressure. Rigging shall be visually inspected for damage before each use and, once every 12 months, preferably at the start of each season, it shall be statically tested to one and one-half times its rated capacity. Alarms shall be tested for correct operation before each use of the system. Gauges and meters shall be visually checked for correct operation at each use. Fire-fighting equipment shall be inspected in accordance with "Fire Detection and Extinguishing Equipment Regulations" of the Canada Shipping Act. Mooring lines shall be visually inspected for damage before each use, and they shall be replaced every 24 months. Floating containment booms shall be visually inspected for damage before each use.

PETROCHEMICAL TRANSFER: LAND OPERATIONS

54. All transfer areas, including — but not limited to — areas for tank truck loading, drum filling and vehicle fuelling, shall have spill collection facilities as outlined in the section "Drum Storage Areas."

55. All transfer points shall be controlled by fast-acting valves so that the flow of the liquid product can be terminated immediately if the hoses or any other equipment should fail or if there is a fire.

56. Transfer operations shall be constantly monitored by trained personnel who shall be in attendance during the entire transfer period.

57. All recommendations made in the section "Petrochemical Transfer: Marine Operations" concerning transfer-point illumination, no-smoking regulations, fire-fighting capabilities, fire extinguishers, and qualified personnel, and relevant points in the preventive maintenance schedule shall apply.

WASTE PETROCHEMICAL HANDLING

58. Bottom-drainage lubricating oil change areas shall be supplied with concrete slabs or some equivalent, such as steel plates, that are suitably graded toward a sump and petroleum separator to ensure that any spillage does not contaminate the surrounding area. Top-drainage lubricating oil change areas, where oil is removed from crankcases by mobile or fixed suction pumps, shall not require special protection.

59. Used lubricating oil shall either be shipped to a refinery for use as feed stock or for re-refining, or burnt in an incinerator specifically designed for the purpose.

60. *An application to dispose of a chemical shall be made to the Agency every time a disposal is contemplated, and the Company must have formal approval of its proposal before the disposal is effected. Generally, the disposal shall conform to recommendations in the Code of Good Practice for Management of Hazardous and Toxic Wastes at Federal Establishments (Environmental Protection Service, Department of the Environment, 1977).*

CONTAMINATED RUN-OFF CONTROL

61. *It may not be practical or possible to collect all petroleum leakages and spills at each small petrochemical storage facility in living and work areas. Run-off water storage pits shall, therefore, be installed immediately adjacent to these areas to collect all run-off so that it may be monitored for petroleum content.*

62. *Storage pits shall be designed to contain a minimum of 48 hours of run-off from the area drained. The rate shall be based on the maximum 24-hour run-off rate for the 10-year storm-return period.*

63. *In sensitive permafrost areas, pits shall be designed to minimize thermal disturbance and degradation of the surrounding soils.*

64. *Permanent storage pits shall be constructed with soil liners to prevent leakage to the environment. Percolation rates shall be less than 5×10^{-6} cm/sec.*

65. *Temporary storage pits shall conform to the percolation rate requirements specified for permanent storage pits. The criteria may be met in the same manner or by the use of oil resistant polyvinyl chloride (PVC) or urethane membranes specifically manufactured for the purpose, but within the restrictions outlined in the recommendations for tankfarms.*

66. *Water from storage pits shall not be released to the environment until it is ascertained that the oil concentration in it is less than 5 parts per million (ppm).*

67. *Surface run-off water from petroleum storage and handling areas that contain petroleum products in excess of the limits specified shall be collected and transported in closed, leak-proof systems to a separator facility. After treatment in the oil-water separation facility, all run-off water shall be drained into a collection pit. The water in this pit shall be inspected to ensure its purity before it is released to the environment. Oil skim on the water shall be removed by commercially available absorbents and incinerated. The concentration of petroleum in discharge water shall be less than 5 ppm.*

68. *Ice and snow contamination by petroleum products shall be kept in storage pits until it melts. Commercial absorbents shall be used to collect the oil, as described above, which shall then be incinerated.*

Contingency Planning for Spill Control

The measures I have outlined above are aimed at spill prevention. Nevertheless, as I explained in Volume One, spills are bound to occur. We also know that, once they do occur, the technology at present available to clean them up is inadequate. Contingency planning is essential to make spill management as effective as technically possible and such planning must be complete, thoroughly understood and ready for immediate implementation.

The submission by Commission Counsel on spill control dealt with the requirements of contingency planning, personnel training and the selection and deployment of clean-up equipment. This was the only comprehensive outline of these subjects that had been developed to that time. However, since then, the Department of the Environment has developed a draft paper entitled "Contingency Planning Guidelines, Oil and Gas Pipelines" (May 1977). I think it is fair to say that in considerable measure these guidelines are based on Commission Counsel's submission to this Inquiry.

69. *The "Contingency Planning Guidelines, Oil and Gas Pipelines," prepared by the Department of the Environment (draft, May 1977), should be adopted as the basis for specific requirements for industry contingency plans.*

I do not think it is necessary to reprint here either the Department of the Environment's draft or Commission Counsel's recommendations because both of them are only guidelines for the preparation of a contingency plan. Such a plan is urgently required and it does not now exist: it must be comprehensive and it must be compatible with other government plans. In the final analysis, the success of the contingency plan will depend on the scope of the planning, the commitment of money, the training of personnel and the limits of technology.

Government agencies across the nation have prepared contingency plans for spills of various sorts. One example is the draft "Government Contingency Plan for Major Oil Spills in the Beaufort Sea" (Environmental Protection Service, Department of the Environment, November 1976), which aims at the coordination of the responses of various levels and departments of government to an accidental spill in the Beaufort Sea. Exactly this sort of coordinating plan will be necessary for a spill anywhere along the proposed pipeline corridor.

70. *The draft "Government Contingency Plan for Major Oil Spills in the Beaufort Sea" should be completed and tested in the field. Similar plans to cover wider regions of the North should also be prepared.*

The preparation of plans to coordinate the work of government departments and agencies is plainly the job of government itself. However, it is equally clear that industry, in this case the pipeline company, will have the first responsibility for and the liability to clean up any accidental spill. In fact, the Pipeline Guidelines specifically require industry to prepare a spill contingency plan in the context not only of a gas pipeline and its attendant facilities, but also an oil pipeline along the same corridor:

> ... effective plans [shall] be developed to deal with oil leaks, oil spills, pipeline rupture, fire and other hazards to terrestrial, lake and marine habitats, that such plans be designed to minimize environmental disturbances caused by containment, clean-up or other operations and to bring about adequate restoration of the environment, that they be designed to deal with minor and major incidents, whether they are single-event or occur over a period of time and that they include contingency plans to cope with major hazards or critical situations. [pp. 15-16]

In addition, the Pipeline Guidelines require proposals of specific contingency plans or information regarding:

a) how the possible loss of oil or gas through pipeline leaks would be routinely detected and stopped quickly (the maximum potential undetected loss from the pipeline should be specified and evidence provided. This value is to be as low as is technologically feasible);
b) how oil which has escaped into the terrestrial, lake or marine environment would be detected, how it would be disposed of and how the elements of the environment affected by the oil would be rehabilitated; ... [pp. 22-23]

The pipeline companies must also:

> ... provide documented evidence that they possess not only the necessary knowledge, but also the capability to carry out the specific proposals. [p. 13]

The contingency plans advanced before the Inquiry by the pipeline companies and the producers in the Mackenzie Delta fall far short of the requirements laid down in the Pipeline Guidelines and of the ultimate requirements for the construction and operation of a pipeline. Obviously, I cannot prepare a comprehensive plan: that is the responsibility of the pipeline company. The Pipeline Guidelines are useful, but they are not specific enough in their directions to industry to ensure that their contingency plans will be comprehensive and compatible with those of government.

71. *The Company shall prepare a spill contingency plan that is comparable to and coordinated with those of the relevant government agencies.*

There are four additional points that warrant further consideration and that should ultimately be included in any planning scheme advanced by industry.

72. *There must be some definition of what constitutes a spill and of the appropriate response, given that the size and nature of spills can vary. The contingency plan must describe not only an appropriate level of response, but also an appropriate type of response, taking into account that, in the North, certain clean-up techniques could cause more harm than the spill itself.*

73. *To assist with project planning and spill response, the Company should establish and file with the Agency a catalogue of all the toxic and hazardous materials that will be used during the construction and operation of the pipeline and its ancillary facilities. The catalogue should include details on the quantities shipped, stored and used in various locations and at specified times; the properties of the substance, the probabilities of a spill and the probable success of a clean-up operation with the equipment on hand.*

This procedure might be developed from the methods outlined in the Battelle Memorial Institute's report *Control of Spillage of Hazardous and Polluting Substances* (United States Government Printing Office, 15090 P0Z10/70).

The reporting of spills has been required by law in the United States since the early 1970s, but, except for spills from ships, it is not yet law in Canada. It must be a requirement for the pipeline project and it would be commendable on a nation-wide basis.

74. *Throughout the preconstruction, construction, operation and abandonment phases of the pipeline project there should be a mandatory spill-reporting scheme for the Company and all its contractors and subcontractors.*

Finally, the contingency plan must be proved effective under actual conditions in the field. It does not matter how persuasive the plan is as a written document, as an organization chart or as a computerized response mechanism; if it does not work in the field, it is useless.

75. *Any comprehensive contingency plan must be field-tested regularly with realistic scenarios of all types of spills. Government or Agency inspectors should spot-check contingency planning preparedness by dropping unannounced into camps and facility sites to conduct mock spill exercises.*

18 Pipe Testing

The technical aspects of testing a pipeline under hydrostatic pressure after it is in place and before it is put into service are based on standard practice and are well covered by existing regulations. There are, however, environmental aspects to the testing of a northern pipeline that require regulation because of the very large volumes of test liquid and its effects on the aquatic environment.

To prevent the test medium from freezing in the pipe, it will be necessary to use either warm water or an antifreeze mixture of water and methanol. Foothills suggested that the antifreeze mixture could be as much as 70 percent methanol, and Arctic Gas suggested 26 percent. In either case, very large volumes of methanol and water will be used. For example, a three-mile length of pipe, the length suggested for a test section, would hold over 1 million gallons. Whether or not this volume is all water or is a water-methanol mixture, there are obvious and major problems related to water withdrawal, the handling of methanol, contingency plans for spills, and the disposal of the warm water or the water-methanol mixture. Most of these problems can be handled by applying the recommendations advanced in the chapters entitled Water Withdrawals, Waste Management, Management of Fuels and Hazardous Substances and The Physical Environment: Water. However, there are some specific issues that warrant mention here.

The first relates to the withdrawal, then disposal, of the large amounts of water that will be required to test the pipe. Millions of gallons of water will have to be withdrawn from one location and disposed of in another several miles away. This prospect raises a number of biological concerns, such as the impact on the location from which the water is withdrawn, and the possibility of transferring water from one watershed to another. If a water-methanol mixture is used, it will be made up at one point, then reused in successive sections of the pipeline before it is ultimately discharged. A test with warm water will require not only the volume of water needed for the test, but also water to flush and warm each section of the pipe before it is tested. This method will require much more water, and it will preclude the reuse of the test liquid, which is possible within a closed system if the water-methanol mixture is used. In either case, the discharge of such large quantities of water could create significant environmental problems, such as melting of river ice at the point of discharge, melting of snow cover over the ice or along stream banks, erosion of bank material, and, when the water has cooled, an increased thickness of river ice that may alter spring break-up patterns.

The second, and perhaps the most troublesome, issue is related to the toxic nature of methanol and, in particular, to its high biological oxygen demand. Although contaminants may be picked up from within the pipeline, even with a warm water test, they probably represent a minor problem in comparison with the toxic and asphyxiating nature of methanol. The pipeline companies have said that, after testing is complete, the methanol will be concentrated by distillation, then burned or used for other purposes; the water from the mixture will either be sprayed onto land or frozen water surfaces or metered into suitable watercourses. Alternatively, the mixture might be diluted with more water, until it contains less than one percent methanol by volume, then disposed of in suitable watercourses. This latter technique has been severely criticized because it would require inordinately large volumes of water and because the total volume of methanol would create a high oxygen demand in the receiving environment.

I am not satisfied that the toxicity of methanol to fish and fish eggs is adequately understood, and I conclude that the possible effects of disposing of the methanol mixture or a distillate residue have not been adequately dealt with. Both Arctic Gas and Foothills have, in my opinion, underestimated the practical problems associated with disposing of the enormous quantities of methanol waste. In particular, they have minimized the high demand for biological oxygen that the methanol will make. As noted in the report of the National Energy Board, small-scale studies of the effects of such a discharge do not provide any assurance that the environmental effects of a large-scale discharge can be overcome. The possible effects on water quality and fish are troubling, and they require the utmost caution.

The third issue involves contingency plans for an accidental spill during testing. Again, the toxicity of methanol is the cause of gravest concern, although a warm water spill would cause melting and erosion, and it could cause problems of thermal shock. The transportation, transfer and storage of the test liquids will have to comply with the recommendations and guidelines presented in the chapter entitled Management of Fuels and Hazardous Substances. I assume, of course, that the most rigorous procedures to maintain quality control will be employed during the construction period to minimize the risk of pipe failure, but special and comprehensive measures must also be developed to contain a spill and to minimize its effects on the environment, should a spill occur during any part of the testing process. No such measures exist in the documentation presented to me, and it appears that the pipeline companies have seriously underestimated the importance of planning for this possibility.

With these points in mind, and recognizing that other chapters of this report cover many issues related to testing the pipeline, I put forward the following recommendations.

1. Before construction of the pipeline begins, the Company shall prepare for approval by the Agency detailed plans for pressure testing. In addition to information required by existing regulations, these plans shall detail the environmental effects and the measures that will be used during a typical water or water-methanol hydrostatic test sequence to mitigate these effects.

2. Pipe testing shall be carried out only under a permit from and in the presence of a representative of the Agency. The Company shall make site-specific and separate applications to the Agency to test the pipe for each spread season during which these tests will be conducted. Each application shall be consistent with and keyed to the overall plans and the recommendations specified in The Physical Environment: Water, and in Fish, Water Withdrawals, Waste Management, and Management of Fuels and Hazardous Substances.

3. Each application to test the pipe shall note clearly and concisely the location or locations at which the following operations are proposed: withdrawal; pretreatment or heating of water; the mixing of methanol and water; the filling of test section or sections; the storage of water or water-methanol mixture in the pipe between tests or from one construction season until the next; the emptying of test section or sections; and the treatment and disposal of the test medium. Each application shall also detail the equipment and procedures to be used, the quantities and temperatures of water and methanol involved, and the dates and times of the proposed operations.

The potential toxicity of the effluent from pipe testing operations must be investigated before any effluent is discharged. The procedures for the toxicity test should be specified by the Toxicity Coordination Committee of the Environmental Protection Service, Department of the Environment, and should include provisions similar to those outlined in the Petroleum Refinery Effluent Regulations and Guidelines (prepared by the Environmental Protection Service, 1974).

4. The water-methanol test mixture shall be disposed of by distillation, and the distillate shall be burned or used in some approved way, and the residue liquid shall be effectively treated before it is discharged. Disposal of the test mixture by dilution shall be prohibited.

Because of the large volumes and high biological oxygen demand of residues that contain methanol, the treatment standards, if they are to protect the environment, may well have to exceed the effluent standards prescribed in Waste Management.

5. Before disposal, the Company shall treat all test liquids, including the water used to heat the pipeline, to reduce concentrations of oils, organic carbon compounds and particulates to acceptable levels.

6. The Company shall store the methanol test mixture between tests, or from one construction season to the next, in steel tanks or bladder tanks in accordance with the recommendations made in Management of Fuels and Hazardous Substances: Spill Prevention. Mixtures stored in completed sections of pipeline shall be stored only in sections that have been successfully pressure tested and have been approved by the Agency for storage purposes.

7. The Company shall submit detailed contingency plans for each spread season during which hydrostatic tests will be conducted, outlining methods to contain and recover spills of warm water, water-methanol or pure methanol, should the pipe or any associated equipment fail during testing. These plans will include methods of detection, notification, decision-making, containment, countermeasures, clean-up and disposal of test media, as well as plans for restoration that adequately reflect concerns for vegetation, surface waters, and wildlife habitats. All plans must be approved by the Agency. Catchment devices may have to be installed before the pipe is tested to prevent any spilled fluid from reaching a waterbody that may be highly sensitive to pollution.

8. The Company shall submit to the Agency for approval plans for the location and repair of failures during pressure testing.

The repair of any failure in the pipe during the testing of it shall depend on access to the site of the failure. The Company should not assume that the construction season will be extended for the repair of any section of pipe that fails during testing. This limitation is particularly important in areas that are seasonally critical to wildlife and fish and in areas to which access is by snow roads.

19 Facilities Complexes and Equipment Operations

Many witnesses at the formal and community hearings described the impact that construction and operation of compressor stations and associated pipeline facilities and equipment is likely to have on the physical, biological and human environment. I have dealt elsewhere with transportation, the physical environment and the location of the pipeline in relation to wildlife, all issues that have direct bearing on the complexes of facilities and the operation of equipment during pipeline construction and operation. Aircraft control is integral to both this chapter and the chapter on Transportation; the subject is dealt with separately because of its complexity and its central importance to effective environmental control in the region.

In this chapter, I shall focus on compressor stations and associated facilities in their relation to the environment. I recognize the artificiality of this categorization in view of the complex interrelationship of all aspects of the environment, of which a fuller appreciation is given in the chapters of Part Two of this volume. In this chapter, I shall simply present some concerns and recommendations related to specific aspects of the project.

The impact of the construction and operation of the facilities that are associated with the pipeline will depend on two factors, with which I shall deal in turn. The first is the location and design of facilities — particularly of compressor stations — in relation to terrain sensitivities, fish and wildlife habitats, migration routes and aesthetic factors. The second relates to the operation of the equipment that is associated with those facilities.

Facilities Complexes: Location and Design

Compressor stations will be located along the pipeline at intervals of approximately 50 miles at hydraulically optimum points chosen on the basis of pipe and station size and on gas volumes; the position of the stations may then be adjusted slightly to accommodate site-specific geotechnical considerations. The degree of flexibility in choosing and adjusting station sites is said to be limited if hydraulic balance and throughput efficiency are to be maintained.

Compressor station sites will be the focal points of activity during the construction and operation of the pipeline because frequently they are also the location of airstrips, heliports, temporary and permanent roads, wharves, stockpile sites, borrow pits, camps and permanent staff quarters. They are, therefore, called facilities complexes.

From a broad, regional perspective, the pipeline is a linear development across the northern landscape with nodes of activity at 50-mile intervals. From a local perspective, however, these nodes are the focal points of many environmental concerns. For example, a facilities complex could sprawl from a wharf site on the Mackenzie River to stockpile sites on the right-of-way and include heliports, airfields and borrow pits. It may include several miles of connecting roads and encompass tens of square miles of land. Such complexes were characterized at the Inquiry as mini-industrial developments and from an environmental perspective, they must be viewed in this way.

Activities at these facilities will be at a high level during the construction phase, and they will persist at a lower level, punctuated periodically by special maintenance and emergency operations, throughout the life of the pipeline. There may also be sustained bursts of activity at compressor sites if the gas pipeline is looped or if an oil pipeline is built. Should these events occur, the whole construction scenario would be repeated — perhaps with greater environmental consequences.

Construction of the pipeline cannot be considered as a single event. Even after construction is completed, there will be some disrupting and disturbing activity, and that activity will be particularly pronounced at the facilities complexes.

Biologists and other people at both the formal and community hearings voiced concern over the levels of logistical and construction activity at these facilities complexes and over their potential effects on the environment and on society. These witnesses expressed concern about the effect of disturbance by transport activities, noise and increased human access during critical life stages of birds, fish and mammals; the impact on fish, aquatic biota and habitat, of run-off, sedimentation and increased siltation caused by the disruption of drainage and the construction of facilities on gravel pads; the threat to bird and fish populations posed by spills of fuel and hazardous substances; and the aesthetic results of the location and design of these facilities. In particular, native people were concerned about the possible impacts on their resources and their way of life.

Overall Plan

The various engineering and environmental aspects of facilities complexes have not yet been brought together in a clear and comprehensive way. An overall plan is, therefore, essential if the extent of the activities, their interrelationship and their impact are to be properly understood by everyone associated with their design, approach and regulation.

1. *Before the final design phase, the Company shall prepare for approval by the Agency a comprehensive, but concise, overall plan for the project's transportation facilities, including airstrips, heliports, temporary and permanent roads, wharves, stockpile sites, borrow pits, camps and permanent staff quarters. This plan shall take into account the other overall plans requested elsewhere in this report. The Agency may request the Company to resubmit parts of this overall plan if, for any reason, they do not meet with its approval. The Company shall undertake to keep this overall plan up to date to reflect the latest policies and actions of the Company, the Agency and government.*

2. *The overall plan shall show in map form the location of all project facilities related to the pipeline right-of-way, the Mackenzie River, existing communities and existing or proposed facilities not related to the project, such as the Mackenzie Highway, land lines, winter roads, borrow pits and wharves. The overall plan shall also specify the design standards to be applied, the general work schedule for each facility and, if requested by the Agency, the total estimated capital cost and the annual operation and maintenance cost of each facility.*

In addition, the overall plan shall outline the rationale that was used to determine the design standard and location for each particular facility and the reasons why the Company has chosen to build new wharves and stockpile sites or to use existing facilities; to use temporary or permanent wharves and stockpile sites; to use gravel roads or snow roads; to build new airports or heliports or to use existing facilities; to use airstrips or heliports; and to use new or existing rights-of-way for roads or other linear facilities.

The overall plan shall list all of the assumptions that the Company has made regarding the availability of existing facilities and the approximate volume of project-related traffic that such facilities will sustain during the construction

period (broken down into monthly or seasonal periods, as appropriate) and during pipeline operation (broken down on a quarterly basis); all of the assumptions that the Company has made regarding facilities that parties not associated with the pipeline company may build, for example, extensions to the Mackenzie Highway and facilities built by the gas producers in the Delta.

3. *The overall plan shall be approved by the Agency before the Company submits site-specific applications for construction and operation of facilities.*

Site-specific Applications

4. *The Company shall file with the Agency site-specific applications for the construction and operation of each compressor station and for other facilities. Each of these applications shall be integrated into the overall plan. Because the operations of all facilities at compressor stations are generally interrelated, site-specific applications shall be submitted on the basis of a complex of facilities centred on a compressor station, unless otherwise approved by the Agency. That is to say, applications for activities at each compressor station site and for all associated facilities that serve that site and the adjacent right-of-way shall be filed as a group.*

5. *Each application shall include a concise summary of all engineering, socio-economic and environmental information that was used in site selection; construction drawings and specifications that comply with the relevant design and environmental standards of the government and the Agency; the schedule of construction and the duration of use of all facilities; the maximum anticipated volumes of traffic and camp populations for various periods during construction and operation; and the exact location of the sources of borrow material and of haul routes, together with the quantities and quality of this material. Each application shall state whether or not the facilities will be required during the operations and maintenance phase of the pipeline. Each application shall include plans for the abandonment of facilities that are not required after construction and for the eventual abandonment of all facilities when the useful life of the project has ended.*

Location and Design Considerations

The cumulative level of activities at the facilities complexes and the period over which these activities will take place have the potential for the creation of unacceptable environmental disturbance. The location and design of these complexes is fundamental to a successful resolution of the environmental concerns that they raise. For example, in the chapter, The Physical Environment, I describe the importance of valleys in the northern ecosystem. Valleys are as important to the local ecosystems that the pipeline will cross as the facilities complexes are to the pipeline itself, for they are also nodes of activities — geological, hydrological, biological, cultural and socio-economic — within an ecosystem. This is why I recommend in the chapter on The Physical Environment that, wherever possible, facilities (particularly groups of facilities) should be kept out of valleys.

6. The location and design of facilities complexes shall conform to the recommendations I have made in Parts One and Two of this report to protect local people's activities and the terrain, waterbodies, wildlife and fish. In general, location and design shall take into account the specific characteristics of the local and regional environment, including geotechnical characteristics, wildlife and fish habitat and migrations, local land and water use, archaeological resources, and the aesthetic values of landscapes and waterbodies. In view of the central importance of valleys to the regional landscapes, ecosystems and land use patterns of local people, particular care should be taken to avoid adverse environmental effects on valleys.

7. Upon abandonment of a facility, it shall be removed and the area shall be restored, as directed by the Agency.

Many particular concerns and recommendations related to facilities complexes are dealt with elsewhere in this report, but a few issues arose during the course of the Inquiry that warrant particular mention here.

ROADS, AIRSTRIPS AND HELIPORTS

Biological experts testified that their greatest concern with respect to roads, airstrips and heliports is that they will increase access to formerly isolated areas and will pose a serious threat to the viability of populations of caribou, moose and Dall's sheep that have survived mainly because large parts of their habitats are inaccessible.

8. During construction, the Company shall limit the use of all roads, airstrips and heliports under its jurisdiction to vehicles and aircraft that are associated with the pipeline project. Access to facilities built by the Company for its own use shall be limited to authorized personnel of the Company, Agency or government. The Company shall take all reasonable steps to discourage access by any other persons.

9. After construction and during the operation of the pipeline, the Company shall limit access to the roads, airstrips and heliports that will be required for its operation and, using methods approved by the Agency, shall remove or otherwise obstruct access to facilities that are not required. Where local people and government authorities agree that project access roads to previously inaccessible areas are beneficial, such roads shall be left intact after pipeline construction is completed.

Well-travelled roads, steep embankments, and, to a lesser extent, airstrips act as barriers to migrating caribou. Not only will such barriers increase exposure of caribou to hunters and predators, they may cause minor diversions in line of travel,

long-term changes in migration patterns, and even abandonment of part or all of a traditional range. Roads can also be barriers to fish if stream crossings are not properly designed.

10. The Company shall design and maintain roads so that easy passage of fish and mammals is assured. Culverts shall be designed so that the passage of fish is not impeded. (See Fish.) The Company shall not use snow clearing techniques that leave long, unbroken stretches of snowfence or deep drifts and snowbanks that could impede the movements of caribou. Snowfencing shall be removed in spring before the migrating caribou arrive.

When surface and subsurface drainage is affected, as it may be by the construction of gravel pads, the result may be erosion and sedimentation. These, in conjunction with run-off water that may contain fuels or other toxic substances, could disturb waterbodies and could pose a hazard to aquatic ecosystems.

11. To protect waterbodies from impacts associated with the construction and operation of roads, airstrips and heliports, an undisturbed buffer strip 300 feet wide, or as specified by the Agency, shall be left between each facility and adjacent waterbody.

12. The construction and operation of roads, airstrips and heliports shall not adversely affect local drainage patterns. (See Terrain Considerations: Drainage and Erosion.)

WHARF AND STOCKPILE SITES

The environmental problems associated with wharves and stockpile sites focus on two items: the disturbance to fish harvesting, and the disturbance of aquatic resources by siltation or by spills of fuels.

13. Because stream and river mouths are frequently areas used by local people for fishing and are often areas of high aesthetic, archaeological and recreational value, wharves shall be located at least 1,500 feet away from the estuaries of streams and rivers, unless otherwise approved by the Agency.

14. To minimize the problems related to drainage and erosion and their adverse effects on waterbodies and fish, stockpile sites shall be located 300 feet from the shoreline, unless otherwise approved by the Agency.

15. In selecting sites for wharves and stockpile sites, the Company shall consider the requirements for effective control of accidental fuel spills. For example, areas of fast water and limited access, and areas that have important biological or sociological features susceptible to spills shall be avoided. (See Management of Fuels and Hazardous Substances.)

16. Unless otherwise approved by the Agency, all storage areas for bulk fuel and chemicals shall be located at least 1,000 feet from any waterbody. To reduce the risk of a spill entering a waterbody, storage facilities for fuels and chemicals shall be located on the part of the site farthest from the water. (See Management of Fuels and Hazardous Substances.)

17. To reduce the risk of leaks not being detected and to facilitate maintenance and repair, all fuel piping systems at wharves, stockpile sites and camps shall be located above ground, except at places, such as road crossings, where short sections of the pipe shall be installed in culverts.

CONSTRUCTION CAMPS

In the socio-economic chapters of this report, I make some recommendations that pertain to the operation of camps. The control of alcohol and of access to communities by camp personnel are examples. On the environmental side, I am most concerned about locating and operating camps so that their adverse effects on terrain, waterbodies, mammals and fish are kept to a minimum.

18. To minimize the area disturbed, camps shall, where possible, be located at stockpile sites, wharves or compressor station sites. Applications to locate camps elsewhere shall be supported by documentation explaining why the camp cannot be located at a preferred site.

19. The camps built or used by the Company shall provide their own support facilities, such as power and water supply, their own sewage treatment and disposal, first aid stations, and recreational facilities.

Compressor and Related Noise

In the chapter on The Physical Environment, I discussed the adverse effects of noise in general. I now wish to address the specific problems of high intensity noise produced in the operation of compressor stations, and to make recommendations on how these problems can be avoided or reduced.

Not all compressor stations will be the same: all stations will have compressors, but the horsepower will vary; some stations will have heat exchangers to chill the gas, but others will not. The noise will, therefore, vary in pitch, intensity and duration from station to station. Gas turbine engines produce high frequency, directional noise at the air intake and low frequency, non-directional noise at the exhaust. Heat exchanger fans direct noise upward and pipes emit high-frequency, pure-tone noises. Vent valves when "blown down" produce intense noise levels — at and beyond the threshold of pain — although the duration is short and the occurrence is infrequent. Control valves and various auxiliary pieces of equipment contribute lower intensity noise.

Because there are so many sources of noise at compressor stations and because the ultimate noise level is so dependent on final design, I do not propose to specify details of noise control. Rather, I will highlight noise problems from an environmental (as opposed to worker safety) perspective and discuss the objectives of ameliorative measures.

20. To minimize disturbance to wildlife and people and to maintain the environmental attributes of the region, the best practicable technology shall be employed for compressor station noise abatement.

The pipeline companies have undertaken to restrict ambient noise levels at the compressor station fence line of compressor stations to 60 dBA. The National Energy Board, while accepting this, foresees that further noise abatement measures might be necessary to prevent adverse environmental effects. Industry's commitment to restrict sound to a maximum of 60 dBA can be interpreted as evidence that such attenuation can be achieved. Evidence brought before me clearly indicates that it is technically possible to attain even lower levels. Carl Koskimaki, testifying for Arctic Gas, said that "maximum silencing" techniques could reduce fence line noise levels from the 59-67 dBA range to around 50 to 53 dBA (F3937).

It is difficult to judge how much noise abatement will be necessary to protect birds and wildlife from unacceptable disturbance. The problem is site-specific and depends both on the nature of the installation and on the local environmental sensitivities. The evidence I heard emphasized the sensitivity of birds, in particular snow geese, to compressor station noise. Dr. William Gunn, an ornithological consultant to Arctic Gas, suggested that, at compressor stations adjacent to habitat frequented by significant numbers of birds, noise levels should not exceed 50 dBA at a distance of 1,000 feet. Various figures have been quoted by other specialists. Clearly, there are circumstances that warrant reducing noise below conventional abatement standards.

21. Compressor stations located in environmentally sensitive areas and areas used extensively by local people shall incorporate special noise abatement designs and operating measures to reduce the disturbance effects to levels that permit normal use of the regional environment. The determination of these site-specific levels shall rest initially with the Company, and prior to completion of design, all the supporting information leading to the design levels shall be submitted to the Agency for approval.

CUMULATIVE EFFECTS

As with all other environmental impacts, each source of noise must be considered in the present and future context of cumulative impact. Although compressor stations will be major sources of noise pollution, they will be only one factor in a much broader setting. Noise will emanate from each part of a facilities complex. In the future, looping, additional compressor units, an oil pipeline, a highway, roads and more people may augment the problem. In the Mackenzie Delta, ongoing petroleum exploration and development will be a major factor, especially in view of the environmental sensitivity of the area during certain times of the year.

Station layout and design, equipment specification, and operating procedures are nearly as important as noise suppression devices. It is costly and perhaps technically impossible to make changes after a problem arises; therefore, careful planning and design are essential. Furthermore, the cumulative impact is handled more effectively and economically by proper initial design of all contributing sources rather than by overly strict constraints on subsequent additions.

22. *Noise abatement plans for pipeline facilities shall incorporate cumulative considerations of all sources of noise. This consideration shall encompass all company and private activities that can be expected to occur in the region of impact throughout the life of the pipeline project. Particular attention shall be given to facilities in the Mackenzie Delta as they relate to ongoing petroleum developments and to the cumulative effect on migratory birds using the area during nesting, moulting and staging.*

MONITORING

Installation of noise attenuation devices and implementation of abatement procedures will not necessarily ensure compliance with site-specific environmental constraints. Much of the design is theoretical and, as I have explained, noise emissions are complex and difficult to predict. There is a need both to test the noise levels at each site shortly after start-up and to monitor the levels on a long-term basis to ensure that acceptable cumulative levels are not exceeded.

23. *The Company shall monitor the noise level of each compressor station as prescribed by the Agency and shall report the results to the Agency within six months of start-up of each station. The Company shall monitor the noise level periodically throughout the life of the project as required by the Agency and in any case within six months of any modification that is likely to alter noise emissions.*

BLOWDOWN NOISE

From time to time, the pipeline at compressor stations and meter stations will be blown down to atmospheric pressure. and meter stations. These blowdowns occur rather infrequently during normal maintenance operations, and also under emergency conditions. The pressure of the gas in the pipeline causes vented gas to escape at very high — even supersonic — velocity. Noise levels of 140 dBA (beyond the threshold of pain) are reached and exceeded. For obvious reasons, unattenuated blowdown noise is totally unacceptable in sensitive wildlife areas, where native people are hunting, fishing or trapping, or near settlements and recreation areas.

24. *At all compressor stations, the Company shall install the best practicable noise attenuation equipment to reduce blowdown noise to levels that will minimize the disturbance to humans and to wildlife.*

25. *As part of the final design, the Company shall submit plans, designs and operating procedures (including expected frequency of maintenance and emergency false-alarm blowdowns) for compressor stations, meter stations or other project facilities where blowdown can be expected during the life of the pipeline.*

Emissions from Facilities

Changes in air quality that are associated with major construction projects are generally temporary or localized in nature, and they are not, therefore, considered to be one of the more serious environmental issues. But, because the ambient air quality of the Mackenzie Valley and Western Arctic is still virtually unimpaired, the next major source of industrial air pollution takes on greater significance than the magnitude of the emissions alone would otherwise merit.

COMPRESSOR STATIONS

The Arctic Gas pipeline project would require a 30,000-horsepower compressor station every 50 miles, usually accompanied by a 17,000-horsepower chilling unit. We can assume that a future gas pipeline project in the Mackenzie Valley will be of comparable magnitude. Natural gas, which is among the cleanest of fuels, would be used to power the pipeline. But each station would emit nearly 1,000 tons of exhaust gases per hour for a total of about 400 thousand tons per operating day for the whole pipeline North of 60. Of this 400 thousand tons, about two million Imperial gallons is water vapour or steam. The volumes are impressive. Furthermore, these emissions will continue and even increase for at least two decades.

Concern about compressor station emissions focuses on the potential problems of ice fog and concentrations of nitrogen dioxide.

26. *In final design preparations, the Company should include site-specific analyses to ensure that all its compressor stations comply with the Clean Air Act: Ambient Air Quality Objectives (The Canada Gazette, Part II, Vol. 108, No. 11, and Vol. 109, No. 3). (See The Physical Environment.)*

The National Energy Board concurs with this recommendation, but in its report does not state explicitly whether it is the "maximum desirable level" or the less stringent "maximum acceptable level" of nitrogen dioxide that it fears may be exceeded. For reasons stated in the chapter on The Physical Environment, I believe the "maximum desirable level" is appropriate in the Mackenzie Valley from a purely environmental standpoint. I cannot comment on the practicability of achieving this level because the detailed technical design considerations are the responsibility of others. But I must note that, if it is not practicable here, it is probably not applicable anywhere, and in that case, it should be reassessed.

27. *Air quality over the long term should be monitored and, in particular, the problems associated with ice fog near communities and at transportation facilities should be assessed. Relocation of pipeline facilities or other preventive measures that can be implemented only during the initial design and construction phases may be the only way to ameliorate unacceptable conditions.*

OTHER EMISSIONS

The construction phase of the project may also cause air quality problems, although combustion emissions produced during this phase will be of smaller volume and of much shorter duration than during pipeline operation. Incinerators, space heaters, vehicles, construction equipment and open fires will burn mainly gasoline, diesel fuel and similar substances. Their use will produce relatively low velocity and low temperature emissions of various kinds, which will stay near ground level. Dispersion above even a shallow inversion layer is unlikely. Such emissions contribute both the nuclei and the water vapour that are essential to ice fog formation, and they contribute pollutants that accumulate as inversion conditions persist, eventually exceeding established ambient air quality objectives, even though emission standards for individual pieces of equipment may have been met.

I understand that emission guidelines or standards are being drafted by the Environmental Protection Service, Department of the Environment.

28. The Agency should consult with the Company and the Department of the Environment with respect to requirements for emission control devices and to the maximum permissible levels of emission for construction equipment and vehicles.

Emission control devices are adjusted at the factory by the manufacturers of vehicles and equipment to meet government requirements. Of course, these devices may be rendered less effective or useless if tampered with later. In recognition of this problem, Ontario has enacted legislation to prevent removal or alteration of the devices so that they fail to comply with regulations (Ontario, Statutes of Ontario, *The Environment Protection Act, 1971,* c.86 as amended by c.94, 1973). This law could be used by the Agency as a model to develop measures to prevent tampering with approved and specified settings of emission control devices on construction equipment and vehicles used on the project.

Equipment Operations

The aspects of the pipeline project that I have described — that is, the aspects relating to physical plant — are only one part of the environmental impact associated with facilities complexes. Construction and maintenance of the pipeline right-of-way and operation of the facilities will depend on the use of a variety of equipment with attendant environmental consequences. Construction involves local and long-distance hauling by truck, barge, aircraft and helicopter. Stations and bases will be supplied by barge and truck, access to the right-of-way will usually be by truck or helicopter, travel along the right-of-way will involve off-road vehicles, and most line patrols will be carried out by light aircraft. The effects of all these operations will occur during all seasons, they will be widespread, and each will raise particular environmental concerns.

The potential risks to waterbodies, terrain, fish, birds and mammals will be great if the construction and operation activities associated with these operations are not carefully planned and controlled. Although the environmental impacts and mitigative measures related to the operation of equipment tend to be activity-specific and site-specific, we can gain an overall perspective by discussing the issue according to the three types of vehicles involved: road vehicles, off-road vehicles and barges. Aircraft pose a special problem that I deal with in a separate chapter, Aircraft Control.

There are two general recommendations that are important in meeting the environmental concerns that I set out in the chapters on The Physical Environment, Wildlife, and Fish.

29. The Company shall assess the environmental effects and limitations of all equipment used for construction and operation of the pipeline and shall select equipment that is least disruptive.

30. The Company shall establish clear environmental and scheduling guidelines for equipment deployment and operation during all aspects of construction and operation.

Road Vehicles

A great many vehicles are required on any pipeline project. Arctic Gas planned to use 350 tractor-trucks, a corresponding number of trailer units, and 1,500 trucks during the contruction phase. Local transportation and maintenance activities at each compressor station site and at the regional headquarters sites will require road vehicles, such as cars and light trucks, and work equipment, such as graders and loaders. The operation of these road vehicles poses various environmental problems. For instance, in the chapter on Wildlife, I describe how road traffic can disturb wildlife and act as barriers to migrations of mammals. There are also indirect problems: vehicles using snow roads and temporary winter stream crossings can damage terrain and water resources; and fuels and other hazardous substances could pose local environmental problems if they were spilled during transportation. I have dealt with these types of problems and the mitigative measures throughout this report. The recommendations that follow are meant to supplement those specific aspects by providing a general approach to the operation of road vehicles.

31. Unless otherwise approved by the Agency, road vehicles shall be operated only on public roads or other suitably prepared surfaces within designated rights-of-way or on lands covered by permit.

32. Operation of road vehicles shall be scheduled to avoid adverse impacts on terrain and wildlife. (See Terrain Considerations: Snow Roads, and Wildlife.)

Off-road Vehicles

Off-road or low ground pressure vehicles comprise various wheeled or tracked vehicles designed for use in muskeg, and over rock, rough ground and snow-covered terrain. They will be used to transport equipment and supplies along the pipeline right-of-way, and for normal and emergency inspection, maintenance and repair work. Hundreds of pieces of equipment, such as backhoes, bulldozers, side-booms, graders, earth movers, loaders and specialized trucks, will be required during construction and, to a lesser extent, will be used in operation and maintenance of the pipeline.

The main environmental concern is that the ground surface vegetation mat may be damaged. This could lead to erosion, disruption of surface and shallow subsurface drainage, disruption of thermal regimes in soil and to the deposition of sediment on land or its discharge into waterbodies. The manner in which the vehicles cross watercourses, particularly in summer, also raises concern for fish. In general, these vehicles have a very high potential for disturbance or harassment of wildlife. All these concerns relate to the type of vehicles and, perhaps more importantly, to the way in which they are operated. There will be a great need to ensure that vehicle operators are well-advised of the environmental hazards and do, in fact, operate all off-road vehicles in an environmentally conscientious manner.

33. Use of off-road vehicles shall comply with plans developed in conjunction with, and supervised by, the relevant territorial or federal wildlife, fish and land use agencies, or the Agency, as appropriate. Such plans shall specify types of vehicles, frequency of passage, and times and areas of avoidance. A particular aspect to be addressed is contingency planning for summer travel along the right-of-way. Such planning shall consider travel that may be required due to a pipeline rupture or other technical or environmental situation that requires prompt corrective action.

34. All off-road vehicles shall be operated with particular care to avoid damage to the vegetation mat and drainage courses in both permafrost and non-permafrost areas. Travel along the pipeline right-of-way shall be confined, as far as practicable, to the winter months when there is sufficient frost penetration and snow cover to provide adequate protection of the ground surface.

35. All operators of off-road vehicles shall be familiar with and follow techniques to minimize disturbance to terrain, watercourses, wildlife and fish. Anyone harassing wildlife shall be subject to immediate dismissal.

36. To allow passage of off-road vehicles during routine and emergency operations, and to keep disturbance from such vehicles to a minimum, the Company shall construct drainage and erosion control devices, shoo-fly roads and other devices.

AIR CUSHION VEHICLES

Air cushion vehicles (hovercraft) may be used for access to the right-of-way for normal and emergency repairs, particularly in the Mackenzie Delta. The advantages of using such vehicles in summer, during floods and during freeze-up and break-up are obvious, but there could be adverse environmental effects, principally related to terrain damage and noise.

Terrain damage can be caused by the air cushion itself or by the vehicle or tractor towing the air cushion vehicle. Several passes by a machine, the air cushion skirt of which is in contact with the ground, can damage vegetation and, in permafrost areas, can cause a slight increase in the depth of thaw of the soil. The ability of large, heavily laden air cushion vehicles to navigate on steep slopes is limited and can also lead to terrain damage.

The noise problem is particularly troublesome because periods when use of air cushion vehicles offers the greatest advantages frequently coincide with periods of high sensitivity for birds. These vehicles are extremely noisy to operate. One pass of a towed air cushion vehicle produces a noise greater than 56 dBA over a swath 3,200 feet wide, with lesser disturbance, (between 50 and 56 dBA) for a further 1,600 feet on either side, for a total width of 6,400 feet (Commission Counsel 1976, "Project Operation: Transportation Requirements," p. 11).

Clearly, air cushion vehicles have distinct environmental disadvantages that offset their logistic advantages.

37. The use of air cushion vehicles during pipeline construction and operation shall be subject to special approval by the Agency. The Company shall submit to the Agency detailed information on the use and control of such vehicles, including the type and size of equipment, travel corridors, frequency of passage and times and areas of avoidance for wildlife reasons.

38. Air cushion vehicles shall avoid critical wildlife and bird habitat areas when they are occupied. (See Wildlife.) Of particular concern are the areas in the Mackenzie Delta that are important for nesting and staging birds, and offshore areas used by white whales for calving and nursing.

Barges

As I describe in the chapter on Transportation, the barging requirements of the pipeline and gas plants give rise to concerns about strains on normal community resupply services. But there are environmental concerns as well.

In the lower Mackenzie Delta, there are several marine areas that are critical to wildlife. The western portions of the Mackenzie River estuary, particularly Mackenzie, Shallow and Shoalwater bays, are important nursing and rearing areas for white whales and during summer more than 4,000 occupy these areas. The warm shallow waters and plentiful food provide ideal habitat for cows with calves. Similarly, from July through September, many thousands of waterfowl require the shelter of river islands, coastal lagoons, spits and offshore islands for moulting and staging.

The protection that needs to be accorded wildlife in the area is, in most instances, site-specific. In Volume One, I discussed the need for a whale sanctuary in west Mackenzie Bay and in the chapter on Wildlife in this volume I discuss the site-specific measures necessary to protect critical bird areas. In spite of these prohibitions, however, it would appear that wildlife can coexist with marine transport in most areas if the situation is controlled.

39. *Marine traffic shall be limited to specific shipping corridors through Mackenzie Bay, Shallow Bay, Shoalwater Bay and the lower Mackenzie Delta. Buoyed channels currently maintained by Transport Canada through Mackenzie, Shallow and Shoalwater bays should be reviewed to ascertain whether they can accommodate the substantially greater volumes of traffic that would result from a pipeline and related transportation needs in the Delta area without unduly damaging the natural environment. If, for wildlife reasons, the channels cannot be enlarged or extended, they should be relocated as soon as possible to ensure that the channels are well-known before major developments get underway.*

A second problem related to marine transport in the context of pipeline construction is spills of petroleum and other toxic materials. Large spills of fuel into the Mackenzie River, the Mackenzie Delta, or the Beaufort Sea could mean the widespread destruction of waterfowl and fish and their habitats. The performance of river operators to date has been good, but a surge of traffic will increase risks because greater volumes of fuels will be handled and experienced labour may be in short supply. A continuing high standard of transport and unloading operation will be necessary if environmental damage is to be avoided.

40. *During the construction and operation phases of the pipeline, Company personnel involved with operating, loading or unloading barges shall follow procedures recommended in Management of Fuels and Hazardous Substances.*

20 Aircraft Control

The adverse effects of aircraft on mammals and birds have been described strongly and unequivocally by many biologists who presented evidence to the Inquiry. Their concerns centre on the critical habitats and life stages that make individuals of rare species or concentrated populations of other species sensitive to disturbance. They spoke of harassment by aircraft that swoop or circle over mammals or birds, but their overriding concern focused on the effects of low-level flight by helicopters and fixed-wing aircraft. The elevation, frequency, routing and timing of such flights and the location of airstrips all have the potential to cause disturbance.

The use of aircraft at low altitudes and under visual flight rules (VFR) is an important and integral part of life and commerce in the North today. The use of aircraft is increasing and will continue to increase with even greater activity by government, industry, sportsmen, tourists and others. The heavy volume of air traffic, and particularly of helicopter flights, that construction activities can generate along the pipeline route and at gas gathering facilities can lead to seriously adverse effects on the birds and mammals of the region.

Disturbance caused by aircraft is one of the basic environmental concerns described in Volume One of my report. I said:

It is often thought that, because of the immense geographic area of the North, construction of a gas pipeline or establishment of a corridor could not cause major damage to the land, the water or the wildlife. But within this vast area are tracts of land and water of limited size that are vital to the survival of whole populations of certain species of mammals, birds and fish at certain times of the year. Disturbance of such areas by industrial activities can have adverse biological effects that go far beyond the areas of impact. This concern with critical habitat and with critical life stages lies at the heart of my consideration of environmental issues. [p. xi]

Uncontrolled aircraft flights are probably the most serious form of disturbance to mammals and birds. In a recently published article, Calef et al. outlined the effects of aircraft on barren-ground caribou:

Aircraft disturbance is merely one of many results of human activity which could have a variety of deleterious effects on caribou. These effects can be divided into three categories:
1. Those causing immediate physical injury or death.
2. Those resulting in increased expenditures of energy, or changes in the physiological condition of the animals, which reduce their rates of survival or reproduction.
3. Those resulting in long-term changes in behaviour, including, especially, the traditional use of ranges.

Low-level flight or "buzzing" elicits panic responses from caribou, which may then injure themselves by stumbling or colliding with one another. Cows just before parturition, and young calves, are particularly susceptible to such injury. Sustained running results in an unusual depletion of energy reserves which could be particularly harmful during periods of stress such as late winter or when the caribou are being harassed by insects. Running during cold weather promotes pulmonary disorders in reindeer ... and therefore presumably in caribou. These are the obvious and immediately injurious consequences to caribou of their making sustained escape responses.

The long-term and more subtle effects of aircraft disturbance cannot be predicted at present. Some species such as wolves can become completely habituated to aircraft according to G. Haber who studied wolves in McKinley National Park, Alaska. ... On the other hand, repeated disturbance by aircraft could cause animals to abandon a range, as automobile and railway traffic apparently have caused them to in Norway. ... Furthermore, little is known of the long-term effects of disturbance on the physiology of ungulates. Geist ... has cited several examples of long-term deleterious effects on metabolism and hormone balance of ungulates exposed to disturbance. [Calef et al., 1976, p. 210]

These kinds of concerns about aircraft disturbance also apply to other wildlife species including Dall's sheep on their wintering and lambing ranges, snow geese during spring and fall staging, waterfowl and falcons while nesting, and ducks, geese and swans while moulting.

The pipeline companies recognize these concerns to be valid and serious, and they propose measures to avoid or mitigate disturbance during the critical life stages of various species. They emphasize, quite rightly, that most of their construction activities, including air traffic, will be confined to the winter season, and they will therefore avoid the most sensitive times of the year for most species. They say that aircraft under their control will maintain minimum altitudes wherever and whenever there might be disturbance to wildlife, and they outline plans to limit the impact of patrol flights along the right-of-way during operation of the pipeline by modifying the mode, pattern and frequency of flights.

It is uncertain what the total amount of air traffic will be because, although the requirements of the pipeline for air support can be defined generally, it is not possible to forecast the amount of air traffic that other activities will generate. The volume of traffic associated with continued exploration for oil and gas in the Mackenzie Delta region is potentially very large, and much of it could be made up of the repeated point-to-point flights that, at certain times of year, could have devastating effects on wildlife populations. The considerably increased use of aircraft in connection with the pipeline, added to the substantial volume of other air traffic throughout the Mackenzie Valley, has the potential for seriously adverse effects on mammal and bird populations.

Although my discussion concentrates on the environmental effects of aircraft flights that are related to the pipeline project, these flights cannot be considered in isolation from all other air traffic. Controls on project-related flights will help to reduce adverse impact, but, if other flights should be allowed to operate without restraint, it is questionable whether or not the impact on wildlife by aircraft can be reduced to a tolerable level.

1. The government should devise and enforce measures to protect birds and mammals from aircraft disturbance. To ensure the ongoing health of wildlife populations, consideration should be given to applying controls not only to air traffic associated with construction and operation of the pipeline, but also to other air traffic in the North.

Restraints on Aircraft Flights

Measures to Limit Disturbance from Project-related Flights

The sensitivities of various species change with the time of year and the stages of their annual cycle. Nonetheless, a considerable degree of protection could be achieved by establishing flight corridors selected to avoid sensitive wildlife, by adhering to minimum-altitude restrictions outside the designated corridors, and by carefully selecting the locations of airfields.

The information that is available on the sensitivity of various species of wildlife to the noise of aircraft is inadequate for an objective determination of minimum flight altitudes that will limit or avoid such disturbance. However, a guide is necessary and from the evidence before the Inquiry, 1,500 feet seems to be appropriate.

Airfields are centres of low-altitude aircraft movements that can be particularly disturbing to mammals and birds during sensitive periods in their annual cycles.

2. All aircraft flights connected with the pipeline project shall be flown at no less than 1,500 feet above ground level between take-off and landing except for flights along designated corridors in which lower minimum heights may be permitted.

3. A number of aircraft corridors, in both time and space, shall be established so that a certain number of flight paths will be available at all times without reference to the regulatory authorities. All such corridors shall have a minimum flight altitude of 500 feet unless specifically designated otherwise. In general, a corridor two miles wide and centred on the pipeline right-of-way should be designated and, as far as possible, it should avoid areas occupied by sensitive bird or mammal populations. To the degree that sensitive areas and times cannot be avoided, the corridor shall be subject to site- and time-specific routing and altitude flight restraints as designated by the Agency.

4. Airfields related to the pipeline project should be located to avoid areas in which there are bird or mammal populations that are sensitive to disturbance by noise and shall be at least three miles from such areas, unless specifically authorized by the Agency. Runways should be oriented so that landing and take-off paths avoid overflight of sensitive areas.

DELIBERATE HARASSMENT

The "buzzing" or chasing by aircraft of individual animals or groups of birds or mammals can be exceedingly harmful to them. For example, disturbance of nesting birds can lead to death of the young and it can cause mammals to abort or to be separated from their young. The Company should ensure that pilots know that such actions, including flights at low levels, are prohibited and subject to disciplinary action.

5. Deliberate harassment of wildlife by aircraft shall not be permitted within pipeline system lands or in any other areas. Pilots, in the direct or indirect employ of the Company, who harass wildlife shall be immediately suspended from any further flying on the project and they shall be reported to the Agency for prosecution.

The effect of harassment on wildlife is so severe that this recommendation should be extended to cover all aircraft in the region.

Measures to Limit Disturbance to Specific Species from Project-related Flights

Many specific proposals for the protection of mammals and birds from disturbance by aircraft were presented to the Inquiry. In addition to the restrictions on altitude, flight frequency and airstrip location, they included recommendations that aircraft should avoid certain areas at certain periods of time. The problems will persist into the operation phase of the pipeline because monitoring flights will be most numerous in the spring during and immediately following break-up when many bird species are most sensitive.

In Volume One of my report, I proposed a wilderness park in the Northern Yukon: it will achieve some of the desired protection. Similarly, the bird sanctuaries I recommended in the Mackenzie Delta and Mackenzie Valley will provide the Canadian Wildlife Service with authority to apply the controls that are needed there. In this volume, I outline, in the chapter on Wildlife, measures that are needed to protect birds and mammals from disturbance in general. I now make recommendations to protect specific species from aircraft disturbance.

RAPTORS

6. Airstrips and helicopter pads should be located so that all approaches and take-offs will avoid Raptor Protection Zones (as defined in Wildlife: Birds).

7. Aircraft should maintain an altitude of at least 3,000 feet above ground level while over any Raptor Protection Zone during a sensitive period. Lower level flights shall be routed around the zone. Pipeline surveillance flights at less than 3,000 feet above ground level and helicopter landings shall be prohibited within a Raptor Protection Zone during any sensitive period, except as specifically authorized by the Agency.

WATERFOWL

8. Air traffic over critical staging and nesting sites shall be subject to specific altitude and frequency restrictions during periods of occupancy.

9. During the periods in spring and fall when islands in the Mackenzie River are used as staging areas by flocks of waterfowl, aircraft shall avoid areas occupied by birds, and any flights within 2 miles of such areas shall maintain an altitude of 2,000 feet above ground level.

10. During fall staging of flocks of snow geese, aircraft shall avoid areas occupied by these birds and any emergency flights within 2 miles of such areas shall maintain altitudes of 5,000 feet.

MAMMALS

11. Aircraft shall maintain a minimum altitude of 2,000 feet above ground level wherever there are calving caribou or lambing Dall's sheep.

Control, Implementation and Enforcement

The above recommendations are, in effect, operating standards that should be complied with if disturbance to wildlife is to be minimized. But the setting of standards is only part of the solution. We must also assess the effectiveness of those standards in individual cases, and devise means of enforcing them.

At present, the only attempt to restrain aircraft operation is within the migratory bird sanctuaries, where the Canadian Wildlife Service requires that aircraft should fly at a minimum altitude of 1,500 feet above ground level. Transport Canada has informed pilots of this limitation in its Notices to Airmen (NOTAMS), but takes no responsibility for enforcing this limitation, and the Canadian Wildlife Service has very limited means of enforcement. In evidence before the Inquiry, Harold Heacock of Transport Canada emphasized the difficulty of enforcing minimum flight altitudes and other environmental controls on aircraft using visual flight rules, particularly while flying during bad weather conditions.

Thus, despite the alarm with which biologists regard the effects of disturbance on birds and mammals by aircraft, only limited and relatively ineffective measures can now be taken to protect them, even in the geographical areas that are of the greatest concern.

My objective is to recommend terms and conditions that will limit the impact of a pipeline and energy corridor along the Mackenzie Valley. However, as I explained at the beginning of this chapter, the problems created by the air traffic generated by the pipeline project cannot be considered in isolation from those created by all other aircraft in the area.

Flight Control Group

Because aircraft disturbance poses an immediate threat to wildlife, and because there is a general lack of regulatory control in this regard, it is essential that government implement a flight control program. Flights associated with the pipeline project are only one small part of the overall problem; the program created to control flights should, therefore, be broad enough to regulate all aircraft activity that poses a threat to wildlife in the area. I recognize that such controls will be unpopular and an inconvenience during certain times of the year, but we must understand that the benefits derived from industrial development in the North carry a price. In a case like this, we must now make a choice: either we develop some means of regulating disturbance or we will suffer the loss of a substantial portion of our greatest northern wildlife resources. No one has seriously suggested that all aircraft activities be stopped: rather, they must be controlled so that critical areas and critical life stages of wildlife are protected. I think that a flight control group is the means to do this. The following recommendation for setting up this group is one of critical importance for the control of aircraft related to the pipeline project. But its implementation would be of value in protecting wildlife from any aircraft disturbance in the North. I have therefore written the recommendation for general application, whether there is a pipeline project or not.

12. To control the environmental effects of all air traffic in the region, including project-related air traffic, a Flight Control Group should be established immediately. To minimize inconvenience to pilots, this Group should be the only point of contact for flight operators. To be effective and comprehensive this group must coordinate closely with Transport Canada, which controls flying from a safety point of view.

The Flight Control Group shall be the basic mechanism for ensuring that environmentally hazardous flying does not occur. In this regard, it should prepare specific measures to protect birds and mammals. The Flight Control Group should involve the federal and territorial governments, and during pipeline construction the Company and the Agency, in identifying the locations and in monitoring the movements of wildlife. On the basis of local observations, field staff of all those involved should be used to predict when and where conflict with human activities might occur and to advise the Group that flight plans may have to be modified to avoid these times or areas.

The Flight Control Group should set up and administer procedures that will include a daily preview of the flight plans of all project-related flights and other flights as required to ascertain whether or not the flights are likely to disturb wildlife populations unduly. The group shall approve flight plans on a case-by-case basis taking into account changing environmental conditions, and the effectiveness of various degrees of restrictions.

In view of the particular wildlife sensitivities in the Mackenzie Delta and recognizing that a great deal of oil and gas activity is concentrated there, the Flight Control Group shall pay particular attention to that area.

Enforcement

Although the Flight Control Group, as recommended, would regulate flights to limit disturbance on wildlife, it will face the same problems of enforcement that exist today. This is a difficult problem that requires careful consideration by government. Although no solutions have been advanced before this Inquiry, it is apparent that measures could be devised. For example, provisions such as those that exist in Air Navigation Order Series V, Number 10, which restricts take-off and landing in designated park areas, may be appropriate.

13. A means of enforcing the regulations and directives prepared by the Flight Control Group regarding aircraft movements should be devised. This enforcement mechanism should be in operation before pipeline construction begins.

14. To ensure comprehensive protection of the environment, compliance with the directions of the Flight Control Group should be made a condition of every drilling licence, land use permit, or similar authorization to carry out work in the area involving aircraft flights.

Company Plans for the Use of Aircraft

To protect birds and mammals, it is necessary to identify problems and to ensure timely planning for the regulation of flights.

15. Before the final design phase, the Company shall submit for approval by the Agency an overall plan for the use of project-related aircraft during the period of construction. Final plans shall be submitted six months in advance of each season's construction. Both the overall plan and the final plans shall detail such items as the routing and frequency of flights, the time of year, the type of aircraft and their flying heights; the landing areas and the pattern of aircraft movement into and out of those areas; and the corridors to be used for low-altitude flights. They shall also describe the potential disturbance of aircraft flights to sensitive wildlife populations, and the measures that are proposed to mitigate this kind of disturbance.

16. Six months before construction is completed, the Company shall submit for approval by the Agency plans for the use and control of aircraft during the operating life of the pipeline.

Pilot Education

The implementation of all the recommendations above should ensure that use of aircraft in the region is compatible with the protection of critical habitats and of wildlife during critical life stages. However, it will always be difficult to protect widely dispersed wildlife populations. General protection can probably be accomplished best through the education of pilots.

In evidence presented to the Inquiry on behalf of Transport Canada, Heacock suggested that one way to reduce possible adverse effects by aerial activities on wildlife would be to:

Mount an extensive publicity campaign to impress on all pilots, contractors, etc., the importance of protection of wildlife in the area and the serious consequences that may result from any unnecessary disturbance of birds or mammals.

Most pilots flying in the north country realize the importance of all mammals in relation to native welfare, and that policing action would be most difficult. Obtaining their full cooperation would appear to be the most likely means of minimizing disturbance to wildlife. If such a publicity program is considered desirable, Transport Canada could provide a nation-wide coverage through [its] air information publications. [F21186]

17. The Agency shall complement its restraints on low-level language, read the same books, and make the same choices in life.

The settlement of native claims offers a uniquely Canadian challenge, certainly the greatest challenge we face in the North. It is by this means alone that we can fairly pursue frontier goals in the northern homeland.

APPENDICES

APPENDIX 1
The Inquiry Process

The Inquiry Process

It is often said that commissions of inquiry have had little or no impact on public policy in Canada. I think this is wrong, as a glance at our history will show. The report of the Rowell–Sirois Commission, appointed in 1937, led to a rearrangement of taxing powers between the federal government and the provinces. The Rand Inquiry into the dispute between the Ford Motor Company and the United Auto Workers in Windsor in 1949, which resulted in the Rand formula, has been regarded ever since as a watershed in labour-management relations in Canada. The Hall Commission on Health Services had and continues to have a great impact on governments, the health professions, and the provision of health services in our country. The recommendations of the Norris Commission, which investigated the disruption of shipping on the Great Lakes, resulted in a major union being placed under government trusteeship.

Commissions appointed by provincial governments have also been influential. The Meredith Commission, appointed in 1911 in Ontario, led to the establishment of Workmen's Compensation Boards first in Ontario and then throughout the country. The Hall–Dennis Commission, appointed by the government of Ontario, and the Parent Commission, appointed by the government of Quebec, have both had a great impact on education in Canada.

There have also been joint federal-provincial commissions of inquiry, such as the McKenna–McBride Commission, whose recommendations regarding Indian reserve lands in British Columbia were adopted, for good or ill, by both governments.

We are all aware of the continuing influence in our federal system today of the recommendations of the Royal Commission on Bilingualism and Biculturalism. The recommendations of the LeDain Commission have been influential in moulding social attitudes toward the non-medical use of drugs in our society. Then, of course, the recommendations of the Royal Commission on the Status of Women constitute a standard against which the progress of the federal government and the provincial governments toward the enactment of legislation to establish equality for women can be measured.

Thus the work of commissions of inquiry has had a significant influence on public policy in Canada. They have brought new ideas into the public consciousness. They have expanded the vocabulary of politics, education and social science. They have added to the furniture that we now expect to find in Canada's storefront of ideas. And they have always had real importance in providing considered advice to governments. This is their primary function. But in recent years, Commissions of Inquiry have begun to take on a new function: that of opening up issues to public discussion, of providing a forum for the exchange of ideas.

Gerald E. LeDain, who headed the Royal Commission on the Non-Medical Use of Drugs, discussed this emerging function in a lecture delivered at Osgoode Hall Law School on March 15, 1972:

> It was our search for the issues and a general perspective, as well as a sense of social feasibility — what the society was capable of — that made us conduct the kind of hearings we did.... We were looking also for the range of attitudes and wanted to hear from those most deeply involved. These hearings made a deep impression on us. At times they were very moving. One of the things we discovered is that we need public opportunities for the exchange of views on vital issues. The hearings provided a public occasion for people to say things to each other that they had obviously never said before. I think that a public inquiry can respond to the need for some extension of the regular electoral process on the social level, a process in which the public can contribute to the identification and discussion of the issues. [*Law and Social Change*, edited by Jacob Ziegel, p.84]

The Law Reform Commission of Canada, in a working paper published earlier this year, enlarged upon this function of commissions of inquiry:

> Finally, as democratic as Parliament may be, there is still an important need in Canada for other means of expressing opinions and influencing policy-making — what Harold Laski called "institutions of consultation." There are, of course, the

"traditional ways"; establishing pressure groups, giving speeches, writing to the newspaper, and so on. But these traditional means are not always adequate. Today the need for other avenues of expression and influence is often focussed in greater demands for *public participation*. Increased participation allows those individuals and groups to express their views to public authorities. It also provides more representative opinion to decision-makers, so as to properly inform them of the needs and wishes of the people. [Law Reform Commission, *Commissions of Inquiry*, p.15]

If commissions of inquiry have become an important means for public participation in democratic decision-making as well as an instrument to supply informed advice to government, it is important to consider the way in which inquiries are conducted and whether they have the means to fulfil their perceived functions. Given the interest the public has had in the Mackenzie Valley Pipeline Inquiry, it may be useful to say something about the way in which it was conducted.

The Inquiry's Mandate

The Mackenzie Valley Pipeline Inquiry was appointed to examine the social, economic and environmental impact of a gas pipeline in the Northwest Territories and the Yukon, and to recommend the terms and conditions that should be imposed if the pipeline were to be built. We were told that the Arctic Gas pipeline project would be the greatest project, in terms of capital expenditure, ever undertaken by private enterprise. We were told that, if a gas pipeline were built, it would result in enhanced oil and gas exploration activity all along the route of the pipeline throughout the Mackenzie Valley and the Western Arctic.

But the gas pipeline, although it would be a vast project, was not to be considered in isolation. The Government of Canada, in the Expanded Guidelines for Northern Pipelines (tabled in the House of Commons on June 28, 1972), made it clear that the Inquiry was to consider what the impact would be if the gas pipeline were built and if it were followed by an oil pipeline.

So the Inquiry had to consider the impact on the North of an energy corridor that would bring gas and oil from the Arctic to the mid-continent. In fact, under the Pipeline Guidelines, we had to consider two corridors, one corridor extending from Alaska across the Northern Yukon to the Mackenzie Delta, and a second corridor from the Mackenzie Delta along the Mackenzie Valley to Alberta.

The Inquiry, when it was established, was unique in Canadian experience because, for the first time, we were to try to determine the impact of a large-scale frontier project before and not after the fact. The Inquiry was asked to see what could be done to protect the North, its people and its environment, if the pipeline project were to go ahead.

Let me repeat the words of the Order-in-Council: social, environmental and economic impact. I dare say they conferred as wide a mandate upon the Inquiry as any government has ever conferred upon any Inquiry in the past. The merit in

such a wide mandate is clear. Impacts cannot be forced into tidy subject compartments. The consequences of a large-scale frontier project inevitably combine social, economic and environmental factors. In my opinion a sound assessment could not have been made if the analysis of impact had been divided up, if, for instance, environmental impact had been hived off for separate analysis.

The Pipeline Application Assessment Group

Concurrently with the establishment of the Inquiry, the Government of Canada established a Pipeline Application Assessment Group. This group, headed by Dr. John G. Fyles of the Geological Survey of Canada, consisted of public servants seconded by the Department of Indian Affairs and Northern Development, the Department of Energy, Mines and Resources, and the Department of the Environment, and by the Governments of the Northwest Territories and the Yukon Territory, and others outside the public service, who were retained in a consultative capacity. The task of the group was to review the material filed by Arctic Gas, the consortium seeking to build the pipeline. In their initial filing, in March 1974, Arctic Gas deposited with the government 32 volumes of material amounting to thousands of pages of technical information. The Assessment Group spent eight months reviewing this material and prepared a report to assist the Inquiry and the National Energy Board in its work, as well as government departments and agencies. Once the Inquiry got under way, many members of the Assessment Group transferred to the Inquiry staff.

Environment Protection Board

I should also mention the Environment Protection Board. The precursors of Arctic Gas and Foothills funded a group of scientists and engineers, all of them men of the highest competence in their various fields, to provide an independent examination of the environmental impact of a gas pipeline from Prudhoe Bay through the Mackenzie Valley to Alberta. The group, known as the Environment Protection Board and headed by Mr. Carson Templeton of Winnipeg, a distinguished engineer, was provided with $3.5 million, and after four years of study, published a lengthy report that was, in many respects, critical of the Arctic Gas proposal.

The report of the Environment Protection Board was of great assistance to the Inquiry. The Board was an intervenor at the Inquiry, and its members and staff gave evidence.

The oil and gas industry was responsible for this innovation. The industry established the Board, funded it, and did not seek in any way to interfere with its work or to dictate what should appear in its report. This represents a new departure for private industry. The precedent was followed at the Alaska Highway Pipeline Inquiry by Foothills Pipe Lines (Yukon) Ltd., which established and funded a similar board of scientists and engineers, once again headed by Mr. Templeton.

The Board wrote a report for Foothills, the report was made public, and the members of the Board testified at the Inquiry.

Preliminary Hearings

Preliminary hearings were held soon after the establishment of the Mackenzie Valley Pipeline Inquiry. At that time, I wrote to Arctic Gas, the environmental groups, the native organizations, the Northwest Territories Association of Municipalities, the Northwest Territories Chamber of Commerce, the Government of the Northwest Territories and the Government of the Yukon. I advised them of my appointment, and asked them for any submissions they wished to make regarding the way in which the Inquiry should be conducted. In April 1974, I held hearings at Yellowknife, Inuvik and Whitehorse, and in May, at Ottawa, and again at Yellowknife in September. Thirty-seven submissions were made at the preliminary hearings. These were very useful: it became apparent that the environmental groups and the native organizations would require time to get ready for the main hearings, and that they, as well as the Northwest Territories Association of Municipalities and the Northwest Territories Chamber of Commerce, would require funds to prepare for and to participate in the hearings. It also became evident that rules would have to be laid down for the production of all the information in the possession of government, industry and other interested parties. I therefore issued rulings on these matters, which are reproduced in Appendix 2 of this volume.

Production of Studies and Reports

The Government of Canada gave the Inquiry the power to issue subpoenas to get the evidence it needed. We sought to ensure that all studies and reports in the possession of the pipeline companies and the other parties should be produced, so that no study or report bearing on the work of the Inquiry would be hidden from view. I ruled that each party — the pipeline companies, and each of the intervenors — would have to prepare a list of all of the studies and reports in their possession relating to the work of the Inquiry, and that the lists should be circulated among all the participants. The Government of Canada, of course, had in its possession many studies and reports relating to the work of the Inquiry. Commission Counsel was therefore made responsible for providing a list of them.

This procedure allowed any party to call upon any other party to produce a copy of any study or report that was listed. If a party were to refuse to produce a document, then an application could be made to the Inquiry for a subpoena. Of course, any claim of lawful privilege would have had to be considered by the Inquiry. All concerned cooperated: no one had to apply for a subpoena at any time during the Inquiry.

In recent years, the Government of Canada has carried out a multitude of studies through its Environmental-Social Committee, Northern Pipelines, Task Force on Northern Oil

Development. These studies cost $15 million. The oil and gas industry has carried out studies on the pipeline that we were told cost something like $50 million. Our universities have been carrying on constant research on northern problems and northern conditions. It would have been no good to let all these studies and reports just sit on the shelves. Where these reports contained evidence that was vital to the work of the Inquiry, it was essential that they be opened and examined in public, so that any conflicts could be disclosed, and where parties at the Inquiry wished to challenge them, they had an opportunity to do so. It meant that opinions could be challenged and tested in public.

It also raised the quality of debate at the Inquiry. Arctic Gas supported their application with much detailed and valuable technical information and indeed with considerable original research. This material, together with the reports of the Pipeline Application Assessment Group, the Environment Protection Board and government studies, permitted the Inquiry to engage in a detailed analysis of issues — to get to the heart of matters as diverse as frost heave and the seasonal movements of marine mammals — rather than deal with them at the level of vague generalization.

As a consequence, all parties at the Inquiry had to be equipped to analyze all of this material and to be in a position to respond to technical questions arising from it. This raises the matter of funding intervenors.

Funding Intervenors

An inquiry of this scope has to consider many interests. If such an inquiry is to be fair and complete, all of these interests must be represented.

A funding program was established for those groups that had an interest that ought to be represented, but whose means would not allow it. On my recommendation, funding was provided by the Government of Canada to the native organizations, the environmental groups, northern municipalities, and northern business, to enable them to participate in the hearings on an equal footing (so far as that might be possible) with the pipeline companies — to enable them to support, challenge, or seek to modify the project.

These groups are sometimes called public interest groups. They represent identifiable interests that should not be ignored, that, indeed, it is essential should be considered. They do not represent the public interest, but it is in the public interest that they should be heard. I ruled that any group seeking funding had to meet the following criteria:

1. There should be a clearly ascertainable interest that ought to be represented at the Inquiry.

2. It should be established that separate and adequate representation of that interest would make a necessary and substantial contribution to the Inquiry.

3. Those seeking funds should have an established record of

concern for, and should have demonstrated their own commitment to, the interest they sought to represent.

4. It should be shown that those seeking funds did not have sufficient financial resources to enable them adequately to represent that interest, and that they would require funds to do so.

5. Those seeking funds had to have a clearly delineated proposal as to the use they intended to make of the funds, and had to be sufficiently well-organized to account for the funds.

In funding these groups, I took the view that there was no substitute for letting them have the money and decide for themselves how to spend it, independently of the government and of the Inquiry. If they were to be independent, and to make their own decisions and present the evidence that they thought vital, they had to be provided with the funds and there could be no strings attached. They had, however, to account to the Inquiry for the money spent. All this they have done.

Let me illustrate the rationale for this by referring to the environment. It is true that Arctic Gas carried out extensive environmental studies, which cost a great deal of money. But they had an interest: they wanted to build the pipeline. This was a perfectly legitimate interest, but not one that could necessarily be reconciled with the environmental interest. It was felt there should be representation by a group with a special interest in the northern environment, a group without any other interest that might deflect it from the presentation of that case.

Funds were provided to an umbrella organization – the Northern Assessment Group – that was established by the environmental group to enable them to carry out their own research and hire staff, and to ensure that they could participate in the Inquiry as advocates on behalf of the environment. In this way, the environmental interest was made a part of the whole hearing process. The same applied to the other interests that were represented at the hearings. The result was that witnesses were examined and then cross-examined not simply to determine whether the pipeline project was feasible from an engineering point of view, but to make sure that such things as the impact of an influx of construction workers on communities, the impact of pipeline construction and corridor development on hunting, trapping and fishing, and the impact on northern municipalities and northern business, were all taken into account.

The usefulness of the funding that was provided has been amply demonstrated. All concerned showed an awareness of the magnitude of the task. The funds supplied to the intervenors, although substantial, should be considered in the light of the estimated cost of the project itself, and of the funds expended by the pipeline companies in assembling their own evidence.

I do not suggest that the funding of intervenors is appropriate in all inquiries – that would depend on the nature of the inquiry. But I can speak to its usefulness in this instance.

Hearings

We sought to avoid turning the Inquiry into an exclusive forum for lawyers and experts. Unless you let outsiders in, an inquiry can become a private, club-like proceeding. This problem presents itself most acutely when you want to hear from the experts but when you want equally to hear from ordinary people who could be affected by the impact of the project.

It was inevitable that conflict would arise if the hearing process in which the public would be entitled to participate was the same as that at which the evidence of engineers, biologists, economists and so on, would be heard and cross-examined – a process necessitating the pre-eminent role of lawyers. That conflict had to be resolved. We therefore decided to hold two types of hearings: formal hearings and community hearings.

We decided to hold formal hearings at Yellowknife, where expert witnesses for all parties could be heard and cross-examined, and where the proceedings would, in many ways, resemble a trial in a courtroom. It was at Yellowknife that we heard the evidence of the experts: the scientists, the engineers, the biologists, the anthropologists, the economists – the people who have studied northern conditions and northern peoples.

The formal hearings began with an overview of the North. Commission Counsel presented a series of witnesses, all of them authorities in their fields, who discussed in a general way the geography, history, flora, fauna, and economy, of the Mackenzie Valley and the Western Arctic. For the Inquiry and the participants, this evidence provided a useful back-drop against which to place the detailed evidence that came later.

At the formal hearings, all the participants were represented: the two pipeline companies, the native organizations, the environmental groups, the Northwest Territories Association of Municipalities and the Northwest Territories Chamber of Commerce. All were given a chance to question and challenge the things that the experts said, and all were entitled, of course, to call expert witnesses of their own. Lawyers represented most of the participants. But non-lawyers acted as counsel for some groups, and quite effectively, too: Carson Templeton for the Environment Protection Board, Jo McQuarrie for the Northwest Territories Mental Health Association and David Reesor for the Northwest Territories Association of Municipalities.

At the same time, community hearings were held in each city and town, settlement and village in the Mackenzie Valley, the Mackenzie Delta and the Northern Yukon. We held hearings at 35 communities in the Mackenzie Valley and the Western Arctic. At these hearings, the people living in the communities were given the opportunity to speak in their own language and in their own way. I wanted the people in the communities to feel that they could come forward and tell me what their lives and their experience led them to believe the impact of a pipeline and an energy corridor would be.

In this way, we tried to have the best of the experience of both worlds: at the community hearings, the world of everyday, where most witnesses spend their lives, and, at the formal hearings, the world of the professionals, the specialists, and the academics.

I appointed Michael Jackson, Special Counsel to the Inquiry, as Chairman of a Committee on Community Hearings. This Committee comprised representatives of each of the participants and it considered such matters as the timing of community hearings — (having regard, among other things, for the seasonal activities of northern people), the procedure to be adopted at such hearings, and the role of the participants and their lawyers.

One of the first matters the Committee had to deal with related to the issue of cross-examination of witnesses. The object of the community hearings was to give all people an opportunity to express their concerns without worrying about what they might well regard as harassment by lawyers. The Committee suggested a variety of ways in which the function of cross-examination could be fulfilled by procedures that would not dissuade people from testifying. One such technique was to invite representatives of both Arctic Gas and Foothills to make a presentation to the Inquiry whenever it appeared to them that people were misinformed or whenever they wished to correct what they felt was a mistaken view of their proposals. In this and other ways, without it ever being necessary formally to restrict the right to cross-examination, the community hearings were conducted, not within a procedural framework in which only lawyers felt comfortable, but within a framework which permitted northern people, native and white, to participate fully.

Many people in the communities of the North do not speak English, and could be understood only through interpreters. For them, the experience of testifying was sometimes strange and difficult, and we did not want to place any impediment at all in the way of their speaking up and speaking out. A fairly wide latitude was given. Even at the formal hearings, we did not insist upon a too rigid observance of legal rules of admissibility, for that might have squeezed the life out of the evidence. I see no difficulty in this. The reasons for insisting upon a strict observance of rules of evidence at civil or criminal trials, do not obtain at a public inquiry relating to questions of social, environmental and economic impact. What is essential is fairness and an appropriate insistence upon relevance.

In order to give people — not just the spokesmen for native organizations and for the white community, but all people — an opportunity to speak their minds, the Inquiry remained in each community as long as was necessary for every person

who wanted to speak to do so. In many villages a large proportion of the adult population addressed the Inquiry. Not that participation was limited to adults. Some of the most perceptive presentations were given by young people, concerned no less than their parents about their land and their future.

I found that ordinary people, with the experience of life in the North, had a great deal to contribute. I heard from almost one thousand witnesses at the community hearings — in English (and occasionally in French), in Loucheux, Slavey, Dogrib, Chipewyan and in the Eskimo language of the Western Arctic. They used direct speech. They seldom had written briefs. Their thoughts were not filtered through a screen of jargon. They were talking about their innermost concerns and fears.

It is not enough simply to read about northern people, northern places and northern problems. You have to be there, you have to listen to the people, to know what is really going on in their towns and villages and in their minds. That is why I invited representatives of the companies that wanted to build the pipeline to come to these community hearings with me. Arctic Gas and Foothills sent their representatives to every hearing in every community.

The contributions of ordinary people were therefore important in the assessment of even the most technical subjects. For example, in Volume One, I based my discussion of the biological vulnerability of the Beaufort Sea not only on the evidence of the biologists who testified at the formal hearings, but also on the views of the Inuit hunters who spoke at the community hearings. The same is true of sea-bed ice scour, and of oil spills; they are complex, technical subjects but our understanding of them was nonetheless enriched by testimony from people who live in the region.

It became increasingly obvious that the issue of impact assessment is much greater than the sum of its constituent parts. For example, when North America's most renowned caribou biologists testified at the Inquiry, they described the life cycle, habitat dependencies and migrations and provided a host of details about the Porcupine caribou herd. Expert evidence from anthropologists, sociologists and geographers described the native people's dependency on caribou from entirely different perspectives. Doctors testified about the nutritional value of country food such as caribou, and about the consequences of a change in diet. Then the native people spoke for themselves at the community hearings about the caribou herd as a link with their past, as a present-day source of food and as security for the future. Only in this way could the whole picture be put together. And only in this way could a sound assessment of impact be made.

When discussion turned to issues relating to social and cultural impact, economic development, and native claims, the usefulness of obtaining the views of local residents was equally important. This was nowhere more apparent than in the consideration of native claims. At the formal hearings, land use and occupancy evidence was presented through prepared testimony and map exhibits. There the evidence was scrutinized and witnesses for the native organizations were cross-examined by counsel for the other participants. By contrast, at the community hearings, people spoke spontaneously and at length of both their traditional and their present-day use of the land and its resources. Their testimony was often painstakingly detailed and richly illustrated with anecdotes.

The most important contribution of the community hearings was, I think, the insight it gave us into the true nature of native claims. No academic treatise or discussion, formal presentation of the claims of native people by the native organizations and their leaders, could offer as compelling and vivid a picture of the goals and aspirations of native people as their own testimony. In no other way could we have discovered the depth of feeling regarding past wrongs and future hopes, and the determination of native people to assert their collective identity today and in years to come.

We had not heard the native people speak with such conviction of these things in recent years. Thus it is not surprising that the allegation should have been made that the testimony given by the native people was not genuine, that in some fashion they had been induced to say things they did not believe. Of course, such allegations reflect a lingering reluctance to take the views of native people seriously when they conflict with our own notions of what is in their best interests. But the point is this: such allegations, advanced in order to discredit the leaders of the native organizations, lose their force when measured against the evidence of band chiefs and band councillors from every community in the Mackenzie Valley and the Western Arctic, and against the evidence of the hundreds of native people who spoke to the Inquiry. These allegations have not, indeed, been made by anyone who was at the community hearings.

From the beginning, it was clear that we were dealing with an issue of national interest and importance. The Order-in-Council establishing the Inquiry contemplated hearings in the provinces as well as in the northern territories. We received many requests from Canadians in the South who wished to have an opportunity to contribute to the debate. So we took the Inquiry to ten of the major cities of Canada, from Vancouver in the west to Halifax in the east. These hearings took approximately one month. Thus the Inquiry, and through it the government, was able to draw on the views of a multitude of ordinary Canadians.

The Media

The Inquiry faced, at an early stage, the problem of enabling the people in the far-flung settlements of the Mackenzie Valley and the Western Arctic to participate in the work of the Inquiry. When you are consulting local people, the consultation should not be perfunctory. But when you have such a vast area, when you have people of four races, speaking seven languages, how do you enable them to participate? How do you keep them informed? We wished to create an Inquiry without walls. And we sought, therefore, to use technology to make the Inquiry truly public, to extend the walls of the hearing room to encompass the entire North. We tried to bring the Inquiry to the people. This meant that it was the Inquiry, and the representatives of the media accompanying it — not the people of the North — that were obliged to travel.

At the same time, we made it plain to the media that we regarded them as an essential part of the whole process. We sought to ensure that they were given every opportunity to provide an account of what was being said by all parties at the Inquiry. We tried to counter the tendency, all too frequent in the past, to treat the work of a Commission of Inquiry as a private affair. So we invited the press, radio, television and film makers into the hearing room. They did not obtrude: this was a public inquiry. The things that were said were the public's business, and it was the business of the media to make sure that the public heard those statements. Of course, this approach cannot always be followed. Certainly in the case of a purely investigatory inquiry, where specific allegations of wrongdoing have been made, different considerations prevail.

The CBC's Northern Service played an especially important part in the Inquiry process. The Northern Service provided a crew of broadcasters who broadcast across the North highlights of each day's testimony at the Inquiry. Every day there were hearings, they broadcast both in English and in the native languages from wherever the Inquiry was sitting. In this way, the people in communities throughout the North were given a daily report, in their own languages, on the evidence that had been given at both the formal hearings and the community hearings. The broadcasts meant that when we went into the communities, the people living there understood something of what had been said by the experts at the formal hearings, and by people in the communities that we had already visited. The broadcasters were, of course, entirely independent of the Inquiry.

No one could be expected to understand all the intricacies of the pipeline proposal and its consequences, but so far as we could provide some understanding of the proposal and what it would mean to northerners, we attempted to do so. The media in a way served as the eyes and ears of all northerners, indeed of all Canadians, especially when the Inquiry visited places that few northerners had ever seen and few of their countrymen had even heard of.

Commission Counsel and Inquiry Staff

Commission Counsel, Ian Scott, Q.C. (who was assisted throughout by Stephen Goudge), took the position that he was independent, and free to test and to challenge the evidence of witnesses of all parties. In addition, he regarded it as his job to ensure that all relevant evidence was assembled and presented to the Inquiry so that no vital area was left unexplored. He questioned witnesses in order to establish the content and implications of every theory of social, environmental and economic impact. To secure this objective, the Inquiry staff were largely under the direction of Commission Counsel. They were engaged in reviewing the evidence that was brought forward at the hearings, and in assembling the evidence to be presented to the Inquiry by Commission Counsel.

The corollary was, of course, that Commission Counsel and the Inquiry staff were not allowed to put their arguments privately to the Inquiry. I ruled that the recommendations the Inquiry staff wished to develop should be presented to the Inquiry by Commission Counsel at the formal hearings. This the staff did at the close of the formal hearings, when their 800-page submission was made public.

Ordinarily, the proposals of Commission Counsel would not have been made public in this way. However, I felt they should be made public so that all participants at the Inquiry would have the fullest opportunity to challenge, support, modify or ignore their proposals. This procedure has been followed by many regulatory tribunals in the United States and I think it is a good one. It gave the pipeline companies, the native organizations, the environmental groups, northern business and northern municipalities a chance to criticize the submissions that Commission Counsel put forward on behalf of himself and the Inquiry staff. I, of course, was not bound in any way by the proposals of Commission Counsel, any more than I considered myself bound by the proposals that any other participant made.

Assessment of Impact

One of the complaints made to the Inquiry by northerners from time to time was that there had already been a plethora of committees, task forces, hearings and reports into some at least of the questions that the Inquiry was examining. Indeed, we came across many of them. But each of these reports and studies had largely been confined to a narrow subject. This has been a major flaw in impact assessment. Each department of government has tended to examine the impact of any given proposal solely within the confines of its own departmental responsibilities. Until this Inquiry was appointed, there was no basis on which an overview of the impact of the pipeline project could be made.

There has been another flaw in assessment of impact. Typically, impact assessments have focused on the individual project, and have not taken into account the cumulative effect of the project and the developments that are associated with it or that may follow. In the past, this tendency has been evident in the North, so that even when departments collaborated on a study of impact, that study was unduly confined. This limitation, which distorts rather than enlightens, represents the worst aspect of conventional impact assessment. It also suggests the necessity for developing a methodology that is sufficiently comprehensive to encompass a wide range of variables, a variety of conflicting interests, and a realistic span of time.

If you are going to assess impact properly, you have to weigh a whole series of matters, some tangible, some intangible. But in the end, no matter how many experts there may be, no matter how many pages of computer printouts may have been assembled, there is the ineluctable necessity of bringing human judgment to bear on the main issues. Indeed, when the main issue cuts across a range of questions, spanning the physical and social sciences, the only way to come to grips with it and to resolve it is by the exercise of human judgment.

Inquiries and Government

A final word about the role of the Commission of Inquiry vis-à-vis the role of the Government, the role of the adviser vis-à-vis the role of the decision-maker. A Commissioner of Inquiry has — or ought to have — an advantage that Ministers and senior executives in the public service do not have: an opportunity to hear all the evidence, to reflect on it, to weigh it, and to make a judgment on it. Ministers and their deputies, given the demands that the management of their departments impose upon them, usually have no such opportunity.

A Commissioner of Inquiry is bound to take full advantage of these advantages, remembering that he must leave the final decision to those elected to govern. This is why I felt throughout the Inquiry that it would be wrong to take the evidence summarily or to arrive at a decision in haste. If you do that, you have lost the great advantage that the work of a Commission of Inquiry can offer to government. There are cases, such as the Alaska Highway Pipeline Inquiry, when (for reasons that were well understood) an inquiry must be carried out according to a deadline. But such cases are exceptional.

As the Law Reform Commission has said:

In a parliamentary democracy, Parliament is supreme. There is no matter beyond the competence of the elected representatives of the people. Nor, because Parliament is democratic and representative, is there a forum better able or more qualified for debating and deciding policy questions confronting Canada.

But for some tasks, the legislature may need and seek assistance. Parliament's strength is also its weakness; its political responsiveness to the current concerns of Canadians makes it difficult for legislators to grapple with complex problems that are not of immediate political concern and require considerable time for their solution.

In politics, a day can be a lifetime. There are often no hours to devote to subtle but significant problems, requiring sustained inquiry and thought. The decision may ultimately rest with the legislature; but the legislature needs very good advice. [Law Reform Commission, *Commissions of Inquiry*, p. 14.]

Advisory commissions of inquiry occupy an important

place in the Canadian political system. They supplement in a valuable way the traditional machinery of government, by bringing to bear the resources of time, objectivity, expertise, and by offering another forum for the expression of public opinion.

All of this cost money. The Inquiry, by the end of fiscal year 1976-1977, cost $3,163,344. When this cost is added to the funds that were provided to the native organizations, the environmental groups, northern municipalities and northern business, which came to $1,773,918, you get a total expenditure of $4,937,262 in public funds. I should add that expenditures in the current fiscal year relating largely to preparation and publication of my report put this figure today over $5.3 million.

The work of the Inquiry took many months (the hearings began on March 3, 1975, and ended on November 19, 1976). It had to if the Inquiry was to be fair and complete. Nevertheless, the Inquiry was completed in good time. Volume One, which dealt with the broad issues of social, environmental and economic impact, and contained the basic recommendations of the Inquiry, was available to the Government on May 9 of this year. These basic recommendations appear on the whole to have been acceptable to the Government of Canada. If the assessment made by the Inquiry has prevailed in the minds of decision-makers, it is perhaps in considerable measure a result of the process of the Inquiry.

APPENDIX 2
Inquiry
Documents

There are, of course, several documents that pertain to the Inquiry. It is impossible to reproduce them all here, so I have limited myself to the five most essential items.

The Order-in-Council appointed me as the Commissioner of this Inquiry and defined my mandate.

The letter from the Honourable Jean Chrétien referred the application of Canadian Arctic Gas Pipeline Limited, and the letter from the Honourable Judd Buchanan referred the application of Foothills Pipe Lines Ltd.

The Preliminary Rulings I and II set out the procedures and rules of conduct for the Inquiry.

CANADA

PRIVY COUNCIL · CONSEIL PRIVÉ

P.C. 1974-641

21 March, 1974

WHEREAS proposals have been made for the construction and operation of a natural gas pipeline, referred to as the Mackenzie Valley Pipeline, across Crown lands under the control, management and administration of the Minister of Indian Affairs and Northern Development within the Yukon Territory and the Northwest Territories in respect of which it is contemplated that authority might be sought, pursuant to paragraph 19(f) of the Territorial Lands Act, for the acquisition of a right-of-way;

AND WHEREAS it is desirable that any such right-of-way that might be granted be subject to such terms and conditions as are appropriate having regard to the regional social, environmental and economic impact of the construction, operation and abondonment of the proposed pipeline;

THEREFORE, HIS EXCELLENCY THE GOVERNOR GENERAL IN COUNCIL, on the recommendation of the Minister of Indian Affairs and Northern Development, is pleased hereby, pursuant to paragraph 19(h) of the Territorial Lands Act, to designate the Honourable Mr. Justice Thomas R. Berger (hereinafter referred to as Mr. Justice Berger), of the City of Vancouver in the Province of British Columbia, to inquire into and report upon the terms and conditions that should be imposed in respect of any right-of-way that might be granted across Crown lands for the purposes of the proposed Mackenzie Valley Pipeline having regard to

...2

- 2 -

(a) the social, environmental and economic
impact regionally, of the construction,
operation and subsequent abandonment
of the proposed pipeline in the Yukon
and the Northwest Territories, and

(b) any proposals to meet the specific
environmental and social concerns
set out in the Expanded Guidelines
for Northern Pipelines as tabled in
the House of Commons on June 28, 1972
by the Minister.

HIS EXCELLENCY THE GOVERNOR GENERAL IN COUNCIL
is further pleased hereby

1. to authorize Mr. Justice Berger

(a) to hold hearings pursuant to this Order in
Territorial centers and in such other places
and at such times as he may decide from time to
time;

(b) for the purposes of the inquiry, to summon
and bring before him any person whose
attendance he considers necessary to the
inquiry, examine such persons under oath,
compel the production of documents and
do all things necessary to provide a full
and proper inquiry;

(c) to adopt such practices and procedures for
all purposes of the inquiry as he from time
to time deems expedient for the proper
conduct thereof;

(d) subject to paragraph 2 hereunder, to engage
the services of such accountants, engineers,
technical advisers, or other experts, clerks,
reporters and assistants as he deems necessary
or advisable, and also the services of counsel
to aid and assist him in the inquiry, at such
rates of remuneration and reimbursement as
may be approved by the Treasury Board; and

(e)   to rent such space for offices and hearing
        rooms as he deems necessary or advisable at
        such rental rates as may be approved by
        the Treasury Board; and

2.   to authorize the Minister of Indian Affairs and
        Northern Development to designate an officer of
        the Department of Indian Affairs and Northern
        Development to act as Secretary for the inquiry
        and to provide Mr. Justice Berger with such
        accountants, engineers, technical advisers, or
        other experts, clerks, reporters and assistants
        from the Public Service as may be requested by
        Mr. Justice Berger.

        HIS EXCELLENCY THE GOVERNOR GENERAL IN COUNCIL
is further pleased hereby to direct Mr. Justice Berger
to report to the Minister of Indian Affairs and Northern
Development with all reasonable despatch and file with
the Minister the papers and records of the inquiry as
soon as may be reasonable after the conclusion thereof.

        HIS EXCELLENCY THE GOVERNOR GENERAL IN COUNCIL,
with the concurrence of the Minister of Justice, is
further pleased hereby, pursuant to section 37 of the
Judges Act, to authorize Mr. Justice Berger to act on
the inquiry.

                            Certified to be a true copy

                            Assistant Clerk of the Privy Council

Ottawa, Ontario KIA OH4
April 19, 1974

The Honourable Mr. Justice
  T.R. Berger,
Law Court,
800 W. Georgia,
Vancouver 1, British Columbia.

Dear Mr. Justice Berger:

Further to your appointment as Commissioner to the
Mackenzie Valley Pipeline Hearings, by Order-in-Council
dated March 21, 1974, I wish formally to refer to you the
application made to me on March 21, 1974 by Canadian Arctic
Gas Pipeline Limited for grant of certain interests in
certain lands in the Yukon and the Northwest Territories
and for necessary authorization to construct, own, and
operate a pipeline and connected works.

It is my understanding that you are now in receipt of the
application and the Order-in-Council authorizing your
appointment, and that you have initiated preparatory works in
respect of the hearings.

I am pleased that you have accepted this responsibility as
Commissioner, and I will look forward to your report. When
I can be of assistance to you in this process, do not hesitate
to get in touch with me.

                              Yours sincerely,

                              Jean Chrétien.

July 4, 1975.

The Honourable Mr. Justice T.R. Berger,
Commissioner,
Mackenzie Valley Pipeline Inquiry,
Resources Building,
P.O. Box 2817,
Yellowknife, N.W.T. X0E 1H0

Dear Justice Berger:

By a letter dated April 19, 1974, my predecessor, the Honourable
Jean Chrétien, formally referred to you, further to your
appointment under Order-in-Council P.C. 1974-641, dated
March 21, 1974, an application made on March 21, 1974, by
Canadian Arctic Gas Pipeline Limited for grant of certain
lands in the Yukon and Northwest Territories and for necessary
authorization to construct, own, and operate a pipeline and
connected works.

The Order-in-Council, which established your Inquiry, designated
you to "inquire and report upon the terms and conditions that
should be imposed in respect of any right-of-way that might be
granted across Crown lands for the purpose of the proposed
Mackenzie Valley pipeline.....".

By letter dated May 23, 1975, I advised you that I was sending,
for your information, copies of applications in the same matter
by Foothills Pipe Lines Ltd. and Alberta Gas Trunk Line (Canada)
Limited in respect of a Grant of Interests in Territorial Lands.

I am of the opinion that these more recent applications, because
of their smaller scale, would generally have a lesser social,
environmental, and economic impact than the application by
Canadian Arctic Gas Pipeline Limited which has been formally
referred to you. As a consequence any terms and conditions that
you may recommend should be imposed in respect of a right-of-way
that might be granted across Crown lands for the purposes of the
proposed Mackenzie Valley pipeline should have equal or lesser
application to these applications than to the application of
Canadian Arctic Gas Pipeline Limited. Nonetheless, there may be
areas of significant difference between the two projects which
would warrant you recommending quite different terms and
conditions.

...2

It is, therefore, with these considerations in mind that I
am now formally referring to you the applications of Foothills
Pipe Lines Ltd. and Alberta Gas Trunk Line (Canada) Limited with
a view to your examining any areas of significant difference and
recommending appropriate terms and conditions thereto.

Yours sincerely,

Judd Buchanan.

Preliminary Rulings (I)

I was appointed by the Government of Canada by Order-in-Council dated March 21, 1974, to conduct an inquiry into the social, environmental and economic impact of the proposed Mackenzie Valley natural gas pipeline.

Canadian Arctic Gas Pipeline Limited have applied to the Minister of Indian Affairs and Northern Development under Section 19(f) of the Territorial Lands Act, R.S.C. 1970, c.T-6, for a right-of-way across crown lands in the Yukon and the Northwest Territories. They propose to build a pipeline up the Mackenzie Valley to bring natural gas from Prudhoe Bay in Alaska and from the Mackenzie Delta to markets in Canada and the United States. The Inquiry I am to carry out is authorized by Parliament under Section 19(h) of the Territorial Lands Act. I am to consider the social, environmental and economic impact regionally of the construction, operation and subsequent abandonment of the proposed pipeline in the Yukon and the Northwest Territories, and I am to consider as well the measures which Arctic Gas propose to take to meet the specific social and environmental requirements of the Expanded Guidelines for Northern Pipelines tabled in the House of Commons on June 28, 1972, and I am to report upon the terms and conditions that ought to be imposed in respect of any right-of-way that might be granted to Arctic Gas. It will be for the Government of Canada, on the recommendation of the Minister of Indian Affairs and Northern Development to decide whether to grant a right-of-way to Arctic Gas. It will be for the National Energy Board to determine whether or not to recommend the granting of a Certificate of Public Convenience and Necessity, and for the Government to decide, if such a recommendation is made by the National Energy Board, whether a Certificate should be granted.

Because this Inquiry is unique in Canadian experience, and because of my anxiety that the people of the North and all other Canadians with an interest in the work of the Inquiry should have every opportunity to be heard, and that the Inquiry itself should be thorough and complete, I held preliminary hearings in April and May [1974] in Yellowknife, Inuvik, Whitehorse and Ottawa, to hear submissions on the way the Inquiry ought to be conducted. I have decided to outline my views now on the procedure that we will follow in the Inquiry, and to indicate my views on the questions that were raised relating to the scope of the Inquiry.

The Timetable for the Inquiry

THE EL PASO PROPOSAL

Arctic Gas argued that this Inquiry should be expedited because the El Paso Natural Gas Company intends to apply to the Federal Power Commission in the United States for permission to construct a pipeline to bring natural gas from Prudhoe Bay across Alaska to Valdez, to be liquefied there and then tankered to California. El Paso has already intervened before the Federal Power Commission, where Arctic Gas's sister company, Alaskan Arctic Gas Pipeline Limited, has applied for permission to build a natural gas pipeline from Prudhoe Bay to the Yukon border. El Paso intends to oppose Alaskan Arctic Gas's application in those proceedings (El Paso has not so far sought to intervene in this Inquiry). It was said that if El Paso's proposal were to be approved by the United States authorities, then the economic viability of Arctic Gas's proposal to build a gas pipeline up the Mackenzie Valley intended to bring gas from Prudhoe Bay and the Mackenzie Delta to the United States and Canadian markets, would be jeopardized. So, it was urged, it is essential that this Inquiry be expedited.

My mandate is to conduct a fair and a thorough Inquiry. That must come first. I intend to give all those persons and organizations with an interest in the proposal made by Arctic Gas a fair opportunity to be heard. I will not diminish anyone's right to be heard, nor will I curtail this Inquiry so as to improve Arctic Gas's position in relation to the El Paso proposals in the United States.

But there will not be any undue delay. At the preliminary hearings, all interested parties offered their cooperation to the Inquiry, and indicated their desire to work with the Inquiry. I intend to hold them to that.

THE NATIONAL ENERGY BOARD

Some of the native organizations and some of the environmental organizations argued that this Inquiry should not proceed until the National Energy Board has completed its hearings. This is urged upon the ground that if the National Energy Board were to refuse to grant a Certificate of Public Convenience and Necessity, this Inquiry would be unnecessary.

But if it can be said that this Inquiry should wait upon the outcome of the National Energy Board Hearings, it could equally be said that the National Energy Board should wait upon the outcome of this Inquiry, since the terms and conditions that are laid down by the Minister as the result of this Inquiry may alter the basis upon which Arctic Gas seek a Certificate of Public Convenience and Necessity. How can the National Energy Board decide whether to grant a Certificate of Public Convenience and Necessity, and how can Arctic Gas be expected to proceed with their request for such, without knowing the terms and conditions under which Arctic Gas is entitled to the right-of-way (assuming the Minister decides to grant a right-of-way at all) which it must obtain if it is to go ahead with the pipeline? A recitation of these arguments reveals that the relationship between this Inquiry and the National Energy Board cannot be comprehensively defined at this stage. I do not think it has been shown that this Inquiry ought to wait until the National Energy Board has completed its hearings and made a recommendation to the Government, and the Government has acted upon it one way or the other, before getting under way.

In any event, this Inquiry is not just about a gas pipeline; it relates to the whole future of the North. I am bound to examine the social, economic and environmental impact of the construction of a gas pipeline in the North. But the Pipeline Guidelines do not stop there. They require that the impact of the pipeline should be considered in the context of the development of a Mackenzie Valley transportation corridor.

The influence of a gas pipeline in the development of a Mackenzie Valley transportation corridor and in moulding the social, economic and environmental future of the North will be enormous. The Pipeline Guidelines contemplate the development of a corridor up the Mackenzie Valley to enable the bringing of oil and gas to southern markets. This Inqiury has been established to ensure that the gas pipeline proposal is not considered in isolation. The Mackenzie River has been a transportation system for centuries, first for the native people, then for the white people. The Mackenzie Highway is already under construction, and already reaches beyond the junction of the Liard and the Mackenzie [rivers] at Fort Simpson. The Pipeline Guidelines envisage that, if a gas pipeline is built, an oil pipeline may follow, and that the corridor may eventually include a railroad, hydro-electric transmission lines, and telecommunications facilities. It would be a mistake to dismember the corridor envisaged by the Pipeline Guidelines, and to consider the gas pipeline in isolation.

It is for that reason that I think this Inquiry should not wait upon the outcome of the proceedings before the National Energy Board. This Inquiry, covering the social, environmental and economic impact of the pipeline proposal against the background of the corridor concept, ought to proceed. The Order-in-Council does not impose any restriction upon the commencement of this Inquiry, and I do not think I should impose one.

Hearings

I intend to visit the communities in the Mackenzie Valley, the Delta and the Yukon, likely to be affected by the construction of the pipeline. I intend to do this before the hearings begin. I intend to travel by myself. My visit will be designed to enable me to get to know the people and the way they live, and not to obtain evidence about the impact of the pipeline or their views on the pipeline; that will come later, at the hearings.

FORMAL HEARINGS

I think the formal hearings should begin with an overview of the Mackenzie Valley, the Delta, and the area across the Northern Yukon where the pipeline is to go. Commission Counsel will bring forward this evidence through witnesses called by him for the purpose. The overview evidence would include such matters as the history, culture and economy of the northern peoples; the geography and geological history of the Mackenzie Valley, the Delta and the Yukon; the climate; the geotechnical aspects of northern construction; terrain types, including permafrost; and resources, renewable and non-renewable.

After that the Inquiry will hear the evidence of Arctic Gas. Arctic Gas suggested at the preliminary hearings that they would simply offer formal proof of the material filed in support of their right-of-way application, and then offer their witnesses for cross-examination. That will not be good enough. I expect Arctic Gas to call as witnesses the people who prepared the material and who carried out the field work on which it is based. I expect Arctic Gas's witnesses to be examined in chief in the usual way, to delineate, explain and discuss the material filed, before cross-examination. I should also say that I expect Commission Counsel to examine in chief each of the members of the Assessment Group assembled by the Government of Canada with a view to a complete canvass of all relevant evidence that each of them has to give. The members of the Assessment Group, like the witnesses for Arctic Gas, will be subject to cross-examination. The same procedure will apply to witnesses called by any of the parties at the formal hearings.

COMMUNITY HEARINGS

I intend to hold hearings in each of the communities in the Mackenzie Valley, the Delta and the Yukon that are likely to be affected by the pipeline, to allow the people living in those communities to tell me their views about the proposed pipeline.

The native organizations have said that the formal hearings, at which evidence is to be called relating to the social, environmental and economic impact of the proposed line, should not take place until the community hearings have been completed. I think it would be a mistake to try to impose a rigid framework like that on the scheduling of the community hearings. The purpose of the hearings in the communities is to offer the people living there an opportunity to state in their own languages and in their own way their views about the gas pipeline and the development that it will inevitably bring in its wake.

If the community hearings are going to offer the native people the opportunity they deserve to consider the proposal made by Arctic Gas, the report of the Assessment Group, and the other evidence to be given at the formal hearings, and then to state their case, they ought not to be held before the formal hearings. Instead I think the community hearings ought to be held concurrently with the formal hearings. By that I mean that the Inquiry should break off the formal hearings from time to time to hold hearings in the communities, to ensure that the native people in the communities have an opportunity to answer whatever may be said by the witnesses called at the formal hearings about the social, environmental and economic issues relating to their communities. It seems to me that the people living in the communities will not have the means of knowing the full extent of the material gathered by Arctic Gas, or the means to study it, or to know its specific application to each community, unless the community hearings proceed concurrently with the formal hearings.

At the community hearings I also want to give the native people an opportunity to tell the Inquiry about the impact seismic lines and other kinds of industrial activity have had on the land, on wildlife and the environment, and their own opinions of the likely effect of the construction of the pipeline on the land, the wildlife and the environment. I am anxious that the native people should bring their whole experience before the Inquiry. I do not think they will get that chance if we hold the community hearings first and then go on to the formal hearings.

At the same time I want to make it plain that I do not intend to hold any community hearings until the people living in the communities have had the opportunity of informing and preparing themselves for them. I want to say also that I expect that native persons will be called as witnesses from time to time at the formal hearings. The native people should not be confined to the community hearings for the purpose of presenting their case.

It is my conviction that the formal hearings and the community hearings should be regarded as equally important parts of the same process, and not as two separate processes.

Practice and Procedure

I do not intend to lay down a comprehensive set of formal rules of practice and procedure. But I do want to deal with some of the issues that arose at the preliminary hearings.

INTERVENORS

All of the persons and organizations that made submissions at the preliminary hearings will have the right to intervene and to participate in the Inquiry. They will be notified when hearings are scheduled, and will be given an opportunity to present their submissions at the time and place most convenient to them.

As regards any other persons or organizations wishing to intervene in order to participate on a continuing basis in the hearings or merely to make a submission, advertisements will be placed in the newspapers throughout Canada, and announcements made over radio and television in the North, to notify any persons or organizations wishing to make submissions of the dates and places when they may do so, and prescribing the times within which their submissions, if in writing, should be sent to the Inquiry.

I expect that Arctic Gas, the native organizations, and the environmental organizations will participate in the formal hearings and the community hearings on a continuing basis. But that does not limit the right of any other intervenor to participate on a continuing basis. Every effort will be made by Commission Counsel to work out a timetable for the hearings in consultation with and with the cooperation of the intervenors.

REQUESTS BY THE ASSESSMENT GROUP FOR SUPPLEMENTARY INFORMATION AND MATERIAL

The Assessment Group will prepare, for the purposes of the Inquiry, requests to Arctic Gas for supplementary information and material relating to matters which the Pipeline Guidelines require Arctic Gas to include in their application for a right-of-way and which, in the view of the Assessment Group, have not been dealt with at all in the application, and information and material relating to matters where the Assessment Group is of the view that the application, though it deals with matters required by the Guidelines, does not in all respects come to grips with the requirements laid down by the Guidelines.

These requests will come to the Inquiry. Arctic Gas and the intervenors will be advised by the Inquiry of any request made by the Assessment Group for supplementary information and material, and the same procedure will be followed as regards the answers made by Arctic Gas to such requests. The requests and the answers will be made available to the public.

THE ASSESSMENT GROUP'S REPORT

The report or reports of the Assessment Group containing the Group's analysis of the material filed by Arctic Gas in support of their Application, will be filed with the Inquiry and copies will be made available to the intervenors and the public.

DISCOVERY

Commission Counsel will, in consultation with counsel for the intervenors, develop procedures for discovery of all studies and reports in the possession of the government of Canada as well as of Arctic Gas and the intervenors. Such material must, of course, be relevant to the Inquiry.

As I have said, I expect that at the hearings Arctic Gas, the native organizations and the environmental organizations will be represented throughout. All of them should be prepared to call witnesses early on to discuss in a general way the studies they have carried out and the reports they have prepared, on matters relating to the Inquiry. Commission Counsel will call appropriate witnesses from the public service for the same purpose. On cross-examination it should be possible to obtain complete discovery. Of course, any objections to the production of any studies or reports will be considered by the Inquiry.

SUBPOENAS

As the Inquiry proceeds, should it be necessary, I will exercise my power of subpoena. For the time being I do not intend to lay down any strict rules governing the exercise of that power.

Scope of the Inquiry

A number of arguments arose at the preliminary hearings regarding the scope of my terms of reference.

Let me say at once that the scope of this Inquiry is defined by the Order-in-Council and by the Pipeline Guidelines. Both the Order-in-Council and the Pipeline Guidelines are cast in broadly worded language. They say I am to conduct a social, economic and environmental impact study. It is a study whose magnitude is without precedent in the history of our country. I take no narrow view of my terms of reference.

I am going to indicate my views on the questions raised at the preliminary hearings regarding the scope of the Inquiry. But I am not in any way seeking here to delineate the whole configuration of the Inquiry; rather I am simply trying to settle some of the questions that were clearly present in many minds regarding the scope of the Inquiry.

NATIVE CLAIMS

The principal submission of the native organizations is that no pipeline development should proceed until the land claims of the native peoples have been settled. All of the native organizations that appeared at the preliminary hearings took the position that one of the terms and conditions that this Inquiry ought to recommend to the Minister of Indian Affairs and Northern Development is that there should be no right-of-way granted to Arctic Gas until the native land claims in the Yukon and the Northwest Territories have been settled.

It was suggested by Arctic Gas that the native people ought not to be allowed to advance such an argument in this Inquiry, on the ground it would not fall within my terms of reference to recommend the imposition of such a term or condition. The Order-in-Council says that I am "to inquire into and report upon the terms and conditions that should be imposed in respect of any right-of-way that might be granted across crown lands for the purposes of the proposed Mackenzie Valley pipeline.... " It is said that this Inquiry is limited by these words to the consideration of terms and conditions to be performed or carried out by Arctic Gas.

It is true that the Pipeline Guidelines contemplate that the terms and conditions that the Minister decides to impose upon the granting of a right-of-way shall be included in a signed agreement to be made between the Crown and Arctic Gas. But the Order-in-Council does not confine this Inquiry to a review of the Pipeline Guidelines and of the measures that Arctic Gas are prepared to take in order to meet them. The Order-in-Council requires that the Inquiry consider the social, economic and environmental impact of the construction of a pipeline in the North. That takes the Inquiry beyond the Pipeline Guidelines, and requires a consideration of what the native organizations say ought to be a condition precedent, to be imposed by the Government, as a matter of policy, quite apart from whatever provisions the Government may require, of Arctic Gas or of any other company wishing to build a pipeline, in a signed agreement for a right-of-way.

I am not saying whether the natives' position is well-founded or not. But it is one which they are entitled to urge upon this Inquiry. In fact, it seems to me that it provides an essential focus for the natives' case regarding the impact of the pipeline on their communities and their way of life. Indeed, I would go further. The case Arctic Gas intend to make is that the pipeline can be built without prejudice to the settlement of native land claims. The position taken by the natives offers a focus for the consideration of those terms and conditions — not only those that emerge from the Pipeline Guidelines, but also any others that Arctic Gas is ready to propose — that may enable the pipeline to be built without prejudice to native claims.

Notwithstanding the language of the Introduction to the Social Guidelines (in the Pipeline Guidelines) which appears to make some distinction between the Indian people and the Inuit and the Metis for purposes of settlement of their claims, I take the view that, so far as this Inquiry is concerned, there should be no distinction between the position of the native peoples. All of them are entitled to urge at this Inquiry that there should be no right-of-way granted until their claims have been settled.

THE CORRIDOR CONCEPT

It has been argued by Canadian Arctic Resources Committee that my terms of reference include any gas pipeline proposed by any applicant, and that this Inquiry should not be limited to the proposal that has been made by Arctic Gas. Arctic Gas, on the other hand, have argued that this Inquiry should be limited to an examination of the particular proposal to build a natural gas pipeline that Arctic Gas have made in their application to the Minister for a right-of-way under the Territorial Lands Act.

I do not think that this really gets me very far in ascertaining the limits of the scope of my terms of reference, because the Pipeline Guidelines clearly require an examination of Arctic Gas's proposed pipeline and the route it is to follow in the light of the corridor concept described in the Guidelines. The Pipeline Guidelines relate to the development of a Mackenzie Valley transportation corridor, and not simply to the construction of a gas pipeline.

In any event, the Pipeline Guidelines specifically require a comparison of the proposed pipeline route with alternative pipeline routes. In view of this, I do not think there is really any difference between an Inquiry into the impact of the pipeline proposed by Arctic Gas and an examination generally of the impact of the construction of a gas pipeline up the Mackenzie Valley. The purpose of the corridor, according to the Pipeline Guidelines, is to minimize social and environmental disturbance. It is in that connection that a comparison of the proposed pipeline route with alternate pipeline routes is relevant to this Inquiry.

I am also bound to consider the economic and social impact of the construction of an oil pipeline and to consider the combined effect of the construction of a gas pipeline and an oil pipeline in the corridor.

However, I am not prepared to consider the merits of alternate modes of transportation of the gas, except to the extent that an examination of the advantages and disadvantages of other forms of transportation will be of assistance in determining what terms and conditions ought to be imposed if a right-of-way is granted. For example, a comparison of the extent of environmental degradation that may accompany other modes of transporting the gas may be useful for the purpose of establishing what environmental standards ought to be laid down for the construction of a natural gas pipeline; or a comparison of the opportunities for northern employment that other modes of transportation may offer may be useful for the purpose of determining what terms and conditions ought to be imposed on Arctic Gas or any other pipeline company, in order to generate northern employment, if that is desirable. But such evidence must be relevant to the purposes of the Inquiry.

SUPPLIES AND EQUIPMENT

The purchase and transportation of supplies and equipment and material for the proposed gas pipeline clearly fall within the terms of reference of this Inquiry.

GATHERING LINES AND GAS FIELDS

Even though Arctic Gas has applied only for a right-of-way for the purpose of constructing a trunk pipeline, I regard it as essential to this Inquiry that I should consider evidence regarding the gas fields in the Delta and the gathering lines to be built in the Delta.

I realize that Arctic Gas will be a common carrier, and not a producer, and that the gathering lines will be built by the producers, and not by Arctic Gas. But these lines are so obviously a part of the pipeline system that any consideration of the impact of the gathering lines entails a consideration of the impact of the gathering lines.

But I am not saying that Arctic Gas must bear the burden of adducing this evidence. And I do not know whether the producers will intervene. So it will be the responsibility of Commission Counsel to obtain evidence, pursuant to subpoena if necessary, to enable this Inquiry to consider the location and extent of the gas fields in the Delta, the likely extent of further gas exploration in the Delta and the Beaufort Sea, the likely location, design and construction of the gathering lines and of the processing plants that will be needed to render the gas acceptable to the trunk pipeline, and the social, environmental and economic impact that the development of the gas fields and the construction of these lines will have in the Delta and elsewhere in the North.

PRODUCER REVENUES AND TAXATION

It was urged by Canadian Arctic Resources Committee that I should consider the revenue to the producers that would be generated by the construction of the proposed gas pipeline.

It was said that I should allow evidence to establish the propriety of imposing a term or condition on the construction of the gas pipeline that would require a part of the revenue from the production of gas in the Delta to be dedicated to the improvement of social services in the North. This is the same thing as saying that I ought to conduct an investigation into the income and profits likely to accrue to the producers by the development of the gas fields in the Mackenzie Delta and then make a determination regarding what would be a fair return to the public from the exploitation of the resource.

That lies beyond my terms of reference. The level of royalties and taxes to be imposed upon the gas producers in the Mackenzie Delta is a matter to be decided by Parliament. That is the place to go with arguments about the adequacy of the return to the Crown from the extraction of the gas.

ECONOMIC IMPACT

I do not intend to conduct an examination of the impact of a gas pipeline on the economy of Canada. I am, however, prepared to consider evidence that reveals the particular impact of a gas pipeline on the economy of the North.

It is impossible wholly to disentangle economic consequences from social and environmental consequences. For example, evidence regarding the quantity and quality of the gas in the Delta and the state of natural gas markets, will be of importance for the purpose of determining the life of the pipeline, and such things as the extent to which looping will occur and the number of compressor stations that will be needed. These relate to economic impact of the pipeline, but they relate as well to the social and environmental impact of the pipeline on the North.

But there will be evidence that relates essentially to economic impact. It must, however, be evidence designed to reveal the economic impact on the North. I am prepared to hear evidence of the effect of the gas pipeline on the rate of inflation, capital markets, the foreign exchange rate and other national economic indicators, to enable this Inquiry to ascertain the effect of the gas pipeline on the economy of the North. But such evidence will be allowed for that purpose only.

It was urged that it is impossible to segregate the impact upon the national economy from the impact upon the economy of the North. But the Order-in-Council provides that I am to have regard to the economic impact regionally of the gas pipeline proposal. I think that fixes the limits of the Inquiry. Whatever impact the construction of a gas pipeline may have on Canada's economy, I do not think that the Order-in-Council allows me to explore it. My mandate is to consider the regional economic impact of the pipeline proposals. That means that I am to consider the economic impact especial to the North, and not the economic impact on the nation as a whole.

GREAT BEAR HYDRO PROJECT

Canadian Arctic Resources Committee said that a study had been made by the Northern Canada Power Commission regarding the feasibility of building three dams on the Great Bear River for the purpose of providing hydro-electric power for the pumping stations on the pipeline. According to the evidence, these proposals proceeded on the basis that such hydro power would be produced more cheaply than the natural gas, and that the hydro power could therefore be used to pump the gas, with a consequent saving of natural gas in the operation of the pipeline. Given a customer whose energy requirements would be of such a magnitude, it would be feasible to proceed with the project, and to generate hydro-electric power for Arctic Gas and customers throughout the North.

Such proposals, as outlined to me, were sketchy and incomplete. However, if such a development were to occur, the impact it would have on Fort Franklin, not to mention the whole of the Mackenzie Valley, is obvious. It would constitute, in my view, an "associated and ancillary facility" within the meaning of the Pipeline Guidelines, and would clearly fall within this Inquiry. In any event, if it were built for the purpose of providing hydro-electric power to Arctic Gas, it would be necessary to consider its social, environmental and economic impact. It is obvious that it might be urged upon the Inquiry that a term or condition of the right-of-way would be that electricity generated by the project should be used to pump the gas, in order to conserve gas in the operation of the line, and to make possible the electrification of the Mackenzie Valley.

Should evidence come before me that indicates that such a project will be seriously considered if a right-of-way is granted and a Certificate of Public Convenience and Necessity follows, then I will hear evidence regarding the social , economic and environmental impact of the project.

These will be the limits of the Inquiry in the disputed areas. In concluding what they ought to be, I have been guided by the conviction that this Inquiry must be fair and it must be complete. We have got to do it right. The pipeline, if it is built, will have a great impact on the future of northern development and the shape of northern communities, and the way of life for northern peoples. Not simply because a pipeline is to be built, but because of all that it will bring in its wake. To limit the Inquiry to an examination of Arctic Gas's proposal merely, without considering the background against which that proposal is made, without considering the corridor concept indicated by the Pipeline Guidelines, would be to nullify the basis on which this Inquiry was established.

Issued: July 12, 1974, Yellowknife, Northwest Territories.

Preliminary Rulings (II)

Practice and Procedure

Mr. Scott, Commission Counsel, has presented certain proposals regarding practice and procedure. I held further preliminary hearings at Yellowknife on September 12 and 13, 1974, to consider representations regarding these proposals by counsel for Arctic Gas, counsel for the other participants who appeared, as well as by Commission Counsel. I also considered the submissions made in writing by other participants.

I said in my Preliminary Rulings of July 12, 1974, that I wanted this Inquiry to be fair and complete. I have had that consideration uppermost in mind in deciding upon these issues of practice and procedure. The Rulings I am handing down today are intended to bring about full disclosure of all the evidence, and to give to all concerned the fullest opportunity to present their case.

As soon as the Inquiry has received the report of the Assessment Group assembled by the Government of Canada to analyze the material filed by Arctic Gas in support of their application for a right-of-way, I will set a date for the commencement of the formal hearings of the Inquiry.

Application of the Rules

DEFINITION OF PARTICIPANT

Any person shall be deemed a participant if he appears at any formal hearing of the Inquiry (including preliminary hearings) and gives his name and address to the Inquiry, or if he advises the Inquiry in writing of his intention to appear. Special Counsel shall maintain a list of participants, which shall be available for inspection by any person at the offices of the Inquiry in Yellowknife and in Ottawa.

APPLICATION

These rules shall apply only to the following participants in the Inquiry:
    Canadian Arctic Gas Pipeline Limited
    Foothills Pipe Lines Ltd.
    Canadian Arctic Resources Committee [1]
    Environment Protection Board
    Indian Brotherhood of the Northwest Territories
    Metis Association of the Northwest Territories
    Inuit Tapirisat of Canada
    Committee for Original Peoples Entitlement
    Yukon Native Brotherhood
    Northwest Territories Association of Municipalities
    Commission Counsel

[1] Mr. Anthony and Mr. Lucas, counsel for Canadian Arctic Resources Committee, have advised the Inquiry that the Northern Assessment Group that was established by Canadian Arctic Resource Committee, the Canadian Nature Federation, the Federation of Ontario Naturalists, Pollution Probe, and the Canadian Environmental Law Association, for purposes of this Inquiry, will comply with any Rules of this Inquiry applicable to Canadian Arctic Resources Committee.

These Rules will not apply to any other participants at the formal hearings.

These Rules will not apply to the community hearings.

Overview Hearings

Witnesses called at the overview hearings will not be cross-examined during the overview hearings, unless it is essential to a fair hearing. In any event, all overview witnesses will be subject to recall for further examination and for cross-examination at the formal hearings.

Formal Hearings

DIVISION OF FORMAL HEARINGS

The formal hearings will be divided into four phases.

Phase 1: Engineering and Construction of the Proposed Pipeline

This phase of the hearings will include such matters as the size of the pipeline, its location, the timing of construction, the composition and deployment of construction crews, and the construction of compressor stations.

Phase 2: The Impact of a Pipeline and Mackenzie Corridor Development on the Physical Environment

This phase of the hearings will include the impact on the land, the air and the water, and will cover such things as the effect on permafrost, river crossings, slope stability, and gravel and other borrow locations.

Phase 3: The Impact of a Pipeline and Mackenzie Corridor Development on the Living Environment

This phase of the hearings will include the impact on plant and animal life, including wildlife, mammals and fishes.

Phase 4: The Impact of a Pipeline and Mackenzie Corridor Development on the Human Environment

This phase of the hearings will include social and economic impact.

This division is for purposes of convenience only. The four phases will not necessarily encompass all of the evidence that will be brought forward at the formal hearings. Commission Counsel will therefore invite the participants to consult with him from time to time with a view to determining whether there should be any further division of the hearings within each phase. In any event, it will be open to any participant to call evidence out of order when that is appropriate.

Special Counsel will provide to each participant Notice of Hearing with respect to each of the four phases of the formal hearings and will advise the public generally of the matters to be considered at each phase of the formal hearings.

CALLING EVIDENCE AND EXAMINATION OF WITNESSES

At the formal hearings, as a general rule, Arctic Gas will lead their evidence first, followed by the other participants and Commission Counsel. Arctic Gas will be entitled to call evidence in rebuttal. From time to time, other participants will lead off; when they do, they will have the right to call evidence in rebuttal after the evidence for the other participants has been heard; in any event, the rights of all concerned to bring forward all their evidence on every issue will be preserved.

With respect to witnesses, counsel for any participant calling a witness will examine him in chief; the witness will then be cross-examined by counsel for each of the other participants and by Commission Counsel. Counsel for the participant calling the witness will be entitled to re-examine.

Commission Counsel will have the responsibility of calling the evidence of the members of the Assessment Group assembled by the Government of Canada, with a view to a complete canvass of all relevant evidence that the Group has to give. The Group will be subject to cross-examination.

Commission Counsel will also be responsible for calling the evidence of the public service of Canada not included in the Assessment Group, whose evidence is regarded as necessary to the completeness of the Inquiry.

It will also be the responsibility of Commission Counsel to obtain evidence, pursuant to subpoena if necessary, to enable the Inquiry to consider the location and extent of the gas fields in the Mackenzie Delta, the likely extent of further oil and gas exploration in the Delta and the Beaufort Sea, the likely location, design and construction of the gathering lines there and of the processing plants that will be needed to render the gas acceptable to the trunk pipeline, and the social, environmental and economic impact that the development of the gas fields and the construction of these lines will have in the Delta and elsewhere in the North.

All of the witnesses giving this evidence will be subject to cross-examination, and Commission Counsel will be entitled to re-examine each of them.

Evidence can be introduced through individual witnesses or panels of witnesses.

PLACE OF FORMAL HEARINGS

Yellowknife will be the main centre for the formal hearings. At the same time, I am anxious that as much as possible of the evidence relating to oil and gas activity in the Mackenzie Delta and the Beaufort Sea and relating to the impact of such activity should be heard at Inuvik.

It may be appropriate for some of the evidence at the formal hearings to be heard in Ottawa. In any event, it will be necessary in due course to hold hearings in major southern centres to enable Canadians who cannot appear in the North to express their views.

Community Hearings

Community hearings will be held in each community in the Mackenzie Valley, the Mackenzie Delta and the Yukon likely to be affected by the construction of a pipeline and by corridor development. I have appointed Professor Michael Jackson of the Inquiry staff to act as co-ordinator of the community hearings. He has established a committee, which consists of counsel representing the participants chiefly concerned with the organizing of the community hearings.

With regard to those communities that have a primarily native population, I expect that the native organizations will bring proposals to Professor Jackson's committee as to the way in which the hearings in those communities ought to be conducted. These proposals should be considered by the committee, and the committee's recommendations referred to me.

In the same way, with regard to those communities that have a primarily white population, I expect that the Northwest Territories Association of Municipalities will come forward with proposals regarding the conduct of those hearings and that they will be considered by Professor Jackson's committee and the recommendations of the committee referred to me.

If the committee does not reach agreement on any matter, I will consider the recommendations of each of its members. In any event, I will be prepared to consider the views of any participant regarding the conduct of the community hearings.

The Inquiry is arranging with the Canadian Broadcasting Corporation for summaries of the evidence given at the formal hearings to be broadcast to northern communities likely to be affected by the construction of a pipeline and the development of a Mackenzie Valley transportation corridor. The broadcasts will be on a regular basis, and will consist of summaries of the evidence given at the formal hearings. I expect that these broadcasts will be in English and in the native languages, so that the people in the communities will know what has been said at the formal hearings and will be able to respond to it when the Inquiry reaches the communities.

I should make it plain that I intend at the community hearings to give everyone who wishes to express his point of view, whether it is one widely held in the community or not, an opportunity to be heard.

Evidence Relating to Native Claims

I said, when I handed down my Preliminary Rulings on July 12, that it would be open to the native peoples in this Inquiry to argue that no right-of-way should be granted for a pipeline until their land claims were settled.

Native claims are based on traditional use and occupation. Evidence relating to current use and occupation will obviously include such things as the location of trap lines, fishing camps and hunting grounds, and berry picking areas. I want to hear from the trappers, hunters and fishermen and others in the native communities not only about their present use of the land and the extent of their reliance upon it, but also their views on the likely efficacy of any measures proposed by Arctic Gas to build a pipeline without damaging these native interests; by that I mean that I want to hear the evidence they have to give, and the representations they wish to make, regarding likely interference with trap lines, obstruction of streams, spoliation of hunting grounds and so on.

It seems to me that, in order to be fair to Arctic Gas, such evidence should be laid before the Inquiry, so that Arctic Gas will be in a position to indicate what terms and conditions they are prepared to submit to, what safeguards they are prepared to adopt, and what measures they are prepared to take, in support of their contention that a pipeline can be built without impairing the native people's current use and occupation of the land.

Now, such evidence would be of the first importance to this Inquiry even if the issue of native land claims had never been raised. That brings me to the problem of how to deal fairly with the contention of the native organizations that no pipeline should be built until their land claims have been settled. Their claims are based on traditional use and occupation and, according to Professor Cumming, senior counsel for the Inuit Tapirisat of Canada and the Committee for Original Peoples Entitlement, they include not only lands that are subject to current use and occupation, but extend to lands that they do not use and occupy today. Mr. Sutton, counsel for the Indian Brotherhood of the Northwest Territories and the Metis Association of the Northwest Territories, took the same position. So did Mr. Lueck, counsel for the Yukon Native Brotherhood.

How then can this Inquiry come to grips with a contention that no pipeline should be built until native land claims are settled, when those land claims relate to ancestral lands that the native people no longer use or occupy?

It is not for this Inquiry to decide the legitimate extent of native land claims in the North. But the native organizations have said to this Inquiry that no pipeline should be built until their land claims have been settled. Those who want to build the pipeline are entitled to an opportunity to meet this by showing that the pipeline can be built without prejudice to native land claims.

I think, therefore, that the native organizations should indicate the nature and extent of their land claims. Given that their view is that any settlement ought to acknowledge that the native people have certain rights that they should be entitled to assert in respect of the lands they claim, there should be some indication of the nature of the rights they assert and of their extent. (The land use studies being carried out by the native organizations relate, as I understand it, not only to land that is the subject of current use and occupation, but also to land that, although the native people no longer use or occupy it, they used to. These studies should be of real assistance to the Inquiry. Some of these studies are complete. Some are not yet complete. But, even where they are not complete, the work done so far may well be helpful.) The Inquiry will then be in a position to indicate to the Minister which measures ought to be taken to ensure that the native peoples, in their negotiations with the Government, do not find themselves at any disadvantage owing to the building of the pipeline, and, looking to the consummation of negotiations, which measures ought to be taken to ensure that, whatever the extent of the native interest that may ultimately be recognized by any settlement, it will not be diminished by the construction of the pipeline in the meantime.

It should, of course, be remembered that it will be for the Government of Canada and the native peoples to negotiate a settlement of the native claims in the North. It is only the Government of Canada and the native peoples of the North that are parties to the negotiations to settle native land claims. Nothing said at this Inquiry can bind either side. Any delineation of native claims before the Inquiry will be for the purpose merely of ensuring that the Inquiry can fairly consider the principal contention of the native organizations regarding the construction of the pipeline and the answer that those who propose to build the pipeline have to make to that contention.

Discovery

DISCOVERY OF WITNESSES

Every participant shall, before giving evidence himself or calling witnesses on his behalf, file with Special Counsel, at least two weeks before giving evidence or calling such evidence, a synopsis of the evidence of the witness intended to be called, together with a list of any reports, studies or other documents to which that witness may refer or upon which he may rely.

This Rule was suggested by Commission Counsel to expedite the hearings. It will sometimes be difficult to comply with. If any participant cannot comply with the Rule, that will not necessarily preclude the calling of the witness in question, at the time the witness is presented to the Inquiry, but it may mean the witness will have to be recalled later on for cross-examination.

PRODUCTION OF STUDIES AND REPORTS

All of the participants, except Arctic Gas, expressed their willingness to provide a list of all studies and reports in their possession or power relating to the Inquiry, including those for which privilege might be claimed.

Mr. Goldie, counsel for Arctic Gas, was not prepared to go along with this. Instead, he suggested that, as each of the witnesses for Arctic Gas is called, there should simply be provided a list of all studies and reports that that witness relies upon, or that touch upon his testimony. It was said that this would be sufficient, and that it would be impracticable for Arctic Gas to provide a list of all their studies and reports before the formal hearings begin.

In my judgment, there is a paramount public interest in the fullest disclosure of all the facts, which requires that a list of all studies and reports in the possession or power of Arctic Gas relating to the Inquiry should be supplied to the Inquiry. It was not suggested that this would be impossible; it was simply urged that it would be difficult for Arctic Gas to comply with such a direction.

It would not be satisfactory for Arctic Gas merely to provide a list of studies and reports to accompany the testimony of each witness. If we were to proceed in that way, we would get the material only in a piecemeal fashion. If we do not require a complete list, there can be no guarantee that

there will be full disclosure of all studies and reports prepared by Arctic Gas relating to the Inquiry. It would be open to Arctic Gas to decide for themselves which witnesses they ought to call and thus avoid the necessity of disclosing the existence of a study or a report that might be damaging to their case but that would be useful to the Inquiry. That will be avoided if a complete list is supplied.

I therefore direct that all of the participants to whom these Rules apply, including Arctic Gas, must provide a list of all studies and reports in their possession or power relating to this Inquiry. These lists should be filed with the Inquiry by November 30, 1974, and copies provided to all of the participants to whom these Rules apply. If they are ready earlier, they should be filed as soon as they are ready and distributed to the other participants; in fact, each participant may well decide to circulate a list of all studies and reports in its possession relating to Phase I of the Inquiry, without waiting until its list is ready covering all phases of the Inquiry. I appreciate that by November 30, 1974, some of the participants will not have completed all the studies and reports they intend to prepare. They should, nevertheless, file a list and add to it as they go along. Commission Counsel will be responsible for providing a list of all studies and reports of the Government of Canada.

When the lists have been provided, it will be open to the other participants to demand that any study or report on any list should be produced. If any participant wishes to raise a claim of privilege as the basis for an objection to production at that stage, the Inquiry will of course consider it then. It should be remembered that, under Section 19(f) of the Territorial Lands Act, R.S.C. 1970, c.T-6, any one appointed to conduct an inquiry has the power:

> for the purposes of the inquiry, to summon and bring before him any person whose attendance he considers necessary to the inquiry, examine such persons under oath, compel the production of documents and do all things necessary to provide a full and proper inquiry.

These powers have been conferred on this Inquiry by the Order-in-Council of March 21, 1974.

In addition, any participant may, in the meantime, request of any other participant a copy of any study or report whether or not it appears on the list filed by the participant of whom it is requested, and whether or not such a list has already been filed.

Applications to the Inquiry

Any applications made by participants to the Inquiry for subpoenas or any relief whatever shall be made upon reasonable notice to the Inquiry and to Commission Counsel as well as to any participant directly affected by the application and to any other participant that the Inquiry decides should be given notice of the application. If the hearings are in progress, the application can be made to the Inquiry at the hearing on the day when it is returnable.

Changes in These Rules

The Inquiry retains the power to add to, alter or modify these Rules, or to require that any participant not already bound by them should comply with them in whole or in part, as well as the power to exempt any participant from complying with them in whole or in part.

Inspection by the Public

Copies of the material filed by any participant or other person or organization, including lists of studies and reports, the transcript of the hearings, and copies of the exhibits, will be on file during office hours, and available for inspection by the public at the Inquiry offices in Yellowknife and in Ottawa.

Issued: October 29, 1974, Yellowknife, Northwest Territories, and Ottawa, Ontario.

APPENDIX 3
Acknowledgements

In Volume One, I thanked all the people who contributed to the work of the Inquiry throughout its various phases: the witnesses, the participants, the pipeline companies, the oil and gas industry, native organizations, the environmental groups, northern municipalities, northern business, the territorial governments, the various departments of the federal government, and the Inquiry staff. The spirit of cooperation and the sharing of knowledge, experience and understanding became hallmarks of the Inquiry process.

The Inquiry continued to receive the full support and cooperation from the Department of Indian Affairs and Northern Development and, as a result, has been able to discharge its mandate completely. I am particularly indebted to the support given me by the Ministers responsible for the Department: The Honourable Jean Chrétien under whom the Inquiry was established, the Honourable Judd Buchanan who succeeded Mr. Chrétien, the Honourable Warren Allmand to whom Volume One was submitted, and the Honourable Hugh Faulkner to whom this volume is addressed.

I wish to extend special thanks to the following persons who have contributed to the publication of Volume Two and who have carried the Inquiry to its conclusion.

Consultants:

Frank Basham, George Braden, Hugh Brody, Jim Cameron, Edward Chamberlin, P.K. Chatterji, Steve Goudge, Christopher Hatfield, Ray Haynes, Joan Hornal, Michael Jackson, Rolf Kellerhals, Steve Merrett, Graham Morgan, Ron Pritchard, Peter Usher.

Technical Staff and Public Service Advisors:

John Fyles (Head); Ed Weick (Socio-economic Advisor), Don Gamble (Engineering and Environmental Advisor), Bruce Amos, Larry Burgess, Janice Falls, Sam Gelman, Daphne Greenwood, Julian Hawryzsko, Alan Heginbottom, Fred McFarland, Sheila Meldrum, Dick Morlan, Mary Mussell.

Report Editing:

Rosemary Wallbank; Heather Boucher, Alan Cooke

Report Production:

Shirley Callard; Donna Agostino, Carolyn Bennett, Pauline Boudrault, Linda Bradley, Ruth Carriere, Pat Clement, Patricia Fournier, Terry Kelly, Lorraine Lafontaine, Lise Lavertue, Paul Rowan, Barbara Smith, Mark Thibeault, Kerry Tindle, Annette Whyte.

Report Translation:

Brian Peters; Richard Gratton, Pierre Guérin, Louise Morrison, Michèle Wilson.

Report Publication:

André Lamothe (Printing), Bob Russell (Alphatext), Byrne Scott (Printing), Ken Slater (Design).

All the views expressed and all of the judgments made in this report are my own and for them I bear complete responsibility.

Photographs and Diagrams

Photographs on Cover

Front cover, clockwise from top right:

Snowmobiles at Holman Island (E. Weick); Muskrat skips on stretch boards (R. Fumoleau); White Whales (R. McClung); Caribou on snow field (IDS—G. Calef); Welding pipe (Arctic Gas); Teddy Tsetta of Detah (R. Fumoleau).

Back cover:

Drill rig on artificial island, Beaufort Sea (J. Inglis); Hunter on arctic sea ice (G. Bristow).

Title page, top left:

Dogrib woman testifying (M. Jackson);

Top right:

Yellowknife formal hearing (D. Gamble);

Centre:

Hearing at Rae (M. Jackson).

Photographs in text

Part One:

Hide being stretched and dried (R. Fumoleau).

Part Two:

Northern landscape (DIAND Yellowknife—B. Braden).

Part Three:

Pipe being laid in ditch (Alyeska).

Part Four:

Loucheux child at Old Crow (G. Calef).

Photography

The photography appearing in this report was made possible through the cooperation of the following organizations and photographers.

Alyeska Pipeline Service Company, Anchorage, Alaska.

Bill Braden, Department of Indian Affairs and Northern Development, Yellowknife, NWT.

Gary Bristow, Holman, NWT.

George Calef, Yellowknife (formerly with Interdisciplinary Systems Ltd. (IDS), Winnipeg).

Canadian Arctic Gas Pipeline Limited, Toronto.

René Fumoleau, Yellowknife.

Don Gamble, Ottawa.

Julian Inglis, Department of Indian Affairs and Northern Development, Ottawa.

Michael Jackson, Vancouver.

R. McClung, Fisheries and Marine Service, Department of the Environment, Ste. Anne de Bellevue, Quebec.

E.R. Weick, Ottawa.

Maps

Colour map:

Surveys and Mapping Branch, Department of Energy, Mines and Resources.

Renewable Resources map:

Geological Survey of Canada, Department of Energy, Mines and Resources.

Northern Conservation Areas map:

Alan Heginbottom, Ottawa.

APPENDIX 4
Terminology and Bibliography

Terminology

Throughout this report I have referred to the land claims of the native people as *native claims.*

Often I have referred to native people meaning all of the people of Eskimo and Indian ancestry, whether they regard themselves as Inuit, Dene or Metis. They are, of course, distinct peoples, yet they have an identity of interest with respect to many of the issues dealt with in this report and have often, in such instances, been referred to collectively as *native people.* Where only one of these peoples is meant, that is apparent from the text.

I have usually referred to present-day Eskimo peoples as Inuit: this is in keeping with their wishes today. Although many people of Eskimo ancestry of the Mackenzie Delta call themselves *Inuvialuit,* I have referred to them also as Inuit.

The term *Dene* refers to the status and non-status people of Indian ancestry who regard themselves as Dene. Native people who describe themselves as Metis and who see themselves as having a distinct history and culture, as well as aspirations and goals that differ from those of the Dene, I have referred to as Metis. I have dealt with the people of Old Crow separately because they live in the Northern Yukon, not in the Northwest Territories.

I have referred to the Mackenzie Valley and the Western Arctic. There is of course some overlap here, in that both geographical areas may be regarded as encompassing the Mackenzie Delta. The Mackenzie Valley includes the whole of the region from the Alberta border to the Mackenzie Delta, including the Great Slave Lake and Great Bear Lake areas. The Western Arctic encompasses the whole area on the rim of the Beaufort Sea, including the arctic coast of the Yukon.

I have referred to witnesses by their first name and surname when their names first appear, and thereafter by their surname only, except where the repetition of the first name is essential to avoid confusion. I have given the appellation "Mr." only to Ministers of the Crown. I have referred to witnesses holding doctorates as "Dr."

I have referred to government officials, the leaders of native organizations, band chiefs and others, by the offices they held when they gave evidence to the Inquiry.

I have often referred to *whites* and to the *white man.* It will be apparent that sometimes I mean western man and the representatives of the industrial system. Of course, in such a context the expression *white man* can, in fact, include people of many races. However, the native people throughout the Inquiry referred to the white man. They knew what they meant, and although they no doubt adopted the expression because the representatives of the larger Canadian society who come to the North are almost entirely Caucasian, they have not been inclined to make any finer differentiation. I think the phrase is not at all misleading under these circumstances. The alternative, which I have rejected, would be constantly to use such expressions as *non-native, southern* or *Euro-Canadian.* Instead, I have used these latter expressions where, in the context, no other would do.

Unless I have indicated otherwise, the term *the North* refers to the Northwest Territories and the Yukon Territory. *The South* generally refers to metropolitan Canada.

I have used the expression *we* many times. I have meant by it the non-native population of Canada, north and south, and have sought merely to remind readers that I view the North as one who shares the culture, perceptions and ideas of Canadians as a whole.

Throughout the report, Canadian Arctic Gas Pipeline Limited is referred to as Arctic Gas and Foothills Pipe Lines Ltd. as Foothills. I have treated each of these informal terms as plural, recognizing that groups of companies are involved.

Since the release of Volume One, the Arctic Gas proposal has been rejected by the National Energy Board and by the Government of Canada. So I have proceeded, in Volume Two, on the assumption that a pipeline may be expected to be built from the Mackenzie Delta along the Mackenzie Valley to the Northwest Territories—Alberta border in ten years' time. The reference to "the Company" in Volume Two is a reference to the company or consortium that may advance new pipeline proposals in the future. "The Agency" refers to the regulatory authority that may be established by the federal government to supervise the construction of a Mackenzie Valley pipeline.

I recognize that some people will attach great importance to my use of the words shall and should. In the context of the hundreds of recommendations made in this report, I do not make a great distinction between the two. In general, however, I use "shall" where I feel the subject matter is particularly important. Most of these recommendations apply to the pipeline Company. I use "should" where I consider an issue needs attention and perhaps further definition. Many of my recommendations that apply to government use the word "should."

Bibliography

The following bibliographic references refer to documents and personal communications cited or used in both Volumes One and Two of my report. The bibliography is divided into two sections. The first lists, in alphabetical order by author, all material exclusive of existing legislation. Legislation is listed separately in the second section. The applications of Canadian Arctic Gas Pipeline Limited and of Foothills Pipe Lines Ltd. are given only one entry in the bibliography; the various submissions and amendments are not listed separately.

Where transcripts of the Inquiry hearings are cited, they are identified by the page number preceded by F (formal hearings) or C (community hearings). The Inquiry exhibits are similarly cited with the exhibit number preceded by F or C. The bibliography does not contain a reference to the transcripts, nor does it list all the exhibits received by the Inquiry. The transcripts and the exhibits form the Public Record and are located in the Public Archives, Ottawa.

Aboriginal Land Rights Commission. *Aboriginal Land Rights Commission Report.* Mr. Justice A.E. Woodward, Commissioner. Sydney, Australia, 1974.

Advisory Committee on Marine Resources Research and International Associaton for Biological Oceanography. "Indices for Measuring Responses of Aquatic Ecological Systems to Various Human Influences." *Fisheries Technical Paper,* No. 151. n.p., 1976.

Agreement in Principle Between the Dene Nation and Her Majesty the Queen, in Right of Canada. n.p., 1976.

Alaska Department of Health and Social Services. "Pipeline Impact — Copper Valley Basin, Alcohol Abuse and Alcoholism." Juneau, Alaska, 1974.

American Petroleum Institute. *Standard 650, Welded Steel Tanks for Oil Storage.* 6th edition. Washington, D.C., 1977.

American Public Health Association, *et al. Standard Methods for Examination of Water and Wastewater.* 14th edition. Washington, D.C., 1976.

The Arctic Institute of North America. "Alaska in the 70's, A Conference Report on Alaskan/Canadian Relationships." Montreal, 1976.

Arnold, Robert D. *Alaska Native Land Claims.* Anchorage: Alaska Native Foundation, 1976.

Asch, Michael. "Addendum to the Submission of Michael Asch, May 1976." Evidence presented on behalf of the Indian Brotherhood of the Northwest Territories to the Mackenzie Valley Pipeline Inquiry, Yellowknife, 1976.

————. "Past and Present Land-Use by Slavey Indians of the Mackenzie District." Evidence presented on behalf of the Indian Brotherhood of the Northwest Territories and Metis Association of the Northwest Territories to the Mackenzie Valley Pipeline Inquiry. Yellowknife, 1976.

————. Personal Communication with Peter J. Usher. June 3, 1977.

Attwood, D., *et al. Human Factors, Assessment of the Voyageur ACV in Canadian Coast Guard Marine Applications.* Department of National Defence, Defence Research Board, DCIEM Operational Report No. 73-OR-997. Ottawa, 1973.

Bailey, B.E. *Marine Oils with Particular Reference to those of Canada.* Fisheries Research Board of Canada, Bulletin No. 59. Ottawa, 1952.

Banfield, A.W.F. *The Mammals of Canada.* Second printing. Toronto: University of Toronto Press, 1977.

Barber, L. "The Basis for Native Claims in Canada." Address to the Rotary Club. Yellowknife, October 1974.

Barry, T.W. "Concerns for Birdlife During Oil and Gas Development." Evidence presented on behalf of the Committee for Original Peoples Entitlement to the Mackenzie Valley Pipeline Inquiry. Inuvik, 1976.

Battelle Memorial Institute. *Control of Spillage of Hazardous and Polluting Substances.* Report No. 15090 POZ10/70. n.p.: United States Government Printing Office, 1970.

Beard, Leo R. "Hypothetical Floods," *Hydrologic Engineering Methods for Water Resources Development.* The Hydrologic Engineering Center, Corps of Engineers, United States Army, Vol. 5. Davis, California, 1975.

Beauchamp, Kenneth P. *Land Management in the Canadian North*. Canadian Arctic Resources Committee. Ottawa, 1976.

Bell, Glen. "Fort Franklin Land Use Map." Evidence presented on behalf of the Indian Brotherhood of the Northwest Territories/Metis Association of the Northwest Territories to the Mackenzie Valley Pipeline Inquiry. Fort Franklin, 1975.

—— "Fort McPherson Land Use Map." Evidence presented on behalf of the Indian Brotherhood of the Northwest Territories/Metis Association of the Northwest Territories to the Mackenzie Valley Pipeline Inquiry. Fort McPherson, 1975.

——. "Fort Norman Land Use Map." Evidence presented on behalf of the Indian Brotherhood of the Northwest Territories/Metis Association of the Northwest Territories to the Mackenzie Valley Pipeline Inquiry. Fort Norman, 1975.

——. "Hay River Land Use Map, and List of Trappers." Evidence presented on behalf of the Indian Brotherhood of the Northwest Territories/Metis Association of the Northwest Territories to the Mackenzie Valley Pipeline Inquiry. Hay River, 1975.

Berger, Thomas R. "The Mackenzie Valley Pipeline Inquiry." Reprint from *Queen's Quarterly*, Vol. 83, No. 1 (1976).

Bissett, Don. *Resource Harvests — Hunter-Trappers in the Mackenzie Valley*. Environmental-Social Committee, Northern Pipelines, Task Force on Northern Oil Development, Report No. 74-42. Ottawa, 1974.

Blondin, Gina, *et al.* "Brief Presented to Mr. Justice Thomas Berger, Mackenzie Valley Pipeline Inquiry." Mackenzie Valley Pipeline Inquiry Submission on the Merits No. 189. n.p., [1976].

Brackel, W.D. *Socio-economic Importance of Marine Wildlife Utilization*. Beaufort Sea Project, Technical Report No. 32, Department of the Environment. Victoria, 1977.

Brewer, Max C. "Land Commitments in Alaska." *Arctic*, Vol. 28, No. 4 (1975), pp. 263-74.

Brody, Hugh. *Indians on Skid Row, The Role of Alcohol and Community in the Adaptive Process of Indian Urban Migrants*. Northern Science Research Group, Department of Indian Affairs and Northern Development. Ottawa, 1971.

——. "Paper 1: An Overview." Evidence presented on behalf of the Committee for Original Peoples Entitlement to the Mackenzie Valley Pipeline Inquiry. Yellowknife, 1976.

——. "Paper 2: Alcohol." Evidence presented on behalf of the Committee for Original Peoples Entitlement to the Mackenzie Valley Pipeline Inquiry. Yellowknife, 1976.

——. "Paper 3: Industrial Impact." Evidence presented on behalf of the Committee for Original Peoples Entitlement to the Mackenzie Valley Pipeline Inquiry. Yellowknife, 1976.

——. *The People's Land, Eskimos and Whites in the Eastern Arctic*. Middlesex: Penguin Books Ltd., 1975.

Brown, B.L. Letter to Mr. Justice Thomas R. Berger concerning "Northern Manpower Delivery System," dated January 14, 1977. Canadian Pipeline Advisory Council.

Buchanan, Honourable Judd. "Notes for a Speech by the Honourable Judd Buchanan, P.C., M.P., Minister of Indian and Northern Affairs to the Northwest Territories Council." Yellowknife, 1976.

Calef, George W. "The Urgent Need for a Canadian Arctic Wildlife Range." *Nature Canada*, Vol. 3, No. 3, (1974), pp. 3-11.

Calef, George W., *et al.* "The Reaction of Barren-Ground Caribou to Aircraft." *Arctic*, Vol. 29, No. 4 (1976), pp. 201-12.

Cameron, James. "Comments on: Mackenzie Valley Pipeline Inquiry, Volume II: Terms and Conditions — Wastewater" and covering letter to D.J. Gamble. Northern Technology Centre, Department of the Environment, Edmonton, 1977.

Canada. *Clean Air Act, 1974. Ambient Air Quality Objectives*. Canada Gazette Part II, Vol. 108, No. 11.

——. *Clean Air Act, 1975. Ambient Air Quality Objectives, No. 2*. Canada Gazette Part II, Vol. 109, No. 3.

Canada, Advisory Commission on the Development of Government in the Northwest Territories. *Report of the Advisory Commission on the Development of Government in the Northwest Territories*. A.W.R. Carrothers, Chairman. Ottawa, 1966.

Canada, Canadian Inter-governmental Beaufort Sea Contingency Planning Task Force. "Government Contingency Plan for Major Oil Spills in the Beaufort Sea." Final draft. Ottawa, 1976.

Canada, Commission of Inquiry into the Non-Medical Use of Drugs. *Final Report of the Commission of Inquiry into the Non-Medical Use of Drugs*. G.E. LeDain, Chairman. Ottawa, 1973.

Canada, Department of Indian Affairs and Northern Development. *Canada's National Wildlife Policy and Program*. A statement made by the Minister of Northern Affairs and National Resources in the House of Commons on April 6, 1966. Ottawa, 1966.

————. *Expanded Guidelines for Northern Pipelines*, as tabled in the House of Commons June 28, 1972 by the Honourable Jean Chrétien. Environmental-Social Committee, Northern Pipelines, TAsk Force on Northern Oil Development, Report No. 72-73. [Ottawa, 1972.]

————. *Mackenzie Valley Pipeline Inquiry, Summaries of Proceedings*. 6 vols. Ottawa, 1976.

————. *Report of the Task Force Formed to Study Problems Encountered by Northern Businessmen in Obtaining Federal Contracts*. n.p., 1975.

————. *Statement of the Government of Canada on Northern Development in the 70's*. Presented to the Standing Committee on Indian Affairs and Northern Development by the Honourable Jean Chrétien, Minister of Indian Affairs and Northern Development on March 28, 1972. Ottawa, 1972.

————. "Territorial Quarrying Regulations." Preliminary 6th Draft, [Ottawa, 1977.]

Canada, Department of Indian Affairs and Northern Development, National and Historic Parks Branch. *Byways and Special Places*. n.p., n.d.

Canada, Department of Indian Affairs and Northern Development, Northern Economic Development Branch, Economic Staff Group and MPS Associates Ltd. *Regional Impact of a Northern Gas Pipeline*. 7 vols. Environmental-Social Committee, Northern Pipelines, Task Force on Northern Oil Development, Reports Nos. 73-28 to 73-34. Ottawa, 1973.

Canada, Department of Indian Affairs and Northern Development, Parks Canada. *National Parks Policy*. Ottawa, 1975.

————. *National Parks System Planning Manual*. [Ottawa, 1972.]

————. *A National Wild Rivers System Proposal*. [Ottawa], 1974.

————. *Natural Areas of Canadian Significance — A Preliminary Study*. [Ottawa], 1977.

————. *Possible Applications of Historic Waterways to the Mackenzie River*. Byways and Special Places Program. [Ottawa], 1974.

Canada, Department of Indian Affairs and Northern Development, Special Staff Group on Northern Employment and Economic Opportunities. *Development Agencies for the Northwest Territories*. [Ottawa, 1973.]

Canada, Department of Industry, Trade and Commerce. *Visit to USSR of a Group of Canadian Experts Representing the Pipeline and the Production and Processing Sub-Groups of the Gas Working Group of the Soviet Canadian Mixed Commission on Industrial Application of Science and Technology*. Ottawa, 1975.

Canada, Department of National Health and Welfare, Health Protection Branch, Non-Medical Use of Drugs Directorate, Research Bureau. *Alcohol Problems in Canada: A Summary of Current Knowledge*. Technical Report Series No. 2. Ottawa, 1976.

Canada, Department of National Health and Welfare, Northern Health Service. *Report on Health Conditions in the Northwest Territories*. n.p., 1970 to 1974.

Canada, Department of National Health and Welfare, Nutrition Canada. *Nutrition, a National Priority*. Ottawa, 1973.

Canada, Department of the Environment, Environmental Protection Service. *Code of Good Practice for Handling Solid Wastes at Federal Establishments*. n.p., n.d.

————. *Code of Good Practice for Management of Hazardous and Toxic Wastes at Federal Establishments*. n.p., 1977.

————. *Code of Good Practice on Dump Closing or Conversion to Sanitary Landfill at Federal Establishments*. n.p., n.d.

————. *Guidelines for Effluent Quality and Wastewater Treatment at Federal Establishments*. Report EPS-1-EC-76-1. n.p., 1976.

————. *Petroleum Refinery Effluent Regulations and Guidelines*. Report EPS-1-WP-74-1. n.p., 1974.

————. *Proposed National Ambient Air Quality Objectives, Part I*. August 7, 1976. n.p., 1976.

————. *Recommended Environmental Standards for the Design and Construction of a Mackenzie Valley Gas Pipeline*. Report EPS-1-NW-76-1. n.p., 1976.

Canada, Department of the Environment, Fisheries and Marine Service. *Guidelines Concerning Applications to Remove Gravel From or Adjacent to Streams Frequented by Fish*. n.p., n.d.

————. "Intake Screen Guidelines (1972)." Vancouver, 1972.

Canada, Department of the Environment, Water Quality Branch. *Water Quality Data Report*. Computer printout of data stored in NAQUADAT system, for chemical and physical analysis of water of rivers in the Mackenzie Valley drainage basin, 1965 to 1977. Ottawa, 1977.

Canada, Law Reform Commission of Canada. *Commissions of Inquiry, Administrative Law, Working Paper 17.* Ottawa, 1977.

Canada, Ministry of Transport. "Mackenzie River Valley Transportation." Evidence presented on behalf of Commission Counsel to the Mackenzie Valley Pipeline Inquiry. Yellowknife, 1976.

Canada, Ministry of Transport, Arctic Transportation Agency. *The Effect of Proposed Staging Sites for Pipeline Construction on Mackenzie Valley Transportation.* n.p., 1976.

Canada, National Energy Board. *Reasons for Decision: Northern Pipelines.* 3 vols. Ottawa, 1977.

――. *Mackenzie Valley Hearing.* Orders GH-1-76 and AO-9-GH-1-76. 208 volumes of transcripts. Ottawa, 1976-1977.

Canada, Office of the Prime Minister. "Political Development in the Northwest Territories." Government background paper concerning the appointment of the Honourable Charles M. Drury as Special Representative for Constitutional Development in the Northwest Territories. Ottawa, 1977.

Canada, Privy Council. O.C. 52, January 26, 1891.

Canada, Science Council of Canada. *Northward Looking – A Strategy and a Science Policy for Northern Development.* Report No. 26. Ottawa, 1977.

Canada, Select Committee of the Senate. *Report of the Select Committee of the Senate Appointed to Enquire into the Resources of the Great Mackenzie Basin.* Session 1888. Ottawa: Queen's Printer, 1888.

Canada, Task Force on Northern Oil Development. *Mackenzie Valley and Northern Yukon Pipelines, Socio-Economic and Environmental Aspects.* Environmental-Social Committee, Northern Pipelines, Task Force on Northern Oil Development, Report no. 74-17. Ottawa, 1974.

Canada, Statistics Canada. *Fur Production (23-207 annual).* Seasons 1965-66 to 1975-76. Ottawa, 1967-1977.

Canada, Alberta, Division of Environmental Health, Water and Pollution Control Section. *Surface Water Quality Criteria, Province of Alberta.* n.p., 1970.

Canada, Northwest Territories. *Commissioner's Orders, 477-73 and 181-74.* [1973, 1974.]

Canada, Northwest Territories, Department of Natural and Cultural Affairs, Recreation Division. "Guide to Services and Programs." n.p., n.d.

――. "Recreation Leadership and Leisure Education, A Proposal to the Executive Committee." n.p., 1975.

――. "Report on Recreation Services in the Northwest Territories." n.p., 1975.

Canada, Northwest Territories, Department of Social Development, Alcohol and Drug Program. *Proposal for the Secondary Prevention of Alcohol and Crime Problems.* n.p., 1975.

Canada, Northwest Territories, Petroleum Resource Development Project Group. *Mackenzie Corridor Development Plan.* Environmental-Social Committee, Northern Pipelines, Task Force on Northern Oil Development, Report No. 74-43. Ottawa, 1975.

Canada, Ontario, Ministry of the Environment. *Model Municipal Noise Control By-Law, Revised May, 1976.* Noise Pollution Control Section. Toronto, 1976.

Canadian Arctic Gas Pipeline Limited. Applications and Supporting Documents to the Applications of Canadian Arctic Gas Pipeline Limited to the National Energy Board and to the Department of Indian Affairs and Northern Development. n.p., 1974 to 1977.

――. "Mackenzie Valley Pipeline Inquiry, Outline of Submissions of Canadian Arctic Gas Pipeline Limited." Evidence presented to the Mackenzie Valley Pipeline Inquiry. Yellowknife, 1977.

――. "Northern Staging Area Report." Evidence presented to the Mackenzie Valley Pipeline Inquiry. Yellowknife, 1976.

――. *Responses to National Energy Board Requests for Additional Information.* 9 vols. n.p., 1976.

――. *Responses to Pipeline Application Assessment Group Requests for Supplementary Information.* Toronto, 1974.

――. "Statement of Substance of Evidence to be Presented by a Panel Composed of Dr. J.I. Clark, *et al.* Relating to the Geotechnical Aspects of the Engineering Design in 'Location, Design and Capacity of Facilities,' Section 8, Appendix B." Evidence presented to the Mackenzie Valley Pipeline Inquiry. Yellowknife, 1975.

――. "Written Direct Testimony, Phase 1A, National Energy Board Hearing, Ottawa." Evidence presented to the National Energy Board Hearing. Ottawa, 1976.

Canadian Arctic Resources Committee. *Final Argument and Recommendations – Mackenzie Valley Pipeline Inquiry.* Ottawa, 1976.

Canadian Council on Rural Development. *A Development Strategy for the Mid-North of Canada,* Ottawa, 1976.

――. *Working Papers, Seminar, Environmentally Appropriate Technology for the Mid-North of Canada.* Ottawa, 1976.

Canadian Pipeline Advisory Council. "Submission to Mr. Justice Thomas R. Berger, Commissioner, Mackenzie Valley Pipeline Inquiry on Phase IV, the Human Environment." Evidence presented on behalf of Commission Counsel to the Mackenzie Valley Pipeline Inquiry. Yellowknife, 1976.

Canadian Standards Association. *Standard Z184, Gas Pipeline Systems*. Toronto, 1975.

Chamberlin, J.E. *The Harrowing of Eden, White Attitudes toward Native Americans*. New York: Seabury Press, 1975.

Chrétien, Honourable Jean, Minister of Indian Affairs and Northern Development. *Statement of the Government of Canada on Indian Policy, 1969*. Ottawa, 1969.

Clark, A. McFadyen, ed. *National Museum of Man Mercury Series, Proceedings: Northern Athapaskan Conference, 1971*. 2 vols. Ottawa: National Museums of Canada, 1975.

Committee for Original Peoples Entitlement — Inuit Tapirisat of Canada. "Argument, Terms and Conditions and Recommendations." Evidence presented to the Mackenzie Valley Pipeline Inquiry. Yellowknife, 1976.

The Council for Science and Society. *Superstar Technologies*. Report of a Working Party — Convenor: Geoffrey Chin. London: Barry Rose (Publishers) Ltd., 1976.

Dailey, Tom, and Dave Redman. *Guidelines for Roadless Area Campsite Spacing to Minimize Impact of Human-related Noises*. United States Department of Agriculture Forest Service General Technical Report PNW-35. Portland, Oregon, 1975.

Dear, Michael. "Planning Community Health Services in Arctic Canada." Research Report to the Presidential Committee on Northern Studies, McMaster University. Hamilton, 1976.

Deloria, Vine, Jr. "The Lummi Indian Community: The Fishermen of the Pacific Northwest." Evidence presented on behalf of the Indian Brotherhood of the Northwest Territories to the Mackenzie Valley Pipeline Inquiry. Yellowknife, 1976.

Deprez, Paul. *The Pine Point Mine and the Development of the Area South of Great Slave Lake*. Center for Settlement Studies, University of Manitoba, Series 2, Research Report No. 16. Winnipeg, 1973.

Devitt, W.G. "History of Eduction in the Northwest Territories," *Education North of 60*. The Canadian Superintendent 1964, A Report Prepared by Members of the Canadian Association of School Superintendents and Inspectors in the Department of Northern Affairs and National Resources. Toronto: Ryerson Press, 1965.

Dosman, Edgar J, *The National Interest, The Politics of Northern Development 1968-75*. Toronto: McClelland and Stewart Ltd., 1975.

Dryden, R.L. and J.N. Stein. *Guidelines for the Protection of the Fish Resources of the Northwest Territories During Highway Construction and Operation*. Department of the Environment, Fisheries and Marine Service, Technical Report Series No. CEN/T-75-1. Winnipeg, 1975.

Dunbar, M.J. *Environment and Good Sense, An Introduction to Environmental Damage and Control in Canada*. Montreal and London: McGill-Queen's University Press, 1971.

EBA Engineering Consultants Ltd. "Terrain Study and Thaw Settlement Analysis (Mile 678 to Mile 784)." Foothills Pipe Lines Ltd. n.p., 1976.

Eggleton, Peter L. and Jacques Laframbroise. *Field Evaluation of Towed Air Cushion Rafts*. Ministry of Transport, Report TDA-500-166. Ottawa, 1974.

Environment Protection Board. *Environmental Impact Assessment of the Portion of the Mackenzie Gas Pipeline from Alaska to Alberta*. 4 vols. Winnipeg, 1974.

European Inland Fisheries Advisory Commission. "Report on Finely Divided Solids and Inland Fisheries." *International Journal of Air and Water Pollution*, Vol. 9 (1965), pp. 151-68.

Feit, H. "Use of Official Fur Statistics as Indicators of Fur Bearing Mammal Harvests." Interim Report No. 4 of the Fort George Resource Use and Subsistence Economy Study, Grand Council of the Crees. Montreal, 1975.

Finney, George, *et al. Biological Field Program Report: 1975*. The Lombard North Group Ltd., for Foothills Pipe Lines Ltd. 4 vols. n.p., 1976.

Fison, Susan R. "Socio-economic Impact of the Trans-Alaska Oil Pipeline on Fairbanks, Alaska." Evidence presented to the Alaska Highway Pipeline Inquiry. Whitehorse, 1977.

Flynn, D. "Recreation North." Requested by Northwest Territories Department of Local Government for Presentation to Territorial Council. n.p., 1974.

Foote, D.C. "Exploration and Resource Utilization in Northwestern Alaska before 1855." Unpublished Ph.D. Thesis in Geography. McGill University, Montreal, 1965.

Foothills Pipe Lines Ltd. Applications and Supporting Documents to the Applications of Foothills Pipe Lines Ltd. to the National Energy Board and to the Department of Indian Affairs and Northern Development. n.p., 1975 to 1977.

———. "A Preliminary Study into the Use of Insulation to Alleviate Frost Heave Problems Relevant to the Operation of a Cold Gas Pipeline." n.p., 1976.

Forrest, Ann. "An Evaluation of the Alaska Native Claims Settlement Act." Evidence presented on behalf of the Indian Brotherhood of the Northwest Territories to the Mackenzie Valley Pipeline Inquiry. Yellowknife, 1976.

Forth, T.G., *et al. Mackenzie Valley Development: Some Implications for Planners.* Environmental-Social Committee Northern Pipelines, Task Force on Northern Oil Development, Report No. 73-45. Ottawa, 1974.

Friesen. B. Fred. *Potential Inuit Benefits from Commercial and Sports Use of Arctic Renewable Resources.* Vol. X of *Renewable Resources Project.* Inuit Tapirisat of Canada. n.p., 1975.

Friesen, B.F., and J.G. Nelson. "An Overview of the Economic Potential of Renewable Resources in the Canadian Arctic." Unpublished manuscript. Waterloo, Ontario, 1975.

G.A. Friesen (Canada) Ltd., Health Care Consultants. *Mackenzie River Area Health Services Study.* 2 vols. Calgary, 1974.

Fumoleau, René, OMI. *As Long As This Land Shall Last, A History of Treaty 8 and Treaty 11, 1870-1939.* Toronto: McClelland and Stewart, [1973].

Geist, V. *Mountain Sheep.* Chicago: University of Chicago Press, 1971.

Gemini North Ltd. *Alaska Native Participation in the Trans-Alaska Pipeline Project, A Survey of Manpower Delivery Systems.* Department of Indian Affairs and Northern Development. Vancouver, 1975.

——. *Social and Economic Impact of Proposed Arctic Gas Pipeline in Northern Canada,* 7 vols. Canadian Arctic Gas Pipeline Limited. n.p., 1974.

Glover, M. ed. *Building in Northern Communities: 1974.* Organized by The Arctic Institute of North America. Montreal, 1974.

Godfrey, E. Earl. *The Birds of Canada.* National Museums of Canada. Bulletin No. 203, Biological Series No. 73. Ottawa, 1966.

Gourdeau, Eric. "The Native Use of Resources in the Context of the Proposed Mackenzie Gas Pipeline," Chapter 11, *Research Reports, Environmental Impact Assessment of the Portion of the Mackenzie Gas Pipeline from Alaska to Alberta.* Vol. IV, Environment Protection Board. Winnipeg, 1974, pp. 293-307.

Gunn, W.W.H. "The Need to Preserve the Integrity of the Mackenzie Delta." *Ornithological Studies, Cross Delta Route.* LGL Limited, Environmental Research Associates. n.p., 1975.

Gray, John A. *Stability of Employment and Production Within Canadian Resource-Based Industries.* Center for Settlement Studies, The University of Manitoba. Winnipeg, 1975.

Hansen, H.A. "Utilization of Wildlife by Alaska Natives." Unpublished manuscript, Alaska Bureau of Sport Fisheries and Wildlife. n.p., 1975.

Harlan, R.L. *Hydrogeological Considerations in Northern Pipeline Development.* Environmental-Social Committee, Northern Pipelines, Task Force on Northern Oil Development, Report No. 74-26. Ottawa, 1974.

Hartland-Rowe, R.C.B., and P.B.Wright. *Swamplands for Sewage Effluents — Final Report.* Environmental-Social Committee, Northern Pipelines, Task Force on Northern Oil Development, Report No. 74-4. [Ottawa], 1974.

Heacock, H.A. "A Summary of Transport Canada's Responsibilities and Activities Respecting Aircraft Operations in Northern Canada." Evidence presented on behalf of Commission Counsel to the Mackenzie Valley Pipeline Inquiry. Yellowknife, 1976.

Helm, June. "Traditional Dene Community Structure and Socioterritorial Organization." n.p., 1976.

Hobart, Charles W. "Socio-Economic Overview of the Mackenzie Delta Region." Evidence presented on behalf of the Oil Producers to the Mackenzie Valley Pipeline Inquiry. Inuvik, 1976.

Hunt, Constance. "The Development and Decline of Northern Conservation Reserves." *Contact, Journal of Urban and Environmental Affairs,* University of Waterloo, Vol. 8, No. 4 (1976) pp. 30-75.

Inhaber, H. "Environmental Quality: Outline for a National Index for Canada." *Science,* Vol. 186 (1974), pp. 798-805.

Innis, H.A. *Empire and Communications.* Toronto, 1950.

Interdisciplinary Systems Ltd. "Recommendations for Site Specific Terms and Conditions for the Arctic Gas Proposal." Maps prepared for Northern Environment Foundation. Evidence presented by C.H. Templeton to the Mackenzie Valley Pipeline Inquiry. Yellowknife, 1976.

——. "Recommendations for Site Specific Terms and Conditions for the Foothills Proposal." Maps prepared for Northern Environment Foundation. Evidence presented by C.H. Templeton to the Mackenzie Valley Pipeline Inquiry. Yellowknife, 1976.

Jacobson, Jerald O. "Potential Impact of the Mackenzie Gas Pipeline on Bird Populations in the Yukon and Northwest Territories," Chapter 6, *Research Reports, Environmental Impact Assessment of the Portion of the Mackenzie Gas Pipeline from Alaska to Alberta,* Vol. IV, Environment Protection Board. Winnipeg, 1974, pp. 121-76.

Jakimchuk, R.D. Letter to Mr. Justice Thomas Berger, concerning the Porcupine Caribou Herd and the Dempster Highway. Edmonton, June 19, 1977.

The James Bay and Northern Québec Agreement, Editeur Officiel du Québec. Québec, 1976.

James Bay and Northern Quebec Native Harvesting Research Committee. *Research to Establish Present Levels of Harvesting by Native Peoples of Northern Quebec.* Part I, *A Report on the Harvests by the James Bay Cree,* 2 vols. Part II, *A Report on the Harvests by the Inuit of Northern Québec.* Montreal, 1976.

Jenness, Diamond. *Eskimo Administration.* The Arctic Institute of North America, Technical report No. 14. Montreal, 1964.

———. *People of the Twilight.* New York: MacMillan Company, 1928.

Katz, J. "Proposed Mental Health Legislation, Working Draft." Anchorage, 1975.

Kelsall, J.P. *The Migratory Barren-Ground Caribou of Canada.* Canadian Wildlife Service, Department of Indian Affairs and Northern Development. Ottawa, 1968.

Kerfoot, Helen. "Mackenzie Delta — A Summary Report of Surface Conditions." Final Draft, Geological Survey of Canada. Ottawa, 1975.

Kitto, Franklin Hugo. *New Oil Fields of Northern Canada.* Ottawa: Department of the Interior, 1921.

Klein, David R. "Reaction of Reindeer to Obstructions and Disturbances." *Science,* Vol. 173 (1971), pp. 393-98.

Klohn Leonoff Consultants Ltd. *Preliminary Design for Drainage and Erosion Control for Study Area at MP 311-3.* Foothills Pipe Lines Ltd. Calgary, 1976.

Kuo, Chan-Yan. *A Study of Income and Income Distribution in the Arctic Coast and Baffin Regions of Northern Canada.* Regional Planning Section, Policy and Planning ACND Division, Northern Policy and Program Planning Branch, Department of Indian Affairs and Northern Development. Ottawa, 1973.

LaResche, D., *et al.* "Alaska Mental Health Needs Survey." n.p., n.d.

LeDain, Gerald E. *Law and Social Change: The Role of the Public Inquiry in our Constitutional System.* Osgoode Hall Law School, York University, Annual Lecture Series 1971-1972, ed. Jacob S. Ziegel.

Lovesey, E.J. "Hovercraft Noise and Vibration." *Journal of Sound and Vibration,* 20(2)(1972), pp. 241-45.

Lu, Chang-Mei. *Estimation of Net Imputed Value of Edible Subsistence Production in Northwest Territories.* Department of Indian Affairs and Northern Development, Economic Staff Group. Ottawa, 1972.

———. *A Study of Health in the Northwest Territories.* Regional Planning and Manpower Section, Economic Staff Group, Northern Economic Development Branch, Department of Indian Affairs and Northern Development. Ottawa, 1972.

Lysyk, Kenneth M., *et al. Alaska Highway Pipeline Inquiry.* Ottawa, 1977.

MPS Associates Ltd. "Effect of Changing the Duration of Pipeline Construction on Selected Variables." Evidence presented on behalf of Commission Counsel to the Mackenzie Valley Pipeline Inquiry. Yellowknife, 1976.

Macauley, A.J., and D.A. Boag. "Waterfowl Harvest by Slave Indians in Northern Alberta." *Arctic,* 27(1)(1974), pp. 15-26.

McColgan, I.J. "Air Pollution Emissions and Control Technology — Packaged Incinerators." Combustion Sources Division, Abatement and Compliance Branch, Air Pollution Control Directorate, Department of the Environment. n.p., 1976.

McCullum, Hugh, and Karmel McCullum. *This Land is Not for Sale, Canada's Original People and their Land, A Saga of Neglect, Exploitation, and Conflict.* Toronto: Anglican Book Centre, 1975.

McCullum, Hugh, *et al. Moratorium: Justice, Energy, the North, and the Native People.* Toronto: Anglican Book Centre, 1975.

Mackay, J. Ross. *The Mackenzie Delta Area, N.W.T.* Geological Survey of Canada, Miscellaneous Report 23. Ottawa, 1964.

McLaren, I.A. *The Economics of Seals in the Eastern Canadian Arctic.* Fisheries Research Board of Canada, Arctic Unit, Circular No. 1. Montreal, 1958.

McLean, W.T.R., and M.E. Stiles. *Cost of Living Study for the Northwest Territories.* Marketing Information Services Ltd. Edmonton and Yellowknife, 1974.

McRoberts, E.C. "Some Aspects of a Simple Secondary Creep Model for Deformations in Permafrost Slopes." *Canadian Geotechnical Journal,* Vol. 12, No. 1 (1975), pp. 98-105.

McRoberts, E.C. and N.R. Morgenstern. "The Stability of Slopes in Frozen Soil, Mackenzie Valley, N.W.T." *Canadian Geotechnical Journal,* Vol. 11, No. 4 (1974), pp. 554-73.

———. "Stability of Thawing Slopes." *Canadian Geotechnical Journal,* Vol. 11 (1974), pp. 447-69.

———. *A Study of Landslides in the Vicinity of the Mackenzie River Mile 205 to 660.* Environmental-Social Committee, Northern Pipelines, Task Force on Northern Oil Development, Report No. 73-35. Ottawa, 1973.

McTaggart-Cowan, Ian. "Biota Pacifica 2000," *Mankind's Future in the Pacific,* ed. R.F. Scagel. Vancouver: University of British Columbia Press, 1976.

———. "An 'Overview' with Particular Reference to Fish and Wildlife," *Science and the North.* Ottawa, 1972, pp. 109-11.

Mair, Charles. *Through the Mackenzie Basin.* Toronto: William Briggs, 1908.

Manforce Research Associates. "Trade Unions and the Northern Business Community." n.p., n.d.

Marcotte Research Center. *Project Mental Health: A Study of Opinion North of 60°. Canadian Mental Health Association, Northwest Territories Division.* Saskatoon, n.d.

Milton Freeman Research Limited. *Inuit Land Use and Occupancy Project,* 3 vols. Ottawa: Department of Indian and Northern Affairs, 1976.

Morgenstern, N.R. and J.F. Nixon. "An Analysis of the Performance of a Warm-Oil Pipeline in Permafrost, Inuvik, N.W.T." *Canadian Geotechnical Journal,* Vol. 12 (1975), pp. 199-208.

Morrow, Honourable Justice William G. "Observations on Resource Issues in Canada's North." *Journal of Natural Resource Management and Interdisciplinary Studies,* Vol. 1, No. 1 (1976).

Munro, J.A. *Mackenzie Corridor Development Plan.* Environmental-Social Committee, Northern Pipelines, Task Force on Northern Oil Development, Report No. 74-43. Ottawa, 1975.

Murie, Olaus, J. "Alaska-Yukon Caribou." United States Bureau of Biological Survey, *North American Fauna No. 54.* n.p., 1935.

National Indian Brotherhood. "Declaration on Indian Housing." Policy Paper. n.p., 1974.

———. *Indian Control of Indian Education.* Policy paper presented to the Minister of Indian Affairs and Northern Development. Ottawa, 1976.

Naylor, Larry L., and Lawrence A. Gooding. "Native Hire on the Trans-Alaska Oil Pipeline: April, 1974 to March, 1976.," Fairbanks, Alaska, 1976.

Naysmith, John Kennedy. *Land Use and Public Policy in Northern Canada.* Northern Policy and Program Planning Branch, Northern Program, Department of Indian and Northern Affairs. Ottawa, 1975.

Northern Engineering Services Company Limited. "Depth of Overburden Cover over the Pipe and Pipe Anchorage, Technical and Cost Considerations." Draft. Canadian Arctic Gas Study Limited. [Calgary], 1974.

———. *Drainage and Erosion Control Measures, Description and Proposed Design Principles.* Canadian Arctic Gas Study Limited. Calgary, 1975.

———. *Drainage and Erosion Control: Pilot Design Project.* Canadian Arctic Gas Study Limited. Calgary, 1976.

———. "Frost Heave Information Pursuant to National Energy Board Requests of May 11, 12 and 14, 1976." Canadian Arctic Gas Study Limited. Calgary, 1976.

———. "Interim Report, Slope Stability in Permafrost Terrain." Canadian Arctic Gas Study Limited. Calgary, 1974.

———. *Mechanical Stress Analysis of Buried Pipeline.* 3 vols. Canadian Arctic Gas Study Limited. Calgary, 1975.

———. "Response to Dr. P.J. Williams' Report on Possible Heave of Chilled Gas Pipeline." Canadian Arctic Gas Study Limited. Calgary, 1976.

———. "Stability of Excavated Submarine Slopes in Mackenzie River Delta Sediments." An exhibit to the National Energy Board Hearing, exhibit No. N-PD-359. Ottawa, 1976.

The Northwest Territories Association of Municipalities. "Summary of Recommendations." Evidence presented to the Mackenzie Valley Pipeline Inquiry. Yellowknife, 1976.

Northwest Territories Council, Task Force on Housing. *Report.* n.p., 1972.

Northwest Territories Drug Coordinating Council. *Northwest Territories Drug Coordinating Council Annual Report, April 1974-March 1975.* n.p., 1975.

Novakowski, N.S. "Cemental Deposition as an Age Criterion in Bison, and the Relation of Incisor Wear, Eye-Lens Weight, and Dressed Bison Carcass Weight to Age." *Canadian Journal of Zoology,* 43 (1965), pp. 173-78.

———. Personal Communication with Peter J. Usher. June 7, 1977.

Novakowski, N.S., and V.E.F. Solman. "Potential of Wildlife as a Protein Source." *Journal of Animal Science,* 40(5)(1975), pp. 1016-19.

O'Hara, P.J. "Contingency Planning Guidelines, Oil and Gas Pipelines." Draft, Department of the Environment. n.p., 1977.

————. "Contingency Planning Guidelines, Oil and Hazardous Material Spills, Oil and Gas Pipelines." Second Draft. n.p., 1977.

Olson, Sigurd F. *The Lonely Land.* Toronto: McClelland and Stewart Ltd., 1961.

————. *Runes of the North.* New York: Alfred F. Knopf, 1963.

O'Malley, Martin. *The Past and Future Land, An Account of the Berger Inquiry into the Mackenzie Valley Pipeline.* Toronto: Peter Martin Associates Ltd., 1976.

Palmer, John. *Social Accounts for the North: Interim Paper No. 3; The Measurements of Incomes in the Yukon and Northwest Territories.* Economic Staff Group, Department of Indian Affairs and Northern Development. Ottawa, 1973.

Peacock, Donald. *People, Peregrines and Arctic Pipelines, The Critical Battle to Build Canada's Northern Gas Pipelines.* Vancouver: J.J. Douglas Ltd., 1977.

Pearson, Arthur M. "Habitat, Management, and the Future of Canada's Grizzly Bears." Manuscript. Edmonton, 1976.

Peterson, E.B. "Biological Productivity of Arctic Lands and Waters: A Review of Canadian Literature," *Inuit Land Use and Occupancy Project,* Vol. 2, *Supporting Studies,* Milton Freeman Research Limited. Ottawa: Department of Indian and Northern Affairs, 1976, pp. 85-100.

Pipeline Application Assessment Group. *Mackenzie Valley Pipeline Assessment, Environmental and Socio-Economic Effects of the Proposed Canadian Arctic Gas Pipeline on the Northwest Territories and Yukon.* Department of Indian Affairs and Northern Development. Ottawa, 1974.

Pipeline Impact Information Center Report. Fairbanks North Star Borough. No. 1 (July 1974) to No. 39 (July 1977).

Platt, Joseph B., and C. Eric Tull. "A Study of Wintering and Nesting Gyrfalcons on the Yukon North Slope During 1975 with Emphasis on their Behavior During Experimental Overflights by Helicopters," *Ornithological Studies Conducted in the Area of the Proposed Gas Pipeline Route: Northern Alberta, Northwest Territories, Yukon Territory and Alaska, 1975.* Canadian Arctic Gas Study Limited, Biological Report Series Vol. 35, Chap.I. n.p., 1977.

A Portrayal of our Metis Heritage, ed. Joanne Overvold (Burger). Metis Association of the Northwest Teritories. n.p., 1976.

Poston, H.J. *Waterfowl Populations Observed Along the Proposed Gas Pipeline Route, Richards Island to N.W.T.-Alberta Border.* Canadian Wildlife Service. n.p., 1973.

Poston, H.J., *et al. Atlas of Waterfowl Habitat Maps. Part of a Wildlife Habitat Inventory of the Mackenzie Valley and the Northern Yukon.* Canadian Wildlife Service for Environmental-Social Committee, Northern Pipelines, Task Force on Northern Oil Development. n.p., 1973.

Pufahl, D.E., *et al. Observations on Recent Highway Cuts in Permafrost.* Environmental-Social Committee, Northern Pipelines, Task Force on Northern Oil Development, Report No. 74-32. Ottawa, 1974.

Reed, Hayter. "Introduction," *Annual Report of the Department of Indian Affairs for the Year ending 30th June, 1893. Ottawa, 1894.*

In *Renewable Resources Project.* Inuit Tapirisat of Canada. n.p., 1975:

Vol. I: Scace, Robert C. *Exploration, Settlement and Land Use Activities in Northern Canada: Northern Canada: Historical Review.*

Vol. II: Boreal Institute for Northern Studies. *Canadian Arctic Renewable Resource Mapping Project and Map Supplement.*

Vol. III: Usher, Peter J. *Historical Statistics Approximating Fur, Fish and Game Harvests Within Inuit Lands of the NWT and Yukon 1915-1975, With Text.*

Vol. IV: de Pape, D., *et al. A Socio-economic Evaluation of Inuit Livelihood and Natural Resource Utilization in the Tundra of the Northwest Territories.*

Vol. V: Turkheim, Richard J. *Biophysical Impacts of Arctic Hydro-electric Developments.*

Vol. VI: Brown, S. *Environmental Impacts of Arctic Oil and Gas Development.*

Vol. VII: Van Diepen, Philip. *The Impact of Mining on the Arctic Biological and Physical Environment.*

Vol. VIII: Mann, Donald. *The Socio-economic Impact of Non-Renewable Resource Development on the Inuit of Northern Canada.*

Vol. IX: Butler, Richard. *The Development of Tourism in the Canadian North and Implications for the Inuit.*

Vol. X: Friesen, B. Fred. *Potential Inuit Benefits from Commercial and Sports Use of Arctic Renewable Resources.*

Vol. XI: J.G. Nelson. *Summary of Recommendations.*

Richardson, B. *Strangers Devour the Land, The Cree Hunters of the James Bay Area Versus Premier Bourassa and the James Bay Development Corporation.* Toronto: Macmillan, 1975.

Robinson, J.L. "Land Use Possibilities in Mackenzie District, N.W.T." *Canadian Geographical Journal,* 31(1) (1945), pp. 30-47.

Royal Commission on Labrador. *Report of the Royal Commission on Labrador,* Vol. III, *Economic Factors.* St. John's, 1974.

Rushforth, Scott. "Recent Land-Use by the Great Bear Lake Indians." Evidence presented on behalf of the Indian Brotherhood of the Northwest Territories and the Metis Association of the Northwest Territories to the Mackenzie Valley Pipeline Inquiry. Yellowknife, 1975.

Russell, Frank. *Explorations in the Far North.* Iowa City: University of Iowa, 1898.

Ruttan, Robert A., and John T'Seleie. "Renewable Resource Potentials for Alternative Development in the Mackenzie River Region." Evidence presented on behalf of the Indian Brotherhood of the Northwest Territories to the Mackenzie Valley Pipeline Inquiry. Yellowknife, 1976.

J.E. Rymes Engineering Ltd. *Preliminary Report of Work and Transportation Equipment for Canadian Arctic Gas Study Limited, Operation and Maintenance, Calgary, Alberta.* Calgary, 1975.

Sanders, Douglas E. "Aboriginal Title: A Legal Perspective." Evidence presented on behalf of the Indian Brotherhood of the Northwest Territories to the Mackenzie Valley Pipeline Inquiry. Yellowknife, 1976.

———. "Testimony to the Mackenzie Valley Pipeline Inquiry." Evidence presented on behalf of the Indian Brotherhood of the Northwest Territories to the Mackenzie Valley Pipeline Inquiry. Yellowknife, 1976.

Savishinsky, Joel S. "Kinship and the Expression of Values in an Athabascan Bush Community." *Western Canadian Journal of Anthropology.* 2(1970), pp. 31-59.

Schaefer, Otto. "Letter and Enclosures from Dr. O. Schaefer in Response to Cross-examination of September 15, 1976." Evidence presented on behalf of Commission Counsel to the Mackenzie Valley Pipeline Inquiry. Yellowknife, 1976.

Scott, Michel. *The Socio-Eocnomic Impact of the Pointed Mountain Gas Field.* Northern Policy and Program Planning Branch, Department of Indian Affairs and Northern Development. [Ottawa], 1973.

Scotter, G.W. "Reindeer Husbandry as a Land Use in Northwestern Canada." *Productivity and Conservation in Northern Circumpolar Lands,* eds. W.A. Fuller and P.G. Kevan. IUCN PUblications, New Series No. 16. Morges, Switzerland, 1970.

Scotter, G.W., and E.S. Telfer. "Potential for Read Meat Production From Wildlife in Boreal and Arctic Regions." *Proceedings of the Circumpolar Conference on Northern Ecology,* September 15-18, 1975, Ottawa. National Research Council. Ottawa, 1975.

Sergeant, D.E., and W. Hoek. "Whales in the Mackenzie Delta and Beaufort Sea." Arctic Biological Station, Fisheries and Marine Service, Department of the Environment. Evidence presented on behalf of the Committee for Original Peoples Entitlement to the Mackenzie Valley Pipeline Inquiry. Inuvik, 1976.

Siegfried, André. *Canada,* trans. H.H. Hemming and Doris Hemming. London, 1937.

Simmons, N.M. "Dall's Sheep Harvest in the Richardson Mountains, Northwest Territories." Unpublished manuscript, Canadian Wildlife Service, CWSC 1540. Fort Smith, N.W.T., 1973.

F.F. Slaney & Company Limited. "The 1975 White Whale Study." Preliminary Draft, Imperial Oil Limited. Vancouver, 1975.

Slipchenko, Walter. *Siberia 1971: A Report on the Visit of the Honourable Jean Chrétien, Minister of Indian Affairs and Northern Development and Official Delegation to the Soviet Union, July-August 1971.* Ottawa, 1972.

Slobodin, Richard. *Metis of the Mackenzie District.* Ottawa: St. Paul University, 1966.

Smelcar, Thea. "One Year Later: Pipeline Impact Report, Copper River Valley." Copper River Native Association. Copper River, Alaska, 1975.

Smith, Derek G. *Natives and Outsiders: Pluralism in the Mackenzie River Delta, Northwest Territories.* Department of Indian and Northern Affairs. Ottawa, 1975.

———. Personal Communication with Peter J. Usher. June 3, 1977.

Smith, N., and R. Berg. "Encountering Massive Ground Ice During Road Construction in Central Alaska." *North American Contribution, Second International Permafrost Conference.* 13-28 July 1973. Yakutsk, U.S.S.R. Washington, D.C.: National Academy of Sciences, 1973.

Smith, P.A., and C.J. Jonkel. *Resumé of the Trade in Polar Bear Hides in Canada, 1972-73.* Canadian Wildlife Service, Progress Note No. 43. Ottawa, 1975.

—— *Resumé of the Trade in Polar Bear Hides in Canada, 1973-74.* Canadian Wildlife Service, Progress Note No. 48. Ottawa, 1975.

Smith, P.A., and I. Stirling. *Resumé of the Trade in Polar Bear Hides in Canada, 1974-75.* Canadian Wildlife Service, Progress Note No. 66. Ottawa, 1976.

Smith, T.G., and D. Taylor. *Notes on Marine Mammal, Fox and Polar Bear Harvests in the Northwest Territories, 1940 to 1972.* Environment Canada, Fisheries and Marine Services, Technical Report No. 694. n.p., 1977.

Stager, J.K. *Old Crow, Y.T. and the Proposed Northern Gas Pipeline.* Environmental-Social Committee, Northern Pipelines, Task Force on Northern Oil Development, Report No. 74-21. Ottawa, 1974.

Stanley Associates Engineering Ltd. *Hay River Staging Area Study.* Canadian Arctic Gas Pipeline Limited. n.p., 1977.

—— *Hay River Industrial Development Study.* Canadian Arctic Gas Pipeline Limited. n.p., 1975.

—— *Mackenzie Valley Pipeline Community Impact Study.* The Northwest Territories Association of Municipalities. n.p., 1975.

Stegner, Wallace. "The Wilderness Idea," *Voices for the Wilderness,* ed. William Schwartz. New York: Ballantine Books, 1969. pp.283-89.

Sterling, R.P. Personal Communication with Peter J. Usher. June 7,1977.

Sterrett, K.F. *The Arctic Environment and the Arctic Surface Effect Vehicle.* Corps of Engineers, United States Army, Cold Regions Research and Engineering Laboratory, Report 76-1. Hanover, New Hampshire, 1976.

Strong, Maurice. Article in *The Edmonton Journal.* Sept. 22, 1976.

A Survey of the Contemporary Indians of Canada, ed. H.B. Hawthorn, Vol. II. Department of Northern Affairs and National Resources, Indian Affairs Branch, Ottawa, 1967.

Templeton, Carson. "Final Argument — Submitted by Carson Templeton to the Mackenzie Valley Pipeline Inquiry." Winnipeg, 1976.

Templeton Engineering Company. *Assessment of Environmental Protection Activities on the Mackenzie Valley Gas Pipeline.* Department of the Environment, Environmental Protection Service, Policy and Planning Report EPS-2-NW-76-1. Winnipeg, 1976.

Tener, J.S. *Muskoxen in Canada.* Canadian Wildlife Service, Department of Northern Affairs and National Resources. Ottawa, 1965.

Terminus Limited. "Trans-Alaska Pipeline — Special Study, An Overview Study with Respect to Effectiveness of the Stipulations During the Construction Phase and an Analysis of Experience Gained which may be of use for Grant of ROW for Future Pipeline Projects." United States Department of the Interior, Alaska Pipeline Office. Toronto, 1977.

Thibault, E. *Regional Socio-Economic Overview Study, Yukon Territory.* Environmental-Social Committee, Northern Pipelines, Task Force on Northern Oil Development, Report No. 74-46. Ottawa, 1975.

Thiessen, George. Personal Communication with L. Burgess. August 1977.

Thomas, W.A., ed. *Indicators of Environmental Quality.* Plenum, New York, 1972.

Tocqueville, A. de. *Democracy in America,* ed. Phillips Bradley. New York: Alfred F. Knopf, 1953.

Trudeau, Honorable Pierre. "Transcript of the Prime Minister's Remarks at the Vancouver Liberal Association Dinner." Seaforth Armories, Vancouver, B.C., August 8, 1969.

——. *Notes for an Address by the Prime Minister to the Annual Meeting of the Canadian Press.* Toronto, April 15, 1970.

Udall, Stewart L. *The Quiet Crisis.* New York: Avon Books, 1963.

Underwriters Laboratories of Canada. *Standard S601, Shop Fabricated Steel Above-Ground Tanks for Flammable and Combustible Liquids.* Scarborough, Ont., 1976.

——. *Standard S603, Steel Underground Tanks for Flammable and Combustible Liquids.* Scarborough, Ont., 1976.

——. *Standard S603.1, Protected Steel Underground Tanks for Flammable and Combustible Liquids.* Scarborough, Ont., 1976.

United States, Congress. *A Bill,* Administration of proposed amendments for an "Alaska National Interest Lands Conservation Act." H.R.39, 95th Congress, 1st Session, 1977.

United States, Congress, Senate. *Senate Bill 2917.* 1974.

United States, Department of the Interior. *2(c) Report: Federal Programs and Alaska Natives.* 4 Vols. n.p., n.d.

——. *Alaska Natural Gas Transportation System, Final Environmental Impact Statement,* 9 Vols. Washington, D.C., 1976.

United States, Laws, Statutes etc. *Johnson v. McIntosh.* (1823), 21 U.S., 543, 572.

————. *Worcester v. Georgia.* (1832), 31 U.S., 350 at 369.

United States, National Academy of Sciences and National Academy of Engineering, Environmental Studies Board, Committee on Water Quality Criteria. *Water Quality Criteria, 1972.* Environmental Protection Agency. Washington, D.C., 1973.

United States, President. "Message to the Congress of the United States." Jimmy Carter. May 23, 1977.

University of British Columbia. "Proceedings of the Arctic International Wildlife Range Conference — October 21 and 22, 1970," *University of British Columbia Law Review.* Vol. 6, No. 1, Supplement, June 1971.

University of Waterloo, Faculty of Environmental Studies. "Arctic Land Use Issues," *Contact, Journal of Urban and Environmental Affairs,* Vol. 8, No. 4 (1976).

Usher, Peter J. *The Bankslanders: Economy and Ecology of a Frontier Trapping Community,* Vol. 2, Ecology. Northern Science Research Group, NSRG-71-2. Ottawa: Department of Indian Affairs and Northern Development, 1971.

————. *Economic Basis and Resource Use of the Coppermine–Holman Region, N.W.T.* Northern Coordination and Research Centre, Report NCRC-65-2, Department of Northern Affairs and National Resources. Ottawa, 1965.

————. "Eskimo Land Use Maps." Fifteen maps compiled for the Inuit Land Use and Occupancy Project. Ottawa, 1976.

————. "Evaluating Country Food in the Northern Native Economy." *Arctic,* 29(2)(1976), pp. 105-20.

————. "Historical Statistics Approximating Fur, Fish and Game Harvests in the Mackenzie Valley N.W.T. 1915-1976." Unpublished report to Department of Education, Government of the Northwest Territories. Ottawa, 1977.

————. *Historical Statistics Approximating Fur, Fish and Game Harvests Within Inuit Lands of the N.W.T. and Yukon, 1915-1974, With Text.* Vol. 3 of *Renewable Resources Project.* Inuit Tapirisat of Canada. n.p., 1975.

————. "The Traditional Economy of the Western Arctic." Evidence presented on behalf of the Committee for Original Peoples Entitlement to the Mackenzie Valley Pipeline Inquiry. Yellowknife, 1976.

Vogt, William. *Road to Survival.* New York: William Sloane Associates, 1948. Includes quotation of Thomas Jefferson.

Wacko, William J. "Indian Alcohol and Drug Abuse in Alberta." Alcohol and Drug Consultant, Department of Indian and Northern Affairs. n.p., 1974.

————. *Observations and Recommendations Respecting Alcohol and Drugs in the Northwest Territories.* Department of Social Development, Government of the Northwest Territories. n.p., 1973.

Waddell, Ian. "Organizations the Inquiry has Funded." Memorandum prepared for Mackenzie Valley Pipeline Inquiry. Yellowknife, 1976.

Wah-shee, James J. "A Land Settlement — What Does it Mean?" Speech presented to a conference, "Delta Gas: Now or Later" Sponsored by Canadian Arctic Resources Committee, Ottawa, May 24, 1974.

Walker, E.R. *Oil, Ice and Climate in the Beaufort Sea.* Beaufort Sea Technical Report No. 35, Beaufort Sea Project, Department of the Environment. Victoria, 1975.

Watkins, M. *Dene Nation: The Colony Within.* Toronto: University of Toronto Press, 1977.

Watson, G.H. *et al. An Inventory of Wildlife Habitat of the Mackenzie Valley and the Northern Yukon.* Special Habitat Evaluation Group, Canadian Wildlife Service, Department of the Environment for the Environmental-Social Committee, Northern Pipelines, Task Force on Northern Oil Development, Report No. 73-27. Ottawa, 1973.

Weinstein, M.S. "A Discussion of the Possibility of Using the Official Division des Fourrures Fur Statistics by Trapline for an Assessment of Trapline Use." Interim Report No. 5 of the Fort George Resource Use and Subsistence Economy Study, Grand Council of the Crees. Montreal, 1975.

————. *What the Land Provides.* Report of the Fort George Resource Use and Subsistence Economy Study, Grand Council of the Crees (of Quebec). Montreal, 1976.

Wenzel, George. "Residents' Perceptions of the Health Delivery System in Six Settlements in the Inuvik Region, Northwest Territories." Evidence presented on behalf of the Committee for Original Peoples Entitlement to the Mackenzie Valley Pipeline Inquiry. Yellowknife, 1976.

Wilhm, J. "Range of Diversity in Benthic Macroinvertebrate Populations." *Journal of Water Pollution Control.* Vol. 42 (1970), pp. R221-24.

Williams, P.J. "Frost Heave." Summaries of Evidence of Witnesses to be called by Commission Counsel in Phase I of the Inquiry. Mackenzie Valley Pipeline Inquiry. Toronto, 1975.

————. "Report on Possible Heave of Chilled Gas Pipeline." Evidence presented on behalf of Commission Counsel to the Mackenzie Valley Pipeline Inquiry. Yellowknife, 1976.

Witty, J.R. "Employment and Manpower Considerations." Evidence presented on behalf of Commission Counsel to the Mackenzie Valley Pipeline Inquiry. Yellowknife, 1976.

Wolforth, John. *The Mackenzie Delta — Its Economic Base and Development, A Preliminary Study*. Northern Co-ordination and Research Centre, Department of Indian Affairs and Northern Development. Ottawa, n.d.

Wong, G. "Notes on Alcohol Consumption and Expenditure in the NWT." Alcohol and Drug Program, Department of Social Development, Government of the Northwest Territories. Unpublished. n.p., n.d.

Wood, K. Scott. *An Approach to Social Reporting in the Canadian North*. Department of Indian and Northern Affairs, and Institute of Public Affairs, Dalhousie University. Halifax, 1974.

Wright, J.V. "The Destruction of Canada's Prehistory." *Bulletin of the Canadian Archaeology Association*, No. 1, pp. 5-11.

Yazzie, Ethelou. "The Bilingual/Bicultural Experiment of Rough Rock Demonstration School." Evidence presented on behalf of the Indian Brotherhood of the Northwest Territories to the Mackenzie Valley Pipeline Inquiry. Yellowknife, 1976.

Yellowknife Detoxification Center, Northern Addiction Services. *Rehabilitation Needs of the Alcoholic: Yellowknife Area*. Yellowknife, 1975.

Yupiktak Bista. *Does One Way of Life Have to Die so Another Can Live? A Report on Subsistence and the Conservation of the Yupik Life-Style*. n.p., 1974.

Zemansky, Gilbert M. "Environmental Non-Compliance and the Public Interest." Evidence presented on behalf of the Committee for Original Peoples Entitlement to the Mackenzie Valley Pipeline Inquiry. Yellowknife, 1976.

Legislation: Canada

Act of 1869 (S.C. 32-33, Victoria, Ch.3)

Act of Union

Arctic Waters Pollution Prevention Act

Banff National Park Act 1887

British North America Act

Canada Shipping Act

Canada Wildlife Act

Clean Air Act

Dominion Lands Act

Environment Protection Act (Statutes of Ontario, 1971 and amendments)

Fisheries Act

Indian Act

Manitoba Act

Migratory Birds Convention Act

National Energy Board Act

National Parks Act

National Transportation Act

Northern Inland Waters Act

Northwest Territories Act

Québec Education Act

Revised Ordinances of the Northwest Territories, 1974.

Territorial Lands Act

Yukon Act

Canada Sessional Papers 1871, No. 20.

Imperial Order in Council (in Appendix of R.S.C., 1970)

Royal Proclamation of 1763

Treaty No. 8, 1899. Reprint, Queen's Printer, 1966.

Treaty No. 11, 1922. Reprint, Queen's Printer, 1957.

Legislation: United States

Alaska Community Mental Health Services Act (1975)

Indian Self Determination and Education Assistance Act (1975)

Local Hire Act (Alaska) (1972)

Wilderness Act (1964)